The Logical Approach
to Syntax

ACL-MIT Press Series in Natural Language Processing
Aravind K. Joshi, Karen Sparck Jones, and Mark Y. Liberman, editors

Speaking: From Intention to Articulation
by Willem J. M. Levelt

Plan Recognition in Natural Language Dialogue
by Sandra Carberry

Cognitive Models of Speech Processing: Psycholinguistic and Computational Perspectives
edited by Gerry T. M. Altmann

Computational Morphology: Practical Mechanisms for the English Lexicon
by Graeme D. Ritchie, Graham J. Russell, Alan W. Black, and Stephen G. Pulman

The Core Language Engine
edited by Hiyan Alshawi

Morphology and Computation
by Richard Sproat

Generating Referring Expressions: Constructing Descriptions in a Domain of Objects and Processes
by Robert Dale

The Logical Approach to Syntax: Foundations, Specifications, and Implementations of Theories of Government and Binding
by Edward P. Stabler, Jr.

The Logical Approach to Syntax

Foundations, Specifications, and Implementations of Theories of Government and Binding

Edward P. Stabler, Jr.

A Bradford Book
The MIT Press
Cambridge, Massachusetts
London, England

This book was printed and bound in the United States of America.

Library of Congress Cataloging-in-Publication Data

Stabler, Edward P.
    The logical approach to syntax: foundations, specifications, and implementations of theories of government and binding / Edward P. Stabler, Jr.
        p.   cm.— (ACL-MIT Press series in natural language processing)
    "A Bradford book."
    Includes bibliographical references and index.
    ISBN 0-262-19315-9
    1. Grammar, comparative and general—Syntax. 2. Language and logic. 3. Government-binding theory (Linguistics) 4. Generative grammar. 5. Computational linguistics. I. Title. II. Series.
P291.S6 1992
415—dc20   91-38763
                                                         CIP

Contents

Preface   xiii

Chapter 1

Introduction   1

Part I

Logical Foundations

Chapter 2

Theories about strings   9

2.1 First order theories, definitions, and representations   10

2.2 A context-free language in logic   13

2.3 Semantic limitations of first order definition   23

Chapter 3

Deductive reasoning about languages   27

3.1 Clausal form   28

3.2 Resolution   31

3.3 Application to linguistic examples   36

3.4   Building in equality axioms: SEq
      resolution   40

3.5   Definite clause theories   44

3.6   Decision procedures   55

3.7   The strategy for the current
      project   56

Chapter 4

**Deductive parsing: Context-free
phrase structure   57**

4.1   Difference lists   58

4.2   A correspondence between
      derivations and deductions   61

4.3   Parse trees again, and
      transformations of parse trees
      72

4.4   LR parsing and LR deduction
      75

4.5   A Prolog session with a simple
      (ineffective) parser   80

Chapter 5

**Deductive parsing: Natural
language phrase structure   83**

5.1   Context-free grammars for natural
      languages   83

5.2   Extraposition grammars   92

5.3   Restricted logic grammars   97

5.4   More unresolved problems   99

5.5   A Prolog session with theory XGR
      101

5.6   A Prolog session with the
      metatheory   103

Part II

Formalizing Barriers

Chapter 6

X-bar theory   107   6.1   Origins of X-bar theory   107

                                 6.2   X-bar theory extended to
                                       nonlexical categories   109

                                 6.3   What is X-bar theory about?
                                       113

                                 6.4   A logical formulation of X-bar
                                       theory   118

                                 6.5   Preliminary tests of the
                                       formalization   124

Chapter 7

The theory of movement   125   7.1   Tree transducers   127

                                 7.2   Substitutions and adjunctions
                                       133

                                 7.3   Preliminary tests and discoveries
                                       141

Chapter 8

Government and barriers   145   8.1   Introducing case theory and
                                       government   145

                                 8.2   Domination, c-command, and
                                       m-command   150

8.3   Binding   152

8.4   Subcategorization and θ-marking
      153

8.5   Blocking categories, barriers, and
      government   155

8.6   Preliminary tests of the
      formalization   157

Chapter 9

**Structure preservation, head   9.1   The structure-preserving
movement, and bounding   161   hypothesis   161**

                                         9.2   Head movement   163

                                         9.3   The theory of bounding   169

                                         9.4   Island constraints   173

                                         9.5   A parametric intrinsic barrier and
                                               cumulative violations   175

                                         9.6   Some loose ends   178

Chapter 10

**The empty category principle and   10.1 Affect-α and the ECP as a filter at
minimality   181   LF   181**

                                         10.2 Proper government   185

                                         10.3 Verb raising revisited   188

                                         10.4 Minimality   189

                                         10.5 *that*-trace effects   192

10.6 A-movement and agreement
195

10.7 A modification in the ECP for
raising and passive   196

10.8 Exploring some consequences of the
ECP formalization   202

Part III

Variations and Elaborations

Chapter 11

Determiner phrases   213

11.1 Empirical motivations for a DP
hypothesis   214

11.2 The formalism and preliminary
tests   217

11.3 Subjacency and the strict cycle
condition   219

Chapter 12

**Inflectional phrases and head
movement   223**

12.1 Verb raising and affix lowering in
English   223

12.2 Head movement and the structure
of IP   226

12.3 Exploring some consequences of the
formalization   233

Chapter 13

VP-internal subjects   237

13.1 A restricted theory of movement
and government   238

13.2 Exploring some consequences of the
     formalization   242

13.3 Head government and *that*-trace
     effects   249

13.4 Movement, agreement, and case
     252

Part IV

Computational Models

Chapter 14

**Guided deductions from linguistic   14.1 Representing FB for two proof
theory   257   methods   258

                                           14.2 Theorems about particular
                                                structures   262

                                           14.3 Induction and the
                                                non-well-foundedness of affect-α
                                                266

                                           14.4 General theorems of linguistic
                                                interest   274

                                           14.5 Decidability   282

                                           14.6 Conclusions   282

Chapter 15

**Parsing as constraint satisfaction   15.1 A parsing problem   284
283**

                                           15.2 Parsing as constraint satisfaction
                                                286

                                           15.3 Structure preservation theorems
                                                288

15.4 Structural complexity results
292

15.5 Locality   310

15.6 Structural and locality theorem
deployment   314

15.7 Some psychological considerations
320

15.8 Conclusions and future directions
321

Appendix A

**Proving a negative result from RT
325**

Appendix B

**The first order formalization
337**

Appendix C

A guided proof system   361

Notes   397

Bibliography   411

Index   425

Preface

This text presumes some familiarity with first order logic, with resolution proof methods for first order logic, and with recent work in theoretical syntax. However, some explanation and references to background material have been added to make the text useful to readers who lack background in one or more of these areas. After an introduction Part I briefly explores some of the logical foundations of our formalization and theorem proving methods. Part II presents, in complete detail, a formalization of the principal claims of Chomsky's *Barriers*. Part III demonstrates the flexibility of this formalization by exploring some significant elaborations of the theory that have been proposed recently. And finally, Part IV considers computational applications of the formalization, putting the basic techniques developed in the first part of the book to work.

All the proof techniques described in Part I have been implemented, and their performance is discussed in Part III. In fact, almost all of the claims about consequences of our formal theories have been checked with one or more of the techniques discussed. Some of them were actually unanticipated discoveries found by one of the automated proof systems. All of the trees displayed in the text were drawn by a graphic interface built for these theorem provers. Appendixes provide the complete first order formalization of the theory and a Prolog implementation of a simple guided deduction system.

I have worked on this project intermittently for more than three years, and it has been incubating for much longer, so I have had time to find much generous assistance. I am most indebted to Robert Berwick, Mark Johnson, Fernando Pereira, Chet Creider, William Demopoulos, and E.W. Elcock, who provided valuable advice, specific criticisms of early drafts, and encouragement. At the 1987 Linguistic Institute at Stanford University, Luigi Rizzi inspired me to take on the whole of *Barriers*, besides providing specific assistance on a number of topics. I would also like to thank especially Kathleen Dahlgren, Janet Dean Fodor, Joyce McDowell, Dominique Sportiche, Tim Stowell, and David Weir.

My ideas were further sharpened by discussions of related topics at various times with Wolfgang Bibel, Verónica Dahl, Ed Keenan, Jerry Fodor, Graeme Hirst, David Israel, Howard Lasnik, Hector Levesque, Robert Matthews, Robert May, Zenon Pylyshyn, Eric Ristad, Ray Reiter, Patrick Saint-Dizier, and Edward P. Stabler. Katherine Hill provided invaluable encouragement, stylistic suggestions, and advice on the presentation.

I am also grateful to the students who helped me get rid of many mistakes and suggested ways of improving the presentation of the material: Filippo Beghelli, Kwok-Hung (Daniel) Chan, Paul Forster, Gail Harris, Susan Hirsh, Mark Szwarc, and especially Dorit Ben-shalom and Andi Wu.

Special software and computer support services, above and beyond the call of duty, were provided for me by Paul Forster, M. V. S. Ramanath, Mark Szwarc, David (Magi) Wiseman, and Ning-Yiu (James) Wong. If these people had not put up with my unreasonable demands and expressions of frustration, this work would have taken much longer!

I have a special debt to Jerry Fodor, Noam Chomsky, Mike Harnish, and Adrian Akmajian for getting me started on this adventure.

This work would not have been possible without the intellectual environment and the relief from teaching that was provided by the Canadian Institute for Advanced Research from 1986 to 1989, for which I am very grateful. Some of this research was also done with support from the Natural Sciences and Engineering Research Council of Canada during 1986–1989, and from the Committee on Research of the Academic Senate of the Los Angeles Division of the University of California during 1989–1991.

The Logical Approach
to Syntax

Chapter 1

Introduction

Two fundamental ideas set the stage for this work. The first is that the study of language processing ought to be guided by the study of properties of human languages themselves, properties that linguistic theories tell us about. Linguists typically abstract away from certain "limitations" in human linguistic performance, but these abstractions probably get more attention than they deserve. Constructions that are in some sense grammatical and yet peculiarly difficult because of length, center embedding, garden paths, and so on, are very suggestive, but they should not eclipse the enormously wide range of constructions that people have no trouble with. It is not easy to provide a reasonable account of even the clear and uncontroversial properties of language; the abstractions are not the problem. So it still makes sense to consider what sort of device could compute the structures defined by our best developed lingistic theories, a device without "performance limitations," and only then to consider how such a system could be limited or otherwise perturbed in such a way as to exhibit human-like performance. Given the complex and peculiar character of human languages, it is hard to see how any other strategy could get very far. Attempting to develop a processing model based on a conception of language structure that linguists have overwhelmingly rejected, letting analogies with processors for much simpler artificial languages lead the way, with the idea that any inadequacies could be quickly patched up, would be naive. That strategy may be appealing in the short run but leads to the situation that Zenon Pylyshyn (1984, xv) warns us about:

> Most current, computational models of cognition are vastly underconstrained and ad hoc; they are contrivances assembled to mimic arbitrary pieces of behavior, with insufficient concern for explicating the principles in virtue of which such behavior is exhibited and with little regard for a precise under-

standing of the class of behaviors for which the model is supposed to provide
an explanation.

Though we have quite rich and substantial theories of language, this observation applies
too often to models of language processing. Recent linguistic theory is rich enough to
provide the basis for a good beginning on the problem of how the full range of constructions in a language could be handled. This problem may be more difficult than designing
parsers that have trouble with peculiar sentences in a small subset of English, but it is
not impossible.

The second fundamental premise of the present study is that human languages are
complex enough that it makes sense to begin a computational study with some formal
specification of the linguistic problems to be handled. Even in elementary arithmetic, a
problem does not need to be very complex before formal methods become valuable in
finding a solution, and recent work in computer science has shown the value of proceeding
even more carefully on more complex problems. One influential text in computer science
says, for example, "A program and its proof should be developed hand-in-hand, with the
proof usually leading the way" (Gries, 1981, 164). The value of a more or less formal
proof is a practical one: it can increase our confidence that a guess about how a problem
might be solved is actually correct, that important counterexamples are not overlooked.
In principle, a correct guess can of course be made without a proof, but in a complex
domain, the nature of one's assumptions about the language can be obscure, and the risk
of oversights and misconceptions is significant.

With these two ideas, the goal of the present study is to provide a methodology and
some initial specifications that can guide the development of particular algorithms for
language processing. With this strategy, we can hope to close the gulf between computational models and our best developed linguistic theories. We treat one recent tradition
in linguistic theory in some detail, the "principles and parameters" or "government and
binding" tradition as developed in Chomsky's *Barriers* (Chomsky, 1986a) and related
work. In the powerful and well-understood notation of first order logic, it turns out that
formalizing these theories without drastic simplification is refreshingly straightforward.
Consider, as a preliminary illustration, the basic structure of some recent theories (see
Figure 1.1). In theories of this kind, each sequence of linguistic sounds, each phonetic
form has representations at a number of levels, including at least the following:

D-structure: the level that directly reflects lexical properties, where the recipients of
θ-roles are in their original positions;

S-structure: an intermediate level, where case theory and subjacency apply;

Logical Form: the level at which meaning is most explicitly represented.

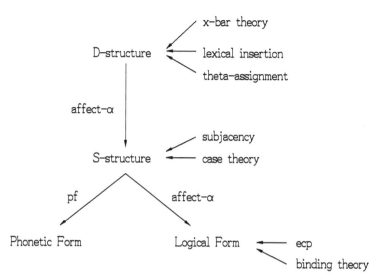

Figure 1.1
The structure of a linguistic theory

These representations are related to each other by affect-α and pf, as shown in the figure, and each level of representation is subject to various well-formedness conditions: X-bar theory imposes some phrase structure constraints on D-structures, and so on. Many of these conditions have restricted, "local" domains of application, that is, they can only apply to some restricted part of a structure at any one time. In theta theory, case theory, binding theory and the ECP, the fundamental locality relations are specified in terms of the notion of *government*, which is roughly the relation between the "head" of a phrase and its complements . A locality condition is also required by subjacency. Chomsky tries to unify these locality conditions with the notion of a *barrier* in a theory that will be the object of study in Part II.

There is no consensus on how the parsing problem for human languages should be specified, exactly, but suppose that we had adopted an account of a language like the one shown in Figure 1.1. Then a preliminary idea about the parsing problem is that it involves finding a constructive proof of a sentence like the following, for any given input phonetic form (PF) τ:

$$\exists DS, SS, LF \quad x\text{-}bar(DS) \wedge$$
$$lexical\text{-}insertion(DS) \wedge$$
$$theta\text{-}assignment(DS) \wedge$$
$$affect\text{-}\alpha(DS, SS) \wedge$$
$$subjacency(SS) \wedge$$

$$case\text{-}theory(SS) \land$$
$$affect\text{-}\alpha(SS, LF) \land$$
$$ecp(LF) \land$$
$$binding\text{-}theory(LF) \land$$
$$pf(SS, \tau)$$

If we can represent the other principles of grammar in a form that mirrors the linguists' proposals as closely as this sentence mirrors the relationships depicted in the figure, then we have a parsing problem that is as rich and well defined as the grammar is. When such a sentence follows from the grammar, the language relates the "sound-meaning" pair τ-LF in such a way that there is a representation of τ at each level of representation, satisfying the appropriate well-formedness conditions.

One can see immediately how different in character this approach is from the prominent earlier approaches. Because first order logic is sufficiently powerful, the formalization of the grammar can be our starting point, and it can be not only faithful to the linguists' intentions but also elegant and transparent. Very little elaboration of the explicit principles of *Barriers* and other proposals is required to allow the formal deduction of interesting results. The demonstration of this point should squelch the unwarranted but repeated rumors that recent theories are not worked out in enough detail to have interesting empirical consequences. Furthermore, unlike certain engineering efforts, this project does not require a complete account of any language. We do not need to base our study on numerous arbitrary decisions about linguistic issues that are not yet understood. On the contrary, since we are interested in how a computational model could exhibit human linguistic sophistication, we want to focus on the properties of language that have been the best established.

There has been a good deal of speculation that maybe the human language processing mechanism does not include any representation of linguistic principles. For example, it has been proposed that some linguistic principles may have a "functional explanation;" that is, they may hold because the basic architecture of the human parsing mechanism is such that languages violating these principles could not be processed.[1] However, while there are perhaps some principles for which such a story might be plausible when taken in isolation (viz., subjacency, and maybe c-command restrictions on binding), anyone acquainted with recent theory knows that few principles have this character. On the contrary, the rich set of principles supposed in current universal grammar form a rather intricate and coherent structure, and it is difficult to see how the whole system could be respected by a learning and language recognition device if not represented propositionally. Jerry A. Fodor (1983, 4-5) summarizes the "standard" story as follows:

...the child is, so to speak, 'born knowing' certain facts about universal constraints on human languages ...it is the fate of the (presumed) innate information to interact with the child's primary linguistic data, and this interaction is presumed to be computational. Now, the notion of computation is intrinsically connected to such semantical concepts as implication, confirmation, and logical consequence. Specifically, a computation is a transformation of representations which respects these sorts of semantic relations...The idea that what is innate has propositional content is thus part and parcel of a certain view of the ontogeny of mental capacities – viz., that in cognitive development, what is endogenously given is computationally deployed.

Perhaps this is only the simplest idea about how the universal principles might be realized. The fact is, though, that no one has been able to make even this "simple" picture work, and since the alternatives appear to be more, not less, difficult to work into any adequate account of human linguistic performance, speculation about alternatives seems premature. In any case, this study is a first step towards the simple, propositional account, and it also provides a methodology with which any of the alternative accounts can be assessed. After studying the very partial account of universal principles presented in Part II, below, the reader is encouraged to consider again how plausible it is that the innate endowment is somehow due to basic facts about parser architecture such as input buffer size.

In sum, with the idea that the complexity of human languages motivates the development of a language processing model that stands in a rigorous correspondence to our best theories of language, we attempt to show that such an approach is feasible by formalizing some particular theories in detail and taking some preliminary steps towards processing models based on these theories. We do not present a finished, efficient parser for English. We only consider the principles that are explicitly presented in *Barriers* and some similar theories, and these comprise only a fragment of what would be needed for any real parsing application. But we use relevant examples of deductions from these theories to show how a theoretically sophisticated parser might be developed. On this approach, the completion of the parser is largely in the hands of linguists, and there, one hopes, those properties of language not yet well understood will come within our grasp through the usual interplay of invention and sustained critical attention.

Though this study is preliminary, we learn some interesting facts about the linguistic theories considered here. In the first place, as already noted, first order logic is powerful enough to allow us to represent most principles of *Barriers* and similar theories quite transparently, in a form that is close to the linguists' original statements of the principles. In this respect, first order logic differs from the standard notations of formal language theory, and also from weaker logics such as the Horn logic used by Prolog. In fact, first order logic is powerful enough that the formalization of influential ideas in the mainstream of theoretical syntax can be worthwhile merely as a way of making those ideas perfectly clear. The bare bones of the proposals are brought into sharp relief, making, for example, a comparison between *Barriers* and the various elaborations in Part III particularly illuminating, showing the character of some recent advances. We discover, in the second place, that specialized automatic theorem provers can be used easily to explore the consequences of these formal theories. Even when established in complete detail, most results that linguists are interested in are easily obtained, although we cannot, even in principle, achieve the goal of formulating a theory from which all linguistic truths can be proven. The difficulties with providing a rigorous decidability result for parsing and similar problems is discussed in Chapters 14 and 15, but a sketch is provided of one way of obtaining such a result for a theory that is more complete than the ones considered here. The use of theorem provers was essential in arriving at the axiomatizations proposed in Parts II and III. These theories are sufficiently complex that hand calculation of formal results is not practical.

Results about the theories and the practical use of the formalizations in guided deductions are not the ultimate goal, of course. What we really want is a better understanding of how humans or any computational system could solve something like the parsing problem for a given natural language, and how this ability could be acquired on the basis of the sort of information children get from their linguistic environments. A basic parsing problem is formulated in terms from the formal theory, and the problem of using it without guidance or simplification is explored. Since we find that, with user guidance, many results can be quickly established directly from first principles, one might think that a parser for a natural language could work analogously, deductively establishing that an input corresponds to well formed grammatical representations. However, when we actually try to design a parsing system that works in this way, the problem is not the length of the derivation of results, but the search for the derivation among many others that do not work out. This is the familiar obstacle in almost all "constraint satisfaction problems," as it is in the simple backtracking methods of context-free parsing. Drawing from the extensive research on constraint satisfaction, new approaches to the parsing problem are suggested which might lead us to a parser that uses first principles directly. This project is very similar to the elimination of spurious local ambiguities in context-free parsing with a finite control automaton and lookahead strings, except the distinctive character of human languages, as reflected in the formal theories, defines exactly what the options are. The difficulties faced here are familiar, but now they have a crisp, rigorous formulation, so they may finally be overcome with further research.

Part I

Logical Foundations

Chapter 2

Theories about strings

*The forms being experimented with come from a closer knowledge of
nature and the outgrowth of the constant search for order.
Design habits leading to the concealment of structure have no
place in this implied order. — Louis Kahn*

Looking over the principles of recent syntactic theories in the "government and binding"
or "principles and parameters" tradition, we see that they mention the presence and
absence of complex properties in trees. It is clear that any transparent representation of
these theories will require a fairly powerful language. First order logic appears to be powerful enough for this purpose. The standard declarative semantics of logic neatly matches
the declarative character of most principles stated by linguists, and so the intended semantics of a first order representation of linguistic theory can be specified easily and
naturally. With this strategy, theories of language can be explicitly represented without
drastic simplifications or reliance on procedural considerations whose substantive import
is only vaguely apprehended. The elegant and transparent representation facilitates the
initial assessment of the correctness of the formalization and provides a valuable flexibility. It should be easy to modify or replace any principle in the formalization. If the
representation is correct, then any surprising results that are derived with sound inference rules will be attributable to the linguistic theory rather than to some peculiarity or
shortcoming in the formalization. Furthermore, a transparent formalization will inherit
the formal simplicity and preserve whatever modularity there is in the structure of the
theory itself.

Apart from merely providing a completely explicit formulation of the central ideas
of linguistic theory, a first order formalization can lead to a usable and provably correct implementation. Automatic first order proof techniques are well developed, and
can be specialized and deployed to explore the consequences of these theories. When
small changes in basic principles have wide ramifications, this can be a valuable tool for
linguists. Chomsky (1986a) has often commented on this feature of recent theory: "As
concepts and principles become simpler, argument and inference tend to become more
complex — a consequence that is naturally very much to be welcomed." In fact, most
research in syntax concerns fragments of theories that are incomplete and only partially

worked out, so one of our challenges is to represent an incomplete theory in such a way that it can be used with a minimum of extension. The formalization of a great deal of material that is irrelevant to the central claims of the theory would be an undesirable burden. Again, the use of first order logic has the advantage that the consequences of a few central ideas can be explored; there is no need to include material that is not needed for the derivation of consequences of immediate interest.

In this chapter, we present some of the basic logical results relevant to understanding the goals and limitations of our formalization and implementation effort.[1] We have a domain of linguistic structures with certain properties which we want to describe. Ultimately, the structures and properties we want to capture will be those that are described by the more or less informal theories in the principles and parameters tradition. We will cast these into precise and formal logical theories. One natural goal for this formalization effort is that each logical theory have as a derivable consequence every true sentence (and *only* true sentences!) about the relevant linguistic domain as it is envisioned by the linguist. This turns out to be unattainable, and so we propose a more modest goal. To explore these matters we use a tiny artificial example: we develop a logical specification of a very simple context-free language. Even in this very simple case, a non-logician may find that some of the subtleties are surprising. A logical theory does not need to be big to be difficult to master.

2.1   First order theories, definitions, and representations

Our logical notation will be standard, except that predicate and function symbols will begin with lower case letters, while variable names will begin with uppercase letters. Another peculiarity in our notation is that we will occasionally write $\psi \leftarrow \phi$ for the material conditional $\phi \rightarrow \psi$, and we will use open formulas to represent their universal closures, except where we explicitly indicate otherwise.

A standard first order language is specified by its nonlogical predicate and function symbols — the quantifiers, logical connectives and so on are invariant from one language to another. Let $\mathcal{L}$ be a first order language with equality. Then a *theory* Γ expressed in that language is just a set of sentences of $\mathcal{L}$. Some of the other standard notions are now defined.

DEFINITION 1 A theory Γ is *closed* iff every consequence of Γ is in Γ. The *closure of* Γ is

$$Cn(\Gamma) = \{s | s \ a \ sentence \ of \ \mathcal{L}, \ \Gamma \models s\}.$$

A language $\mathcal{L}$ is interpreted by a structure $\mathcal{U}$ which assigns each predicate an extension and each function a value in a domain. The truth values of all of the sentences in the language are then determined in the standard ways. We can think of the true sentences, the sentences verified by the structure, as those that correctly describe the structure. This idea is standardly captured as follows:

DEFINITION 2 The theory of an $\mathcal{L}$-structure $\mathcal{U}$ is the set of sentences that the structure verifies, i.e.,

$Th(\mathcal{U}) = \{s | s$ a sentence of $\mathcal{L}$, $\mathcal{U} \models s\}$.

DEFINITION 3 A theory Γ is *complete* iff for every sentence s in $\mathcal{L}$, either $s \in \Gamma$ or $(\neg s) \in \Gamma$.

Obviously, for any structure $\mathcal{U}$, $Th(\mathcal{U})$ is complete. In the current project, the ideal would obviously be to get a theory of the structure which is the linguistic domain with the relevant properties and relations. We would like to represent this theory in a finite or at least decidable form though, so what we really want is an "axiomatization" of this theory.

DEFINITION 4 A recursive set Δ of sentences is an *axiomatization* of Γ iff

$Cn(\Gamma) = Cn(\Delta)$.

A theory is *finitely axiomatizable* just in case it has a finite set of axioms. Obviously, a finitely axiomatizable theory always has an axiomatization containing a single sentence. With a sound and complete proof method, we can derive all and only the consequences of Γ from any axiomatization of Γ. That is, using $\vdash$ for "derives," if Δ is an axiomatization of Γ we have $Cn(\Gamma) = \{s | \Delta \vdash s\}$. From our computational perspective, it is this sort of derivation relation that we are most interested in. Unfortunately, it is not always possible to get an axiomatization of the theory of a structure.

When we cannot get a complete theory of the relevant structure, we could still attempt to correctly define or represent the important linguistic relations. We can make these notions precise.

In any $\mathcal{L}$-structure $\mathcal{U}$, we follow the convention of letting $\bar{a}$ be the name of a, and we let $|\mathcal{U}|$ be the domain of $\mathcal{U}$.

DEFINITION 5 A k-ary relation R in $\mathcal{U}$ is *defined* by formula ϕ (with k free variables) iff for every $a_i \in |\mathcal{U}|$,

$\langle a_1, \ldots, a_k \rangle \in R$ iff $\mathcal{U} \models \phi(\bar{a}_1, \ldots, \bar{a}_k)$.

Since a structure will verify $\neg\phi$ whenever it fails to verify ϕ, this can be expressed as follows: R is defined by ϕ iff for every $a_i \in |\mathcal{U}|$,

$\langle a_1, \ldots, a_k \rangle \in R$ implies $\mathcal{U} \models \phi(\overline{a}_1, \ldots, \overline{a}_k)$, and
$\langle a_1, \ldots, a_k \rangle \notin R$ implies $\mathcal{U} \models \neg\phi(\overline{a}_1, \ldots, \overline{a}_k)$.

Since our goal is to get a theory, an axiomatization, from which we can *deduce* all the truths about the linguistic domain, we are really more interested in a related but stronger syntactic notion:

DEFINITION 6 Formula ϕ in theory Γ *represents* R iff for every $a_i \in |\mathcal{U}|$,

$\langle a_1, \ldots, a_k \rangle \in R$ implies $\phi(\overline{a}_1, \ldots, \overline{a}_k) \in \Gamma$, and
$\langle a_1, \ldots, a_k \rangle \notin R$ implies $\neg\phi(\overline{a}_1, \ldots, \overline{a}_k) \in \Gamma$.

R is *representable* in Γ iff there is such a ϕ in Γ that represents R.

Obviously then, ϕ represents R in $Th(\mathcal{U})$ iff ϕ defines R in $\mathcal{U}$.

Since the set of theorems of an axiomatization are recursively enumerable, Church's thesis tells us that a relation is representable in a consistent axiomatizable theory only if the relation is recursive. It might appear that commonsense observations about human linguistic abilities indicate that human languages are recursive. For example, a competent speaker of English can quickly tell you that a string like *lions sleep* is a good English sentence but *lions* is not. If this ability is computational, and if this decision can be made effectively for every string, then English must be recursive. However, this argument breaks down as soon as one notes that there are grammatical strings of English that competent speakers cannot classify, such as sentences with more than a googol words, or certain deeply center-embedded and garden path sentences, discussed below. Other similar arguments for the recursiveness of human languages also break down under scrutiny.[2] The question can only be settled by a theory about the actual structure of human languages, a theory of the kind we will be attempting to formalize. It would be a mistake to assume in advance that the set of sentences must be recursive. And even if the set of sentences is recursive, other linguistically relevant properties of sentences and other strings, particularly the properties of sentence *structures*, may not be recursive.

Sometimes, we can only get "half" of representability:

DEFINITION 7 Formula ϕ in theory Γ *weakly represents* R iff for every $a_i \in |\mathcal{U}|$,

$\langle a_1, \ldots, a_k \rangle \in R$ iff $\phi(\overline{a}_1, \ldots, \overline{a}_k) \in \Gamma$

R is *weakly representable* in Γ iff there is such a ϕ in Γ that weakly represents R.

Group theory is finitely axiomatizable, complete and decidable, but many other theories do not have these properties. For example, Zermelo-Fraenkel set theory is axiomatizable (though not finitely axiomatizable), but it is incomplete and undecidable. We would like our theories of language to be not only axiomatizable and complete but also decidable. In fact, the former two properties imply the latter:

DEFINITION 8 A theory Γ is *decidable* iff there is an effective method for deciding whether, for any sentence ϕ, $\phi \in \Gamma$ or $\phi \notin \Gamma$.

LEMMA 1 If theory Γ and its complement $\{\phi | \phi \notin \Gamma\}$ are each recursively enumerable, then Γ is decidable.

Proof: Enumerate one element of Γ and then an element of $\{\phi | \phi \notin \Gamma\}$, and so on. Every sentence ϕ will appear in one of these enumerations after finitely many steps. ∎

THEOREM 1 If theory Γ is axiomatizable and complete, Γ is decidable.

Proof: Since Γ is axiomatizable, $\Gamma = Cn(\Gamma_0)$ for some recursive Γ_0. Since Γ is complete, we have $\Gamma_0 \vdash \phi$ or $\Gamma_0 \vdash \neg\phi$ for every sentence ϕ. Since the theorems of any first order axiomatization are recursively enumerable, and since $\phi \in \{\phi | \phi \notin \Gamma\}$ iff $\neg\phi \in Cn(\Gamma_0)$, Γ is decidable by the previous lemma. ∎

There are axiomatizable theories that are not decidable. Consider, for example, the theory that is axiomatized by the empty theory $Cn(\emptyset)$. This is just the set of valid first order sentences, and it is not decidable. It is not complete, in our sense of "complete:" there are sentences ϕ such that neither $\phi \in Cn(\emptyset)$ nor $\neg\phi \in Cn(\emptyset)$. First order logic is said to be "complete" in a different sense: there is an effective procedure for demonstrating that any valid sentence is valid. It is important to distinguish the completeness of proof techniques from the completeness of theories. First order logic has a complete proof technique, but the set of consequences of axiomatizations of first order logic is incomplete as a theory, and first order logic is undecidable because we cannot effectively determine that a sentence is not valid.

2.2   A context-free language in logic

Consider a context-free grammar G with the terminal vocabulary Σ. Using $\Rightarrow^*$ for the relation "derives in 0 or more steps," the language generated by the grammar is standardly defined as the set of strings derivable from the "start" or "sentence" symbol S:

$$L(G) = \{String|\ S \Rightarrow^* String,\ String \in \Sigma^*\}.$$

Suppose that we want to represent in logic the property of being in this language, letting this property be the intended interpretation of some predicate s in our first order language. Then, where $\mathcal{G}$ is the intended interpretation, and using the notation $s^{\mathcal{G}}$ for the interpretation that $\mathcal{G}$ assigns to s, what we want is for the the unary relation $s^{\mathcal{G}}$ to hold of exactly the strings in $L(G)$.

To develop this idea, it will be convenient to consider a simple context-free grammar G:

$S \rightarrow NP\ VP$ *Grammar G*
$S \rightarrow S\ and\ S$
$NP \rightarrow lions$
$VP \rightarrow sleep$

Using the standard representation of sequences or strings as lists, the following is probably the most straightforward logical representation of this simple grammar (where each formula represents its universal closure):

Theory T

$s(S) \leftarrow np(NP) \wedge vp(VP) \wedge append(NP, VP, S)$ (2.2.1)
$s(S) \leftarrow s(S1) \wedge s(S2) \wedge append(S1, [and|S2], S)$ (2.2.2)

$np([lions])$ (2.2.3)
$vp([sleep])$ (2.2.4)

$append([H|T1], L2, [H|T3]) \leftarrow append(T1, L2, T3)$ (2.2.5)
$append([], L, L) \leftarrow list(L)$ (2.2.6)

$list([])$ (2.2.7)
$list([H|T]) \leftarrow list(T)$ (2.2.8)

Does the open formula $s(S)$ correctly represent the relation $s^{\mathcal{G}}$ in the simple logical theory $Cn(T)$? We must first define the intended interpretation $\mathcal{G}$. There is room for creativity here, but we follow one of the simplest approaches. The domain $|\mathcal{G}|$ is the terminal vocabulary of G, sequences over that vocabulary (including sequences containing sequences), and a set of "dotted pairs" which are merely a technical convenience. The interpretation of each nonterminal category Cat is the set of terminal strings that can be derived from Cat in grammar G. We now specify the interpretation more formally. In this definition we use Quine's (1976, §6) "quasi-quotation" to represent concatenations. For example, $\ulcorner a.b \urcorner$ represents the result of concatenating 'a' with '.' with 'b'.

(a) *The interpretation of the function symbols.* All function symbols except the binary . ("cons") and the (0-ary) constant $[]$ ("the empty list") receive the Herbrand interpretation. That is, the 0-ary functions *lions*, *sleep* and *and* denote themselves.

The cons and the empty list provide representations of sequences, as is standard. However, we also need to provide denotations for values of cons that are not sequences, and it will be convenient if these values are distinct for each distinct pair of arguments. For these cases, we use a special interpretation and call them "dotted pairs":

$$h.^{\mathcal{G}}t = \begin{cases} \langle h, t_1, \ldots, t_n \rangle, & \text{if } t \text{ is a sequence } \langle t_1, \ldots, t_n \rangle \ (n \geq 0) \\ \ulcorner (\bar{h}).(\bar{t}) \urcorner, & (\text{"dotted pairs"}) \text{ otherwise} \end{cases}$$
$$[]^{\mathcal{G}} = \langle \rangle$$

The parentheses in the second case of the definition of the cons function serve to guarantee uniqueness of denotations. For example, $a_1.(a_2.a_3) \neq (a_1.a_2).a_3$ in $\mathcal{G}$.

(b) *The interpretation of the predicate symbols.* For each nonterminal Cat in the grammar, our theory contains a unary predicate cat of the same name. In each of these cases,

$$L \in cat^{\mathcal{G}} \text{ iff } Cat \Rightarrow^* L, \ L \in \Sigma^*.$$

The predicates *append* and *list* have the standard interpretations:

$$\langle L1, L2, L3 \rangle \in append^{\mathcal{G}} \quad \text{iff } L3 \text{ is the sequence that results}$$
$$\text{from appending } L2 \text{ to } L1$$
$$L \in list^{\mathcal{G}} \quad \text{iff } L \text{ is a sequence}$$

Now we can return to our question: does $s(S)$ correctly represent $s^{\mathcal{G}}$ in $Cn(T)$? That is, assuming a sound and complete proof method, is it the case that for every x,

$x \in L(G)$ implies $T \vdash s(\bar{x})$, and
$x \notin L(G)$ implies $T \vdash \neg s(\bar{x})$?

We begin by considering weak representation.

PROPOSITION 1 The formula $s(S)$ weakly represents $s^{\mathcal{G}}$ in $Cn(T)$.

Proof: We must prove $x \in L(G)$ iff $T \vdash s(\overline{x})$.
($\Rightarrow$) Clearly $L(G) = \{lions\ sleep\ (and\ lions\ sleep)^n | n \geq 0\}$. We show by induction on n that every member x of this set is such that $T \vdash s(\overline{x})$.

($n = 0$). By 2.2.3 and 2.2.4 we have $np([lions])$ and $vp([sleep])$. And since $\{2.2.7, 2.2.8\}$ $\vdash list([sleep])$, we have $append([], [sleep], [sleep])$. Thus we have $T \vdash append([lions], [sleep], [lions, sleep])$. From these results we can derive $s([lions, sleep])$.

($n = k + 1$). Assume that the result holds for $n = k$. Then we can use 2.2.2, $s(S) \leftarrow s(S1) \wedge s(S2) \wedge append(S1, [and|S2], S)$, letting $S1$ be the string *lions sleep (and lions sleep)*^{k} and letting $S2$ be the string of case $n = 0$, *lions sleep*. Rules 2.2.5-2.2.8 guarantee that there will be a string S such that we have $T \vdash append(S1, [and|S2], S)$, and this is the case $n = k + 1$.

($\Leftarrow$) It is clear, as in the proof of ($\Rightarrow$), that any derivation of $s(\overline{x})$ from T corresponds to a derivation of x from S in G. (The intuitive correspondence is spelled out via the notions of grammatical derivation trees and logical proof trees in §4.2, below.) ∎

PROPOSITION 2 The formula $s(S)$ does not represent $s^{\mathcal{G}}$ in $Cn(T)$.

Proof: Although $T \vdash s([lions, sleep])$, we do not have $T \vdash \neg s([sleep, sleep])$, as can be seen by noting that T is consistent with $s([lions, sleep])$ and with $lions = sleep$, and hence with $s([sleep, sleep])$. ∎

PROPOSITION 3 The theory $Cn(T)$ is not complete.

Proof: By the proof of the previous proposition, $T \nvdash \neg s([sleep, sleep])$ and it is also clear that $T \nvdash s([sleep, sleep])$. ∎

The absence of restrictions on the equality relation in structures that verify T was exploited in the last two results. This weakness is serious. There are even finite models of T: although we can derive from 2.2.7 and 2.2.8 the existence of lists $[], [[]], [[[]]], \cdots,$ there is nothing in the theory to block the assumption that these are all identical to $[]$.

The incompleteness of $Cn(T)$ is different from *essential* incompleteness. Gödel's famous incompleteness result concerns the essential incompleteness of Peano arithmetic:

DEFINITION 9 Theory Γ is *essentially incomplete* if Γ is not complete and no consistent, recursively enumerable extension of Γ is complete.

Since we have not established that $Cn(T)$ is essentially incomplete, we can try to extend T to obtain the completeness that is our goal. It is clear that to represent $s^{\mathcal{G}}$, we need the converses of the conditionals in T, and we need an equality theory. The equality theory must contain pairwise inequalities for all our functions in addition to the standard axioms for equality:

Theory RT

$$s(S) \leftrightarrow (\quad \exists NP, VP$$
$$np(NP) \wedge vp(VP) \wedge append(NP, VP, S)$$
$$\vee \quad \exists S1, S2$$
$$s(S1) \wedge s(S2) \wedge append(S1, [and|S2], S)$$
$$)$$

(2.2.9)

$$np(NP) \leftrightarrow NP = [lions]$$

(2.2.10)

$$vp(VP) \leftrightarrow VP = [sleep]$$

(2.2.11)

$$append(L1, L2, L3) \leftrightarrow (\quad \exists H, T1, T3$$
$$L1 = [H|T1] \wedge L3 = [H|T3] \wedge$$
$$append(T1, L2, T3)$$
$$\vee \quad L1 = [] \wedge L2 = L3 \wedge list(L3)$$
$$)$$

(2.2.12)

$$list(L) \leftrightarrow (\quad L = []$$
$$\vee \quad \exists H, T(L = [H|T] \wedge list(T))$$
$$)$$

(2.2.13)

$$X = X$$

(2.2.14)

$$\neg lions = sleep$$

(2.2.15)

$$\neg lions = and$$

(2.2.16)

$$\neg lions = []$$

(2.2.17)

$$\neg lions = [H|T]$$

(2.2.18)

$$\neg sleep = and$$

(2.2.19)

$$\neg sleep = []$$

(2.2.20)

$$\neg sleep = [H|T]$$

(2.2.21)

$$\neg and = [] \tag{2.2.22}$$

$$\neg and = [H|T] \tag{2.2.23}$$

$$\neg[] = [H|T] \tag{2.2.24}$$

$$[H|T] = [H1|T1] \leftrightarrow H = H1 \wedge T = T1 \tag{2.2.25}$$

$$s(X1) \leftarrow s(X) \wedge X = X1 \tag{2.2.26}$$

$$np(X1) \leftarrow np(X) \wedge X = X1 \tag{2.2.27}$$

$$vp(X1) \leftarrow vp(X) \wedge X = X1 \tag{2.2.28}$$

$$list(X1) \leftarrow list(X) \wedge X = X1 \tag{2.2.29}$$

$$X1 = Y1 \leftarrow X = Y \wedge X = X1 \wedge Y = Y1 \tag{2.2.30}$$

$$append(X1, Y1, Z1) \leftarrow append(X, Y, Z) \wedge X = X1 \wedge Y = Y1 \wedge Z = Z1 \tag{2.2.31}$$

We have one function symbol with positive arity, the cons. The $\leftarrow$ part of 2.2.25 is the standard equality substitution rule for this function, and the $\rightarrow$ part tells us that the function is 1-1. RT has six predicates, and 2.2.26-2.2.31 are merely instances of the standard substitution rule for each of these.

In assessing these first order sentences, it is valuable to keep in mind some basic equivalences. Remember that $\forall(\Phi \leftrightarrow \Psi)$ is equivalent to $\forall(\Phi \rightarrow \Psi) \wedge \forall(\Psi \rightarrow \Phi)$. And if Φ contains a variable X that does not occur in Ψ, then $\forall(\Phi \rightarrow \Psi)$ is equivalent to $\forall((\exists X \; \Phi) \rightarrow \Psi)$.

For example, since we will often leave the universal closure operator implicit, we display a sentence like

$$\forall(\; p(X) \leftarrow \exists Y \; q(X, Y) \;)$$

as

$$p(X) \leftarrow \exists Y \; q(X, Y),$$

except where there could be confusion about whether we intend the sentence or the open formula. The sentence is equivalent to

$$\forall(\; p(X) \leftarrow q(X, Y) \;).$$

However, notice that

$$\forall(\; p(X) \rightarrow \exists Y \; q(X, Y) \;)$$

is not equivalent to

$$\forall(\ p(X) \rightarrow q(X, Y)\ ).$$

Now consider the question: does $s(S)$ correctly represent $s^{\mathcal{G}}$ in $Cn(RT)$? Is it the case that for every x,

$x \in L(G)$ implies $RT \vdash s(\overline{x})$, and
$x \notin L(G)$ implies $RT \vdash \neg s(\overline{x})$?

As we noted, to get this result it is important that the theory provide enough information about equality in $\mathcal{G}$, so we begin with a preliminary result about the representation of this relation. It is clear that the members of the sequence $[], [[]], [[[]]], \ldots$ must be pairwise distinct in any model of RT:

PROPOSITION 4 The formula $X = Y$ represents $=^{\mathcal{G}}$ in $Cn(RT)$.

Proof: We need to show that for any $x, y \in \mathcal{G}$,

$x = y$ implies $RT \vdash \overline{x} = \overline{y}$
$x \neq y$ implies $RT \vdash \neg \overline{x} = \overline{y}$

if x and y are the same, it is clear that $\overline{x}$ and $\overline{y}$ will be the same, and hence $\{2.2.14\} \vdash \overline{x} = \overline{y}$. Notice that 2.2.14 and 2.2.30 allow us to derive the symmetry of equality, $X = Y \leftarrow Y = X$. So if x and y are one of the "basic" elements *lions*, *sleep*, *and*, or $\langle \rangle$, then we have $\vdash \neg \overline{x} = \overline{y}$ from one of the inequalities 2.2.15-2.2.24 and symmetry. We can similarly derive the inequality of basic elements and values of the cons function (i.e. a dotted pair or a sequence). If x and y are distinct values of the cons function, then in some argument they have distinct elements. Repeated applications of 2.2.25 will allow us to derive $\neg \overline{x} = \overline{y}$ in either case, again using one of the inequalities 2.2.15-2.2.24 and symmetry. ∎

PROPOSITION 5 The formula $s(S)$ represents $s^{\mathcal{G}}$ in $Cn(RT)$.

Proof: It is obvious that $s(S)$ weakly represents $s^{\mathcal{G}}$ in $Cn(RT)$. We show that $x \notin L(G)$ implies $RT \vdash \neg s(\overline{x})$. Since, by the previous proposition, we can derive $\neg [lions] = lions$, we can derive $\neg np(lions)$, and similarly for every constant and function expression distinct from $[lions]$. Similarly, we can derive $\neg vp(t)$ for every t distinct from $[sleep]$. Given any $x \notin L(G)$, there will be finitely many pairs $\overline{y}, \overline{z}$ such that $append(\overline{y}, \overline{z}, \overline{x})$, and for each of these, we will be able to show that there is no $\overline{z1}$ satisfying:

$np(\overline{y}) \wedge vp(\overline{z})$ or
$s(\overline{y}) \wedge \overline{z} = [and|\overline{z1}] \wedge s(\overline{z1})$.

Thus we can derive $\neg s(\overline{x})$. ■

Is $Cn(RT)$ complete? A complete theory, an axiomatization of $Th(\mathcal{G})$, is obviously the ideal that we should strive for. If completeness were established, then we would immediately have an alternative proof of the previous proposition, since by the weak representation proposition we know $x \notin L(G)$ implies $RT \nvdash s(\overline{x})$. In this ideal situation, we would have $Cn(RT) = Th(\mathcal{G})$. Unfortunately, this does not hold.

PROPOSITION 6 $Cn(RT)$ is not complete.

Proof: Notice that RT is still not strong enough to allow us to derive either $(\forall X)\neg X = [X]$ or $\neg(\forall X)\neg X = [X]$. We can see this by noting that there are models $\mathcal{G}'$ of RT that have the domain of $\mathcal{G}$ plus one additional element $*$ which is not denoted by any constant in $\mathcal{L}$, but which *is* the value of $*.^{\mathcal{G}'}\langle\rangle$. This structure verifies RT but falsifies $(\forall X)\neg X = [X]$. ■

Given the previous result, it is worthwhile to consider whether there is a slightly stronger theory that is complete. Let GT be RT plus all instances of the following axiom schema for all variables X:

$\neg X = \tau$ *for every term τ properly containing variable X*   (2.2.32)

No finite set of axioms will have the same consequences as GT:

PROPOSITION 7 $Cn(GT)$ is not finitely axiomatizable.

Proof: Notice that the following sentences are all instances of 2.2.32:

$\neg X = [X]$ *remember that $[X]$ is $X.[]$*
$\neg X = [[X]]$ $[[X]]$ *is* $(X.[]).[]$
$\neg X = [[[X]]]$ $[[[X]]]$ *is* $((X.[]).[]).[]$
$\cdots$ $\cdots$

(This set of sentences is similar to the standard first example of a theory that is not finitely axiomatizable.) Note that there is no finite subset $GT_0 \subseteq GT$ such that $Cn(GT_0) = Cn(GT)$. So our result follows if we show that some finite subset $GT_0 \subseteq GT$ axiomatizes GT if there is any finite axiomatization of GT at all.

Suppose that $Cn(GT)$ is finitely axiomatized by some Γ. Then $Cn(GT) = Cn(\Gamma)$, and so $GT \models \Gamma$. By compactness it follows that there is a finite $GT_0 \subseteq GT$ such that $GT_0 \models \Gamma$. Thus we have $Cn(\Gamma) \subseteq Cn(GT_0) \subseteq GT$, and it then follows that $Cn(GT_0) = Cn(GT)$. ∎

PROPOSITION 8 $Cn(GT)$ is not complete.

Proof: Although GT is strong enough to represent identity, there are still many true sentences that cannot be derived in RT. For example, it is clear that we cannot derive

$$\exists Y, Z(X = [Y|Z]) \leftarrow \qquad\qquad (2.2.33)$$
$$\neg(X = [\,] \vee X = lions \vee X = sleep \vee X = and).$$

We can see this by noting that $RT + 2.2.33$ is true in the intended model $\mathcal{G}$, so $RT + 2.2.33$ is consistent, and hence the negation of 2.2.33 cannot be derived from RT by itself. Furthermore, we can construct a model $\mathcal{G}'$ of RT that falsifies 2.2.33. Let $\mathcal{G}'$ have the domain of $\mathcal{G}$ plus one additional element $*$ which is not denoted by any constant in $\mathcal{L}$, and which is the not the value of $x.^{\mathcal{G}'}y$ for any x, y. $\mathcal{G}'$ is a model for RT but not for $RT + 2.2.33$. It follows that 2.2.33 cannot be derived from RT. ∎

We can try the same trick again. That is, we can strengthen the theory to allow us to derive the sentence used in the last proof. Unfortunately, there are many sentences that cannot be derived from GT. Tarski's (1934) "string theory" provides a good inventory of basic properties of domains of strings of symbols, and many of them have not yet been captured by axioms in GT.[3]

In the first place, unit sequences have a special role as the "simplest" nonempty strings. For convenience, let's extend the language with a predicate defined as follows:

$unit(X) \leftrightarrow \exists Y\ X = [Y].$

With this definition and 2.2.32 we can derive

$\neg unit([\,]).$

However, we have missed some fundamental properties of the cons function and the *append* relation:

$$append(X, Y, [Z]) \rightarrow (\quad unit(X) \wedge Y = [\,] \qquad\qquad (2.2.34)$$
$$\vee \quad unit(Y) \wedge X = [\,]$$
$$).$$

Furthermore, the empty sequence has special properties:

$$append(X, Y, []) \rightarrow X = [] \wedge Y = []$$ (2.2.35)

$$append(X, [], X)$$ (2.2.36)

$$append([], X, Y) \leftrightarrow append(X, [], Y)$$ (2.2.37)

There is another principle concerning the results of appending strings that is sometimes called "Tarski's law" (Corcoran et al., 1974). It says that when a string is the result of appending two pairs of strings X, Y and $X1, Y1$, then there is a string Z that is an "interpolant" of these pairs:

$$(\; append(X, Y, L) \wedge append(X1, Y1, L) \;) \leftrightarrow (\qquad \exists Z \; append(X, Z, X1) \wedge$$ (2.2.38)
$$append(Z, Y1, Y)$$
$$\vee \quad \exists Z \; append(X1, Z, X) \wedge$$
$$append(Z, Y, Y1)$$
$$).$$

A little reflection suffices to show that these principles are true in $\mathcal{G}$, and so any complete theory of $\mathcal{G}$ must include them.

"Induction principles" are essential for demonstrating many properties (like 2.2.33). The following second order induction principle is very powerful:

$$\forall \phi \big(\phi([]) \wedge \forall X, Y (\phi(X) \wedge unit(Y) \rightarrow$$ (2.2.39)
$$\exists Z \; append(X, Y, Z) \wedge \phi(Z))) \rightarrow$$
$$\forall X \, sequence(X) \rightarrow \phi(X).$$

Suppose we have a property ϕ such that the empty sequence satisfies ϕ, and for any sequence X that satisfies ϕ the result Z of appending X and any unit sequence Y also satisfies ϕ. Then it follows that everything satisfies ϕ. Following Tarski, Maloney proves that this provides a "categoricity," a guarantee that consistent extensions of this theory will represent properties of strings that hold in isomorphic domains.

Obviously, we cannot use second order induction axioms in our first order approach. Often we can make do with first order instances of this axiom. For example, we can add the version of 2.2.39 that lets ϕ be any open formula with one free variable. This suffices for the results we will be interested in, but, as we will see in the following section, it sacrifices categoricity.

Suppose for a moment that we could use 2.2.39. Let CA be the set of all instances of 2.2.34, 2.2.35, 2.2.36, 2.2.38, and 2.2.39. Let $CT = GT + CA$. The theory is *still* incomplete, and it is essentially so, as we can now see because its relation to theories of arithmetic is clear, and has in fact been formally established.

PROPOSITION 9 CT is essentially incomplete. There is no axiomatization of $Th(\mathcal{G})$.

Proof: Gödel constructed a model of concatenation in arithmetic, and a model of arithmetic is easily constructed in a theory of concatenation like $Cn(CT)$, as shown by Hermes and Quine (1946). Consequently, $Cn(CT)$ has the same essential incompleteness that arithmetic has. See Corcoran et al. (1974) for a survey of these results, presented in terms of a strong relation of "synonymy." ■

2.3   Semantic limitations of first order definition

We could have aimed for a higher goal, the goal of formulating a theory that describes the intended domain and no other, a theory that uniquely determines the intended structure. However, we know that this goal is unattainable in first order logic. A first order theory of the infinite domain of linguistic structures (or *any* infinite domain) cannot characterize its domain even up to isomorphism. This is what is meant by saying that the theory is not categorical. The limitation applies to the simple theories of $\mathcal{G}$ as well as to our theory of English. We briefly present the relevant results.[4]

DEFINITION 10 Two structures $\mathcal{U}$ and $\mathcal{B}$ are *elementarily equivalent,* $\mathcal{U} \equiv \mathcal{B}$, iff

$$Th(\mathcal{U}) = Th(\mathcal{B}).$$

DEFINITION 11 A mapping F of $|\mathcal{U}|$ onto $|\mathcal{B}|$ is a *homomorphism* of $\mathcal{U}$ onto $\mathcal{B}$ iff

(i) for every k-ary predicate $p \in \mathcal{L}$, if $\langle a_1, \ldots, a_k \rangle \in p^{\mathcal{U}}$, then $\langle F(a_1), \ldots, F(a_k) \rangle \in p^{\mathcal{B}}$
(ii) for every k-ary function $f \in \mathcal{L}$, $F(f^{\mathcal{U}}(a_1, \ldots, a_k)) = f^{\mathcal{B}}(F(a_1), \ldots, F(a_k))$.

Two structures $\mathcal{U}$ and $\mathcal{B}$ are *homomorphic* iff there is an homomorphism from $|\mathcal{U}|$ onto $|\mathcal{B}|$.

DEFINITION 12 A mapping F of $|\mathcal{U}|$ onto $|\mathcal{B}|$ is an *isomorphism* of $\mathcal{U}$ onto $\mathcal{B}$ iff F is a 1-1 homomorphism such that

(i') for every k-ary predicate $p \in \mathcal{L}$, $\langle a_1, \ldots, a_k \rangle \in p^{\mathcal{U}}$ iff $\langle F(a_1), \ldots, F(a_k) \rangle \in p^{\mathcal{B}}$.

Structures $\mathcal{U}$ and $\mathcal{B}$ are *isomorphic,* $\mathcal{U} \cong \mathcal{B}$, iff there is an isomorphism from $|\mathcal{U}|$ onto $|\mathcal{B}|$.

DEFINITION 13 Let Φ be a set of sentences in $\mathcal{L}$. The *class of models of* Φ,

$$Mod_{\mathcal{L}}(\Phi) = \{\mathcal{U}|\mathcal{U} \text{ is an } \mathcal{L} - structure \text{ and } \mathcal{U} \models \Phi\}.$$

DEFINITION 14 A class of $\mathcal{L}$-structures $\mathcal{R}$ is *elementary* (EC) iff there is a sentence ϕ of $\mathcal{L}$ such that $\mathcal{R} = Mod_\mathcal{L}(\phi)$.

DEFINITION 15 A class of $\mathcal{L}$-structures $\mathcal{R}$ is Δ-*elementary* (or generalized elementary, EC_Δ) iff there is a set of sentences of $\mathcal{L}$, Φ such that $\mathcal{R} = Mod_\mathcal{L}(\Phi)$.

THEOREM 2 If $\mathcal{U}$ is infinite, then $\{\mathcal{B}|\mathcal{B} \cong \mathcal{U}\}$ is not Δ-elementary.

Proof: Assume $\mathcal{U}$ is infinite and Φ is such that

$$Mod_\mathcal{L}(\Phi) = \{\mathcal{B}|\mathcal{B} \cong \mathcal{U}\}.$$

Since Φ has a model, by the Löwenheim-Skolem theorem, it has a model with at least as many elements as the power set of $\mathcal{U}$, contradicting our assumption that the $\mathcal{L}$-models of Φ are all isomorphic. ∎

COROLLARY 1 For each infinite structure, there exists an elementarily equivalent, nonisomorphic structure.

There is another way to describe the semantic limitation of first order logic, in terms of what can be "expressed:"

DEFINITION 16 Proposition Φ is *expressible in first order logic* iff there is some first order sentence ϕ such that, for all models $\mathcal{U}$, Φ holds in $\mathcal{U}$ iff $\mathcal{U} \models \phi$. In this case, we say ϕ *expresses* Φ.

In this sense, many syntactic claims are are not first order expressible:

There are infinitely many sentences.

There are just finitely many lexical items.

Every lexical item has just finitely many subcategorization frames.

There are just finitely many parameters of language-specific variation,

            and finitely many values for each.

For every variable there is an operator.

For every θ-role there is a recipient.

For every verb phrase there is a subject.

The inexpressibility of each of these can be established by minor variations in the following familiar sort of proof:[5]

PROPOSITION 10 "There are infinitely many sentences" is not expressible in first order logic.

Proof: For $i = 1, 2, \ldots$, it is easy to provide a sentences ψ_i in first order logic with identity that express the proposition that there are at least i sentences in the language. For example,

$\exists X \quad sentence(X)$
$\exists X, Y \quad \neg X = Y \wedge sentence(X) \wedge sentence(Y)$
$\ldots$

Now assume for contradiction that ϕ is a first order sentence expressing the fact that there are infinitely many sentences, and let T be the infinite theory that contains $\neg\phi$ and all of these ψ_i. Every finite subset of T has a model. By compactness, then, T has a model $\mathcal{U}$. But since all ψ_i are true in $\mathcal{U}$, the number of sentences is infinite. But since the model also verifies $\neg\phi$, this contradicts our assumption. ∎

Chapter 3

Deductive reasoning about languages

> *Input systems... perform inference-like operations on representations of impinging stimuli. Processes of input analysis are thus unlike reflexes in respect of the character and complexity of the operations that they perform.*
> *— Jerry Fodor*

There are many different proof methods that could be used to establish consequences of theories like those considered in the previous chapter. Formal proof methods familiar from introductory logic books often involve a number of different inference rules, and part of the challenge in finding a proof is knowing which rules to apply in which order. With practice, some people can get very good at doing these proofs. It is very hard to formalize this expertise, though, and even if it could be formalized, it is not clear that this kind of expertise is appropriate for natural language processing systems, computational systems that can, without conscious human guidance, automatically establish certain consequences of a linguistic theory. Instead of the impressive hit-or-miss techniques of a logician, it is more natural to study computing systems which will methodically search for proofs in a way that is guaranteed to find a proof if there is one. One of the most successful methods of this kind, "resolution," will be introduced here and modified slightly for the peculiarities of our linguistic problems. The question of whether the methods discussed here are really the best for one or another purpose will be considered at length in Part IV, below. For present purposes, it is important to see how automatic proof systems could be designed to perform simple computational tasks like parsing, and how these proof methods can be tailored to the particular characteristics of the tasks at hand.

The most successful and popular automatic proof methods use one simple rule, a sort of generalization of *modus ponens* called "resolution." The price that must be paid for this simple approach is that the axioms used in the proof and the results to be established must all be represented in a certain restricted form, "clausal form." We will not provide a thorough introduction to clausal form and resolution proof methods, but will quickly review the basics.[1] The next chapter will apply these methods to some simple linguistic problems and illustrate how flexible they are.

3.1   Clausal form

Clausal form is essentially a universally quantified prenex conjunctive normal form. To define it precisely we need the following basic notions:

DEFINITION 17 An *atomic formula* is an n-ary predicate letter ($n \geq 0$) followed by n terms.

DEFINITION 18 A *literal* is an atomic formula or the negation of an atomic formula. Literals are sometimes called *positive* or *negative*, with the obvious meaning.

DEFINITION 19 A first order formula is in *conjunctive normal form* (CNF) iff it is a conjunction of disjunctions of literals. (There might be only one disjunct, or only one conjunct.)

DEFINITION 20 A first order formula is in *prenex normal form* (PNF) iff it consists of $n \geq 0$ quantifiers followed by a quantifier-free formula M:

$Q_1 \ldots Q_n \ M.$

The quantifiers $Q_1 \ldots Q_n$ are called the *prefix* of the sentence and the quantifier-free formula M is called the *matrix* of the sentence.

It is easy to show that the following steps will convert any first order sentence into an equivalent PNF sentence, and that the matrix of the PNF sentence can be converted to a CNF formula:

I. Convert the sentence to PNF. This step can be done with the following procedure:

1. Eliminate $\leftrightarrow$ and $\rightarrow$ by using the following valid sentences in the $\rightarrow$ direction to transform all of the applicable subexpressions:

$(F \leftrightarrow G) \leftrightarrow ((F \rightarrow G) \wedge (G \rightarrow F))$
$(F \rightarrow G) \leftrightarrow (\neg F \vee G).$

2. Move $\neg$ "inward" as far as possible, using the following valid sentences in the $\rightarrow$ direction to transform the all of the applicable subexpressions:

$$\neg(\forall X)F \leftrightarrow (\exists X)\neg F$$
$$\neg(\exists X)F \leftrightarrow (\forall X)\neg F$$
$$\neg(F \vee G) \leftrightarrow (\neg F \wedge \neg G)$$
$$\neg(F \wedge G) \leftrightarrow (\neg F \vee \neg G)$$
$$\neg\neg F \leftrightarrow F.$$

3. Rename variables so that no two quantifiers bind the same variable. For example,

$$((\forall X\ p(X)) \wedge (\exists X\ q(X))) \leftrightarrow ((\forall X\ p(X)) \wedge (\exists Y\ q(Y))).$$

4. Place all quantifiers at the beginning of the formula, by applying the following valid rules in the $\rightarrow$ direction to relevant subformulas:

$((\forall X)F) \wedge G \leftrightarrow (\forall X)(F \wedge G)$	*X does not occur in G*
$F \wedge (\forall X)G \leftrightarrow (\forall X)(F \wedge G)$	*X does not occur in F*
$((\exists X)F) \wedge G \leftrightarrow (\exists X)(F \wedge G)$	*X does not occur in G*
$F \wedge (\exists X)G \leftrightarrow (\exists X)(F \wedge G)$	*X does not occur in F*
$((\forall X)F) \vee G \leftrightarrow (\forall X)(F \vee G)$	*X does not occur in G*
$F \vee (\forall X)G \leftrightarrow (\forall X)(F \vee G)$	*X does not occur in F*
$((\exists X)F) \vee G \leftrightarrow (\exists X)(F \vee G)$	*X does not occur in G*
$F \vee (\exists X)G \leftrightarrow (\exists X)(F \vee G)$	*X does not occur in F*

II. Convert the matrix to CNF. Since we have already eliminated $\leftrightarrow$, $\rightarrow$, and already moved negations inward, we need only convert any disjunctions of conjunctions to conjunctions of disjunctions. Use the following valid sentences in the $\rightarrow$ direction to transform subformulas until these rules do not apply any more:

$$(F \vee (G \wedge H)) \leftrightarrow ((F \vee G) \wedge (F \vee H))$$
$$((G \wedge H) \vee F) \leftrightarrow ((F \vee G) \wedge (F \vee H))$$

The CNF/PNF formula that results from this procedure can be further simplified by eliminating existential quantifiers and replacing the existentially quantified variables by appropriate Skolem functions, to yield a "Skolem transform" of the original sentence. This step does not preserve logical equivalence, but it does preserve unsatisfiability. That is, the Skolem transform is unsatisfiable iff the original sentence is. A Skolem transform can be produced with the following procedure:

III. Eliminate existential quantifiers. Given a PNF sentence,

$$Q_1 X_1 \ldots Q_n X_n \ M,$$

apply the following step repeatedly until all existential quantifiers are removed:

Take the leftmost ∃-quantifier Q_r of the prefix. Where $m \geq 0$ is the number of ∀-quantifiers that precede Q_r, replace all occurrences of X_r in M by a new m-ary function symbol $f(X_1, \ldots, X_m)$.

The functions introduced by this procedure are called *Skolem functions*. If $m = 0$ the new 0-ary function symbol f is, of course, a constant.

Since permuting the universal quantifiers of a PNF sentence that contains no existential quantifiers preserves equivalence, we can simply drop the prefix altogether and adopt the convention that the resulting formulas are universally closed. This leaves just a CNF formula, a conjunction of disjunctions of literals:

$$(L_{1_1} \vee \ldots \vee L_{1_i}) \wedge \ldots \wedge (L_{n_1} \vee \ldots \vee L_{n_k}).$$

Each disjunction of such a sentence is called a "clause:"

DEFINITION 21 A *clause* is a disjunction of literals. By convention, free variables in the clause are universally quantified.

Since conjunction and disjunction are commutative, the order of the conjuncts and disjuncts does not matter, and so a set notation for these sentences is often used, representing the sentence as a set of sets:

$$\{\{L_{1_1}, \ldots, L_{1_i}\}, \ldots, \{L_{n_1}, \ldots, L_{n_k}\}\}.$$

The sentence, then, can be represented as a set of clauses, where each clause is itself a set of literals.

Certain kinds of clauses are of particular interest:

DEFINITION 22 A clause is *ground* if it contains no variables. Similarly, a term is ground if it contains no variables.

The empty disjunction is represented by the special symbol □ , and is always false.

A *negative clause* is a clause containing only negative literals.

A *Horn clause* is a clause containing at most one positive literal.

A *definite clause* is a clause containing exactly one positive literal.

Clausal form may be appropriate for certain deductive systems, but it can be rather opaque for conscious human problem-solving. This is easy to show with some simple examples. The procedures described relate the following forms:

$\exists X \forall Y\ loves(X,Y)$ $\{\{loves(f,Y)\}\}$

$\forall X \exists Y\ loves(X,Y)$ $\{\{loves(X,f(X))\}\}$

$p \rightarrow q$ $\{\{\neg p, q\}\}$

$p \leftrightarrow q$ $\{\{\neg p, q\}, \{\neg q, p\}\}$

$p \leftrightarrow (q \leftrightarrow r)$ $\{\{\neg p, \neg q, r\}, \{\neg q, \neg r, p\}, \{\neg p, \neg r, q\}, \{p, q, r\}\}$

The last of these sentences in first order form is perfectly intelligible, but the clausal representation is much longer and more difficult to understand. Besides intelligibility to humans, this example also raises an issue that is relevant to the practicality of using these representations in any computing system: how much can the conversion to clausal form increase the complexity of a first order sentence, where the complexity is measured as, e.g., the number of symbols (i.e. symbol *occurrences*). In this example, a 7 symbol representation is converted to a 39 symbol representation. In fact, the increase in complexity can be exponential, and this can pose problems, as we will discuss in §14.1.

3.2   Resolution

Most clausal theorem provers proceed by finding refutations of sets of clauses, i.e. proofs that the set of clauses is not satisfiable. To prove that a sentence is entailed by a theory in clausal form, the sentence is negated, converted to a set of clauses, and then an attempt is made to show that these clauses together with the theory form an unsatisfiable set. One simple rule, "resolution," provides a sound and complete method for such problems. The rule will be quickly introduced here.

Again, we must begin with some basic notation and definitions.

DEFINITION 23   A *substitution* is an expression $\{X_1/t_1, \ldots, X_n/t_n\}$ for some $n \geq 0$ where $X_1, \ldots, X_n$ are distinct variables, $t_1, \ldots, t_n$ are terms, and no $t_i = X_i$. The empty substitution $(n = 0)$ is written ϵ.

The expression $\{X/t\}$ represents the replacement of all occurrences of X by term t.[2] The components of a substitution $\{X_1/t_1, \ldots, X_n/t_n\}$ are all applied simultaneously. For example, letting

$\sigma = \{X/a\},$

$\nu = \{X/Y\},$

$\xi = \{Y/a\},$ and

$\phi = \{loves(X, f(X))\},$

we have

$$\phi\sigma = (\phi\nu)\xi = \phi(\nu\xi) = \{loves(a, f(a))\}$$
$$\phi\nu = (\phi\nu)\sigma = \{loves(Y, f(Y))\}.$$

It is standard to use $\phi\sigma\nu$ to represent $(\phi\sigma)\nu$. Notice that, in this example, $\phi\sigma\nu \neq \phi\nu\sigma$.

It will be convenient in the sequel to have defined the composition of substitutions. The composition of θ and ξ, written $\theta\xi$ is the substitution ν such that $\phi\nu = (\phi\theta)\xi$ for all expressions ϕ. We provide a constructive definition as follows:

DEFINITION 24 Let $\theta = \{X_1/t_1, \ldots, X_n/t_n\}$ and let $\xi = \{Y_1/u_1, \ldots, Y_m/u_m\}$. Then to form the composition $\theta\xi$ take the expression

$$\{X_1/(t_1\xi), \ldots, X_n/(t_n\xi), Y_1/u_1, \ldots, Y_m/u_m\}$$

and delete any Y_i/u_i such that $Y_i = X_j$ for some $0 \leq j \leq n$, and delete any $X_i/t_i\xi$ such that $X_i = t_i\xi$.

Certain substitution instances of clauses are of particular interest. In particular, we are interested in substitutions that can make two clauses identical singletons, and especially in the substitutions that produce the most general singletons:

DEFINITION 25 A substitution σ *unifies* two sets of literals C_1 and C_2 just in case $C_1\sigma = C_2\sigma = \{L\}$ for some literal L. In this case σ is a *unifier* of C_1 and C_2.

A *most general unifier* (mgu) σ of C_1 and C_2 is a unifier of C_1 and C_2 such that every unifier θ of C_1 and C_2 is such that $(C_1 \cup C_2)\theta = (C_1 \cup C_2)\sigma\theta'$ for some substitution θ'.

For example, letting

$$C_1 = \{p(X), p(g(Y))\}$$
$$C_2 = \{p(Z)\},$$

the following are all unifiers of C_1 and C_2,

$$\sigma_0 = \{X/g(Y), Z/g(Y)\}$$
$$\sigma_1 = \{X/g(a), Z/g(a), Y/a\}$$
$$\sigma_2 = \{X/g(a(b)), Z/g(a(b)), Y/a\}$$
$$\sigma_3 = \{X/g(W), Z/g(W), Y/W\}.$$

but only σ_0 and σ_3 are most general unifiers. Notice that $C_1\sigma_0 = C_2\sigma_0 = \{p(g(Y))\}$ and $C_1\sigma_1 = C_2\sigma_1 = \{p(g(a))\}$. Clearly the second of these can be obtained from the first by application of $\theta' = \{Y/a\}$, but the first cannot be obtained from the second by any substitution.

It is convenient to introduce one more bit of notation before defining resolution.

DEFINITION 26 Given a literal L, if $L = \neg A$ is a negative literal, let $cmp(L) = A$; if L is a positive literal, let $cmp(L) = \neg L$.
Similarly, if C is a set of literals, let $cmp(C) = \{L|\ cmp(L) \in C\}$.

To simplify the definition of the basic inference step, the following convention is standard: to draw a conclusion from two clauses that happen to have some variable in common, equivalent alphabetic variants of the two clauses are formulated before performing the inference. Expressions ϕ and ψ are *variants* of each other iff there are substitutions θ, σ such that $\phi = \psi\theta$ and $\psi = \phi\sigma$. If $X_1, \ldots, X_n$ are all the variables in expression ϕ, a *renaming substitution* for ϕ with respect to a set of expressions S is a substitution $\xi = \{X_1/Y_1, \ldots, X_n/Y_n\}$ where all the Y_i are distinct variables that do not occur in ϕ or S. Obviously, if ξ is a renaming substitution for ϕ, $\phi\xi$ is a variant of ϕ.

Now we are ready to define the resolution inference step.

DEFINITION 27 Let C_1, C_2 be clauses, and let $F_1 \subseteq C_1$, $F_2 \subseteq C_2$. Let ξ_1 be a renaming substitution for C_1 with respect to C_2, and let ξ_2 similarly be a renaming substitution for C_2 with respect to C_1.

If σ is an mgu of $cmp(F_1\xi_1)$ and $F_2\xi_2$, then $R = ((C_1 - F_1)\xi_1 \cup (C_2 - F_2)\xi_2)\sigma$ is a *resolvent* of C_1 and C_2. We say the literals in F_1, F_2 were *resolved upon* to obtain resolvent R, and we call C_1, C_2 the *parents* of R.

If R is any resolvent of C_1, C_2, then R is entailed by $C1$ and C_2. Consider, for example, the syllogism

$\forall X\ man(X) \rightarrow mortal(X)$
$man(socrates)$

———

$mortal(socrates)$.

Expressed in clausal form, it is easy to see that the conclusion of this argument is a resolvent of the premises:

$\{\neg man(X), mortal(X)\}$
$\{man(socrates)\}$

———

$\{mortal(socrates)\}$.

This follows since when $F_1 = \{\neg man(X)\}$, $F_2 = \{man(socrates)\}$, $\{X/socrates\}$ is an mgu of $cmp(F1)$ and $F2$.

As noted above, most resolution systems are used to provide proof by refutation. That is, we assume the negation of what we want to establish and deduce an explicit

contradiction. The canonical explicit contradiction in clausal systems is the empty clause
$\square$. Resolution, as defined above, yields the empty clause immediately from explicitly
contradictory premises. As an example, suppose that we know that Socrates is a man,
and now we want to prove by contradiction that something is a man. So we begin by
assuming that nothing is a man, and derive a contradiction in one resolution step:

$\{\neg man(X)\}$
$\{man(socrates)\}$

___

$\square$.

This establishes that our assumption contradicts our other premises, and so we can
conclude that the assumption is false: something is a man. Notice, furthermore, that
the proof has established that a particular instance of our assumption is false, namely,
the instance obtained by applying the substitution $\{X/socrates\}$ to our assumption.
Consequently we can conclude not only that something is a man; our proof tells us that
Socrates is a man! The substitution $\{X/socrates\}$ is an "answer substitution" in a sense
that will be defined below. The strategy of collecting from the proof the particular
instances of the refuted clauses is very useful; we can use the theorem prover to compute
and display these solutions.

   We can express the soundness and completeness of resolution as follows: there is a
deduction of $\square$ from a theory T just in case T is unsatisfiable. To be precise,

DEFINITION 28 A *deduction of C from a set of clauses T* (by resolution) is a sequence

$\langle C_0, C_1, \ldots, C_n \rangle$

such that $C = C_n$ and every C_i, $0 \leq i \leq n$ is either an element of T or a resolvent of
parents C_j, C_k, $0 \leq i, j < i$.

   In such a deduction, we can let *ancestor* be the transitive, reflexive closure of the
parent relation, and let *descendant* be the inverse of the ancestor relation.

   The following soundness and completeness result is due to Robinson (1965) and is
proven in any of the texts on resolution mentioned in previous notes. Using $\vdash$ to mean
"derives by resolution:"

THEOREM 3 $T \vdash \square$ iff T is unsatisfiable.

   An appropriate definition of "answer substitution" must be a little more complex than
our simple examples above might suggest because of the fact that a refuted clause and
its descendants may be used in more than one resolution step.[3] Consider, for example,
the following theory:

$\{\neg p(X), r(X)\}$
$\{p(a), p(b)\}$

We can prove $\exists X\ r(X)$ by refuting its negation, with the following resolution deduction:

Refutation Γ_1

1. $\{\neg p(X), r(X)\}$ *axiom*
2. $\{p(a), p(b)\}$ *axiom*
3. $\{\neg r(X)\}$ *for refutation*
4. $\{\neg p(X)\}$ *from* $1, 3$
5. $\{p(b)\}$ *from* $2, 4$
6. $\{r(b)\}$ *from* $1, 5$
7. $\square$ *from* $3, 6$

In this example, we have refuted the claim that nothing is r, but not by refuting a particular instance of $\{\neg r(X)\}$. What we have refuted is actually the conjunction of $\{\neg r(a)\}$ and $\{\neg r(b)\}$. There are two "answer substitutions" in this case. This kind of complication is handled by the following approach:

DEFINITION 29 $P = \langle C_0, \ldots, C_m \rangle$ is a *path from C_0 to C_m in deduction Γ with associated substitution* $\xi_1\theta_1 \ldots \xi_m\theta_m$ iff

(i) every element of P occurs in Γ,
(ii) for every $C_i, C_{i+1} \in P$, C_i is a parent of C_{i+1} in Γ, formed by a resolution step using renaming substitution ξ_{i+1} applied to C_i and mgu θ_{i+1}.

DEFINITION 30 *The answer set for S in refutation Γ is the set of clauses*

$\{C_i\Sigma_j|\ C_i \in S,\ C_i \in \Gamma,$
$\qquad \Sigma_j$ associated with path from C_i to $\square$ in $\Gamma\}$.

Let $P_0, \ldots, P_j$ be all the paths from C_i to $\square$. The substitutions $\Sigma_0, \ldots, \Sigma_j$ associated with these paths are the *answer substitutions for C_i in Γ*.

Consider our example Γ_1 again. In this case, the clause to be refuted is $\{\neg r(X)\}$, and there are only two paths from $\{\neg r(X)\}$ to $\square$ in this deduction, since $\{\neg r(X)\}$ serves as a parent only twice, and each of its descendants serves as a parent only once. The two paths are:

$P_1 = \langle \{\neg r(X)\}, \{\neg p(X)\}, \{p(b)\}, \{r(b)\}, \square \rangle,$

with the associated substitution $\Sigma_1 = \{X/a\}$, and

$$P_2 = \langle \{\neg r(X)\}, \square \rangle,$$

with the associated substitution $\Sigma_2 = \{X/b\}$.

The significance of these answers sets is given by the following results:

THEOREM 4 Let Γ be a refutation of $T \cup S$ where

$$A = \{\{L_{1_1}, \ldots, L_{1_i}\}, \ldots, \{L_{n_1}, \ldots, L_{n_j}\}\}$$

is the answer set for S in Γ. Then

$$T \models \forall (cmp(L_{1_1}) \land \ldots \land cmp(L_{1_i})) \lor \ldots \lor (cmp(L_{n_1}) \land \ldots \land cmp(L_{n_j})).$$

Proof: This is established with an induction on the number of resolvents in the deduction in Stabler (1990a).

THEOREM 5 Let S be a set of clauses. If $T \models (S\theta)$ where

$$S = (cmp(L_{1_1}) \land \ldots \land cmp(L_{1_i})) \lor \ldots \lor (cmp(L_{n_1}) \land \ldots \land cmp(L_{n_j})),$$

then there is a refutation Γ of $T \cup S'$ where

$$S' = \{\{L_{1_1}, \ldots, L_{1_i}\}, \ldots, \{L_{n_1}, \ldots, L_{n_j}\}\},$$

with answer set A for S' such that for every $C \in S'$, $C\theta$ is an instance of a clause in A.

Proof: For the proof of this result, based on a "lifting lemma," see Stabler (1990a).

3.3   Application to linguistic examples

In Chapter 2 we tried to construct a complete axiomatization for a simple linguistic structure. A complete theory turns out to be unattainable in principle, but fortunately it is not needed for many applications. However, we often need at least a "representation" of important relations, in the precise sense we defined in Chapter 2. "Weak representation" is not generally enough to determine whether a string is well-formed according to a theory, since, for example, in our formalization of a grammar for English, many well-formedness conditions will require the absence of certain properties. Consequently, to solve certain problems, a proof method will need to be able to establish that some basic relations do not hold, and the existence of such proofs is guaranteed by having a full representation of the relevant notions. The weakest theory considered in the previous chapter that represents the linguistic categories of our simple context-free grammar is $Cn(RT)$. The resolution method can be applied to a clausal form of RT, providing our first illustrations of linguistic results found by an automated proof technique.

RT is first converted to clausal form — a rather tedious business, but easily done by machine. The results become familiar with practice. In this case we get:

Clausal Form Theory $Cl(RT)$

1. $\{np(sk1(A)), \neg s(A), s(sk3(A))\}$
2. $\{\neg append(A, B, C), \neg vp(B), \neg np(A), s(C)\}$
3. $\{vp(sk2(A)), \neg s(A), s(sk3(A))\}$
4. $\{\neg append(A, [and|B], C), \neg s(A), \neg s(B), s(C)\}$
5. $\{np(sk1(A)), \neg s(A), s(sk4(A))\}$
6. $\{append(sk1(A), sk2(A), A), \neg s(A), s(sk3(A))\}$
7. $\{np(sk1(A)), append(sk3(A), [and|sk4(A)], A), \neg s(A)\}$
8. $\{vp(sk2(A)), \neg s(A), s(sk4(A))\}$
9. $\{append(sk1(A), sk2(A), A), \neg s(A), s(sk4(A))\}$
10. $\{vp(sk2(A)), append(sk3(A), [and|sk4(A)], A), \neg s(A)\}$
11. $\{append(sk1(A), sk2(A), A), append(sk3(A), [and|sk4(A)], A), \neg s(A)\}$
12. $\{\neg np(A), A = [john]\}$
13. $\{\neg A = [john], np(A)\}$
14. $\{\neg vp(A), A = [reads]\}$
15. $\{\neg A = [reads], vp(A)\}$
16. $\{A = [], A = [sk5(B, C, A)|sk6(B, C, A)], \neg append(A, C, B)\}$
17. $\{\neg append(A, B, C), \neg D = [E|A], \neg F = [E|C], append(D, B, F)\}$
18. $\{A = [], B = [sk5(B, C, A)|sk7(B, C, A)], \neg append(A, C, B)\}$
19. $\{\neg list(A), \neg B = [], \neg C = A, append(B, C, A)\}$
20. $\{A = [sk5(B, C, A)|sk6(B, C, A)], C = B, \neg append(A, C, B)\}$
21. $\{A = [], \neg append(A, B, C), append(sk6(C, B, A), B, sk7(C, B, A))\}$
22. $\{list(A), B = [sk5(A, C, B)|sk6(A, C, B)], \neg append(B, C, A)\}$
23. $\{A = B, B = [sk5(B, A, C)|sk7(B, A, C)], \neg append(C, A, B)\}$
24. $\{A = B, \neg append(C, A, B), append(sk6(B, A, C), A, sk7(B, A, C))\}$
25. $\{list(A), A = [sk5(A, B, C)|sk7(A, B, C)], \neg append(C, B, A)\}$
26. $\{list(A), \neg append(B, C, A), append(sk6(A, C, B), C, sk7(A, C, B))\}$
27. $\{A = [], A = [sk8(A)|sk9(A)], \neg list(A)\}$
28. $\{\neg A = [], list(A)\}$
29. $\{A = [], \neg list(A), list(sk9(A))\}$
30. $\{\neg list(A), \neg B = [C|A], list(B)\}$

31. $\{A = A\}$
32. $\{\neg lions = sleep\}$
33. $\{\neg lions = and\}$
34. $\{\neg lions = []\}$
35. $\{\neg lions = [A|B]\}$
36. $\{\neg sleep = and\}$
37. $\{\neg sleep = []\}$
38. $\{\neg sleep = [A|B]\}$
39. $\{\neg and = []\}$
40. $\{\neg and = [A|B]\}$
41. $\{\neg[] = [A|B]\}$
42. $\{\neg A = B, \neg C = D, [A|C] = [B|D]\}$
43. $\{\neg[A|B] = [C|D], A = C\}$
44. $\{\neg[A|B] = [C|D], B = D\}$
45. $\{s(A), \neg B = A, \neg s(B)\}$
46. $\{np(A), \neg B = A, \neg np(B)\}$
47. $\{vp(A), \neg B = A, \neg vp(B)\}$
48. $\{list(A), \neg B = A, \neg list(B)\}$
49. $\{A = B, \neg C = B, \neg D = A, \neg D = C\}$
50. $\{append(A, B, C), \neg append(D, E, F), \neg F = C, \neg E = B, \neg D = A\}$

From this clausal form we can easily prove that something is a sentence by refuting $\neg s(A)$, and then we can collect the sentence that this found by the proof. The following refutation suffices, for example:

$\{\neg s(A)\}$	*for refutation*
$\{\neg append(C, D, A), \neg vp(D), \neg np(C)\}$	*by 2*
$\{\neg append(C, D, A), \neg vp(D), \neg C = [john]\}$	*by 13*
$\{\neg append([john], C, A), \neg vp(C)\}$	*by 31*
$\{\neg append([john], C, A), \neg C = [reads]\}$	*by 15*
$\{\neg append([john], [reads], A)\}$	*by 31*
$\{\neg append(D, [reads], E), \neg[john] = [F|D], \neg A = [F|E]\}$	*by 17*
$\{\neg append(E, [reads], B), \neg[john] = [A|E]\}$	*by 31*
$\{\neg append([], [reads], A)\}$	*by 31*
$\{\neg list(A), \neg[] = [], \neg[reads] = A\}$	*by 19*
$\{\neg list([reads]), \neg[] = []\}$	*by 31*
$\{\neg list([reads])\}$	*by 31*

$\{\neg list(E), \neg[reads] = [F|E]\}$ *by 31*
$\{\neg list([])\}$ *by 31*
$\{\neg[] = []\}$ *by 28*
$\square$ *by 31*

Obviously, we have not repeated in this display all the axioms of the theory that are used in the refutation. In the part of the refutation which is displayed, every line (properly, every element of the sequence) except the first is a resolvent, and every resolvent has the immediately previous element in the sequence as one parent and an axiom as the other parent. Also notice that every single literal in the clause to be refuted and in every resolvent is negative, and that every axiom used is a definite clause. Proofs with this form can be found very easily, and will be given special consideration in §3.5. The answer set for $\{\neg s(A)\}$ in this refutation is, of course, $\neg s([john, reads])$.

Proving that something is not a sentence is not so easy, and this may be a surprise. A refutation of $s(A)$ is presented in Appendix A. The refutation there formulates the answer set $s([sleep])$, showing that *sleep* is not a sentence according to our theory. Though this is a simple instance of a non-sentence, the refutation contains 63 resolvents, as compared to the 15 resolvents in the previous refutation, and many of the resolvents are more complex than any in the previous refutation. What is responsible for all of this extra complexity? There is perhaps an intuitive sense in which this result is more informative than the previous one. This one tells us that *sleep* is not identical to *any* sentence of the language. The clause to be refuted in this case is positive, but that, by itself, obviously cannot be the source of the trouble, since the result of replacing every occurrence of a predication involving s in the previous refutation (including the axioms) with its complement is a nice, simple refutation of a positive clause. Thus it is misleading to speak of the difficulty of proving negative results, as is sometimes done in the literature, unless one keeps in mind the other contributing aspects of the situation. Negative results are only difficult to establish when the axioms make the positive cases the simple ones. That is, our negative result, our refutation of a positive literal, is relatively difficult just because it requires that most of the reasoning proceed by using the definitions of RT in the $\rightarrow$ direction. The conclusions drawn are then more complex because the right hand sides of our first order definitions are more complex than the left hand sides, and because these conclusions often contain Skolem functions. If the right hand sides of the definitions were no more complex than the left hand sides, establishing negative results would be as easy as establishing positive results.

In the sort of direct use of linguistic theory being developed in this study, the scientific interest in avoiding disjunctive characterizations has a computational analog: reasoning from formal systems with disjunctions can be very complex. Among linguists, the suggestion that disjunctions in linguistic rule systems (e.g., as expressed with "curly bracket" notation) indicate missed generalizations has usually been associated with the idea that grammars should conform to an expressively restrictive framework, as in, for example, Lakoff (1971) and McCawley (1972). This was one of the original motivations for Chomsky's (1970) X-bar theory and for Bresnan's (1975, 1976) work on conditions on transformations. The concern for restrictiveness was motivated at least in part by learnability issues and has led to the restriction of language-specific aspects of grammar to the values of a finite number of grammatical parameters, specific lexical information, and other "peripheral" material. However, even when learnability is not an issue, the concern to eliminate disjunctions remains. For example, linguists have been very unhappy with disjunctive formulations of the empty category principle, even when assuming that it is a universal principle of grammar, not learned.[4] The special computational difficulty in establishing negative results from axioms that include disjunctions is an interesting additional motivation for these efforts. Disjunctions occur in many applications of theorem proving methods, and so there has been a flurry of recent activity in computer science to find reasonable proof strategies for these problems.[5]

3.4   Building in equality axioms: SEq resolution

Notice that theory RT contains pairwise inequalities for all of the terminal elements of the language. It is difficult to estimate the number of words (or morphemes) that a typical adult speaker knows, in an appropriately weak sense of "know", but if we had 200,000 different words, the knowledge that they were all different from each other would require $\binom{200000}{2} = 19,999,900,000$ inequalities. It seems rather unlikely that humans use an explicit representation of such inequalities. Leaving the psychological issues aside for the moment, the point to notice is that the representation of an appropriate equality theory can be problematic even in very restricted, finite theories. In Chapter 2 we considered equality theories that had no finite axiomatization, such as GT (see Proposition 7 of Chapter 2). The axioms of equality in such theories make interesting results infeasible for any proof method that checks each axiom at each step in the search for a proof. Consequently, it is worth noting that there are alternative proof methods which are specialized for certain theories, remaining sound and complete for these theories but avoiding the need to represent and scan infinitely many axioms. We will consider two special proof methods in this section: "building in" the equality axioms, and using a non-monotonic inference rule. This chapter will then conclude with a brief discussion of resolution-based decision strategies. This last topic has a bearing on our non-monotonic rule, and more generally on our ability to guarantee an effective solution to grammatical problems we may be interested in, problems that will be much harder than the artificial examples we have so far considered.

It is interesting to note that equality was an issue for linguists concerned about the expressive power of transformational rules (Chomsky, 1965, 225-6; Lasnik, 1980, 153). The issue was very serious in transformational syntax before the move to a principles and parameters approach in which expressiveness is, in effect, limited to a choice among a finite number of parameter settings. But now similar issues arise for reasons of computational complexity, and our response to this problem is similar to Chomsky's (1965) response to the earlier one: because certain aspects of the identity relation hold quite generally, we can use deductive systems in which the relation is implicit.

In the present context, the problem is just this: equality axioms, even when they fail to fully represent the equality relation (in our technical sense of "representation") can vastly increase the search space of any general first order theorem prover.[6] Consequently, there has been a good deal of work on building standard equality axioms (reflexivity and the substitutivity axioms) into special, more efficient inference rules in such a way that a sentence has a special derivation from a theory without equality axioms just in case it has a standard derivation from the theory together with those axioms. Our current problems can be handled with these techniques, but we can do better. Consider the equality axioms in $Cn(GT)$. These have the effect of forcing a "free interpretation" of every term: every distinct ground term must denote a distinct element of the domain, and all functions are 1-1. The axioms play no other role in the theory. In this situation, we can get rid of both the standard equality axioms *and* the inequalities which are special to the particular linguistic applications that we have in mind. For example, using a simple inference rule that is sound and complete only relative to this model-theoretic restriction, we can get full representation of $s^{\mathcal{G}}$ with specialized derivations from the following subset of smaller theory RT:

Theory RT_0

$$s(S) \leftrightarrow (\quad \exists NP, VP \tag{3.4.1}$$
$$np(NP) \wedge vp(VP) \wedge append(NP, VP, S)$$
$$\vee \quad \exists S1, S2$$
$$s(S1) \wedge s(S2) \wedge append(S1, [and|S2], S)$$
$$)$$

$$np(NP) \leftrightarrow NP = [lions] \tag{3.4.2}$$
$$vp(VP) \leftrightarrow VP = [sleep] \tag{3.4.3}$$

$$append(L1, L2, L3) \leftrightarrow (\quad \exists H, T1, T3 \tag{3.4.4}$$
$$L1 = [H|T1] \wedge L3 = [H|T3] \wedge$$
$$append(T1, L2, T3)$$
$$\vee \quad L1 = [] \wedge L2 = L3 \wedge list(L3)$$
$$)$$

$$list(L) \leftrightarrow (\quad L = [] \tag{3.4.5}$$
$$\vee \quad \exists H, T(L = [H|T] \wedge list(T))$$
$$)$$

$$[H|T] = [H1|T1] \rightarrow H = H1 \wedge T = T1. \tag{3.4.6}$$

The semantic relationships we are interested in can be defined as follows:

• Where Eq is the set of standard equality axioms for the language of Γ, Γ is *e-unsatisfiable* iff $\Gamma \cup Eq$ is unsatisfiable.
• Where SEq is the set of standard equality axioms together with the axioms defining syntactic equality for the language of Γ, Γ is *SEq-unsatisfiable* iff $\Gamma \cup SEq$ is unsatisfiable.

With this syntactic equality restriction, there is a special, computationally simple approach to equality. We can entirely avoid the substitution rules, including the transitivity and symmetry rules of equality. The sufficient condition for identity in our restricted models is easily expressed. It can be represented simply by the sentence: $X = X$. The necessary condition is the tricky part. We want to say that two things are nonidentical just in case they are named by distinct terms.

We can obtain this effect with a special inference rule. The idea behind the rule is just that $t = t'$ is SEq-satisfiable iff t and t' are unifiable. We can express this as an extension to resolution as follows.

Supplement standard resolution with the following:

(i) If C contains a literal $\neg t = t'$, and σ is an mgu of t and t', then $(C - \{\neg t = t'\})\sigma$ is a resolvent of C.

(ii) If C contains a literal $t = t'$, and $t\sigma$ and $t'\sigma$ are not unifiable, then $(C - \{t = t'\})\sigma$ is a resolvent of C.

A proof of the following result is sketched in Stabler (1989).

THEOREM 6 There is a derivation of $\square$ from Γ using resolution extended with (i) and (ii) iff Γ is SEq-unsatisfiable.

This result is suggestive, but does not suffice for our purposes. In the first place, a simple extension of resolution with (i) and (ii) is unnecessarily inefficient. However, much more efficient proof rules based on essentially the same idea have been presented, using the "E-resolution" methods of Morris, Digricoli and others.[7] The theories of interest to us raise a second, much more serious problem for this approach, however. The problem is simply that although they might have syntactic equality theories, the conversion to clausal form introduces Skolem functions for which the syntactic equality restriction cannot be presumed to hold. When this happens, the previously mentioned proof strategies are not appropriate.

As an example, consider a simpler theory than those presented above, a minimal theory *NN* of natural numbers:

Theory NN

$$nn(X) \leftrightarrow (\ X = 0 \vee \exists Y(X = s(Y) \wedge nn(Y)) \ ).$$

This sentence can be regarded as defining a natural number as 0 and its successors. If the language of the theory contains one other constant, a, which is distinct from zero and all successors as required by the syntactic equality theory for this language, then $NN \cup \{\neg nn(a)\}$ is SEq-unsatisfiable even though it is satisfiable. However, the transformation to clausal form enlarges the language of the theory, introducing a Skolem function, which we call $sk1$ in the following formulation:

Theory Cl(NN)

$\{\neg nn(A), A = 0, A = s(sk1(A))\}$
$\{\neg A = 0, nn(A)\}$
$\{\neg nn(A), nn(sk1(A)), A = 0\}$
$\{\neg nn(A), \neg B = s(A), nn(B)\}.$

The first clause tells us that if $nn(A)$ for some A, then either A is 0 or A is the successor of something in the domain, namely, $sk1(A)$. Obviously, this function must have numbers as its values, and so we have lost the unique names property. Skolem functions are similarly introduced when our theories RT, GT, CA, and CT are converted to clausal form. That is, every theory named in Chapter 2 except T requires Skolem functions in its clausal form, and so syntactic equality does not hold.

The situation is not as bleak as it might seem in these cases. Since Skolem functions are the *only* departure from the unique names restriction, and since these theories "almost" satisfy that restriction, we can still benefit from a specialized rule of inference that exploits a standard theory of equality (or an inference rule that builds in equality) but which takes advantage of the fact that many of the terms must have distinct denotations. We can come as close as possible to syntactic equality, and then provide some general treatment of the equality relation only for those cases (such as Skolem functions) where syntactic equality cannot be presumed. At least, then, the computationally difficult equality problems will not infect everything. Exactly this idea is formalized as "SEq resolution" in Stabler (1989), and has been implemented.[8] SEq resolution can be used when we do not have syntactic equality, but we have a decidable set of terms whose denotations are known to be pairwise distinct.

3.5 Definite clause theories

It is interesting to note that our theory T of the previous chapter is a set of definite Horn clauses. Since there are very efficient definite clause theorem proving techniques, this point is worth exploring.

Remember that a Horn clause is a clause with at most one positive literal, and a definite clause has exactly one literal. Consider $\forall X\ q(X) \to p$. This has a clausal form with a Skolem function $\{p, \neg q(f)\}$, so even though it is not logically equivalent to our original sentence, it is equi-satisfiable, it is Horn, and it is definite. Of course many theories have no Horn clause formulation at all, with or without Skolem functions. For example, $p \vee q$ is equivalent to the non-Horn clausal form $\{p, q\}$. The sentence $p \vee q \leftarrow r$ is equivalent to the non-Horn clausal form $\{p, q, \neg r\}$. Neither of these is equivalent to any set of Horn clauses. Our original theory T is equivalent to a Horn theory, but none of the other named theories of Chapter 2 are.

It is convenient to write Horn clauses in a form which has been become common in discussions of pure Prolog. It can be defined as follows, where $A, A_1, A_2, \ldots$ are atomic formulas, i.e. positive literals:[9]

(i) definite clauses $\{A, \neg A_1, \ldots, \neg A_n\}$, $n \geq 0$, are written in conditional form $A \leftarrow A_1 \wedge \ldots \wedge A_n$. Notice that when $n = 0$ we have the special case of a simple assertion, $A \leftarrow$.

(ii) negative clauses $\{\neg A_1, \ldots, \neg A_n\}$, $n > 0$, are written $\leftarrow A_1 \wedge \ldots \wedge A_n$.

(iii) as before, the *empty clause* is written $\square$, contains no literals, and is always false.

This notation makes only a trivial change from the notation used for theory T:

Theory HT

$$s(S) \leftarrow np(NP) \wedge vp(VP) \wedge append(NP, VP, S) \qquad (3.5.7)$$

$$s(S) \leftarrow s(S1) \wedge s(S2) \wedge append(S1, [and|S2], S) \qquad (3.5.8)$$

$$np([lions]) \leftarrow \qquad\qquad (3.5.9)$$

$$vp([sleep]) \leftarrow \qquad\qquad (3.5.10)$$

$$append([H|T1], L2, [H|T3]) \leftarrow append(T1, L2, T3) \qquad\qquad (3.5.11)$$

$$append([], L, L) \leftarrow list(L) \qquad\qquad (3.5.12)$$

$$list([]) \leftarrow \qquad\qquad (3.5.13)$$

$$list([H|T]) \leftarrow list(T). \qquad\qquad (3.5.14)$$

3.5.1   SLD resolution

Notice that a Horn theory in this form contains no negations. In effect, the arrows partition each clause into the positive literal on the left and the negative literals on the right. This partitioning is useful for resolution proof methods in which a negative and positive literal of different clauses are unified and a resolvent is computed: a literal to the right of an arrow can only be resolved against one to the left of an arrow. The theory HT is a set of definite clauses, and every definite clause theory is satisfiable. The most natural problems involve showing that a negative clause is inconsistent with this theory.

Suppose, for example, that we want to prove that something is a sentence according to our theory HT, i.e. $HT \models \exists X\ s(X)$. We do this by refuting $HT \cup \{\leftarrow s(X)\}$. Leaving the axioms of the theory (the input clauses) out of our display of the deduction, as is often done in simple cases like this one, the deduction can be represented by the clause for refutation and its descendants:

1. $\leftarrow s(X)$ *for refutation*
2. $\leftarrow np(NP) \wedge vp(VP) \wedge append(NP, VP, S)$ *from* 1, (3.5.7)
3. $\leftarrow vp(VP) \wedge append([lions], VP, S)$ *from* 2, (3.5.9)
4. $\leftarrow append([lions], [sleep], S)$ *from* 3, (3.5.10)
5. $\leftarrow append([], [sleep], S)$ *from* 4, (3.5.11)
6. $\leftarrow list([sleep])$ *from* 5, (3.5.12)
7. $\leftarrow list([])$ *from* 6, (3.5.14)
8. $\Box$ *from* 7, (3.5.13)

Composing the most general unifiers from this proof, we find that we have refuted $\leftarrow s([lions, sleep])$. In other words, we have proven that there is a sentence according to this theory, namely the string *lions sleep*. Notice that the proof begins with the clause to be refuted and that every following step is the resolvent of an axiom of HT, an input clause, and the immediately preceding resolvent. If a negative clause is inconsistent with a definite clause theory, there will always be a refutation of this simple form, with a single answer substitution.

DEFINITION 31 *Binary resolution* is resolution in which exactly one literal from each parent is resolved upon.

Linear resolution is resolution that pursues deductions by generating descendants of one clause, the "goal" or "top" clause.

Input resolution is resolution that uses derived clauses only once, always resolving them with an axiom, an input clause.

SLD resolution is binary, linear, input resolution, where the clause to be refuted is negative, the axioms are definite clauses, and every resolution step involves a negative parent clause and a definite input clause, resolving upon a literal in the negative parent which is selected as a function of that parent.

If a definite clause theory is inconsistent with a negative clause C, there is always a binary, linear, input resolution deduction of $\square$ from C. The fact that there is always a single answer substitution in such refutations follows from the fact that the refutation is linear and that the clause to be refuted is the goal. There will always be a unique path from the clause to be refuted to $\square$ in such a deduction. Pure Prolog uses these efficient techniques, and is based on *SLD resolution*.[10] This is the basic logical foundation of Prolog's success. Notice that the method does not apply to Horn clause satisfiability in general, but only to refutations of a negative clause from a definite clause theory.[11]

Since the refutations of negative clauses from definite clause theories can always have this simple structure, the proof techniques can be relatively efficient. It is unfortunate that our open formula $s(S)$ only weakly represents $s^{\mathcal{G}}$ in HT. In some cases this suffices, but adding limited negation and a non-monotonic inference rule gets us more.

3.5.2 SLD resolution with negation as failure

We have weak representation of $s^{\mathcal{G}}$ in HT, so a simple strategy suggests itself. Suppose we infer $\neg \phi$ whenever ϕ is not provable. Since, if $x \notin L(G)$, $T \nvdash s(\overline{x})$, this rule seems to allow us to infer exactly the right sentences from our simple theories, T or HT, sentences like $\neg s([sleep])$. Notice that this rule, a "negation as failure" rule, is "non-monotonic" in the sense that, with this rule, the addition of axioms can remove some theorems. This strange rule appears to give us something like strong representation from a weak theory, though, and so it is worth considering what difficulties it poses.

In the first place, we need to be careful about which sentences ϕ we allow this rule to apply to. From the fact that we cannot deduce 2.2.32 from T we would not want to infer the negation of 2.2.32. In the second place, although the set of derivable consequences of a first order theory is recursively enumerable, in general the complement of that set is not. Horn theories are similarly semi-decidable. Yet it is exactly the non-deducible sentences whose negations we are allowed to infer. In general, this rule cannot be effectively applied. We might, however, have a theory which not only weakly represents a relation but also is such that the failures to prove negative cases all terminate after finitely many steps. Clearly, this can be difficult to ensure. There is still a great deal of controversy about the best non-monotonic strategies. We will confine ourselves to a brief and informal introduction to Horn clause theories and one non-monotonic inference rule.

We extend the Prolog form for Horn theories to "general logic theories" by allowing negation to occur to the right of the arrows (in the "antecedents"). As with Horn theories, we partition these theories into programs and goals:

DEFINITION 32 A *general logic program* is a set of clauses of the form

$$A \leftarrow L_1 \wedge \ldots \wedge L_n$$

where $n \geq 0$, A is a positive literal (i.e. an atom), and each L_i is a positive or negative literal. A *general goal* is a clause of the form

$$\leftarrow L_1 \wedge \ldots \wedge L_n$$

where $n > 0$, and each L_i is a positive or negative literal.

Some care is required here, since $\leftarrow \neg q$ is logically equivalent to $q \leftarrow$ and $p \leftarrow \neg q$ is logically equivalent to the non-Horn clause $p \vee q$. In Prolog form, a negative literal to the right of an arrow corresponds to a positive literal in clausal form. However, we will define our special inference rule on our extended Prolog form: general programs and general goals. This form allows us to represent non-Horn clauses.

The simplest idea does not work. We could modify SLD resolution just by extending it with a special treatment of negative literals to the right of the arrow:

(Naive NF) Use SLD resolution except whenever a negative literal $\neg A$ is selected, proceed not by resolution but by attempting to refute $\leftarrow A$. If the attempt to refute $\leftarrow A$ fails finitely then $\leftarrow \neg A$ is refuted.

We can see that this strategy is unsound with a simple example like the following. Consider the general program

$$p(a) \leftarrow$$
$$q(b) \leftarrow$$
$$r1 \leftarrow \neg p(b)$$
$$r2 \leftarrow \neg p(X)$$

and the general goal ← $r1$. With our simple extension of SLD resolution, we find no
refutation of ← $p(b)$ and this comprises a refutation of ← $\neg p(b)$, and so we can refute
← $r1$. This is the behavior we intended. Now notice that the last rule of our theory
is equivalent to the first order form $r2 \leftarrow \exists X \; \neg p(X)$. Since we have already proven
that $\neg p(b)$ (by refuting ← $\neg p(b)$), we should certainly be able to prove $\exists X \; \neg p(X)$ and
thereby refute ← $r2$. However, our simple inference rule does not do this. Consider the
goal ← $\neg p(X)$. Following our strategy, we look for a refutation of ← $p(X)$, but this
time we find one, and so we fail to find a refutation of ← $\neg p(X)$. The goal ← $r2$ has no
refutation and this comprises a refutation of ← $\neg r2$.

Notice that, with negation as failure, we have the peculiar situation in which incompleteness leads to *unsound* results, because the refutation of a goal can depend not only
on successful refutations, successful deductions of □ from subgoals, but also on failures
to find a refutation. Failures to find a refutation license the applications of the negation
as failure rule.

Clearly we must use a more sophisticated strategy than naive NF. We might be able
to tolerate some incompleteness, but unsoundness is not acceptable. The problem with
the naive strategy can be avoided if we never select for refutation a negative literal that
contains a variable. This has the effect that a goal like ← $\neg p(X)$ cannot begin any
deduction; the selection rule cannot select the literal containing a variable. In fact, it is
important to say here that the deduction cannot even "fail" in the sense that its proof
tree terminates with goals that lead to no further resolvents. Since this goal does not
even "fail" in this sense, it cannot license the deduction of ← $\neg\neg p(X)$. The computation
does not "fail," it *aborts*.

There is a slightly weaker restriction that is also safe:

(SLDNF) [12] Use SLD resolution, except whenever a negative literal $\neg A$ is selected for
refutation, attempt to refute ← A. If there is no refutation of ← A, this refutes ← $\neg A$.
If ← A is refuted without binding any variables in A, then fail to find a refutation of
← $\neg A$. If every refutation of ← A binds some variable in A, then *abort* the deduction.

To characterize the derivable sentences of this sort of system, Clark formalizes the
intuition that the non-monotonic rule presumes that the definite clause theory includes
"complete" information about the positive instances of every relation that it formalizes
(Clark, 1978; Lloyd, 1987). Rather than simply noting that the predicates of the definite
clause theory must be weakly represented, Clark provides a theory, "the completion of
the definite clause theory," whose logical consequences include everything that SLDNF
allows us to deduce from the definite clause theory.

DEFINITION 33 Let P be a set of general clauses not containing the equality predicate $=$. Then the *completion of* P, $Comp(P)$, is defined as follows. First we transform each sentence ϕ in P. Every ϕ will have the form

$$p(t_1, \ldots, t_n) \leftarrow L_1 \wedge \ldots \wedge L_m$$

for some $m, n \geq 0$. Where variables $Y_1, \ldots, Y_d$, $d \geq 0$, are the variables in ϕ, and $X_1, \ldots, X_n$ do not occur in ϕ, the transformation of ϕ is

$$p(X_1, \ldots, X_n) \leftarrow \exists Y_1, \ldots, Y_d$$
$$(X_1 = t_1) \wedge \ldots \wedge (X_n = t_n) \wedge L_1 \wedge \ldots \wedge L_m$$

Now we collect all the transformed clauses with the same predicate p to the left of the arrow:

$$p(X_1, \ldots, X_n) \leftarrow E_1$$
$$\ldots$$
$$p(X_1, \ldots, X_n) \leftarrow E_k$$

The completed definition of predicate p, $Comp(p)$, is then

$$p(X_1, \ldots, X_n) \leftrightarrow E_1 \vee \ldots \vee E_k.$$

Finally, the completion of the theory P is the set of completed definitions of its predicates, together with an equality theory SEQ_P that defines syntactic equality in P:

$$Comp(P) = \{Comp(p) | p \in P\} \cup SEQ_P$$

For any theory P, the equality theory SEQ_P is defined relative to the set of constants and function symbols in the language of P as follows. We have the following axioms, for all distinct constants, a, b, functions f, g and predicates p:

		Theory SEQ_P
$X = X$		(3.5.15)
$\neg a = b$		(3.5.16)
$\neg a = f(X_1, \ldots, X_n)$		(3.5.17)
$\neg f(X_1, \ldots, X_n) = g(Y_1, \ldots, Y_m)$		(3.5.18)
$\neg X = \tau$	*for all τ containing X*	(3.5.19)
$f(X_1, \ldots, X_n) = f(Y_1, \ldots, Y_n) \leftrightarrow X_1 = Y_1 \wedge \ldots \wedge X_n = Y_n$		(3.5.20)
$p(X_1, \ldots, X_n) \leftarrow p(Y_1, \ldots, Y_n) \wedge X_1 = Y_1 \wedge \ldots \wedge X_n = Y_n$		(3.5.21)

Notice that SEQ_P is infinite whenever the language of P contains even a single function symbol of positive arity, because of the schema 3.5.19.

Clark establishes a soundness result which can be stated as follows (Clark, 1978; Lloyd, 1987):

THEOREM 7 (Soundness of negation as failure) Let P be a general program and G be a general goal. If there is a derivation of $\square$ from $P \cup \{G\}$ using SLDNF resolution, then $Comp(P) \cup \{G\}$ is unsatisfiable.

We do not have the completeness result for SLDNF resolution that we might like. Consider the following example (from Lloyd, 1987):

Theory NF

$p(X) \leftarrow$
$q(a) \leftarrow$
$r(b) \leftarrow$

We can derive $\square$ from this theory and $\leftarrow p(b), \neg q(b)$, but we cannot derive $\square$ from $\leftarrow p(X), \neg q(X)$. We should be able to! The completion of NF is the union of SEQ_{NF} and the following:

Theory Comp(NF)

$p(X) \leftrightarrow \exists Y\ X = Y$
$q(X) \leftrightarrow X = a$
$r(X) \leftrightarrow X = b$

Clearly, the union of $Comp(NF)$ and the set containing only the general goal $\leftarrow p(X) \wedge \neg q(X)$ is unsatisfiable. Note that in first order logic this general goal would be written $\forall X\ \neg p(X) \vee q(X)$, but the first two sentences of $Comp(NF)$ tell us that $\neg p(b)$ and $q(b)$ are false, so $Comp(NF) \cup \{\leftarrow p(X) \wedge \neg q(X)\}$ is unsatisfiable.

Notice that we could extend the negation as failure strategy to make it complete as follows: whenever a non-ground negative literal is selected, find a substitution σ that makes it ground, and proceed with the deduction (composing σ in the answer substitution with the substitutions from resolution steps). This strategy is effective since the ground substitutions can be enumerated; it is simply infeasible. Notice the similarity with our special equality rules of the previous subsection in which we considered the possibility of "building in" the equality theory we need. This incompleteness is not too serious, because we can formulate our theories in such a way that it will rarely manifest itself. That is, we can exploit the following restricted completeness result:

PROPOSITION 11 If SLDNF resolution never aborts deductions from general goal G and general program P, then it will deduce $\square$ just in case $P \cup \{G\}$ is unsatisfiable.

Proof: See Clark (1978) or Lloyd (1987).

We consider strategies for ensuring the condition of this proposition in later sections. When the computation never aborts, we have a sound system with a restricted completeness result, but Lloyd (1984, 76) aptly points out that it would have been nice to get a bit more than this:[13]

> Note that bindings are only made by successful calls of positive literals. Negative literal calls can never create bindings; they only succeed or fail. Thus negation as failure is purely a test. As such, it is a rather unsatisfactory substitute for (logical) negation.

The completion of a theory seems quite natural in many cases. Indeed, it is easy to show that $Comp(HT)$ is logically equivalent to the theory GT of the previous section. (They are identical except for some superfluous equations of variables, equations that can be removed by resolution with the clause $\{X = X\}$.) Why should these two theories be equivalent? The answer is not simply that $Comp(HT)$ is a "completion" of HT and that GT was developed as the first step towards a complete theory of the domain $\mathcal{G}$. A complete theory of $\mathcal{G}$ could perfectly well contain distinct terms with the same denotation. The reason that there was no such pair of terms was simply a matter of convenience.

Consider, for example, adding to the language of CT and HT a new constant j with the same denotation in $\mathcal{G}$ as $[lions]$. The complete theory $Th(\mathcal{G})$ would then include $j = [lions]$, $np(j)$ and $list(j)$. Let HT' be HT plus the sentence $np(j) \leftarrow$. Then $Cn(Comp(HT'))$ would include $\neg j = [lions]$, since it has inequalities for every distinct pair of constants and functions. The motivation for the inclusion of these inequalities in the completion is not some guess about what the intended model is, but the goal of properly characterizing the theorems that can be deduced from HT' with SLDNF inference. Notice that $list(j)$ is not among the SLDNF-deducible consequences of HT'. The SLDNF derivation of $list(j)$ is blocked because the completion does not, and cannot, have any equation of distinct functions, like $j = [lions]$. So one perspective on the inequalities in Clark's completion is, to put it roughly, that those inequalities block the application of substitution principles in a way that properly characterizes the consequences derivable with SLDNF resolution from a theory without equality. It really is just lucky coincidence that a natural theory of $\mathcal{G}$, or a theory of any similar domain, does not call for distinct terms denoting the same thing: this was convenient because it happens that standard grammars (like our grammar G of the previous section) use unique terms, and we used an *append* predicate rather than an append function. Theories of arithmetic, on the other hand, typically have *many* distinct terms with the same denotation, such as $s(0)$ and $s(0) + 0$, because they use a sum function rather than a sum predicate.[14]

The completion of a theory allows us to see exactly the respect in which SLDNF inference is nonmonotonic. Consider the definite clause theory

$nn(0) \leftarrow$
$nn(s(X)) \leftarrow nn(X).$

With SLD resolution, we can show that this theory is inconsistent with $\leftarrow nn(s(s(0)))$. Adding negation as failure, we can use SLDNF inference to refute $\leftarrow \neg nn(a)$: there is no refutation of $\leftarrow nn(a)$, so we take $\leftarrow \neg nn(a)$ to be refuted. Obviously, if we add $nn(a) \leftarrow$ to the theory, SLDNF inference will not longer allow us to refute $\leftarrow \neg nn(a)$. But notice that the addition of an axiom to this theory corresponds to adding an additional disjunct to the completed definition of nn, not an additional axiom. Standard inference rules for first order logic are monotonic. Adding an axiom to a monotonic system never decreases the size of the set of derivable consequences of the system, but it is no surprise that adding an additional disjunct to a definition of a relation can change the provable positive and negative instances of the relation.

Completions of theories are not always so natural as $Comp(HT)$ might suggest. In the first place, under the intended interpretation, a Horn clause theory can be correct without providing weak representation of all of its relations. In this case, the completed definitions of those relations will simply be false. It is valuable to note that in this situation we can still get sound results when the negation as failure rule is restricted to those predicates that, under the intended interpretation, correspond to relations that *are* weakly represented. Suppose we have a procedure that tells us whether a predicate, under our intended interpretation, corresponds to a relation that is weakly represented or not. Then we can define the following inference rule:

(Selective SLDNF) [15] Use SLD resolution except when a negative literal $\neg A$ is selected for refutation. In that case, if the predicate of A is not weakly represented, then *abort* the deduction. Otherwise, attempt to refute $\leftarrow A$. If there is no refutation of $\leftarrow A$, this refutes $\leftarrow \neg A$. If $\leftarrow A$ is refuted without binding any variables in A, then fail to find a refutation of $\leftarrow \neg A$. If every refutation of $\leftarrow A$ binds some variable in A, then *abort* the deduction.

Since it is clear that the completion is only needed to cover refutations of negative literals and results that depend on these refutations, it is no surprise that the following restricted result can be established (see Chan, 1986 for a proof):

DEFINITION 34 The *partial completion of P* is the set:

$$PComp(P) = \{Comp(p)|p \ a \ weakly \ represented \ predicate \ in \ T\} \cup SEQ_P$$

THEOREM 8 If Selective SLDNF resolution never aborts deductions from general goal G and general program P, then it will deduce $\square$ just in case $P \cup PComp(P) \cup \{G\}$ is unsatisfiable.

A more serious problem with completions has been raised in a number of critiques. The following sort of example is often noted (Sheperdson, 1987; Flannagan, 1986). The definite clause theory

$$p \leftarrow \neg p$$

is logically equivalent to p but the completed definition of this predicate is the contradiction

$$p \leftrightarrow \neg p.$$

To take a slightly more interesting case, consider the definite clause theory (called "DB_2" in Flannagan, 1986):

Theory DB_2

$$p(a, b) \leftarrow$$
$$p(X, Y) \leftarrow \neg p(Y, X)$$

This theory has the following two sentences in its completion

$$\neg a = b$$

$$p(X, Y) \leftrightarrow (\quad X = a \land$$
$$\qquad\qquad\quad Y = b$$
$$\quad \lor \quad \exists W, Z$$
$$\qquad\qquad\quad Y = W \land$$
$$\qquad\qquad\quad X = Z \land$$
$$\qquad\qquad\quad \neg p(W, Z)$$
$$\qquad)$$

Again, this theory is unsatisfiable: letting $X = Y = W = Z = a$ we can deduce

$p(a,a) \leftrightarrow \neg p(a,a)$.

In view of examples like these, one critic of negation as failure makes the following remark:

> Thus, the value of even the concept of [the completion of a data base] is suspect ... Notice that we are not saying that the value of a theory ... diminishes just because it might be inconsistent. Arithmetic might be inconsistent. We are saying that the value of a theory is seriously diminished if it is very likely to be inconsistent ... the simplicity of DB_2 shows that, in general, we are bound to disbelieve the consistency of [the completion of a data base]. (Flannagan, 1986)

This conclusion is too strong. The problem can be avoided if appropriate care is taken in assessing the completion itself. The point is that we should not adopt the strategy of attending only to the truth of a definite clause formulation, naively assuming that negation as failure will produce acceptable results. The value of negation as failure is that it provides a relatively efficient proof strategy for something more than the Horn clause subset, although it should be remembered that in the worst case this proof strategy is not even effective. Furthermore, this proof strategy cannot be directly applied to theories that do not respect the syntactic equality.

Let's express this last point more carefully. It is tricky because there are (Skolem-function-free) definite clause theories T whose completions $Comp(T)$ have clausal forms containing Skolem functions. Our little theory of natural numbers (theory NN of page 43) is a case in point. SLD resolution extended with negation as failure can apply in these cases soundly, but possibly incompletely. However, many of the first order theories considered in Chapter 2, for example, have clausal forms containing Skolem functions and are *not* the completions of any definite clause theory. Theory CT (of page 22), for example, contains sentences, such as instances of 2.2.33, which are not in the completion of any Horn theory. The completion must introduce its own equality relation, and it is not one that includes or entails 2.2.33, though it is compatible with 2.2.33. If we are interested in completeness, or in the consequences of theories that are not the completion of any general clause theory, we can use one of the inference techniques mentioned above, such as SEq resolution.

3.6   Decision procedures

First order logic has effective proof procedures that are sound and complete, but these will not and cannot, in general, effectively determine that a sentence has no proof. The same holds for Horn clause theories. However, many sentences of first order logic *are* decidable. For example, many but not all the results that we might want to establish in a simple grammatical domain like $\mathcal{G}$ are decidable. Yet our proof procedures cannot be guaranteed to make the decision. It will be recalled from the proof of Theorem 1 of Chapter 2 that one way of getting a decision in complete theories is to simultaneously seek proofs of both the sentence and its negation. There are much more efficient strategies. For example, Joyner (1976) has shown that there are more efficient resolution-based strategies for certain decidable classes of sentences. Basically, Joyner exploits the fact that if the empty clause is not among the resolvents after all of them have been explored, it follows that the original theory is satisfiable. Following work by Kowalski and Hayes (1969), Joyner introduces restrictions on the resolution procedure that block the exploration of certain sets of resolvents where it can be demonstrated that these sets do not contain the empty clause, and he shows that for certain classes of first order sentences, these restrictions suffice to make the decision about satisfiability effective without removing the completeness of the proof procedure in the general case.

Unfortunately, though, our theories of $\mathcal{G}$ are essentially incomplete, and the same holds of the theory we formalize in later sections. Thus Theorem 1 of the previous chapter does not guarantee a decision on an arbitrary problem. In fact, since we cannot show our theories to be decidable in general, the task will be to consider whether certain interesting classes of problems are decidable, and then to consider whether they are feasible. Though we cannot decide the satisfiability of the conjunction of our theory with an arbitrary sentence (the "goal" to be refuted), the usefulness of the theory in applications depends on the decidability of certain problems. Decidability is also essential for handling one of the most serious problems with the negation as failure rule. Negation as failure is not, in the general case, an inference step that can be effectively applied precisely because we have no guarantee that failed attempts to establish a result will fail in a finite number of steps. It is interesting to consider whether there is a useful class of problems such that we can guarantee a decision about the availability of a SLD resolution proof. In this context, Clark (1978) and others have studied the same problem: is there any interesting class of Horn problems for which we can guarantee a decision after a finite number of steps? We will return to these issues after formalizing the theory and specifying some of the problems that we would like to decide.

3.7   The strategy for the current project

We have discussed a number of proof techniques: resolution, resolution modified with
special equality rules, SLD resolution, and SLD resolution extended with negation as
failure. Implementations of these proof methods are all available, as is the conversion from
first order form to clausal form. In the next chapter we explore the use of these methods
on problems involving simple artificial languages. In Part II we we formalize a linguistic
theory in first order logic, and here the ability to check our tentative formulations of these
theories by deriving expected consequences has served behind the scenes as an invaluable
aid to eliminating errors in the formalization.[16] As discussed in §3.4, the formalization
conforms to the "syntactic equality" or "unique names" restriction, avoiding the use of
many names for a single object, in order to avoid unnecessary reasoning with equality.
After the formalization has been presented, we will return to the interesting question
of whether significantly better methods are available for deductive models of natural
language processing.

Chapter 4

Deductive parsing:
Context-free phrase structure

> *When the thing sufficiently lives for you then start to plan it with instruments, not before. To draw during the conception or sketch, as we say, experimenting with practical adjustments to scale, is well enough if the concept is clear enough to be firmly held in the meantime... If the concept is lost as the drawing proceeds, throw all away and begin again...*
> — *Frank Lloyd Wright*

In this chapter we develop a logical representation of context-free grammar (CFG) phrase structure parsing problems, and in the course of this exercise we introduce some technical tools that will be useful in our attempt to construct a linguistically sophisticated approach to human language processing.

We have considered the use of specialized proof techniques for increasing the feasibility of proofs from certain theories, theories that contain equality axioms that restrict the class of models to those that provide unique names for each (named) element of their domains. Even when these special theorem proving methods are used, though, efficiency can be a serious problem. We begin by introducing a second efficiency-enhancing strategy, "program transformations," or, as they might more appropriately be called in our case, "theory transformations." We will transform our list representations of sequences into "difference list" representations. This alternative representation of sequences is much more efficient, and proof-theoretically more elegant. We formalize a transformation from grammars to theories that uses this idea, and then we demonstrate the correctness of the resulting theories.

After treating the problem of recognizing a language generated by an arbitrary context-free grammar, we consider the problem of parsing these languages, formulating derivation trees for the strings in the language. Since we represent the grammatical relations such as sentencehood with logical theories, and since certain proofs from these theories exhibit a very simple correspondence to derivations from the grammar, it turns out that the parsing problem is essentially the problem of representing the set of proofs of a theory. We introduce a general technique for representing the proofs of a Horn clause theory and then apply the technique to parsing. Automatic proof methods which construct the instances of the clauses they refute can then be used to construct derivation trees. Since metatheoretic techniques can cause confusions (and even inconsistencies!), this material is treated in detail. They are of sufficient interest to warrant the attention.

4.1   Difference lists

When Γ and Γ' are two distinct but logically equivalent theories, a class of results can be more efficiently proven from Γ than from Γ'. This observation is the basic idea behind "program transformations" in logic programming. It can be useful to transform a theory into a different but logically equivalent form in order to facilitate the proofs of certain results. The measures of efficiency are typically the length of the shortest proof, and the number of deductive steps in the search for the shortest proof. These measures depend, of course, on the proof method. We focus here on improving the efficiency of resolution proofs, but, at least for the problems considered here, it will be clear that the proposed representations will be more efficient for a wide range of natural proof methods.[1]

Preserving logical equivalence is an unnecessarily strict constraint on efficiency enhancing transformations. Transformations that preserve logical equivalence obviously cannot change the language of a theory, for example, but it is well known from work on transformational methods for procedural programs that changes in data structures can be very valuable, and the inventory of functions and predicates comprise the data structures of a logical theory. In this section we consider a data structure transformation. It is inspired by noting that a lot of *append*ing gets done in proofs from HT and the related theories we have considered. Clark and Tärnlund introduce a more efficient representation of sequences for domains like the one we have considered: "difference lists."[2] We represent a sequence $S = \langle t_1, \ldots, t_k \rangle$ as the difference between a pair of sequences $S0, S1$ such that $S0 = \langle t_1, \ldots, t_k, \ldots, t_n \rangle$ and $S1 = \langle t_{k+1}, \ldots, t_n \rangle$. Extending our theory with a "difference" function symbol, sequence S in this case could be denoted by $S0 - S1$; S is the sequence that remains when final segment $S1$ is removed from sequence $S0$. (It is convenient to extend this idea to dotted pairs as well, letting $(a.b) - b$ denote the sequence $[a]$.)

In this extended theory, we could reformulate HT as follows:

$$s(S0 - S) \leftarrow np(S0 - S1) \wedge vp(S1 - S)$$
$$s(S0 - S) \leftarrow s(S0 - [and|S1]) \wedge s(S1 - S)$$

$$np([lions|S] - S) \leftarrow$$
$$vp([sleep|S] - S) \leftarrow$$

$$list([]) \leftarrow$$
$$list([H|T]) \leftarrow list(T).$$

Extending our model $\mathcal{G}$ to capture the intended interpretation of the new binary function symbol $-$, each sentence of this theory is equivalent to the corresponding sentence of HT, and it is easy to show that we have weak representation of $s^{\mathcal{G}}$.

This strategy can introduce some difficulties, though, because the use of the difference function gives us many different ground terms with the same denotation. Consider for example:

$[lions, sleep]$
$[lions, sleep] - []$
$[lions, sleep, and] - [and]$
$[lions, sleep, and, and] - [and, and]$
$\ldots$

Having distinct terms for each named element of the domain can simplify proofs and models enormously, so a modification in our predicates is preferable to the introduction of the difference function. Using two distinct predicate arguments to hold a pair of difference lists does not impair readability:

Theory DG

$$s(S0, S) \leftarrow np(S0, S1) \wedge vp(S1, S) \tag{4.1.1}$$

$$s(S0, S) \leftarrow s(S0, [and|S1]) \wedge s(S1, S) \tag{4.1.2}$$

$$np([lions|S], S) \leftarrow \tag{4.1.3}$$

$$vp([sleep|S], S) \leftarrow \tag{4.1.4}$$

Not only are proofs from this theory simpler because no instances of the append relation need to be established, but we also have a very simple and elegant correspondence between grammatical derivations of nonterminal strings x and SLD refutations of $s(\overline{x}, [])$. We will define and exploit this correspondence in our parsing theory below. First, to make our presentation relatively complete, let's specify the intended model $\mathcal{DG}$ for theory DG:

(a) The interpretation of the function symbols. As in $\mathcal{G}$.

(b) The interpretation of the predicate symbols. For each nonterminal Cat in the grammar, our theory contains a binary predicate cat of the same name. In each of these cases, $\langle s, s' \rangle \in cat^{\mathcal{DG}}$ iff one of the following conditions holds:

(b.i) $s = \langle t_1, \ldots, t_k, \ldots, t_n \rangle$, $s' = \langle t_k, \ldots, t_n \rangle$, and $t_1, \ldots, t_k$ is a string of terminal categories L such that $Cat \Rightarrow^* L$, or

(b.ii) $s = \ulcorner h.t \urcorner$ (a dotted pair), $s' = t$, and h is a terminal category such that $Cat \Rightarrow^* h$.

The last clause, (b.ii) allows $\models_{DG} np(lions.lions, lions)$, which, although a deviant case, is an instance of 4.1.3.

It is not too hard to see that deductions of $s(\overline{x})$ from DG correspond exactly to grammatical derivations of terminal string x from nonterminal S. Obviously, this correspondence is not peculiar to our grammar G, but will hold for every similarly represented context-free grammar. To define this sort of correspondence, we first define a mapping from context-free grammars to logical theories that weakly represent all nonterminal categories of the grammar. Later, after we have defined proof trees, we will demonstrate that the deductions from the theories correspond in structure to the derivations from the grammar. The correctness of DG will follow as a corollary to that stronger result.

DEFINITION 35 **Definition of τ_g:**[3]

(i) For any grammar, G, $\tau_g(G) = \{\tau_g(R) | R$ *a rewrite rule of* $G\} \cup \{X = X \leftarrow\}$.

(ii) For every nonterminal category Cat of G, $\tau_g(G)$ contains a binary predicate of the same name but written in lower case, cat. For each rule R of the grammar of the form

$$NT \rightarrow Cat_1 \ldots Cat_k,$$

if $k = 0$ then $\tau_g(R) = nt(S_0, S_k) \leftarrow S_0 = S_k$. Otherwise, $\tau_g(R) = nt(S_0, S_k) \leftarrow A_1 \wedge \ldots \wedge A_k$ where $S_0, S_1, \ldots$ are distinct variables and for each $0 < i \leq k$,

$$A_i = \begin{cases} cat_i(S_{i-1}, S_i) & \text{if } Cat_i \text{ is a nonterminal;} \\ S_{i-1} = [cat_i | S_i] & \text{if } Cat_i \text{ is a terminal.} \end{cases}$$

For example, the result of applying the transformation to Grammar G of §2.3 is the following:

Theory $\tau_g(G)$

$s(S0, S2) \leftarrow np(S0, S1) \wedge vp(S1, S2)$
$s(S0, S3) \leftarrow s(S0, S1) \wedge S1 = [and|S2] \wedge s(S2, S3)$
$np(S0, S1) \leftarrow S0 = [lions|S1]$
$vp(S0, S1) \leftarrow S0 = [sleep|S1]$
$X = X \leftarrow$

Notice that these clauses are not quite the same as those of DG. The equalities in $\tau_g(G)$ are superfluous in the presence of EQ, where this is the equality theory defined for Clark's completion of $\tau_g(G)$, an equality theory which imposes the unique names restriction as discussed in the previous chapter.

We will need the following result:

LEMMA 2 For every r, there is exactly one ϕ such that $\tau_g(r) = \phi$. In other words, τ_g^{-1} is a mapping.

Proof: This follows immediately from the definition of τ_g, assuming that the sequence of variables $S_0, S_1, \ldots$ is fixed for every application of the definition. ∎

4.2 A correspondence between derivations and deductions

Given any context-free grammar G, it is a simple matter to define the set of derivation trees of G. We will represent trees with terms of the form *root/subtrees* where *root* is a label and *subtrees* is a term denoting a non-empty sequence of trees that are immediately dominated by the node labeled by *root*.

DEFINITION 36 Consider a context-free grammar $G = \langle N, \Sigma, S, P \rangle$.[4] Tree t is a *derivation tree of G* just in case

(i) its root is labeled S,
(ii) if a node labeled Cat immediately dominates nodes $Cat_1, \ldots, Cat_n$ (in that order), then $Cat \to Cat_1, \ldots, Cat_n$ is a rewrite rule in P, and
(iii) every leaf node is labeled either with a terminal category (an element of Σ) or with a non-terminal C which can be rewritten with the empty string (i.e., the production $C \to \lambda$ is an element of P).

PROPOSITION 12 All interior nodes of a derivation tree are labeled with nonterminals.

Proof: Follows immediately from definition. ∎

DEFINITION 37 The *yield* of a tree is the (possibly empty) sequence of terminal categories that label the leaves of the tree, in order.

PROPOSITION 13 $L(G) = \{x | x$ *is the yield of a derivation tree of G*$\}$.

Proof: Since $L(G) = \{x | S \Rightarrow^* x, \ x \in \Sigma^*\}$, this proposition follows immediately from the definitions just given. ∎

It is also a simple matter to define proof trees corresponding to successful SLD refutations. Remember that in SLD refutations, the axioms of the theory ("input clauses") are commonly left out, even though they play a role in the derivation of every resolvent.

DEFINITION 38 Let G be a goal, a negative clause, $\leftarrow A$ where A is an atom. Let Ψ be
an SLD refutation $\langle G_0, G_1, \ldots, G_n \rangle$, $(G_0 = G, G_n = \Box)$ using input clauses $C_1, \ldots, C_n$
with unifiers $\theta_1, \ldots, \theta_n$ whose composition we will call θ. Then a *proof tree corresponding
to* Ψ is a tree such that: in Ψ, G_{i-1} $(0 < i \le n)$ is resolved with the head of input
clause $C_i = C \leftarrow C_{i_1} \wedge \ldots \wedge C_{i_m}$ $(m \ge 0)$ iff there is a node in the tree labeled $C\theta$
with m daughters labeled $C_{i_1}\theta, \ldots, C_{i_m}\theta$. (We regard the literals that label the tree as
universally closed.)

This is a standard notion of a proof tree (cf., e.g., Shapiro, 1984). It is easy to show that
for any SLD refutation Ψ of a theory, there is exactly one proof tree corresponding to
Ψ. Given any particular proof tree t and a computation rule R, there is a theory with
at least one SLD refutation via R that corresponds to t.

Now we can undertake to establish the correspondence between proof trees of $\tau_g(G)$
and grammatical derivations from G. Consider the following example:

Theory S

$man(X) \leftarrow male(X) \wedge human(X)$
$male(X) \leftarrow$
$human(X) \leftarrow$

The following is a refutation of $\leftarrow man(A)$ from this theory:

$\leftarrow man(A)$
$\leftarrow male(A) \wedge human(A)$
$\leftarrow human(A)$
$\Box$

This refutation corresponds to the proof tree in Figure 4.1. We interpret the proof tree
as indicating that, in S, $\forall man(A)$ can be proven by proving $\forall male(A)$ and $\forall human(A)$,
which in turn can be proven directly from unit clauses. In our textual notation, this tree
is represented by

$man(A)/[male(A)/[], human(A)/[]]$.

The examples we are more interested in are the proof trees corresponding to refutations
of $s(x, [])$ from $\tau_g(G)$. For $x = [lions, sleep]$ we have, for example, the refutation indicated
by the proof tree in Figure 4.2. Obviously, this corresponds exactly to the derivation tree
for the string *lions sleep*. The following proposition expresses the relation that holds:

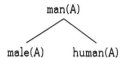

Figure 4.1
Proof tree for ← $man(A)$

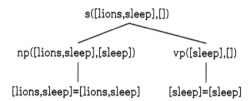

Figure 4.2
Proof tree for ← $s([lions, sleep], [])$

PROPOSITION 14 Consider the following sets:

$Trees(\tau_g(G)) = \{t | t$ is a proof tree with root $s(x, [])$ for some $x\}$

$\quad Trees(G) = \{t | t$ is a derivation tree for $G\}$

There is a simple relabeling g such that for any tree t, $t \in Trees(\tau_g(G))$ iff $g(t) \in Trees(G)$.

Proof: Consider the following mapping g from proof trees to grammatical derivation trees

$$g(root) = \begin{cases} Cat & \text{if root is labeled } cat(s, s') \text{ or } [cat|s] = [cat|s]; \\ undefined & \text{otherwise} \end{cases}$$
$$g(root/[t_1, \ldots, t_n]) = g(root)/[g(t_1), \ldots, g(t_n)]$$

Using the definition of τ_g it is easy to show by an induction on the depth of the tree that if t is a proof tree in $Trees(\tau_g(G))$, then $g(t)$ is a derivation tree for G. Furthermore, noting that the elements in the equated sequences all occur in the terminal string and hence occur in derivation trees as leaves, we can see that for any derivation tree t' for G, there can only be one proof tree t in $Trees(\tau_g(G))$ such that $g(t) = t'$. We can see that $g^{-1}(t')$ is a proof tree t such that

(a) the root is $g^{-1}(S) = s(\overline{x}, [])$ where x is the yield of t', and in general, for each nonterminal node Cat, $g^{-1}(Cat) = cat(\overline{x}, \overline{y})$ where $x - y$ is the yield of the subtree dominated by the corresponding Cat in t' and y is the sequence of terminal categories which follows that yield in the string x;

(b) for each terminal, leaf node Cat, $g^{-1}(Cat)$ is the equation $[cat|\overline{y}] = [cat|\overline{y}]$ where y is the sequence of terminal categories which follows this occurrence of cat in the string x. ∎

PROPOSITION 15 $s^{\mathcal{G}} = \{x | \langle x, \langle \rangle \rangle \in s^{\mathcal{DG}}\}$

Proof: Using the correspondence g of the previous proposition, it is easy to show that tree t is a proof tree with root $s(\overline{x}, [])$ just in case $g(t)$ is a derivation tree corresponding to the derivation of x from G. ∎

4.2.1   Parsing and CFG derivation trees

Given a language specified by a context-free rewrite grammar, $L(G)$, it is standard to distinguish two rather different problems that are often of practical interest. The first is the *recognition* problem: is there an algorithm that effectively decides whether or not an arbitrary terminal string x is in $L(G)$? Note that such a decision algorithm need not use grammar G at all; sometimes it is more efficient to base a recognition algorithm for $L(G)$ on a different grammar G' such that $L(G) = L(G')$. The *parsing* problem, on the other hand, is the problem of effectively constructing a representation of the derivation of x from G just in case there is one. Parsing is typically the operation we are interested in. We code into the grammar the appropriate structural descriptions of grammatical strings and then effectively formulate those descriptions with a parser. The structural descriptions are typically trees.

We can name exactly the sets that must be correctly represented in any adequate representation of a recognition or parsing problem for a grammar:

DEFINITION 39 The *recognition problem for G* is $\{x | x \in L(G)\}$.

DEFINITION 40 The *parsing problem for G* is

$\{\langle x, t \rangle | t$ *is a derivation tree of G with yield x*$\}$.

We have already treated the recognition problem for an arbitrary context-free grammar G. We have the following as corollaries of our previous proposition:

COROLLARY 2 $s(S, [])$ in $\tau_g(G)$ weakly represents the recognition problem for G.

COROLLARY 3 $s(S, [])$ in $Comp(\tau_g(G))$ represents the recognition problem for G. In other words, using negation as failure (which can be ineffective), $s(S, [])$ represents the recognition problem for G.

Now we turn to the parsing problem. In typical introductions to formal language theory or compiler theory, the parsing problem is never formalized, but is treated informally and then implemented. It is formalized in translation theory and in tree automata theory, but these subjects are often neglected. The lack of an intelligible, declarative specification can lead to serious errors, though. Many people read Earley's (1970) famous paper on efficient context-free parsing, even reading his proofs, without noticing the error in the tree construction procedure of his parser.[5] In our relatively rigorous logical approach, we have already formulated logical theories whose proof trees correspond to grammatical derivation trees, so the logical formulation of the parsing problem can take the form of a metatheory, a theory about proofs from $\tau_g(G)$. We take up a couple preliminaries first.

To (weakly) represent the parsing problem in logic, we must at least have terms that denote trees. For this purpose, we can extend our *logical language* with the same notation that we have been using for trees in our metalanguage. We represent trees in the logic with terms of the form *root/subtrees* where *root* is a term (typically one that denotes itself) and *subtrees* is a term denoting the possibly empty sequence of trees that are immediately dominated by the node labeled by *root*. Formally, then, the slash is a binary function symbol written in the convenient infix notation. For example, $a/[b, c]$ is a simple binary tree. The term $a/[]$ is a tree with no branches, with a root labeled a.[6]

The formal interpretation of the function symbol / can be specified in a way that will be suitable for every intended interpretation of a language containing the symbol. The interpretation of the constant [] and the cons function is as specified in §2.2, above. Then our "standard" interpretation I of / is the following:

$$I(r/s) = \begin{cases} \text{the tree with root labeled} \\ \quad I(r) \text{ and subtrees } I(s) & \text{if } I(s) \text{ is a sequence} \\ \ulcorner (\overline{r})/(\overline{s}) \urcorner, & \text{otherwise.} \end{cases}$$

In a tree $r/[t_1, \ldots, t_n]$, r is the label of the root vertex, $t_1, \ldots, t_n$ $(n > 0)$ are trees, and an arc connects the root labeled r to the root of each t_i $(0 < i \leq n)$, in order. Notice that we resort to a Herbrand-like, syntactic interpretation whenever t is not a sequence with at least one element, as we did in the interpretation of lists. This interpretation preserves the unique name property. We will sometimes leave out the parentheses when no confusion will result.

Given this notation for trees, it is easy to define standard structural relations on the nodes of a tree. For example, we can define the standard subtree, parent and ancestor relations with the following axioms:

$$
\begin{aligned}
subtree(Sub, Tree) \leftrightarrow \quad (\quad &Sub = Tree \\
\vee \quad &\exists Node, Seq, Sub1 \\
&Tree = Node/Seq \wedge \\
&member(Sub1, Seq) \wedge \\
&subtree(Sub, Sub1) \\
)&
\end{aligned}
\tag{4.2.5}
$$

$$
\begin{aligned}
member(Element, Seq) \leftrightarrow (\quad &\exists Seq1 \; Seq = [Element|Seq1] \\
\vee \quad &\exists Element1, Seq1 \\
&Seq = [Element1|Seq1] \wedge \\
&member(Element, Seq1) \\
)&
\end{aligned}
\tag{4.2.6}
$$

$$
\begin{aligned}
parent(Parent, Node, Tree) \leftrightarrow \quad &\exists Seq, Seq0 \\
&subtree(Parent/Seq, Tree) \wedge \\
&member(Node/Seq0, Seq)
\end{aligned}
\tag{4.2.7}
$$

$$
\begin{aligned}
ancestor(Anc, Node, Tree) \leftrightarrow (\quad &parent(Anc, Node, Tree) \\
\vee \quad &\exists Mid \\
&parent(Anc, Mid, Tree) \wedge \\
&ancestor(Mid, Node, Tree) \\
)&
\end{aligned}
\tag{4.2.8}
$$

These familiar relations are actually not needed for the simple parsing problems of this chapter, but they will play a fundamental role in the formulation of linguistic principles in later sections. The point to note here is just that our notation allows us to formalize basic properties of trees in the standard way.

4.2.2 Context-free parsing with a metatheory

We have shown that deductions of $s(\overline{x})$ from DG correspond exactly to grammatical derivations of terminal string x from nonterminal S, and that this correspondence holds whenever the logical theory is the result of applying our mapping τ_g to a context-free grammar. This leads us to notice that *the parsing problem for G is a matter of specifying the structure of proofs from DG.* That is, we need a logical theory about proofs from the theory *DG*, a *metatheory* in which there are terms that denote proofs from *DG*. Since *DG* is a Horn theory, it turns out that we can use the simple structure of SLD resolution to define these metatheories precisely. We will then be in a position to demonstrate the relation between the proof trees and the grammatical derivation trees. This relation is useful in a number of different applications (Stabler, 1990), but here we use it to represent the parsing problem for context-free grammars.

There are standard techniques for defining proof trees of a theory. We will begin with one of the simplest. We define a general transformation that maps any Horn clause theory S into a theory $\tau_m(S)$ that specifies proof trees of S. Under the intended interpretation, terms of $\tau_m(S)$ have exactly the same length and the same structure as the terms of S that they refer to. The interpretation of these terms is given by a symbol-for-symbol bijection.[7] This makes the semantics and the proofs in the metatheory $\tau_m(S)$ extremely simple. But it is clear that this same property makes self-referential formulas impossible in a standard logic, for notice that we immediately have the consequence that no finite expression can properly contain a name of itself.[8]

We first define a syntactic transformation τ_m that maps a theory S into a different theory $\tau_m(S)$ which specifies the proof trees of S. The intended semantic interpretation of the output of this transformation will then be defined. Finally, some of the important properties of τ_m are established.

We begin by motivating our approach with a simple example. The function τ_m transforms a logical theory expressed in Horn clauses into another theory which defines deductions in the original theory. The basic idea of the transformation is really quite simple and well known. The proof is represented by a variable added as a new argument to every predicate in the body of a clause, and by a term added as argument to every predicate in the head of a clause, as illustrated in the following example:[9]

Theory S

$\leftarrow man(X)$
$man(X) \leftarrow male(X) \wedge human(X)$
$male(X) \leftarrow$
$human(X) \leftarrow$

Theory $\tau_m(S)$

$\leftarrow man(X, Proof)$
$man(X, man(X)/[Q, R]) \leftarrow male(X, Q) \wedge human(X, R)$
$male(X, male(X)/[]) \leftarrow$
$human(X, human(X)/[]) \leftarrow$

The instance of $\leftarrow man(X, Proof)$ found to be inconsistent with the other clauses in $\tau_m(S)$ is one in which X is instantiated to a variable and $Proof$ is instantiated to (some alphabetic variant of) the term: $man(A)/[male(A)/[], human(A)/[]]$. In the tree notation defined in the last section, this term represents the tree we already displayed above. As we noted there, we can interpret this as a proof tree indicating that, in S, $\forall man(A)$ can be proven by proving $\forall male(A)$ and $\forall human(A)$, which in turn can be proven directly from unit clauses. We can establish that this technique is sound and complete in a clear sense: we can use this transformation to define all and only the proof trees of the original theory.

Notice that the language of $\tau_m(S)$ is not the same as the language of S. It includes new predicates, and a number of new function symbols. In our example, the unary function symbols man, $male$ and $human$, the binary (infix) function $/$, and the list functions (which are, in canonical form, . and []) appear in the transformed theory and not in the original theory. We can define the language L' of $\tau_m(S)$ in terms of the language L of S as follows.

Let $name$ be a bijection from the n-ary ($n \geq 0$) predicate symbols of L onto a set of n-ary function symbols that do not occur in L. Then the *set of function symbols of L'* is the union of the function symbols of L with the set F of new n-ary function symbols,

$$F = \{f^n \mid f^n = name(P^n) \ for \ some \ predicate \ P^n \ in \ L\},$$

together with a set T containing three new function symbols (whose arity we have indicated with superscripts):

$$T = \{.^2, []^0, /^2\}.$$

The first two symbols in T are the standard binary "list constructor" and the 0-ary "empty list;" if these functors already occur in S, different symbols can be used to avoid ambiguity. To simplify the presentation, we assume that the symbols in T do not occur in L or F. We assume that L does not use any symbol both as an n-ary function symbol and as an n-ary predicate symbol, so $name$ can be the syntactic identity function.

The set of predicate symbols of L' is the set (again using superscripts to indicate arity):

$$\{P^{n+1} \mid P^n \ a \ predicate \ in \ L\}.$$

DEFINITION 41 **Definition of τ_m:**

(i) For any set of Horn clauses, S, $\tau_m(S) = \{\tau_m(C) | C \in S\}$.

(ii) For any Horn clause C such that for some $k > 0$,

$$C \mathrel{=} \leftarrow A_1 \wedge \ldots \wedge A_k$$
$$\tau_m(C) \mathrel{=} \leftarrow A'_1 \wedge \ldots \wedge A'_k$$

where if the predicate of A_i is an n-ary predicate P $(n \geq 0)$, then A'_i is the $n + 1$-ary predicate P with the n arguments of A_i as its first arguments and with a new variable as its last argument.

(iii) For any Horn clause C such that for some $k \geq 0$,

$$C \mathrel{=} A_0 \leftarrow A_1 \wedge \ldots \wedge A_k$$
$$\tau_m(C) \mathrel{=} A'_0 \leftarrow A'_1 \wedge \ldots \wedge A'_k$$

where

(a) if the predicate of A_i $(k \geq i \geq 1)$ is an n-ary predicate P $(n \geq 0)$, then A'_i is the $n + 1$-ary predicate P with the n arguments of A_i as its first arguments and with a new variable as its last argument, and

(b) if the predicate of A_0 is an n-ary predicate P $(n \geq 0)$, then A'_0 is the $n + 1$-ary predicate P with the n arguments of A_0 as its first arguments and with $A_0/[V_1, \cdots, V_k]$ as its last argument, where $V_1, \cdots, V_k$ are the k new variables introduced by step (a).

Notice that according to this definition, τ_m is not really functional, since the choice of "new variables" is not determined by the source clause. It is clear, however, that all the values of $\tau_m(C)$ for any C are variants of one another. Since we are interested in the entailments of the values of $\tau_m(S)$, any one of these values will suffice.

One other point that should be noted is that τ_m introduces some redundancy: the representation of the proof repeats information that is specified in other arguments of the predicates. We could eliminate some of this redundancy in various ways. The reason for keeping the redundancy in τ_m is, intuitively, that it keeps the "tree-building" part of the theory separate from the arguments needed to define the entailments. This formulation facilitates the consideration of sound ways of building something less than, or something rather different from complete proof trees, as discussed in the sections below on parsing and covering grammars.

4.2.3 A semantic interpretation of the metatheory

Transformations like τ_m are common in logic programming, but they are often introduced as proof-theoretic tricks, without a semantic theory. Since the semantics is not provided, the metatheoretical strategies are often more complex than this one, and the intended semantics can be far from clear. The basic metatheoretic idea has been well explained, however, as in the following passage,

> Typically this sort of thing is done using string operations like concatenation, so that the conjunction of P and Q would be represented by something like '('$|P|$'∧'$|Q|$')' ... There is a much more elegant way to do the encoding, however, which is due to McCarthy (1962). For purposes of semantic interpretation of the object language, which is what we want to do, the details of the syntax are largely irrelevant. In particular, the only thing that we need to know about the syntax of conjunctions is that there is *some* way of taking P and Q and producing the conjunction of P and Q. We can represent this by having a function And such that $And(P, Q)$ denotes the conjunction of P and Q. To use McCarthy's term, $And(P, Q)$ is an *abstract syntax* for representing the conjunction of P and Q. We will represent all the logical operators of the object language by functions in an abstract syntax. (Moore, 1980, 79)

Tarski (1934) actually used exactly this approach in his work on formal truth definitions, and a similar idea is implicit in Gödel's (1931) formal representation of syntactic expressions. We are doing the same thing, but instead of representing such things as conjunctions of propositional calculus atoms, we represent proof trees of (universally closed) predicate calculus atoms. This raises some minor technical difficulties to which we now turn.

The following definition from Stabler (1990) defines an interpretation I' with domain D' in terms of our original theory S, its language L, and its interpretation I. This definition can then be used to state precisely our claims about the soundness and completeness of this metatheoretic strategy.

(a) *The domain.* D' is the well formed expressions of L together with the proof trees over L and sequences of proof trees over L.

(b) *The interpretation of the function symbols.* All function symbols except those in

$$T = \{.^2, []^0, /^2\}.$$

receive the Herbrand interpretation. That is, 0-ary functions are mapped into themselves, and each n-ary function ($n > 0$), f, is associated with the mapping from $t_1, \ldots, t_n$ to the function expression $f(t_1, \ldots, t_n)$.

The interpretation of the function symbols in T is specified above.

(c) *The interpretation of the predicate symbols.* Following standard practice, expressions ϕ of L containing free variables are interpreted relative to an assignment ξ of variables of L to elements of D: $I(\phi)_\xi$ is then defined for all expressions ϕ in L.

We accordingly define I' in terms of I and assignments ξ. Every n-ary predicate symbol p^n is assigned a set of n-tuples in D' as follows:

$\langle a_1, \ldots, a_n \rangle \in I'(p^n)$ *iff for every* ξ,

$$\langle I(a_1)_\xi, \ldots, I(a_{n-1})_\xi \rangle \in I(p^{n-1}),$$

and a_n *is a proof tree corresponding to*

a refutation of $\leftarrow p(a_1, \ldots, a_{n-1})$ *in* S

This semantic theory is very simple — so simple, in fact, that we do not quite have the property that we were hoping for. It is not the case that $I \models S$ iff $I' \models \tau_m(S)$. In the theory $\tau_m(S)$ of §4.2, for example, it is clear that under the intended interpretation $I' \not\models human([], human([])/[]) \leftarrow$, and so $I' \not\models human(X, human(X)/[]) \leftarrow$, and yet this is a clause in $\tau_m(S)$. In short, under our intended interpretation, our transformed theories are false. We have introduced new objects like the empty sequence into the domain, and so it is no longer true that everything is human even if it was true in the original, intended domain.

We could look for a different interpretation I'' with the property that $I \models S$ iff $I'' \models \tau_m(S)$, but this is obviously not very appealing, since we do not want an interpretation that verifies $human([], human([])/[]) \leftarrow$. A more appealing strategy is to define a different transformation τ with the property that $I \models S$ iff $I' \models \tau(S)$, but any such theory will be more complex than the transform we have defined. Fortunately, the fact that $I' \not\models \tau_m(S)$ does not really matter for our practical purposes, and it is common for logic programmers to neglect conditions that will properly restrict the provable instances of a goal.[10] For example, the standard definition of the *append* relation is the following:

$append([], X, X) \leftarrow$
$append([X|Y], Z, [X|W]) \leftarrow append(Y, Z, W)$

When these clauses are added to any theory whose intended domain includes anything other than lists, the first clause is false. These consequences could be ruled out by adding a condition requiring that the arguments of *append* all be lists, but for most purposes this is unnecessary. The same is true for the result of applying τ_m. We must keep in mind that $\tau_m(S)$ is only an approximation to the correct theory; we must be careful to properly restrict the instances of provable goals. The danger is just that when a logic program contains many such approximations, the programmer may forget the limitations of his axiomatization and get unsound results.

For this reason, it is worth trying to characterize the range of problems on which τ_m is correct. Notice that the problematic case $human([], human([])/[]) \leftarrow$ is not in the range of τ_m, since $human([])$ is not an expression in the language L of S. It contains the constant $[]$ which is in L' but not in L. If we restrict our attention to refutations of goals that are in the range of τ_m, we will never get an unsound result. So given a theory S and goal G, we do have a sound and efficient method for getting representations of proofs of G in S. We can state these ideas precisely, as follows.[11]

PROPOSITION 16 (Noninterference) $S \models \forall C$ iff, for some substitution η for variables that do not occur in C, $\tau_m(S) \models \forall \tau_m(C)\eta$.

PROPOSITION 17 (Representation Correctness) Let $G = \leftarrow A$ where A is atomic, and let $\tau_m(G) = \leftarrow A'$. Then $\tau_m(S) \models \forall A'\eta$ iff η, when restricted to variables in A', is a substitution $\{Proof/Tree\}$ such that $Proof$ is the variable introduced into A' by τ_m, and $Tree$ is a proof tree corresponding to a refutation of $\{G\} \cup S$.

To conclude, we consider again our simple example to see that the interpretation we have provided is very close to what was promised. We can refute

$$\leftarrow man(X, man(X)/[male(X)/[], human(X)/[]])$$

from the theory $\tau_m(S)$, and so

$$\forall X \ man(X, man(X)/[male(X)/[], human(X)/[]])$$

is entailed by the theory, but this is the misleading result. Since the values of the variable in this term should really be restricted to the terms of the language of S, the correct idea is that when X is assigned any term in the language of S,

$$man(X)/[male(X)/[], human(X)/[]])$$

is a proof in S. In particular, then, if $x_L, y_L, \ldots$ are any variables of the object theory, we conclude that $man(x_L)/[male(x_L)/[], human(x_L)/[]])$ is a proof in S. That is, $\forall man(x_L)$ can be proven in the object theory by proving $\forall male(x_L)$ and $\forall human(x_L)$, which in turn can be proven directly from unit clauses. This is the interpretation we wanted.

4.3   Parse trees again, and transformations of parse trees

We now have a provably correct technique for obtaining metatheories that define the proof trees of any definite clause theory. We can now apply this general technique to the problem we started with. In our earlier discussion of the recognition problem, we established that derivations of x from G correspond to proofs of $\tau_g(s(\overline{x}, []))$ from $\tau_g(G)$. So now, using our correctness result for $\tau_m(\tau_g(G))$, we can easily represent the parsing problem. Returning to our grammar example, we have

Theory $\tau_g(G)$

$s(S0, S2, s(S0, S2)/[NP, VP]) \leftarrow np(S0, S1, NP) \wedge vp(S1, S2, VP)$
$s(S0, S3, s(S0, S3)/[Sa, Eq, Sb]) \leftarrow s(S0, S1, Sa) \wedge$
$$= (S1, [and|S2], Eq) \wedge s(S2, S3, Sb)$$
$np(S0, S1, np(S0, S1)/[Eq]) \leftarrow= (S0, [lions|S1], Eq)$
$vp(S0, S1, vp(S0, S1)/[Eq]) \leftarrow= (S0, [sleep|S1], Eq)$
$= (X, X, X = X/[]) \leftarrow$

This is already very close to a representation of the parsing problem. The sentence $s(X, [], P)$ weakly represents a relation between strings and logical proofs, but we are interested in the relation between strings and grammatical derivation trees. Notice that the values of τ_m for each clause of the theory have such a simple structure that it is an easy matter to consider modifications in our structural representations. That is, we could recognize $L(G)$ while generating structural descriptions that do *not* correspond to proofs from $s(\overline{x}, [])$. For example, recall the relabeling correspondence g between proof trees and derivation trees. If we, in effect, apply g to the subtrees in each clause of our metatheory, we can represent the corresponding derivation trees directly, without ever specifying the proof trees:

Theory $\tau_{mg}(\tau_g(G))$

$s(S0, S2, s/[NP, VP]) \leftarrow np(S0, S1, NP) \wedge vp(S1, S2, VP)$
$s(S0, S3, s/[Sa, Eq, Sb]) \leftarrow s(S0, S1, Sa) \wedge$
$$= (S1, [and|S2], Eq) \wedge s(S2, S3, Sb)$$
$np(S0, S1, np/[Eq]) \leftarrow= (S0, [lions|S1], Eq)$
$vp(S0, S1, vp/[Eq]) \leftarrow= (S0, [sleep|S1], Eq)$
$= ([X|Y], [X|Y], X/[]) \leftarrow$

Clearly, it would be a trivial matter to specify a mapping τ_{mg} that would have this value for argument $\tau_g(G)$. We now easily get the following corollaries:

COROLLARY 4 $s(S, [], Tree)$ in $\tau_m(\tau_{mg}(G))$ weakly represents the parsing problem for G.

COROLLARY 5 $s(S, [], Tree)$ in $Comp(\tau_{mg}(\tau_g(G)))$ represents the parsing problem for G.

Assuming an effective decision procedure for sentences of the form $s(\overline{x}, [])$ for $x \in \Sigma^*$ in $\tau_g(G)$, this comprises a provably correct recognizer for G. Assuming an effective decision procedure for sentences of the form $s(\overline{x}, [], Tree)$ for $x \in \Sigma^*$ in $\tau_{mg}(\tau_g(G))$, this comprises a provably correct parser for G.

Notice that we could have modified the structural representations represented by $\tau_m(\tau_g(G))$ with something more dramatic than the mere relabeling does. In fact, this is a valuable logic programming technique. It is commonly used, for example, to build flat trees of the form:

$$S_a/[S_1, and/[], S_2, and/[], \ldots, and/[], S_n]$$

rather than "right-embedded" trees of the form:

$$S_a/[S_1, and/[], S_b/[S_2, and/[], \ldots]].$$

The modification of the previous theory to achieve this effect is left as an exercise for the reader.

A related exercise is to construct a parser for the same language (producing either flat or nested trees) that does not do an infinite search for a refutation of the goal $\leftarrow s([sleep, sleep], [], T)$ using the Prolog depth-first proof strategy.

The strategy of building structural representations that do not correspond exactly to the grammar being used to guide the parse is a familiar one. This is most valuable when the relation between the parse trees of the parser's grammar and the output trees is easy to compute. In some cases of this kind we say that the grammar guiding the parser "covers" the grammar of the language whose parse trees are being constructed.

This connection with formal language theory is established with the following basic concepts:[12]

DEFINITION 42 We use the notation $S \overset{\pi}{\Rightarrow} w$ to indicate that there is a leftmost derivation of w from S using the productions in sequence π. $S \Rightarrow^\pi w$ iff there is a rightmost derivation of w from S using the productions in sequence π.

DEFINITION 43 A *homomorphism* h from V_1^* to V_2^* is a mapping from V_1 to V_2^* that is extended to V_1^* in the following way: it maps the empty string to itself, and $h(xa) = h(x)h(a)$ for all $x \in V_1^*$ and all $a \in V_1$.

DEFINITION 44 Let $G_1 = \langle N_1, \Sigma, S_1, P_1 \rangle$ and $G_2 = \langle N_2, \Sigma, S_2, P_2 \rangle$. Grammar G_2 *left covers* G_1 if there is a homomorphism $h : P_2 \to P_1$ such that all of the following hold:

(i) $L(G_1) = L(G_2)$,

(ii) If $S_2{}^{\pi} \Rightarrow w$, then $S_1{}^{h(\pi)} \Rightarrow w$, and

(iii) If $S_1{}^{\pi} \Rightarrow w$, then there is some π' such that $S_2{}^{\pi'} \Rightarrow w$ and $h(\pi') = \pi$.

DEFINITION 45 Let $G_1 = \langle N_1, \Sigma, S_1, P_1 \rangle$ and $G_2 = \langle N_2, \Sigma, S_2, P_2 \rangle$. Grammar G_2 *right covers* G_1 if there is a homomorphism $h : P_2 \to P_1$ such that all of the following hold:

(i) $L(G_1) = L(G_2)$,

(ii) If $S_2 \Rightarrow^{\pi} w$, then $S_1 \Rightarrow^{h(\pi)} w$, and

(iii) If $S_1 \Rightarrow^{\pi} w$, then there is some π' such that $S_2 \Rightarrow^{\pi'} w$ and $h(\pi') = \pi$.

These definitions indicate a range of cases in which the "covering" strategy could easily be applied. The idea is a valuable one. We will encounter a number of variations on this strategy later.

4.4 LR parsing and LR deduction

It is worth mentioning, if only briefly, another relation between CFG parsing and deduction. The discussion of parsing and deduction in this chapter might seem to suggest that deductions must always be found with a top-down, backtracking method, as in Prolog. It is well-known that these methods are inefficient. Computing a parse tree with this method can require a number of steps that is an exponential function of the number of words in the string to be parsed. Nothing in the logic, however, requires a top-down non-deterministic approach. On the contrary, the logic is completely neutral with regard to the order in which the parse is computed. Earley's parsing algorithm, much more efficient in the worst case than backtracking methods, inspired the proof method for negative clauses and definite clause theories presented by Pereira and Warren (1983). The most efficient context-free parsing methods, however, are tabular. The grammar is used to calculate a table which, in effect, tells us which production to use at each point in the construction of the parse. Let's consider how LR(k) tabular recognition methods can be extended to deduction. The name signifies that the methods, in effect, proceed from Left to right through the input string, deterministically finding a Rightmost parse in reverse, on the basis of testing the next k symbols of the unprocessed input string.

4.4.1 LR(k) parsing

LR recognition methods can naturally be viewed as a refinement of bottom-up shift-reduce recognition. We will not present a rigorous account, since these methods are nicely described elsewhere (e.g., Aho and Ullman, 1977; 1972). Roughly, the idea is this: we recognize an input string by shifting a word w from the input onto a stack and then attempting to apply the productions of the grammar backwards, "reducing" the terminal items on top of the stack to a category C, or shifting more elements from the input, and so on, with the goal of reducing everything on the stack to S after having consumed all the elements of the input string. For example, consider the following grammar:

1. $S \rightarrow NP\ VP$ *Grammar G_1*
2. $NP \rightarrow N$
3. $NP \rightarrow N\,PP$
4. $PP \rightarrow P\,NP$
5. $VP \rightarrow sleep$
6. $N \rightarrow lions$
7. $N \rightarrow paws$
8. $N \rightarrow claws$
9. $P \rightarrow with$

To recognize *lions with claws sleep* with a shift-reduce method, we first shift *lions* onto the stack, leaving a situation which can be represented as follows:

			lions		with	claws	sleep	

Now we can reduce *lions* to N, getting

			N		with	claws	sleep	

Here we can either reduce N to NP or shift again. To correctly decide what to do we need more information than we have on the stack. We do not know which rule with N on the right hand side should be used unless we can look at more of the input string. For this grammar, we can always make the right decision about what to do if we look just one symbol ahead into the input, i.e., the grammar is LR(1). The instructions about what rule to use are encoded in an LR(1) table for the grammar, which is often displayed in a format shown in Table 4.1. The $ in this table is a special symbol that signifies that there is no more input. The empty positions in the table signify error conditions: if these are reached, the LR recognizer halts and the input is not in the language of the grammar. The use of the table can be explained by continuing with our example.

Beginning with state 0 on the stack, we have a configuration which can be displayed as follows:

			0		lions	with	claws	sleep	

Table 4.1

state	$	claws	lions	paws	sleep	with	N	NP	P	PP	S	VP
0		sh6	sh5	sh4			2	10			12	
1		re9	re9	re9								
2					re2	sh1			3	8		
3		sh6	sh5	sh4			2	7				
4					re7	re7						
5					re6	re6						
6					re8	re8						
7					re4							
8					re3							
9	re5											
10					sh9							11
11	re1											
12	acc											

State symbol 0 is on top of the stack, and the whole input is waiting to be processed. Looking in the table in the row of state 0 with *lions* as the next symbol, we find *sh5*, which means that we should shift a symbol from the input and go into state 5:

| | | 0 | lions | 5 |

| with | claws | sleep | |

Now we read the action from the row for state 5 when the next symbol is *with*: it is *re6*, which indicates that we should reduce with production number 6. This removes 5 and *lions* from the stack, exposing state 0. Now we read from the row of state 0 which state to go into when a *N* is about to be put onto the stack — this part of the table is to the right of the double lines. We are to go into state 2, so the configuration is now:

| | | 0 | N | 2 |

| with | claws | sleep | |

Continuing in this way:

| | | 0 | N | 2 | with | 1 |

| claws | sleep | |

| | | 0 | N | 2 | P | 3 |

| claws | sleep | |

| | 0 | N | 2 | P | 3 | claws | 6 |

| sleep | |

| | | 0 | N | 2 | P | 3 | N | 2 |

| sleep | |

	0	N	2	P	3	NP	7		sleep	
		0	N	2	PP	8			sleep	
			0	NP	10				sleep	
		0	NP	10	sleep	9				
		0	NP	10	VP	11				
			0	S	12					

When we reach state 12 with nothing left in the input, the table prescribes the action *acc*, i.e., the input string is accepted.

4.4.2 LR(k) deduction

The correspondence between derivations from CFGs and refutations that as established in §4.2 shows immediately how LR(k) tables can be regarded as instructions for finding refutations deterministically by proceeding from left to right through input, where the input is now the first argument of the sentence predicate. This method builds a rightmost proof tree in reverse deterministically on the basis of testing the next k symbols of the input.

Consider the previous example. Applying τ_g to G_1 we obtain a recognizer for the language of G_1, a theory that weakly represents our grammatical relations:

$$\textit{Theory } \tau_g(G_1)$$

c0. $X = X \leftarrow$
c1. $s(S0, S2) \leftarrow np(S0, S1) \wedge vp(S1, S2)$
c2. $np(S0, S3) \leftarrow n(S0, S1)$
c3. $np(S0, S2) \leftarrow n(S0, S1) \wedge pp(S1, S2)$
c4. $pp(S0, S2) \leftarrow p(S0, S1) \wedge np(S1, S2)$
c5. $vp(S0, S1) \leftarrow S0 = [sleep|S1]$
c6. $n(S0, S1) \leftarrow S0 = [lions|S1]$
c7. $n(S0, S1) \leftarrow S0 = [paws|S1]$
c8. $n(S0, S1) \leftarrow S0 = [claws|S1]$
c9. $p(S0, S1) \leftarrow S0 = [with|S1]$

The proof tree corresponding to the SLD resolution refutation of $\leftarrow s([lions, with, claws, sleep], [])$ from this theory is shown in Figure 4.3. (We have abbreviated the lists that occur in some of the equations to make the figure smaller). To construct a similar

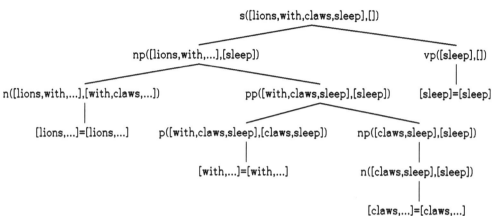

Figure 4.3
Proof tree for $\leftarrow s([lions, with, claws, sleep], [])$

refutation in LR order, we use the LR table shown above, and we use a stack as part of the "control system" that determines which resolvents to compute, except that this stack is allowed to have complex objects (or pointers to complex objects) as elements. The reduction steps correspond to a special instance of resolution which is called (positive, unit-resulting) "hyperresolution" (Robinson, 1965a). A hyperresolution step takes a clause called the *nucleus* with negative literals $L_1, \ldots, L_n$, $n > 0$ and resolves upon all of these negative literals at once, using positive clauses $P_1, \ldots, P_n$ as the other parents, which are called the *electrons*. Hyperresolvents thus never contain any negative literals. Hyperresolution is complete.[13]

Here is the procedure for LR parsing by deduction:

1. Extract the first argument of the sentence predicate to be refuted: this sequence is the input. (The second argument is presumed to be [].)

2. Beginning in state 0, proceed as in LR recognition, except reinterpret the indicated actions as follows:

shN: As in LR recognition, shift the next input symbol onto the stack and go into state N.

reN: Let $L_1, \ldots, L_k$ be the literals in the antecedent of clause cN. Pop the elements $t_1, s_1, \ldots, t_k, s_k$ off the stack, as in LR recognition, exposing some state s, where s_k is the state symbol on top of the stack, t_k, the symbol immediately under it, and so on. We now compute a new stack element, which will be a hyperresolvent. Every literal in the antecedent of cN is resolved upon as follows: if L_i is an equation, resolve with clause $c0$; otherwise, resolve with t_i. Put the resulting hyperresolvent on top of the stack. Find the new state from the table by looking in the row of state s under column x where x is the predicate in the hyperresolvent now on top of the stack, and put the new state on top of the stack.

acc: Resolve the (non-state) symbol remaining in the stack with the clause to be refuted and halt.

Applying this procedure to our example, we obtain a refutation of $\leftarrow s([lions, with, claws, sleep], [])$. That is, the sequence that results from placing this clause in a sequence followed by the resolvents that are computed by following the given procedure (in order), produces the following resolution refutation:

$c10.$	$\leftarrow s([lions, with, claws, sleep], [])$	$for\ refutation$
$r1.$	$n([lions\|L], L)$	$by\ c6, c0$
$r2.$	$p([with\|L], L)$	$by\ c9, c0$
$r3.$	$n([claws\|L], L)$	$by\ c8, c0$
$r4.$	$np([claws\|L], L)$	$by\ r2, c3$
$r5.$	$pp([with, claws\|L], L)$	$by\ r4, r2, c4$
$r6.$	$np([lions, with, claws\|L], L)$	$by\ r1, r5, c3$
$r7.$	$vp([sleep\|L], L)$	$by\ c5, c0$
$r8.$	$s([lions, with, claws, sleep\|L], L)$	$by\ r6, r7, c1$
$r9.$	$\square$	$by\ r8, c10$

If we construct a tree of the parent relations that hold among the hyperresolvents that are computed in this refutation, there is again a simple correspondence to the context-free derivation tree, and hence also to the tree in Figure 4.3 which was computed with a standard, nondeterministic, top-down SLD refutation procedure.

This relation between LR recognition techniques and resolution can obviously be extended to LR parsing, to $LR(k, t)$ and similar deterministic recognition and parsing methods (Szymanski and Williams, 1976), and to other methods that allow "conflicts" in the tables (Tomita, 1986). In fact, this kind of approach to theorem proving can be generalized to non-CFG and even non-linguistic problems. These matters merit further exploration, but are beyond the scope of the present project.[14] The important point is that a logical representation of a problem leaves many processing options open.

4.5 A Prolog session with a simple (ineffective) parser

The theory $\tau_g(G)$ can be directly represented in Prolog, as shown in the following "listing," and run as a program, though the results are not what one would like. In particular, Prolog is ineffective in this case, going into an infinite loop on some simple and legitimate inputs. This problem with Prolog is well-known and fairly easy to avoid by reformulating the axioms or by using a different proof procedure.

In this Prolog notation, the $\wedge$ is replaced by a comma and the $\leftarrow$ is replaced by :-.

```
| ?- listing.

s(A,B,s/[C,D]) :-
      np(A,E,C),
      vp(E,B,D).
s(A,B,s/[C,D,E]) :-
      s(A,F,C),
      =(F,[and|G],D),
      s(G,B,E).

np(A,B,np/[C]) :-
      =(A,[lions|B],C).

vp(A,B,vp/[C]) :-
      =(A,[sleep|B],C).

=([A|B],[A|B],A/[]).

yes
| ?- s([lions,sleep],[],T).

T = s/[np/[lions/[]],vp/[sleep/[]]]

% we can display our tree representations in pretty-printed form:

| ?- s([lions,sleep],[],T),pp_tree(T).
s
    np  lions
    vp  sleep

T = s/[np/[lions/[]],vp/[sleep/[]]]

| ?- s([lions,sleep,and,lions,sleep],[],T),pp_tree(T).
s
    s
        np  lions
        vp  sleep
    and
    s
        np  lions
        vp  sleep

T = s/[s/[np/[lions/[]],vp/[sleep/[]]],and/[],s/[np/[lions/[]],vp/[sleep/[]]]]

| ?- s([sleep,sleep],[],T).

% Prolog enters an infinite search here
```

Chapter 5

Deductive parsing: Natural
language phrase structure

> *When an inquiry becomes so convoluted, we must suspect that we are*
> *proceeding in the wrong way. We must return to go, change gears, and*
> *reformulate the problem, not pursue every new iota of information*
> *or nuance of argument in the old style, hoping all the time that our*
> *elusive solution simply awaits a crucial item, yet undiscovered.*
> — *Stephen Jay Gould*

In this chapter we present a very brief and incomplete introduction to some of the techniques that have been used in feasible applications of logic to language processing problems, specifically the problem of parsing fragments of English. The presentation of a few progressively more complex language processing systems is intended to illustrate a line of development that has little hope of success. Sticking to descriptions of the superficial phrase-structure of natural languages, using simple and psychologically implausible generative devices, we cannot handle the complexity of human languages. Such methods were left behind by theoretical linguists decades ago. A computational linguist, even one with short term engineering goals, cannot afford to neglect the past three decades of research in theoretical linguistics. The second purpose of this section is to obtain from some of the pioneering efforts, particularly those that have been logic-based, some technical tools that will be useful in our later attempts to construct an approach to language processing that can be linguistically sophisticated and not entirely lacking in formal and computational rigor.

5.1   Context-free grammars for natural languages

We now can represent the parsing problem for any context-free language. Formal techniques for parsing these languages are well understood. Do context-free grammars suffice for representing the parsing problem for natural human languages like English or French or Swahili? This question is not quite clear. The first thing to notice is that these questions are useless without some idea of what counts as grammatical sentences of any language. In the first place, there is dialect variation. So we might, for example, assume that there are many languages, which we could number so that each individual speaks $English_i$ or $French_i$ or whatever. Still there is some imprecision in our original question about whether there is a context-free grammar which represents the parsing problem for any particular speaker's natural language. We should distinguish among the following different questions:

(1) For each natural language, is there a context-free grammar that generates all and only grammatical sentences of that language? (In this case we say that the language is *weakly context-free.*)

(2) For each natural language, is there a context-free grammar G such that the derivation trees of G are appropriate structural descriptions for all and only the grammatical sentences of the language? (In this case we say that the language is *strongly context-free.*)

(3) Suppose that for each natural language L, there is a context-free grammar G such that the derivation trees of G are appropriate structural descriptions for all and only the grammatical sentences of L. Is such a grammar G a psychologically plausible representation of human linguistic knowledge of L?

These questions are much better than our original ones, but they are still unclear, because even when we choose a particular speaker, the question of whether a string is grammatical in that speaker's language or not often seems to lack a clear answer. Furthermore, the second and third questions are unclear insofar as it is not clear, in advance, what the "appropriate" structural representations of English sentences are. Initially, we will aim for structural representations that seem intuitively reasonable, but we can aim to characterize the structural representations of a language that are psychologically real, ones that are appropriate for models of language comprehension and production. Once matters are put this way, we can see that it would be a mistake to expect hard and fast answers. The statements of the problems presuppose notions that only a linguistic theory, a psychological account of human language, can answer. Until some of the linguistic theory has been presented, we really have no option but to appeal to intuitions about grammaticality that may need to be called into question later. For the time being, then, we will proceed, keeping these issues in mind.

Some of the basic difficulties in defining a language like English should be noted right away, since they motivate some fundamental aspects of linguistic methodology (which is not to say that they cannot be challenged). In the first place, we will initially aim to characterize the grammatical sentences, rather than the sensible ones. Chomsky (1956; 1957) illustrated the point with the famous example,

Colorless green ideas sleep furiously.

This is a perfectly grammatical sentence though it is poetry or nonsense, while

Furiously sleep ideas green colorless.

is not grammatical. And both of the following are grammatical:

The ape has an arm.
The arm has an ape.

but the following is ungrammatical:[1]

* Has an arm.

Moving to some more interesting cases, notice that in English we have the capability of modifying any noun phrase with a sentence-like structure, as in:

This is the house that Jack built.

Intuitively, *the house* is modified by another part of the sentence, *that Jack built*, which itself is a clause containing a subject and a verb. These sorts of modifiers can be added to modify parts of a modifier, and so on, as in

This is malt that lay in the house that Jack built.
This is rat that ate the malt that lay in the house that Jack built.
This is cat that killed the rat that ate the malt that lay in the house that Jack built.
. . .

These clauses are right-embedded in the sentence structure, and these all seem like good sentences. Since there does not seem to be any definite limit to the number of right-embedded clauses we can add, we assume that there is no limit. It follows that the language contains infinitely many strings, and some of them, in fact infinitely many of them, are such that no human could speak or understand them. We just abstract away from the limitations on memory and attention that limit us to sentences of rather small, finite lengths.[2]

Another, similar construction provides slightly more interesting examples: nested, or center-embedded clauses, where the modifier is placed into the middle of the clause it modifies. Consider the sentences:

The house was built by Jack.
The house the malt lay in was built by Jack.
The house the malt the rat ate lay in was built by Jack.
The house the malt the rat the cat killed ate lay in was built by Jack.
. . .

In these cases, the comprehensibility decreases much more quickly with increasing depth of embedding, but nevertheless these sentences are usually regarded as grammatical. It seems plausible that this difficulty may be accounted for not in terms of the principles defining grammatical structures, but in terms of some special difficulty in processing these structures. Chomsky (1963) noticed that while unbounded right-embedding is within the capability of regular grammars and can be recognized by finite state machines, unbounded center embedding requires an infinite machine, such as a machine with an infinite "stack." He says:

> From these observations we must conclude that the *competence* of a native speaker cannot be characterized by a finite automaton...Nevertheless, the *performance* of the speaker or hearer must be representable by a finite automaton of some sort. The speaker-hearer has only a finite memory, a part of which he uses to store the rules of his grammar (a set of rules for a device with unbounded memory), and a part of which he uses for computation in actually producing a sentence or "perceiving" its structure. (Chomsky, 1963, §4.6)

The same point is emphasized again in the following passage:

> No automaton with bounded memory can produce all and only the grammatical sentences of a natural language; every such device, man presumably included, will exhibit certain limitations. (Miller and Chomsky, 1963)

These abstractions away from the limitations of speakers are fundamental in current theoretical linguistics. In each of the constructions we have considered, the situation is the following. We have a simple and natural description of some construction, but the description also covers some sentences which are not acceptable. However, we notice that the unacceptability of these cases seems to correlate with a property of the sentence which could plausibly place unusual demands on the memory or attention of the speaker-hearer. Furthermore, a description of exactly the cases that are acceptable is considerably more complex and unnatural than the simple description. In such cases, it seems reasonable to assume that the speaker is using the simple and natural characterization and the unacceptability of some of the sentences covered by that characterization should be attributed to limitations in the human language processing mechanism.

To get a feeling for the subtlety of the abstraction away from performance, it is worth noting some other sentences that are claimed to be grammatical even though they would not generally be regarded as acceptable. Consider:

The horse raced past the barn fell

This string seems ungrammatical until one notices that it has the same structure as

The cart driven around the park squeaks.

These sentences are called "garden path" sentences because they seem to trick the unsuspecting listener or reader into an initial misanalysis that then proves difficult to abandon. Other cases which have this character are the following:

The prime number few.
John gave the man a dog bit the bandage.
The boy got fat melted.
Does this butcher knife handle frozen foods too.
The dealer sold the forgery complained.
The granite rocks during earthquakes.
I told the girl the boy seduced the story.
Without her contributions to the fund would be inadequate.

These various kinds of garden path sentences have played an important role in investigations of human parsing mechanisms.[3]

While there seems to be something special about the difficulty of center embedded and garden path sentences, it is easy to construct grammatical sentences that are too complex in other ways to be acceptable. Some of these cases have gotten special attention in studies of processing complexity. The following sorts of constructions are considered by Barton et al. (1987) and Ristad (1991), for example. We can use the term *police police* for police who police other police. But then the following sentences can be seen to be perfectly grammatical:

Police police police police.
Police police police police police.
. . .

The use of many pronouns in various constructions can also be very awkward:

Some stewards say at the airport a KGB man met Jane, who the mechanic expected them to talk to her about.
Some stewards say at the airport a KGB man met Jane, who the officer, the agent, and the mechanic suspected he expected them to talk to her about.
Some stewards say at the airport a KGB man met Jane, who the officer, the agent, and the mechanic suspected he expected them to talk to her about, and the crew, the pilot, and the co-pilot knew they traded them to her for, and so do some stewardesses.
. . .

As a last sort of case, it is easy to produce unacceptable levels of complexity in VP-ellipsis constructions. The following examples are not too awkward:

Jack corrected his spelling mistakes before his teacher did.
Jack corrected his spelling mistakes before his teacher did, and Ted did too.

But further elaboration of the same construction results in strings like:

Harry claims that Jack corrected his spelling mistakes before his teacher did and Ted did too, but Bob doesn't.
Sue believes that Harry claims that Jack corrected his spelling mistakes before his teacher did and Ted did too, but Bob doesn't, but Mary doesn't.

Acceptability judgements are a good guide to grammaticality only in very simple cases.

5.1.1 The context-freeness of natural languages

The question of whether the sentences of a natural language can generally be generated by some context-free grammar, our question (1), is of marginal interest unless it contributes to the syntactic theory of natural languages and ultimately to the project of finding a psychologically plausible representation of human linguistic knowledge. The basic question is worth at least brief consideration, though we will see by the examples of the theories discussed in Parts II and III that the relevant considerations have little or no bearing on central issues in syntactic theory.

It turns out to be rather difficult to show that natural languages are not generally weakly context-free. Bar-Hillel and Shamir (1960) noted that constructions with "respectively" seem to have a non-context-free character. A proper formulation of their argument was proposed by Langendoen. Suppose we regard subject-verb agreement as a syntactic matter, so that

* *The men smokes*

is an ungrammatical string in English. Then consider the sentences

* *The woman and the men smoke and drinks, respectively.*
The woman and the men smokes and drink, respectively.
* *The woman, the men and the woman smoke and drink and smoke, respectively.*
The woman, the men and the woman smokes and drink and smokes, respectively.
. . .

If these grammaticality judgements are correct — a very dubious proposition — then English is not context-free. This can be established by the following argument. The intersection of any context-free language with any regular language is context-free.[4] So consider the intersection of the grammatical strings of English with the regular language

$(a, b)^+$ *and* $\{a, b\}$ $(c, d)^+$ *and* $\{c, d\}$

where

$a = $ *the woman*
$b = $ *the men*
$c = $ *smokes*
$d = $ *drink.*

The result of this intersection is the set of all strings xy such that $x \in \{(a, b)^+ $ *and* $ \{a, b\}\}$ and y is the corresponding string with c for a and d for b. This language can be shown to be non-context-free using the pumping lemma for context-free languages. Such a language is said to exhibit *cross-serial* dependencies since the acceptability of each element in y depends on a corresponding earlier element in x, and these dependencies cross each other. These crossing dependencies contrast with, for example, the "nested dependencies" of a language like $a^n b^n$ where the acceptability of the string of b's can be determined by letting the first b depend on the nth a, the second b depend on the $(n - 1)$th a, and so on. These dependencies do not cross each other, and so, unlike unbounded crossing dependencies, unbounded nested dependencies can be defined by a context-free grammar.

The assumptions about the set of grammatical strings of English that this last argument requires, though, seem to be unsupportable. One of the few well-known and well-supported arguments for a claim that a natural language is not context-free is presented by Shieber (1985). He argues that a dialect of Swiss-German spoken near Zurich contains a cross-serial construction. The language contains sentences with transliterations (i.e. word-by-word translations) like the following

We the children Hans the house let help paint.

with the meaning

We let the children help Hans paint the house.

Furthermore, agreement in case-marking between the noun phrases and the corresponding verbs is required. So we have agreement relations between each NP_i and VP_i in arbitrarily long sequences of the form:[5]

$NP_1\ NP_2 \ldots NP_n\ VP_1\ VP_2 \ldots VP_n.$

This cannot happen in a context-free language.

Since there appear to be natural languages that are not generated by any context-free language, it follows that there are natural languages for which there is no context-free grammar G such that the derivation trees of G are appropriate structural descriptions for all and only the grammatical sentences of the language. That is, a language that is not weakly context-free is certainly not strongly context-free, and since some natural languages are not weakly context-free, they are not strongly context-free either. A negative answer to our question (1) implies a negative answer to our question (2). It is worth noting, however, that it is much easier to establish the negative answer to question (2). There appear to be certain constructions whose structural descriptions cannot be specified with a context-free grammar even though the corresponding strings can be generated by a context-free grammar. Examples of this kind are discussed in §9.2.

5.1.2   Context-free grammars and linguistic theory

We can conclude from the previous section that although there do appear to be some non-context-free constructions in natural languages, these are not very common. No persuasive example of non-context-freeness in English has been found. However, even if English were strongly context-free, this would not imply that context-free grammars were psychologically plausible representations of an English speaker's knowledge. For example, the smallest context-free grammar for English might contain more than a googol category symbols or rules. In fact, it is not hard to provide informal arguments that have roughly the this form. There are simple features of English syntax which do not have any simple expression in a context-free grammar. Arguments showing the inadequacy of context-free grammars for representations of natural languages have been presented and debated in detail elsewhere. Here, we will sketch one of the standard examples in just enough detail to motivate the departures from context-free parsing methods that we want to consider below.[6]

It is easy to see that in simple, declarative sentences, the verb *put* requires a direct object and a locative phrase of some kind:

I put the car in the garage.
I put it inside.
* *I put the car.*
* *I put it.*
* *I put in the garage.*
* *I put inside.*

We say that *put* "subcategorizes" for these constituents. Somehow, we need to represent this fact in our grammar. But notice that the regularity seems to be violated by simple questions with the verb *put*. The sentence

Where did you put the car?

has no locative phrase following the verb, and

What did you put inside?

has no direct object following the verb. However, in these cases, it is natural to regard the missing constituent as having moved to the front of the sentences in the form of a *wh*-word. This perspective receives further justification from the observation that the fronted *wh*-word can occur *only* when there is, in effect, an empty position somewhere in the sentence from which it could have come:

* *What did you put the car in the garage?*

There are a couple of points which make it look unlikely that there will be an elegant context-free account of this simple regularity in English syntax. In the first place, a *wh*-word can correspond to a constituent position arbitrarily far away from the beginning of the sentence, as shown by the following examples:

Who$_i$ did you put t$_i$ in the trunk?
Who$_i$ did you want Wanda to put t$_i$ in the trunk?
Who$_i$ did you want the police to think you wanted Wanda to put t$_i$ in the trunk?
...

In these examples, we have noted the position from which the *wh*-word labeled i has been moved with a "trace" t_i, an element which is not pronounced or written in the terminal string. There is some motivation for assuming that an "empty" category actually occurs in these positions, so we will continue to mark them in this way.

A similar kind of *wh*-movement seems to occur in relative clauses. For example, in

The man who$_i$ you put t$_i$ in the trunk is unhappy.
The man who$_i$ you wanted Wanda to put t$_i$ in the trunk is unhappy.
...

And both kinds of *wh*-movement can occur at once,

What$_i$ did the man who$_j$ you put t$_j$ in the trunk put t$_i$ in his pocket?
What$_i$ did the man who$_j$ you put t$_j$ in the trunk put t$_i$ in the pocket of the thug who$_k$ t$_k$ had forgotten her gun?

We could try to express this kind of regularity directly: after satisfying subcategorization principles, we allow a *wh*-word to move from any position in a string to the front of the sentence or to the front of the clause in which it occurs. As we will see, this suggestion is not even close to right, but it gets some cases and is simple enough that it was almost immediately incorporated into language processing systems.

5.2 Extraposition grammars

A simple extension of context-free parsing methods has been proposed for processing sentences in which wh-phrases have moved to the left. When a *wh*-phrase occurs, the parser simply waits for a position later in the sentence from which that *wh*-phrase could have come. This idea was used in "Augmented Transition Networks" (ATNs) (Woods, 1970), and an essentially similar idea is implemented by the passing of a gap feature in certain versions of GPSG and related theories (Gazdar et al., 1985). ATNs can be represented quite directly in logic, as noted in Pereira and Warren (1980), but here we are interested just in this strategy for handling movements. Pereira (1981; 1982) showed how this strategy could be simply represented with his "extraposition grammars." We will describe the basic idea behind the logical implementation of these grammars here.

ATNs handle moved constituents with a special HOLD list that holds the *wh*-phrases for which positions are being sought. A very similar effect can be obtained in a logical representation by associating with each grammatical predicate a pair of lists $H0, H$ such that $H0$ is the list of unplaced *wh*-phrases found earlier in the string and H is the list of *wh*-phrases that still need to be placed somewhere later in the string. We can let this pair of lists represent a single sequence which we call the "extraposition list." Consider, for example, the following tiny theory which is similar to theory DG of §4.1 in the previous chapter:

Theory XG

$$s([what|S0], S, H0, H) \leftarrow s(S0, S, [what|H0], H) \tag{5.2.1}$$

$$s(S0, S, H0, H) \leftarrow np(S0, S1, H0, H1) \wedge vp(S1, S, H1, H) \tag{5.2.2}$$

$$vp(S0, S, H0, H) \leftarrow v(S0, S1, H0, H1) \wedge np(S1, S, H1, H) \tag{5.2.3}$$

$$v([reads|S], S, H, H) \leftarrow \tag{5.2.4}$$

$$np([john|S], S, H, H) \leftarrow \tag{5.2.5}$$

$$np(S, S, [what|H], H) \leftarrow \tag{5.2.6}$$

As in the previous section, we can assume that we will always be representing a sentence with a pair of sequences $\overline{x}, []$ and we can assume that we are interested in finding parses of the sentence based on the assumption that initially, no *wh*-phrases need to be placed, and that none should remain to be placed at the end of the string either. Hence, we consider only proofs beginning with negative clauses of the form $\leftarrow s(\overline{x}, [], [], [])$. Given this interest it is natural to add the following rule to our theory:

$$s(S) \leftarrow s(S, [], [], []) \tag{5.2.7}$$

Then we can refute the following clauses, for example:

$\leftarrow s([john, reads, john])$
$\leftarrow s([what, reads, john])$

(With some strain, these strings can be seen not only as grammatical but also to make some sense in English: imagine that *john* is not only the name of a person but also of a book, and that mechanical devices and asexual aliens sometimes read this book.)

Consider the following refutation of this last clause:

$\leftarrow s([what, reads, john])$
$\leftarrow s([what, reads, john], [], [], [])$
$\leftarrow s([reads, john], [], [what], [])$
$\leftarrow np([reads, john], S1, [what], H1) \wedge vp(S1, [], H1, [])$
$\leftarrow vp([reads, john], [], [], [])$
$\leftarrow v([reads, john], S1, [], H1) \wedge np(S1, [], H1, [])$
$\leftarrow np([john], [], [], [])$
$\Box$

The course of this refutation is much like the course of an ATN parse. In effect, the

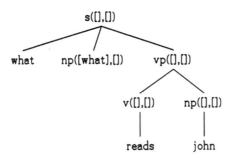

Figure 5.1
Proof tree for $s([what, reads, john], [])$

initial *what* is first put into the extraposition list. Then it is noticed that this phrase can be placed into the subject position — in fact, it must be so placed. Then the verb phrase *reads john* is recognized, and the recognition is complete. We can use the transformation of the previous section to draw the proof tree of Figure 5.1 corresponding to our refutation, but to improve readability we leave out the first two arguments of each predication and provide a special treatment for the clauses corresponding to terminal expansions, 5.2.4, 5.2.5.

Because we have an inadequate representation of English verb phrase structure, we can also refute clauses whose strings do not correspond to English sentences, such as $\leftarrow s([what, john, reads])$. It is well known that when a *wh*-phrase moved to the front of a sentence, some form of auxiliary verb needs to be placed before the subject. When there is no auxiliary verb, an appropriate form of *do* occurs, perhaps as the result of a special operation that we can call "*do*-support." So we should accept *what does john read* rather than *what john reads*. Such complications are not essential to explaining the basic approaches to handling movement relations in logic, and so we will not consider them here.

Letting the inadequacy in our treatment of the verbs go for the moment, this approach is wonderfully simple, so let's consider whether we can get a little more out of it. In the first place, it is easy to extend the grammar to get relative clauses. We introduce two new categories: *cp* is, in effect, the category of questions, and *rel* is the category of relative clauses.

Theory XGR

$$s(S) \leftarrow s(S, [], [], []) \tag{5.2.8}$$

$$s(S) \leftarrow cp(S, [], [], []) \tag{5.2.9}$$

$$cp([who|S0], S, H0, H) \leftarrow s(S0, S, [who|H0], H) \tag{5.2.10}$$

$$cp([what|S0], S, H0, H) \leftarrow s(S0, S, [what|H0], H) \tag{5.2.11}$$

$$s(S0, S, H0, H) \leftarrow np(S0, S1, H0, H1) \wedge vp(S1, S, H1, H) \tag{5.2.12}$$

$$vp(S0, S, H0, H) \leftarrow v(S0, S1, H0, H1) \wedge np(S1, S, H1, H) \tag{5.2.13}$$

$$v([reads|S], S, H, H) \leftarrow \tag{5.2.14}$$

$$v([likes|S], S, H, H) \leftarrow \tag{5.2.15}$$

$$np(S0, S, H0, H) \leftarrow det(S0, S1, H0, H1) \wedge n(S1, S, H1, H) \tag{5.2.16}$$

$$np(S0, S, H0, H) \leftarrow \tag{5.2.17}$$

$$det(S0, S1, H0, H1) \wedge n(S1, S2, H1, H2) \wedge rel(S2, S, H2, H) \tag{5.2.18}$$

$$np(S, S, [what|H], H) \leftarrow \tag{5.2.19}$$

$$np(S, S, [who|H], H) \leftarrow \tag{5.2.20}$$

$$det([the|S], S, H, H) \leftarrow \tag{5.2.21}$$

$$det([every|S], S, H, H) \leftarrow \tag{5.2.22}$$

$$det([some|S], S, H, H) \leftarrow \tag{5.2.23}$$

$$det([no|S], S, H, H) \leftarrow \tag{5.2.24}$$

$$n([woman|S], S, H, H) \leftarrow \tag{5.2.25}$$

$$n([man|S], S, H, H) \leftarrow \qquad\qquad\qquad (5.2.26)$$
$$n([book|S], S, H, H) \leftarrow \qquad\qquad\qquad (5.2.27)$$
$$rel([who|S0], S, H0, H) \leftarrow s(S0, S, [who|H0], H) \qquad\qquad (5.2.28)$$
$$rel([that|S0], S, H0, H) \leftarrow s(S0, S, [that|H0], H) \qquad\qquad (5.2.29)$$

Now we can refute a much wider and more interesting range of clauses:

$\leftarrow s([what, the, man, reads])$
$\leftarrow s([some, man, who, reads, the, book, likes, the, woman])$
$\leftarrow s([the, man, who, every, woman, likes, reads, the, book])$
$\leftarrow s([what, the, man, who, the, woman, likes, reads])$

(Remember that in the first and last of the following examples we really should apply *do*-support, adding *does* and changing *reads* to *read*.) We seem to be making some progress, but in addition to grammatical nonsense strings, we have some ungrammatical nonsense strings as shown by the refutation of

$\leftarrow s([what, the, man, who, likes, reads, the, book])$.

(This string would not be any good even if "do-support" had applied.) In effect, our refutation finds that the *who* can be placed in the embedded subject position and *what* can be placed into the embedded object position, as the object of *likes*. The problem here is not with the theory but with the idea that a *wh*-phrase can be moved to the front of a string from anywhere in the sentence. Notice that we can also refute

$\leftarrow s([the, man, who, the, woman, likes, the, book, reads])$.

Here, the *who* is placed as the object of *reads*.

Pereira notes that some restrictions are needed to rule out examples like these. They correspond to violations of Ross's (1967) *complex NP constraint*, which rules out movement relations that cross an NP boundary when the NP has the form $NP/[Det, N, Rel]$. In such a case, the N is said to be the *head* of the NP. Ross's complex NP constraint says there can be no movement across an NP node when that NP has a (non-empty) head. Both of the bad examples mentioned in the previous paragraph violate this constraint.

The bad examples can be ruled out with a simple technique suggested by Pereira. We simply change the rule for *rel* so that it puts an element * on the extraposition list to block access to the items waiting to be placed.[7] This element can then be removed when the relative clause has been parsed, so long as nothing added to the extraposition list during the parse of the relative clause is still waiting to be placed. The following replacements for 5.2.28 and 5.2.29 have this effect:

$$rel([who|S0], S, H0, H) \leftarrow s(S0, S, [who, *|H0], [*|H]) \tag{5.2.30}$$

$$rel([that|S0], S, H0, H) \leftarrow s(S0, S, [that, *|H0], [*|H]) \tag{5.2.31}$$

This theory is much better than the original, but we can see that simple extensions of this theory will recognize some strings that are ungrammatical, where the ungrammaticality does not come simply from the inadequacy in our representation of English verbs. Suppose that we add prepositional phrase modifiers with rules like the following:

$$np(S0, S, H0, H) \leftarrow det(S0, S1, H0, H1) \wedge \tag{5.2.32}$$
$$n(S1, S2, H1, H2) \wedge pp(S2, S, H2, H)$$

$$pp(S0, S, H0, H) \leftarrow p(S0, S1, H0, H1) \wedge np(S1, S, H1, H) \tag{5.2.33}$$

$$p([about|S], S, H, H) \leftarrow \tag{5.2.34}$$

Then we can refute the following (which needs "do-support"):

$$\leftarrow s([what, the, man, read, the, book, about])$$

by placing the *what* as the object of the preposition that modifies the book. This derivation should be blocked. This example is a little tricky, because there is a grammatical structure for the string, one in which the prepositional phrase modifies the verb or the sentence. Extraction is possible from prepositional phrases in these positions, but these positions are not even covered yet by our grammar. We want to block the movement of the object of a prepositional phrase out of the NP it modifies.

This last example shows that we have not quite captured Ross's complex NP constraint. We could fix this problem by putting dummy elements into the extraposition list as we did for the *rel* category, but notice that this would have the undesirable consequence of blocking all extractions out of a prepositional phrase. Examples like the following show that this would be a mistake:

Who$_i$ did you read about t_i?
Who$_i$ did you tell me to ask about t_i?

. . .

Furthermore, even if we made an *ad hoc* change to handle prepositional phrases by distinguishing those that modify NPs from all the others, there are other cases that simple extensions of our grammar will not block. Suppose we extend our grammar so that it can recognize sentential complements, such as those in the following sentences:

The officer asked where I hid the keys.
You wonder how I fixed the car.

We need to block extraction in these cases as well:

* *What$_i$ did the officer ask where I hid t$_i$.*
* *What$_i$ do you wonder how I fixed t$_i$.*

Turning again to linguistic theory, it is easy to find principles that block movements in all of these cases. Some first steps in this direction are taken in the "restricted logic grammars" of the next section.

5.3   Restricted logic grammars

A grammar formalism called *restricted logic grammars* is designed to provide a couple of straightforward extensions of extraposition grammar (Stabler, 1987a). We will develop some of these extensions a piece at a time. In the first place, we would like to have more powerful constraints on movement. We begin with the following ideas:

(a) A moved constituent must *c-command* its trace, where node α *c-commands* β iff α does not dominate β but the first node with more than one child (i.e., the first "branching" node) that dominates α dominates β.

(b) No rule can relate a constituent X to constituents Y or Z in a structure of the form

$$\ldots Y \ldots [_{\alpha} \ldots [_{\beta} \ldots X \ldots] \ldots] \ldots Z \ldots$$

where α and β are "bounding nodes." (In English, we will assume that the bounding nodes are S and NP.)

These conditions are simplified versions of principles developed in the tradition of Chomskian syntax. The first is related to principles of binding theory, and the second to the "subjacency principle."

Notice that these principles do suffice to handle the cases of overgeneration that we have mentioned so far. Acceptance of string (∗1) is blocked by (b), since the required movement of *what$_i$* must cross an NP and an S boundary:

* *What$_i$ does [$_{np}$the man who$_j$ [$_s$t$_j$ likes t$_i$]] read the book.*   (*1)

Acceptance of string (∗2) is blocked by the first condition, since the required movement is to a site that is not c-commanded. That is, the first branching node that dominates *who$_i$*, namely *rel*, does not dominate t$_i$:

* *The man [$_{rel}$who$_i$ [$_{np}$the woman likes the book]] reads t$_i$.*   (*2)

Acceptance of string (∗3) is blocked by (b):

* $What_i$ [$_s$ did the man read [$_{np}$ the book about t_i]].   (*3)

We have not extended our grammar to allow sentential complements yet, but it is clear that acceptance of strings (∗4) and (∗5) should be blocked by (b):

* $What_i$ [$_s$ did the officer ask where [$_s$ I hid t_i].   (*4)
* $What_i$ [$_s$ do you wonder how [$_s$ I fixed t_i]].   (*5)

It looks like these principles might be roughly on the right track, so let's consider how they could be represented in an extension of *XGR*.

Pereira's trick for blocking extractions from relative clauses can be extended in a straightforward way to block extractions across two bounding nodes. Instead of putting a dummy element into the extraposition list when we begin parsing a relative clause, we can put dummy elements into the extraposition list whenever we begin parsing a bounding category, and then allow placement of a *wh*-phrase across one but not across two of these dummy elements. We can also block movement to non-c-commanding positions if we check to make sure that the new *wh*-phrase has been removed before the end of the first branching node dominating any moved constituent. In *XGR* this would mean that a special test must be performed before completing the recognition of a *cp* or *rel*. This check need only ensure that the new *wh*-phrase picked up at the beginning of the category has been placed and is no longer in the extraposition list. This check is tricky, because a *wh*-phrase can be at the head of the extraposition list when *rel* or *cp* is complete. It just cannot be a *wh*-phrase that was introduced inside of that category. This can be enforced by somehow assigning each *wh*-phrase a unique index $i, j, k, i_1, \ldots$ (as we have done in the presentation of our examples), and making sure that a *wh*-phrase with a new index is not waiting to be placed at the completion of a *rel* or *cat*.[8]

This last strategy is a bit complex, but the approach is still inadequate. Our principle (b), or rather its implicit logical representation, blocks the recognition of strings like the following:

Who_i [$_s$ do you think [$_s$ I said [$_s$ I read about t_i]]]?
$What_i$ [$_s$ did the man with a gun say [$_s$ I should do t_i]]?

It turns out that we can recognize these strings without giving up (b) if we allow a movement to take place in a number of steps. One way to get this effect in our approach is to give S bounding nodes a special status. Notice that the S boundaries play an essential role in blocking acceptance of (∗1), (∗3), (∗4), (∗5). In (∗1), (∗4), (∗5) there are *two* movements out of an S:

* *What$_i$ does [$_{np}$the man who$_j$ [$_s$t$_j$ likes t$_i$]] read the book.*   *(*1)*
* *What$_i$ [$_s$did the officer ask where [$_s$I hid t$_i$].*   *(*4)*
* *What$_i$ [$_s$do you wonder how [$_s$I fixed t$_i$]].*   *(*5)*

This suggests that we might give the category S a special treatment, allowing no more than one *wh*-phrase to cross each. That is, after one *wh*-phrase moves across an S-node, it becomes a blocking category like NP. Unfortunately, this would provide no way to eliminate

* *What$_i$ [$_s$did the man read [$_{np}$the book about t$_i$]]*   *(*3)*

There are other bad strings that are not ruled out by the c-command restriction and (b), such as

* *Who$_i$ do you think that t$_i$ saw Bill?*

We will leave these problems unresolved for the moment.

5.4   More unresolved problems

In fact, the approach described looks less and less natural when the range of unresolved problems is surveyed.[9] Consider, in the first place, rightward movements such as we see in constructions like the following:

The man t$_i$ arrived [who I told you about]$_i$
What book t$_i$ arrived [about the arms race]$_i$

We want to allow these, while disallowing

* *The woman [who likes [the man t$_i$]] arrived [who I told you about]$_i$*
* *What woman [who likes [the book t$_i$]] arrived [about the arms race]$_i$?*

The strategy of coding parts of the syntactic structure in the extraposition list must be supplemented in some way to handle such cases, and the structural conditions on rightward movement must be enforced as well. That is, the strategy of allowing empty categories only if a suitable moved constituent has already been found must be supplemented with the much less efficient strategy of allowing empty categories whenever a suitable moved constituent might be found later in the sentence. This addition will allow spurious empty categories to be posited only to be rejected later. There is a more efficient but less elegant trick: to leave NPs indeterminate in certain respects in case we discover a modifier displaced to the right (e.g., Stabler, 1987; Berwick, 1983).

Another thing that RLGs were designed to allow is crossing relations between moved constituents and their original sites. It is easy to verify that the grammars shown above allow only properly nested dependencies, and so an extension seems to be required to allow cases like

What$_i$ do you know how$_j$ to read t_i t_j?

Unfortunately, the mechanism that allows such constructions in RLGs also allows ungrammatical strings like the following:[10]

* *Who$_i$ do I wonder whether$_j$ she was t_i t_j?*
* *What$_i$ did he ask [in which place]$_j$ I hid t_i t_j?*
* *[The theorem]$_i$ was discovered why$_j$ t_i to be unsolvable t_j?*

So RLGs hardly begin to provide an adequate account of movement relations. They have no natural way of blocking the acceptance of bad strings, and this problem, of course, indicates also that the system has no natural way to block certain bad analyses of good strings. The latter problem is perhaps the more serious in most practical applications.

It is worth mentioning one other kind of problem that this approach does not address. Linguists have been abandoning the view that grammaticality is an all-or-nothing matter. For example, using ?, ??,..., *, **,... to indicate, respectively, increasingly severe departures from perfect grammaticality, the sentences just displayed are better ranked as follows:

? *Who$_i$ do I wonder whether$_j$ she was t_i t_j?*
?? *What$_i$ did he ask [in which place]$_j$ I hid t_i t_j?*
** *[The theorem]$_i$ was discovered why$_j$ t_i to be unsolvable t_j?*

In fact, these examples are subsumed in fairly robust generalizations about patterns of acceptability. As discussed in later chapters, certain especially severe departures from grammaticality can be identified as "ECP violations" (with ungoverned subject traces):

** *Who$_i$ did you wonder that t_i left?*
** *Who$_i$ do you wonder how$_j$ t_i fixed the car t_j?*

These examples seem worse than other violations of principle (b).

Cinque (1990) has suggested that linguistic theory should account for the difference between two large classes of cases. The first class he calls extractions from "strong islands" (subject islands, complex NP islands, adjunct islands):

* *Which books$_i$ did talking about t_i become difficult?*
* *To whom$_i$ have you found someone who would speak t_i?*
* *To whom$_i$ did you leave without speaking t_i?*

These all seem less acceptable than extractions from "weak islands" (i.e. wh-islands, negative islands, factive islands, extraposition islands):

?? To whom$_i$ didn't they know when to give their present t$_i$?
? To whom$_i$ didn't you speak t$_i$?
? To whom$_i$ do you regret that you could not speak t$_i$?
?? To whom$_i$ is it time to speak t$_i$?

There is some variation from speaker to speaker on these relative judgements, but the general pattern of contrasts seems to hold. To account for these contrasts we cannot simply fail to parse all but the perfect strings. Apparently, we need a system that will parse a range of less than perfect strings, noticing that certain structures have less than ideal properties. Comparative judgements like these have guided the development of recent linguistic theory, as described in Parts II and III, and this theory provides the means to draw the relevant distinctions. From this perspective, the most natural assumption is that the same principles that define degrees of acceptability are used by the parser, in some form or other, to define the available structures. A system of this kind is one goal of the remainder of this text.

5.5   A Prolog session with theory XGR

Our theory XG R can be directly entered as a Prolog program:

```
% Theory XGR

s(S) :- s(S,[],[],[]).
s(S) :- cp(S,[],[],[]).

cp([who|S0],S,H0,H) :-
    s(S0,S,[who|H0],H).
cp([what|S0],S,H0,H) :-
    s(S0,S,[what|H0],H).

s(S0,S,H0,H) :-
    np(S0,S1,H0,H1) ,
    vp(S1,S,H1,H).

vp(S0,S,H0,H) :-
    v(S0,S1,H0,H1) ,
    np(S1,S,H1,H).

v([reads|S],S,H,H).
v([likes|S],S,H,H).

np(S0,S,H0,H) :-
```

```
    det(S0,S1,H0,H1) ,
    n(S1,S,H1,H).
np(S0,S,H0,H):-
    det(S0,S1,H0,H1),
    n(S1,S2,H1,H2),
    rel(S2,S,H2,H).
np(S,S,[what|H],H).
np(S,S,[who|H],H).

det([the|S],S,H,H).
det([every|S],S,H,H).
det([some|S],S,H,H).
det([no|S],S,H,H).

n([woman|S],S,H,H).
n([man|S],S,H,H).
n([book|S],S,H,H).

rel([who|S0],S,H0,H) :-
    s(S0,S,[who|H0],H).
rel([that|S0],S,H0,H) :-
    s(S0,S,[that|H0],H).

/* the following two rules block complex NP constraint violations
rel([who|S0],S,H0,H) :-
    s(S0,S,[who,'*'|H0],['*'|H]).
rel([that|S0],S,H0,H) :-
    s(S0,S,[that,'*'|H0],['*'|H]).
*/
```

We can use the simple Prolog proof strategy to refute some of the negative clauses mentioned above:

```
| ?- s([some,man,reads,every,book]).
```

```
yes
| ?- s([who,reads,every,book]).
```

% string not accepted if there is no place to put the wh-phrase:

```
| ?- s([who,the,man,reads,every,book]).
```

```
no
| ?- s([what,the,man,reads]).
```

```
yes
```

%%%% a complex-NP constraint violation --- accepted by this system:

```
| ?- s([what,the,man,who,likes,reads,the,book]).
```

```
yes

%%%% here is a deeply center embedded example:

| ?- s([what,the,man,who,every,woman,who,some,man,
        who,the,book,reads,likes,likes,reads]).

yes
```

5.6 A Prolog session with the metatheory

Let's apply our metatheory translator, τ_m, to XG R to get a parser, or rather a representation of the proof trees of XG R. The metatheory $\tau_m(XGR)$ is the following:

```
s(A,s(A)/[B]) :-
    s(A,[],[],[],B).

s(A,s(A)/[B]) :-
    cp(A,[],[],[],B).

cp([who|A],B,C,D,cp([who|A],B,C,D)/[E]) :-
    s(A,B,[who|C],D,E).

cp([what|A],B,C,D,cp([what|A],B,C,D)/[E]) :-
    s(A,B,[what|C],D,E).

s(A,B,C,D,s(A,B,C,D)/[E,F]) :-
    np(A,G,C,H,E),
    vp(G,B,H,D,F).

vp(A,B,C,D,vp(A,B,C,D)/[E,F]) :-
    v(A,G,C,H,E),
    np(G,B,H,D,F).

v([reads|A],A,B,B,v([reads|A],A,B,B)/[]).

v([likes|A],A,B,B,v([likes|A],A,B,B)/[]).

np(A,B,C,D,np(A,B,C,D)/[E,F]) :-
    det(A,G,C,H,E),
    n(G,B,H,D,F).

np(A,B,C,D,np(A,B,C,D)/[E,F,G]) :-
    det(A,H,C,I,E),
    n(H,J,I,K,F),
    rel(J,B,K,D,G).

np(A,A,[what|B],B,np(A,A,[what|B],B)/[]).
```

```
np(A,A,[who|B],B,np(A,A,[who|B],B)/[]).

det([the|A],A,B,B,det([the|A],A,B,B)/[]).

det([every|A],A,B,B,det([every|A],A,B,B)/[]).

det([some|A],A,B,B,det([some|A],A,B,B)/[]).

det([no|A],A,B,B,det([no|A],A,B,B)/[]).

n([woman|A],A,B,B,n([woman|A],A,B,B)/[]).

n([man|A],A,B,B,n([man|A],A,B,B)/[]).

n([book|A],A,B,B,n([book|A],A,B,B)/[]).

rel([who|A],B,C,D,rel([who|A],B,C,D)/[E]) :-
    s(A,B,[who|C],D,E).

rel([that|A],B,C,D,rel([that|A],B,C,D)/[E]) :-
    s(A,B,[that|C],D,E).
```

Again, Prolog can refute the negative clauses mentioned in the text, providing the effect of a parser. We "prettyprint" our example proof tree to make it more readable:

```
| ?- s([every,man,reads,the,book],P),pp_tree(P).

s([every,man,reads,the,book])
    s([every,man,reads,the,book],[],[],[])
        np([every,man,reads,the,book],[reads,the,book],[],[])
            det([every,man,reads,the,book],[man,reads,the,book],[],[])
            n([man,reads,the,book],[reads,the,book],[],[])
        vp([reads,the,book],[],[],[])
            v([reads,the,book],[the,book],[],[])
            np([the,book],[],[],[])
                det([the,book],[book],[],[])
                n([book],[],[],[])
```

Part II

Formalizing Barriers

Chapter 6

X-bar theory

> *Since a grammar is a theory of a language, and simplicity and generality are primary goals of any theory construction, we shall naturally try to formulate the theory of linguistic structure to accommodate rules that permit the formulation of deeper generalizations. — Noam Chomsky & George A. Miller*

We now undertake the project of formalizing the leading ideas of Chomsky's *Barriers*. The formalization will be organized roughly according to the text of *Barriers*, so we begin with X-bar theory.

6.1 Origins of X-bar theory

The traditional grammatical categories (noun, verb, subject, predicate, object, etc.) have not turned out to be quite appropriate for the formal account of natural language syntax. The set of categories used in theoretical linguistics is still evolving, but some of the basic considerations are clear. We want to identify categories that allow us to state the regularities in the syntax of human language without allowing us to state regularities that never occur in natural languages. Therefore a proposal about the appropriate categories ought to be evaluated with regard to whether it is sufficiently rich to allow the statement of important generalizations without facilitating the definition of strange structures that never occur in any human language.

The first formulation of X-bar theory is proposed by Chomsky in his "Remarks on Nominalization" (1970). He points out that there are significant differences between "derived nominals" like *John's criticism of the book* and "gerundive nominals" like *John's criticizing the book*. There is more productivity in the case of gerundive nominals. They can contain aspectual auxiliary verbs, as in *John's having criticized the book*, and they can occur with a range of adverbial phrases, as in *John's criticizing the book too often* or *John's criticizing the book without understanding it*. Derived nominals do not have these properties: * *John's having criticism of the book*, * *John's criticism of the book too often*. Observations like these prompt Chomsky to propose that gerundive nominals should be generated from underlying sentence-like structures, while derived nominals are not, contrary to previously held views. The relation between the verb *criticize* and the nominal form *criticism* is to be accounted for not by a transformation, but by a lexical rule of some kind.

The structure of a derived nominal is thus something like

$[_{np}[_{det}John's]\ [_{n}criticism]\ [_{pp}of\ the\ house]]$.

This is the underlying, basic structure of such phrases, and they are not derived from anything containing sentential constituents like *the criticism that John has which is of the house*. We have already noted that derived nominals cannot contain aspectual verbs, although sentences can. As for the final prepositional phrase, even though in this case there may seem to be a relation to a relative clause, there are other cases where this account of PPs in noun phrases does not seem plausible, as in *the weather in England, the author of the book, the bottom of the barrel* or *his advantage over his rivals*.

In fact, almost any category can occur with a following PP, as in

I $[_{vp}fixed\ the\ fender\ with\ a\ crowbar]$.
I am $[_{ap}happy\ about\ it]$.

And so we might propose rules like the following:

$NP \rightarrow N\ PP$
$VP \rightarrow V\ PP$
$AP \rightarrow A\ PP$.

But there is a regularity here that should be captured. Another problem with this proposal is that there is reason to suppose that the N and PP form a constituent even when there is a determiner phrase, as in

$[_{np}[_{det}several\ of\ John's][_{\alpha}proofs\ of\ the\ theorem]]$.

We need a $+N$ category α "higher" than N but "lower" than NP. These ideas are captured in X-bar theory.

The original X-bar theory identified three primitive lexical categories — N, V, and A — each of which has two phrasal categories. The category N occurs in an intermediate category N' (which is pronounced *N-bar*) and a maximal category N'' (which is usually called NP), and similarly for V and A. The lexical category X in such a structure is said to be the *head* of the phrases X' and X'' that contain it. This approach was later extended to four lexical categories, based on two features, each of which has one of two values:

N is a category X with the features $[+N, -V]$

V is a category X with the features $[-N, +V]$

A is a category X with the features $[+N, +V]$

P is a category X with the features $[-N, -V]$

This theory has empirical consequences. We predict that linguistic generalizations will all be statable as generalizations about categories X with some (nondisjunctive) specification of features. For example, there might be a generalization about a category X (which is a generalization about N, V, A, and P) or about a category X[+N] (which is about N and A), but not a generalization about only the categories N and V. X-bar theory can then be regarded as making a claim about what categories dominate others, or rather, how any *head X* must project to X' and X''. X together with a sequence of *complements* is immediately dominated by X', and X' together with a sequence of *specifiers* is immediately dominated by X''.

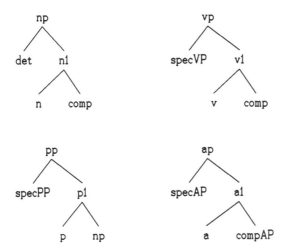

Figure 6.1
Lexical categories in English

6.2   X-bar theory extended to nonlexical categories

For convenience, we will use the old notation of NP, VP, AP, and PP for N'', V'', A'', P'', respectively, but we will continue to regard these categories as the second bar level projections of the lexical heads. It will also be more convenient to use the notation N1, V1, A1, and P1 for N', V', A' and P', respectively. The claims of X-bar theory, together with any specification of the ordering parameters dictate a certain homogeneity among

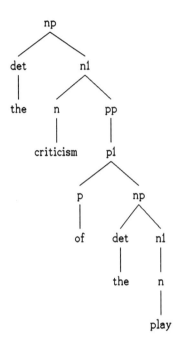

Figure 6.2
A simple NP

the major syntactic categories. In English, for example, Figure 6.1 shows the structures
of the lexical categories. Notice that *det* (for "determiner") is shown here as a specifier
of NP, but there could be no specifier, or more than one specifier. Rather than go into
what might occur as a specifier of VP in English (if anything), the specifier position has
been indicated with the label *specVP*, and similarly for the other categories. On this
view, the lexical categories all have a similar basic structure, though we need an account
of the acceptable specifiers and complements. On this approach, an NP like *the criticism
of the play* has the structure shown in Figure 6.2.

Stowell (1981) proposes that X-bar theory should be extended to nonlexical or *functional* categories, and a similar idea is developed in *Barriers*. In particular, S is regarded
as *I″*, which we will call IP, where its head, I, is the inflectional element (such as tense or
aspect). We say in such a case that S is the maximal projection of inflection. And *S′* is
regarded as *C″*, which we will call CP, whose head is a complementizer C. And similarly
we will use I1 and C1 to represent *I′* and *C′*. Then a simple declarative sentence in English has the structure shown in Figure 6.3. That is, NP is the specifier of IP, and VP is
the complement. For *S′* structures, that is, sentences together with a prefixed (possibly
empty) complementizer, we now have the structure shown in Figure 6.4. Thus, CP is

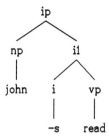

Figure 6.3
A simple IP

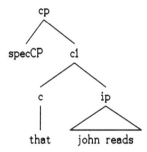

Figure 6.4
A simple CP

the "maximal projection" of the nonlexical category C, and the complement in a CP is an IP. Notice that in the last tree display we did not show the internal structure of the IP. We will often neglect such internal structure in constituents when it is not relevant to the matter at hand.

Chomsky assumes that both the specifiers and complements of any category are maximal projections. Notice that we have used the label *det* as the specifier of NP, and for the moment we will just regard *det* or *d* as a special sort of maximal projection. Actually, the account of specifiers should be reworked to fit the new approach, but Chomsky does

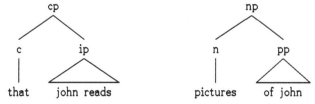

Figure 6.5
Structures without specifiers

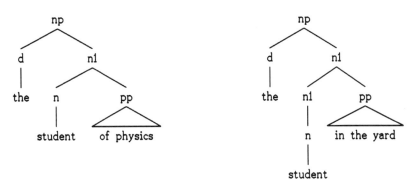

Figure 6.6
Complement and adjunct PPs in NP

not focus on this in *Barriers*.[1] Chomsky suggests that specifiers are optional, while the complements are determined according to the subcategorization features of the heads of the lexical items. When there is no specifier, we allow the occurrence of the intermediate level category to be omitted. For example, the trees in Figure 6.5 are well-formed.

One more wrinkle is needed in the story. Chomsky (1986a, 3) suggests these X-bar constraints apply at D-structure, though they may fail to apply after certain movements (adjunctions) have taken place. Adjoining a subtree *sub* to another subtree *cat/seq* produces either *cat/[sub, cat/seq]* or *cat/[cat/seq, sub]*. This movement and others will be discussed in detail in the next chapter, but here we want to allow for some similar structures to be "base-generated." That is, some such structures are allowed to occur at D-structure, before any movements have occurred. Adjunct modifiers can be assumed to occur in a structural position that would result from an adjunction. For example, *the student of physics* is naturally regarded as an NP with a PP complement, but *the student in the yard* is regarded as an NP with a PP adjunct modifier, as shown in Figure 6.6.[2]

Finally, the trees that we have displayed have a certain left-to-right order among the nodes that has not yet been required by anything. In *Barriers* (p91n3) it is suggested that the orderings might be specified by certain language-specific "parameters of X-bar theory." For example, in English, heads tend to precede their complements, and specifiers tend to precede the heads. So we will presume that the needed ordering relationships can be specified with two parameters, each of which can have one of two values: the head can precede or follow the specifiers, and the head can precede or follow the complements. In English, the specifiers of X'' precede X', while the complements follow X. The X-bar dominance relations are sometimes regarded as universal, holding in every human language, but the ordering is of course language-specific and can be violated by "marked" constructions.[3]

6.3   What is X-bar theory about?

The structures we have displayed are trees, but it is not generally accepted that linguistic representations are trees. For example, Chomsky (1984, 14-15, 57) suggests that D-structures have the properties of tree structures, but suggests that reanalysis and reconstruction processes may yield representations that are not trees. Since reanalysis and reconstruction get little attention in *Barriers*, trees will suffice for present purposes. For those who are worried about trees, however, it is worth digressing to briefly mention some alternative ideas.

6.3.1   Phrase markers, reduced phrase markers, and trees

The relation between syntactic structures and various set-theoretic constructions called "phrase markers" deserves some attention. Chomsky (1955, §§53-54; 1956, §5) proposes "phrase marker" representations of context-free derivation structures, where a phrase marker is the set of all the lines in all the derivations that correspond to a single derivation tree. For example, the tree in Figure 6.3 corresponds to the following phrase marker:

$\{ip,\ np\ i1,\ john\ i1,\ np\ i\ vp,\ john\ i\ vp,\ np\ i\ read,$

$\quad john\ i\ read,\ np\ \text{-}s\ read,\ john\ \text{-}s\ read\}$

Each element of this set corresponds to a horizontal "cut," or "factorization" of the tree. The analogous vertical notion is the idea of a *path*, which is just a sequence of nodes $\langle a_0, a_1, \ldots, a_n \rangle$ such that for all $0 \le i \le n$, a_i is the parent of a_{i+1}. Clearly, given the familiar notion of precedence, no node in a path precedes any other node in that same path. So we can say,

DEFINITION 46 A *factorization* of a tree T is a sequence $P = \langle a_0, a_1, \ldots, a_n \rangle$ such that

(i) a_i precedes a_{i+1} in T (for all $0 \le i \le n$), and
(ii) no node can be added to the sequence without violating (i).

With this idea we can define a phrase marker as follows:

DEFINITION 47 The *phrase marker* of a tree T is the set of all factorizations of T.

Clearly, these phrase markers carry the same information as a tree, but they are highly redundant and hence formally clumsy and, for most purposes, computationally inefficient.
   The "reduced phrase markers" (RPMs) of Lasnik and Kupin (1977) are quite different. They are much simpler, so much simpler in fact that they do not suffice to represent syntactic relationships that are central in current syntactic theory. An RPM is roughly the set of all factorizations of T that contain at most one nonterminal element. After

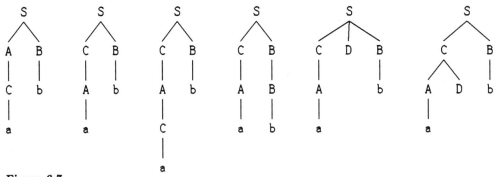

Figure 6.7
Six trees with the same RPM

presenting a precise definition, Lasnik and Kupin (1977, 179) point out that the 6 trees of
Figure 6.7 and infinitely many others all correspond to one and the same RPM, namely,

$$\{S,\ A\ b,\ C\ b,\ a\ B,\ a\ b\}$$

This first pair of the six trees shows that RPMs are unable to distinguish the positions of
two nodes in cases of exclusive domination; the second pair of trees shows that RPMs are
unable to distinguish repetitions in cases of exclusive domination; and the last pair shows
that RPMs are unable to distinguish the position of a node that does not dominate a
terminal. This last pair is especially interesting. When empty nodes occur, RPMs do not
provide enough information to decide whether two nodes are sisters, whether an arbitrary
node is branching (i.e., has more than one daughter), whether a c-command relation
holds, etc. To avoid these problems, Lasnik and Kupin stipulate that empty categories
at D-structure actually dominate special terminals Δ, that every transformation leaves
behind a special terminal element *t*, and that deletions similarly leave terminals Δ.

This approach begins to seem rather forced and unnatural. If we are going to have to
reinterpret our theories about empty categories in this way, imposing a special distinction
between terminals and nonterminals, we want to know the motivation. So it is relevant
to observe at this point that Lasnik and Kupin (1977) presented this work before the
movement from formal universals to substantive universals had taken hold, and their
goal was to provide a restrictive characterization of transformations, where these were
regarded as a set of "structural description - structural change" rules. Now that parameters of language-specific variation are identified and presumed to interact with universal
principles of movement, this motivation for a restrictive formalism is gone. Consequently,
there is no longer any point in reconstruing linguistic claims about empty categories as
claims about special "terminals." Lasnik and Kupin, however, do make some substantial claims which could still hold in current theories. Because of their special empty

"terminals," they do not intend any strange claims about any inability to detect sisterhood, c-command, government and other relations involving these categories. They are committed, however, to the idea that no linguistic principles need to know whether A dominates B or B dominates A unless the domination relation is not exclusive. Unfortunately, this idea conflicts with many proposals in recent syntax. For example, it conflicts with the X-bar theory that we are currently considering, since that theory requires that XP dominate an X, and it does not allow the reverse even when the domination is exclusive (i.e., when there are no specifiers or complements). As we will see, immediate domination is a notion that plays a role in a number of linguistic concepts.

6.3.2 Unordered trees

Although immediate domination does seem to play a role in syntax, Marantz (1989, 114-115) and others have suggested that linear precedence does not. So, again, the idea is that something weaker than ordered trees would suffice for syntax. Trees without linear precedence relations (what mathematicians might call finite, labeled, rooted, unordered trees) would suffice. The only significant feature is the hierarchical relations. It is quite possible that linear precedence is irrelevant to syntactic levels of structure, D- and S-structure, and appears only at the level of phonological or phonetic form (PF), which was mentioned just briefly in §1. This development would require no change in our formalism, except for the relocation of the language-specific precedence restrictions to PF.[4] That is, as far as the theory is concerned, we could regard the left-to-right ordering shown in our displays as an imposition of the orthographic linearity of English text, as it is in most depictions of family trees. This linearity would be a matter to which no computation is sensitive. This idea that precedence could be relocated to PF apparently conflicts with proposals mentioned above. It will be recalled that we considered deriving precedence restrictions from properties of θ and case assignment, relations which are central in current syntactic theory. But this is a dispute that we need not engage. In formalizing *Barriers* and similar theories, we can use trees with no regard for their precedence relations.

6.3.3 Structures formed by reanalysis

English is unusually permissive about stranding prepositions, but stranding must be blocked in some cases to allow for contrasts like the following:

This solution is argued for by many linguists.
John was taken advantage of by Bill
Mary was spoken to by the professor.
The expert was sent for.

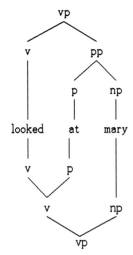

Figure 6.8
A non-tree reanalysis structure

The bed was slept in.
* Dinner is drunk brandy after by Bill
* Many hours were argued with Bill for by Harry
* A living is taught for by many writers.
* His destination was arrived at late last night.
* The auditorium was gone into by many people.
* Their claims are not tallied with by this data.

Since the good constructions here, called "pseudopassives" or "prepositional verb constructions," are only sometimes allowed in English and are relatively rare in other languages, it is often proposed that the extraction of NP from PP is generally blocked, and that it occurs in pseudopassives because the verb and preposition can be reanalyzed as a single complex verbal constituent. This story about reanalysis may seem rather *ad hoc*, designed to fit recalcitrant data in some few languages, but reanalysis has been used to account for other data in a wide range of languages. Reanalysis theories have been proposed to account for similar phenomena in Dutch and Vata (Koopman, 1983, §3.1.4; 1990), and for "clitic climbing" constructions in French (Kayne, 1975, 269), Spanish (Contreras, 1979), Italian (Rizzi, 1978), Dutch and German (Haegeman and van Riemsdijk, 1986).[5]

Deciding among these options or offering another is beyond the scope of our investigation, but it is easy to see how the non-tree structures that some linguists have proposed, if it turns out that they are in fact empirically well-motivated, could be represented with a modest extension of the tree notation introduced in the previous chapter. For example, one idea is that the resulting VP structures could be represented with a graph like the one in Figure 6.8 (Koster, 1986, 277). The two sequences of constituents, depicted above and below the terminal string shown, are not ordered by the precedence relation. We could represent such structures by putting all the constituents of both sequences inside the VP, so that it would contain not only a simple V and PP, but also the complex V and the empty NP. To keep the precedence ordering in the tree everywhere except for the reanalyzed constituent, we need only extend our notation very slightly. For example, we could use the operator + to indicate an unordered union of two ordered sequences, and represent the unordered tree of Figure 6.8 with the following notation:

```
s /[
    np /[ john/[] ],
    vp /
        [     v /[ looked/[] ],
            pp /[
                p /[ at/[] ],
                np/[ mary/[] ]]]
    +
        [     v /[
                v /[ looked/[] ],
                p /[ at/[] ]],
            np/[ mary/[] ]]].
```

It would be straightforward to define *parent*, *ancestor*, and other relations for these new structures.

A similar kind of multiple structure might be proposed as the result of "reconstruction" at a level of "logical form" (LF), a level of representation that is the basis for interpretation. Chomsky (1981, 89; 1982, 55) proposed that in some cases where a wh-phrase has moved, such as

Whose mother did you see?,

a "reconstruction rule" applies to put part of the moved constituent back into its original position:

Whose did you see mother?

This reconstructed structure is needed at LF for some purposes, but the original structure is needed for other purposes. In this case, we might say, as in reanalysis, that both structures are in some sense there. It would be nice to avoid reanalysis and reconstruction altogether, but many linguists have argued for these structure-changing operations.[6]

6.4   A logical formulation of X-bar theory

We have already introduced our tree notation and defined basic structural relations in §2.2, above. In our formalization of linguistic theory, the node labels will be grammatical categories. As mentioned above, one special type of tree that we will need to consider below is produced by "adjoining" a subtree *sub* to another subtree *cat/seq* to produce either *cat/[sub, cat/seq]* or *cat/[cat/seq, sub]*. May (1985) suggests that these trees are unusual in that we always want to treat the two nested subtrees dominated by *cat* as a single constituent. In order to treat adjunction structures in this way, we distinguish each occurrence of a category in a tree. In our formalism this is accomplished by providing the grammatical categories with a first argument which will number the occurrence of that category in any tree.[7] A properly numbered tree to which no adjunction has applied will have unique numbers at each node. The categories are also associated with features which are specified by a sequence in a second argument. So, for example,

$$x(s(s(0)), n, 1, [agr : sing + 3, case : nom, index : 1])$$

denotes a bar level 2 category n, that is an NP, with occurrence number 1 and the agreement features singular and third person, nominative case, and index 1. For convenience, in our discussion and in our tree displays we will usually use familiar abbreviations of the categories and bar level: *np*, *n1*, *n*, *vp*, *v1*, *v*, *ap*, *a1*, *a*, *pp*, *p1*, *p*. So, for example, the previously displayed category will often be represented in our notation as:

$$np(1, [agr : sing + 3, case : nom, index : 1]).$$

The following is a simple tree labeled with linguistic categories (with no associated features), and containing an adjunction structure — that is, containing a node with two segments:

```
x(s(s(0)),v,1,[]) /[
     x(0,v,2,[])/[],
     x(s(s(0)),i,3,[]) /[
          x(s(s(0)),n,4,[])/[],
          x(s(s(0)),i,3,[]) /[
               x(s(0),i,5,[])/[]]]].
```

This works fine in the logic, but in our discussion and displays we will sometimes use the following more readable notation as a convenient shorthand for the previous term:

```
vp(1,[]) /[
     v(2,[])/[],
     ip(3,[]) /[
          np(4,[])/[],
          ip(3,[]) /[
               i1(5,[])/[]]]].
```

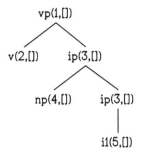

Figure 6.9
A tree with an adjunction

Most often, though, we will display the even more readable trees, such as those of Figure 6.9, which stand in an obvious 1-1 correspondence to the logical terms.

The feature lists that can occur as the final arguments of the node labels deserve a little more attention. We construe them as "attribute:value" pairs as is standard in the literature. We will sometimes want to assign a feature to a node. For example, we might want to assign $index : 1$ to the node

$$x(s(s(0)), n, 1, [agr : sing + 3, case : nom]).$$

We would want this assignment to be blocked if the node already had an index feature with a value distinct from 1. This effect can be achieved by defining a new relation as follows:

$$feature(AV, Node0, Node) \leftrightarrow \exists Att, Val, L, C, F0, F \qquad (6.4.1)$$
$$AV = Att : Val \wedge$$
$$Node0 = x(L, C, N, F0) \wedge$$
$$(\quad member(Att : Val, F0) \wedge F = F0$$
$$\vee \quad \forall Val0 \; \neg member(Att : Val0, F0)$$
$$\wedge F = [Att : Val | F0]$$
$$) \wedge$$
$$Node = x(L, C, N, F).$$

This formulation presupposes the standard axiomatization of *member*, which was presented in §4.2. Given these axioms (and the equality theory) we can prove, for example,

$$feature(index : 1,$$
$$x(s(s(0)), n, 1, [case : nom]),$$
$$x(s(s(0)), n, 1, [index : 1, case : nom])$$
$$).$$

Attribute-value structures have been extensively studied, but they do not play a large role in the theory developed here. We will not need to make use of negative or disjunctive features, and this allows us to avoid some thorny issues.[8]

Returning to the specifics of the theoretical framework, the following axioms allow us to distinguish theoretically relevant subsets of categories in the standard way:[9]

$$lexical(Node) \leftrightarrow \exists L, Cat, N, F \qquad (6.4.2)$$
$$Node = x(L, Cat, N, F) \wedge$$
$$member(Cat, [v, n, a, p])$$

$$maximal(Node) \leftrightarrow \exists Cat, N, F \qquad (6.4.3)$$
$$Node = x(s(s(0)), Cat, N, F)$$

$$minimal(Node) \leftrightarrow \exists Cat, N, F \qquad (6.4.4)$$
$$Node = x(0, Cat, N, F).$$

Remember that here and throughout we let our variables be any atomic expression beginning with an uppercase letter; we assume all of our sentences are universally closed; and we often represent integers as successors of 0 ($1 = s(0), 2 = s(s(0)), \ldots$).

We come at last to the principles of X-bar theory. Our formalization will attempt to mirror the *Barriers* formulation as closely as possible. It is natural to try to use something like the logical formulations of phrase structure rules to represent X-bar theory, but the X-bar principles are really rather different. They allow arbitrarily long sequences of unspecified categories to be dominated by a single node, and they provide no ordering information at all. The ordering information is provided by a separate parameter. The ordering is trivial, so let's formalize that first:

(o1) A language-specific parameter specifies whether the sequence of specifiers precedes or follows the head, and another specifies whether the sequence of complements precedes or follows the head.

We can simply use two unary predicates, each of which is satisfied by exactly one of 0 or s(0). Using the predicates *head_spec* and *head_compl*, the English setting of these language-specific parameters can be represented with the following sentences:[10]

$$head\_spec(X) \leftrightarrow X = 0 \qquad (6.4.5)$$
$$head\_compl(X) \leftrightarrow X = s(0) \qquad (6.4.6)$$

It will be convenient to have defined a couple of related predicates. We can define a predicate that will, in effect, use the ordering parameters to separate the head from the specifiers in the sequence of subtrees dominated by an XP. The following predicate, *separate*, will remove the last *Element* from a *List* leaving a *Remainder* when $N = 0$ and will remove the first *Element* when $N = s(0)$:

$$separate(N, Head, List, Rem) \leftrightarrow (\quad N = 0 \wedge last(Head, List, Rem) \qquad (6.4.7)$$
$$\vee \quad N = s(0) \wedge List = [Head|Rem]$$
$$)$$

$$last(Element, List, Remainder) \leftrightarrow (\quad \exists E1, E2, Rest, Rem \qquad (6.4.8)$$
$$List = [E1, E2|Rest] \wedge$$
$$Remainder = [E1|Rem] \wedge$$
$$last(Element, [E2|Rest], Rem)$$
$$\vee \quad List = [Element] \wedge$$
$$Remainder = []$$
$$).$$

These axioms will allow us to make use of the idea that if the value of *head_spec* is $s(0)$ then the head precedes the specifier, but if it is 0 then the head follows the specifiers, and similarly for complements.

Now we turn to X-bar theory proper. We want to require that lexical items are projected appropriately, allowing adjunction to intermediate and maximal categories, and allowing maximal and minimal projections at D-structure to be empty, or "bare" nodes, dominating nothing. We can formulate the basic claims as follows:

(x0) Every X0 node is either empty with no features or the parent of a lexical item with the category and features specified for that item in the lexicon.[11]

(x1) Every X1 node with lexical features F is either the parent of exactly one X with F (the head) and a sequence of XPs (complements), or else the parent of an identical node X1 and exactly one XP (adjunct).

(x2) Every XP with features F is such that one of the following holds: (i) it is the parent of nothing and F is empty, or (ii) it is the parent of a sequence of XPs (specifiers) and exactly one X1 with F, or (iii) it is the parent of a sequence of XPs (complements) and exactly one X with F, or (iv) it is the parent of an identical node XP and exactly one other XP.

Remember that the mentioned sequences of XPs can be empty.

It is convenient to define a predicate that holds of any sequence of maximal categories:

$$xps(L) \leftrightarrow (\quad L = []$$

$$\lor \quad \exists Tree, Seq$$
$$L = [Tree|Seq] \land$$
$$xp(Tree) \land$$
$$xps(Seq)$$
$$)$$

(6.4.9)

This presupposes a predicate xp which we have not defined yet. This predicate will apply to any well-formed maximal projection.

Principle (x0) provides the link to lexical information, projecting each non-empty category according to lexical information, and requiring all empty X0 categories to be featureless:

$$x0(X0) \leftrightarrow \exists Cat, N, F, Seq$$

$$X0 = x(0, Cat, N, F)/Seq \land$$
$$(\quad Seq = [] \land F = []$$
$$\lor \quad \exists Word$$
$$Seq = [Word/[]] \land$$
$$lexicon(Word, Cat, F)$$
$$).$$

(6.4.10)

Principle (x1) is more complex, but can be represented in a similar style, and it uses the predicate $x0$ to impose an appropriate condition on the subtree containing the head of each intermediate category T:

$$x1(X1) \leftrightarrow \exists Cat, N, F, Subtrees$$

$$X1 = x(s(0), Cat, N, F)/Subtrees \land$$
$$(\quad \exists Position, N0, L, Remainder$$
$$head\_compl(Position) \land$$
$$separate(Position, x(0, Cat, N0, F)/L, Subtrees, Remainder) \land$$
$$xps(Remainder)$$
$$\lor \quad \exists L, XP$$
$$(\quad Subtrees = [x(s(0), Cat, N, F)/L, XP]$$
$$\lor \quad Subtrees = [XP, x(s(0), Cat, N, F)/L]$$
$$) \land$$

(6.4.11)

$$x1(x(s(0), Cat, N, F)/L) \wedge$$
$$xp(XP)$$

).

Principle (x2) shows how to extend this account to maximal projections, yielding the most complex definition in our account, and one of the most complex in syntactic theory:

$$xp(XP) \leftrightarrow \exists Cat, N, F, T, Ts, Pos, Nn, L, Rem, XP1 \hspace{3cm} (6.4.12)$$
$$(\hspace{0.5cm} XP = x(s(s(0)), Cat, N, F)/[]$$
$$\vee \hspace{0.5cm} XPTree = x(s(s(0)), Cat, N, F)/[T|Ts] \wedge$$
$$head\_spec(Pos) \wedge$$
$$separate(Pos, x(s(0), Cat, Nn, F)/L, [T|Ts], Rem) \wedge$$
$$xps(Rem) \wedge$$
$$x1(x(s(0), Cat, Nn, F)/L)$$
$$\vee \hspace{0.5cm} XP = x(s(s(0)), Cat, N, F)/[T|Ts] \wedge$$
$$head\_compl(Pos) \wedge$$
$$separate(Pos, x(0, Cat, Nn, F)/L, [T|Ts], Rem) \wedge$$
$$xps(Rem) \wedge$$
$$x0(x(0, Cat, Nn, F)/L)$$
$$\vee \hspace{0.5cm} XP = x(s(s(0)), Cat, N, F)/[T|Ts] \wedge$$
$$(\hspace{0.5cm} [T|Ts] = [x(s(s(0)), Cat, N, F)/L, XP1]$$
$$\vee \hspace{0.5cm} [T|Ts] = [XP1, x(s(s(0)), Cat, N, F)/L]$$
$$) \wedge$$
$$xp(x(s(s(0)), Cat, N, F)/L) \wedge$$
$$xp(XP1)$$

).

Each disjunct in the right-hand side of this definition corresponds to one of the cases in principle (x2), stated above.

The relation between a head and its maximal projection is easily formalized in this framework, as is the relation between a head and its intermediate projection (if any). Following common usage of the term "specifier," it is convenient to think of specifier as a relation between the specifier node and all projections of a head, XP, X1, and X. The complement relation can be treated similarly. For example, a complement of a verb can also be called a complement of the intermediate and maximal projections of that verb. Definitions of these relations, $head\_xp(X, XP, Tree)$, $head\_x1(X, X1, Tree)$, $specifier(Specifier, Xn, Tree)$ and $complement(Complement, Xn, Tree)$ are presented in Appendix B. They will be used in later chapters.

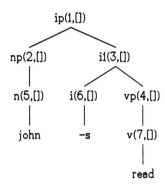

Figure 6.10
A properly projected IP

6.5 Preliminary tests of the formalization

The formalization now allows us to deduce the results we would expect. For example, we can prove that the tree of Figure 6.3 does not satisfy xp. The node labels do not conform to our specification. The tree of Figure 6.10, though, does satisfy xp, and provably so, if the lexicon has or entails the following:

$lexicon(john, n, [])$
$lexicon(\text{-}s, i, [])$
$lexicon(read, v, [])$.

(Remember that the node labels shown in Figure 6.10 are the more readable abbreviations for the $x(Level, Category, Number, Feature)$ notation specified in §6.3.) Of the tree in Figure 6.10, we can also prove that category 6 is the head of category 1, that category 5 is the head of category 2, and that category 7 is the head of category 4.

Checking with an informal proof sketch that such results do in fact follow from our formalization is a good exercise for the reader. As the simpler problems from previous chapters have shown that even some of the simplest results can require rather tedious proofs. Remember, for example, the proof shown in Appendix A and discussed in §3.3. Automatic theorem provers are an invaluable tool for checking the consequences in detail, as described in §3.7 and §14.

Chapter 7

The theory of movement

Penser, c'est tout d'abord situer et comparer: encore les deux
opérations se laissent-elles ramener á une seule, car
la comparaison initiale est le rapport d'un lieu á un autre.
— O.V. de L.-Milosz

In this section, we introduce the movement rule move-α. It is most natural to define movements relations on trees. They are the most difficult aspect of linguistic theory to formalize naturally, but even here the first order formalization is fairly elegant. Whereas our structural definitions have stayed very close to the linguists' formulations, the treatment of move-α requires a little more creativity. Roughly, move-α simply says to move any constituent to any other position in the tree, leaving a trace.

Traces and other "empty" categories that are "phonologically null" are one of the most important and distinctive parts of the structures posited by the theories of syntax considered here. They play an important role in a number of linguistic principles. For example, traces allow us to maintain a simple version of the *projection principle*. This principle says that the subcategorization requirements of lexical items are satisfied at every level of representation. We noted in §5 that the required direct object of *put* in

Who$_i$ did you put t$_i$ in the trunk?

seems to have been moved to sentence-initial position, but if we presume that a trace was left in the original location of the wh-phrase, then a direct object is still there. The trace in direct object is not pronounced, and it is co-indexed with the sentence-initial wh-phrase, and can serve to satisfy the projection principle.

Let's quickly consider one other principle that is simplified by the assumption of traces and other empty categories. There is a principle of binding theory, principle A, which says that an anaphor must be bound in its governing category. We will define binding in §8.3, but for the moment, since the "anaphors" include the reflexive pronouns (*myself, yourself, herself,...*), we can take this principle as requiring that each reflexive pronoun have an antecedent that is included in the lowest IP that includes the reflexive pronoun. Letting identity of subscripts indicate a sharing of "index features" which marks the pronoun-antecedent relation, this principle accounts for the pattern in the following examples:

Ronald$_i$ believes himself$_i$.
* *Nancy$_i$ believes himself$_j$.*
Nancy thinks [$_{ip}$Ronald$_i$ believes himself$_i$].
* *Ronald$_i$ thinks that [$_{ip}$Nancy$_j$ believes himself$_i$].*

Now consider the following sentences

Who[$_{ip}$ believes himself]?   (a)
Who wants [$_{ip}$to believe himself]?   (b)

If we can assume that there are NP positions to be antecedents for these reflexive pronouns, then we can preserve principle A in something like its original form.[1]

The last argument has a basic flaw, however. Why not just assume that principle A
applies at D-structure? Then we could account for the previous examples without the
assumption of traces, but it is easy to find cases where this will not work. Consider, for
example, the following structures.

They$_i$ seem to each other$_i$ [$_{ip}$t$_i$ to be devoted to the cause].
Nancy$_i$ knows [which picture of herself$_i$] [$_{ip}$ Ronald likes t$_i$].

Rather than abandoning principle A in the light of these examples, the usual assumption
is that the principles applies after movement (in at least some cases). These structures are
well-formed, and it is clear that they violate principle A before, but not after, movement.
Contrast, for example,

* *It seems to each other$_i$ that [$_{ip}$they$_i$ are devoted to the cause].*
* *Nancy$_i$ knows [$_{ip}$ Ronald likes the picture of herself$_i$].*

Thus we can maintain our previous argument for the view that traces allow us to keep a
certain simplicity in the binding principles.[2]

One argument for traces that was, at least initially, very appealing because it was less
theory-internal, comes from certain contraction phenomena which are assumed to take
place at "PF," a non-syntactic level of representation. Consider the following examples
from Chomsky (1981, §3.2.2):

The students want PRO to visit Paris.
The students wanna visit Paris.
They want Bill to visit Paris.
* *They wanna Bill visit Paris.*
Who do they want t$_i$ to visit Paris.
* *Who do they wanna visit Paris.*

These facts seem to indicate that the presence of a trace blocks contraction, in essentially the same way as the "overt" NP, *Bill.* This appealing argument runs into problems, though, because sometimes traces seem to allow contraction, as in

Who$_i$ do they want t$_i$ to visit?
Who do they wanna visit?
John$_i$ used t$_i$ to win.
John use'ta win.

We have not discussed case theory yet, but these last examples can be taken to suggest that only traces with case block contraction. This nicely explains why PRO and traces of NP-movement do not block contraction, while traces of wh-movement and clitic movement do block contraction. Unfortunately, further study shows that these matters are actually very tricky, and so this argument is controversial.[3]

To formalize move-α, we need to be more precise about the ways in which a moved category can be removed and reattached. Chomsky stipulates that only maximal and minimal categories (as defined in §6.4) are *visible* to move-α, and distinguishes two sorts of movements: substitutions and adjunctions. These are fairly easy to understand intuitively, but when spelled out in detail they are surprisingly complex. The most natural formalization we have discovered is based on a standard approach to the specification of root-to-frontier tree transducers (*R-transducers*).[4] In fact, the development of Chomskyan syntax was one of the inspirations for the development of tree automata theory (Rounds, 1970; Gécseg and Steinby, 1984).

7.1 Tree transducers

Tree automata are a natural generalization of standard string automata. Strings can be regarded as the special case of unary trees — trees in which every node dominates at most one other node; a finite state recognizer is then a unary tree automaton. Generalizing to all finite trees, a standard (finite-state) R-transducer can be defined with a set of productions or "transitions" that can be written as rules of the form:

$$(a_0, input\_label/[tree_1, \ldots, tree_n]) \rightarrow (output\_label/[(a_1, tree_1), \ldots, (a_n, tree_n)])$$

where each a_i is an element of a set of states A, the *input_label* is an element of the non-terminal vocabulary of the input trees if $n > 0$ or of the terminal vocabulary if $n = 0$; and the *output_label* is an element of the terminal or nonterminal vocabulary of the output trees.[5] The initial states are elements of a distinguished set $A' \subseteq A$. Intuitively, to transduce a tree, we apply an initial state to the root and propagate the state changes through the tree as specified by the transition rules. Thus the descent down each path is just like the operation of a conventional string transducer. The transition shown above, then, can be regarded as saying that beginning from initial state a_0 the tree,

$$input\_label/[tree_1, \ldots, tree_n]$$

is transformed into

$$output\_label/[(a_1, tree_1), \ldots, (a_n, tree_n)]$$

just in case each of the subtrees $tree_i (0 < i \leq n)$ is transformed into a tree $(a_i, tree_i)$ beginning from state a_i. That is, state a_0 transforms the root node $input\_label$ to the node $output\_label$, and passes the states $a_1, \ldots, a_n$ down the respective branches from the root.

A pertinent example will illustrate the idea. Consider a (nondeterministic, nondeleting, nonlinear) R-transducer that maps input trees labeled with (binary) nonterminals $\{a, b\}$ and terminals $\{c, d, \emptyset, t\}$ into output trees with the same alphabet, substituting a terminal node d for a $\emptyset$ in the input tree on condition that a t is substituted for a node d in the input tree. This R-transducer can be defined with four states, which we can call *subst*, *identity*, *zero_d* and *d_zero*. Intuitively, *subst* is the state that applies to the root to produce a substitution of node d for a $\emptyset$ and a substitution of a t for a node d; *identity* leaves the tree unchanged; *zero_d* applies to a tree to change some d in the tree to a t, and *d_zero* applies to a tree to change some $\emptyset$ in the tree to a d. The set of initial states $A' = \{subst\}$.

For simplicity, when a_i $(i > 0)$ is a final state that has no outgoing transitions, we can leave it out of the notation of the rule. Then the following productions suffice to define the desired transduction between trees:

$$(subst, a/[t_1, t_2]) \rightarrow a/[(subst, t_1), (identity, t_2)]$$
$$(subst, a/[t_1, t_2]) \rightarrow a/[(identity, t_1), (subst, t_2)]$$
$$(subst, a/[t_1, t_2]) \rightarrow a/[(zero\_d, t_1), (d\_zero, t_2)]$$
$$(subst, a/[t_1, t_2]) \rightarrow a/[(d\_zero, t_1), (zero\_d, t_2)]$$
$$(subst, b/[t_1, t_2]) \rightarrow b/[(subst, t_1), (identity, t_2)]$$
$$(subst, b/[t_1, t_2]) \rightarrow b/[(identity, t_1), (subst, t_2)]$$
$$(subst, b/[t_1, t_2]) \rightarrow b/[(zero\_d, t_1), (d\_zero, t_2)]$$
$$(subst, b/[t_1, t_2]) \rightarrow b/[(d\_zero, t_1), (zero\_d, t_2)]$$

$$(zero\_d, a/[t_1, t_2]) \rightarrow a/[(zero\_d, t_1), (identity, t_2)]$$
$$(zero\_d, a/[t_1, t_2]) \rightarrow a/[(identity, t_1), (zero\_d, t_2)]$$
$$(zero\_d, b/[t_1, t_2]) \rightarrow b/[(zero\_d, t_1), (identity, t_2)]$$

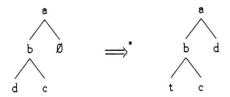

Figure 7.1
Trees related by a simple transduction

$(zero\_d, b/[t_1, t_2]) \rightarrow b/[(identity, t_1), (zero\_d, t_2)]$
$(zero\_d, d/[]) \rightarrow t/[]$

$(d\_zero, a/[t_1, t_2]) \rightarrow a/[(d\_zero, t_1), (identity, t_2)]$
$(d\_zero, a/[t_1, t_2]) \rightarrow a/[(identity, t_1), (d\_zero, t_2)]$
$(d\_zero, b/[t_1, t_2]) \rightarrow b/[(d\_zero, t_1), (identity, t_2)]$
$(d\_zero, b/[t_1, t_2]) \rightarrow b/[(identity, t_1), (d\_zero, t_2)]$
$(d\_zero, \emptyset/[]) \rightarrow d/[]$

$(identity, a/[t_1, t_2]) \rightarrow a/[(identity, t_1), (identity, t_2)]$
$(identity, b/[t_1, t_2]) \rightarrow b/[(identity, t_1), (identity, t_2)]$
$(identity, c/[]) \rightarrow c/[]$
$(identity, d/[]) \rightarrow d/[]$
$(identity, \emptyset/[]) \rightarrow \emptyset/[]$
$(identity, t/[]) \rightarrow t/[].$

The following is a derivation of $a/[b/[t/[], c/[]], d/[]]$ from $a/[b/[d/[], c/[]], \emptyset/[]]$ (these trees
are shown in Figure 7.1):

$(subst, a/[b/[d/[], c/[]], \emptyset/[]])$
$\quad \Rightarrow a/[(zero\_d, b/[d/[], c/[]]), (d\_zero, \emptyset/[])]$
$\quad \Rightarrow a/[b/[(zero\_d, d/[]), (identity, c/[])], (d\_zero, \emptyset/[])]$
$\quad \Rightarrow a/[b/[t/[], (identity, c/[])], (d\_zero, \emptyset/[])]$
$\quad \Rightarrow a/[b/[t/[], c/[]], (d\_zero, \emptyset/[])]$
$\quad \Rightarrow a/[b/[t/[], c/[]], d/[]].$

This transduction on trees can easily be formalized in logic, treating the four states
as relations and using variables that range over subtrees. Consider the following one-
formula-for-one-rule representation of the previous example:

$subst(S1, T1) \wedge identity(S2, T2) \rightarrow subst(a/[S1, S2], a/[T1, T2])$
$identity(S1, T1) \wedge subst(S2, T2) \rightarrow subst(a/[S1, S2], a/[T1, T2])$

$zero\_d(S1, T1) \wedge d\_zero(S2, T2) \rightarrow subst(a/[S1, S2], a/[T1, T2])$
$d\_zero(S1, T1) \wedge zero\_d(S2, T2) \rightarrow subst(a/[S1, S2], a/[T1, T2])$
$subst(S1, T1) \wedge identity(S2, T2) \rightarrow subst(b/[S1, S2], b/[T1, T2])$
$identity(S1, T1) \wedge subst(S2, T2) \rightarrow subst(b/[S1, S2], b/[T1, T2])$
$zero\_d(S1, T1) \wedge d\_zero(S2, T2) \rightarrow subst(b/[S1, S2], b/[T1, T2])$
$d\_zero(S1, T1) \wedge zero\_d(S2, T2) \rightarrow subst(b/[S1, S2], b/[T1, T2])$

$zero\_d(S1, T1) \wedge identity(S2, T2) \rightarrow zero\_d(a/[S1, S2], a/[T1, T2])$
$identity(S1, T1) \wedge zero\_d(S2, T2) \rightarrow zero\_d(a/[S1, S2], a/[T1, T2])$
$zero\_d(S1, T1) \wedge identity(S2, T2) \rightarrow zero\_d(b/[S1, S2], b/[T1, T2])$
$identity(S1, T1) \wedge zero\_d(S2, T2) \rightarrow zero\_d(b/[S1, S2], b/[T1, T2])$
$zero\_d(d/[], t/[])$

$d\_zero(S1, T1) \wedge identity(S2, T2) \rightarrow d\_zero(a/[S1, S2], a/[T1, T2])$
$identity(S1, T1) \wedge d\_zero(S2, T2) \rightarrow d\_zero(a/[S1, S2], a/[T1, T2])$
$d\_zero(S1, T1) \wedge identity(S2, T2) \rightarrow d\_zero(b/[S1, S2], b/[T1, T2])$
$identity(S1, T1) \wedge d\_zero(S2, T2) \rightarrow d\_zero(b/[S1, S2], b/[T1, T2])$
$d\_zero(\emptyset/[], d/[])$

$identity(S1, T1) \wedge identity(S2, T2) \rightarrow identity(a/[S1, S2], a/[T1, T2])$
$identity(S1, T1) \wedge identity(S2, T2) \rightarrow identity(b/[S1, S2], b/[T1, T2])$
$identity(c/[], c/[])$
$identity(d/[], d/[])$
$identity(\emptyset/[], \emptyset/[])$
$identity(t/[], t/[]).$

Each of these relations relates pairs of trees in terms of their subtrees. Thus the first rule says that for all $S1, S2, T1, T2$, if tree $T1$ is a result of applying *subst* to $S1$ and $T2$ is a result of applying *identity* to $S2$, then $a/[T1, T2])$ is a result of applying *subst* to $a/[S1, S2]$. This claim is clearly true, and so our representation is a correct theory about the R-transducer defined above, but it has two shortcomings.

In the first place, this theory cannot be regarded as a complete representation of the R-transduction we defined above. Our "definitions" of the states provide sufficient but not necessary conditions.[6] In the case of grammars and automata, the "only if" is built into the standard treatment: a string is in the range of a transducer if *and only if* it can be derived from an input. To get this in the logical representation, we must provide it explicitly. It can be provided using Clark's (1978) method for "completing" a theory (discussed in §3.5, above), but it is often left out because it is not needed to derive certain consequences.

The second shortcoming of our initial representation is that the desired transduction has a much more concise representation, particularly if we want to extend the vocabulary. To define the same movement of d to $\emptyset$ over trees with larger alphabets, the size of the R-transducer specification would necessarily grow. Unsurprisingly, this transduction on trees can easily be formalized in logic in a much more concise fashion that treats most nodes similarly, regardless of the number of their branches. Rather than having separate rules that pass the *subst* state down each of a node's branches, we use some simple "list-processing" relations to define a single, general rule. The relation

$$select(Position, Seq, Element, Seq0)$$

holds when $Seq0$ is the sequence that results when the specified $Element$ is removed from the specified $Position$ of Seq:

$$select(Position, List, Selected, Remainder) \leftrightarrow \qquad\qquad (7.1.1)$$

$$
\begin{aligned}
(\quad & Position = s(0) \land \\
& List = [Selected | Remainder] \\
\lor \quad & \exists Head, Tail, Rest, Position1 \\
& \quad Position = s(s(Position1)) \land \\
& \quad List = [Head | Tail] \land \\
& \quad Remainder = [Head | Rest] \land \\
& \quad select(s(Position1), Tail, Selected, Rest) \\
).
\end{aligned}
$$

This relation can be used, in effect, to select a subtree, and then to insert a transformation of the subtree into the place from which it came.[7]

With the *select* predicate, we can define *subst*, intuitively, as the state that either transforms exactly one selected subtree by application of *subst*, or else transforms one subtree with *d_zero* and another with *zero_d*. The *identity* state leaves a tree unchanged, and so we do not need it:

$$
\begin{aligned}
subst(Tree0, Tree) \leftrightarrow \\
& \exists Node, Seq0, Seq, Position1, Selected1, RestSeq1 \\
& \quad Tree0 = Node/Seq0 \land \\
& \quad Tree = Node/Seq \land \\
& \quad select(Position1, Seq0, Selected1, RestSeq1) \land \\
& \quad (\quad \exists Transformed \\
& \qquad\quad subst(Selected1, Transformed) \land
\end{aligned}
$$

$$\qquad\qquad select(Position1, Seq, Transformed, RestSeq1)$$
$$\lor\quad \exists Position2, Selected2, RestSeq2$$
$$\exists Transformed1, Transformed2, Seq1$$
$$\qquad select(Position2, RestSeq1, Selected2, RestSeq2)\land$$
$$\qquad zero\_d(Selected1, Transformed1)\land$$
$$\qquad d\_zero(Selected2, Transformed2)\land$$
$$\qquad select(Position2, Seq1, Transformed2, RestSeq2)\land$$
$$\qquad select(Position1, Seq, Transformed1, Seq1)$$
$$)$$

$$zero\_d(Tree0, Tree)\leftrightarrow$$
$$(\quad \exists Node, T0, T0s, Seq, Position$$
$$\exists SelectedTree, RestSeq, Transformed$$
$$\qquad Tree0 = Node/[T0|T0s]\land$$
$$\qquad select(Position, [T0|T0s], SelectedTree, RestSeq)\land$$
$$\qquad zero\_d(SelectedTree, Transformed)\land$$
$$\qquad select(Position, Seq, Transformed, RestSeq)\land$$
$$\qquad Tree = Node/Seq$$
$$\lor\quad Tree0 = d/[]\land$$
$$\qquad Tree = t/[]$$
$$)$$

$$d\_zero(Tree0, Tree)\leftrightarrow$$
$$(\quad \exists Node, T0, T0s, Seq, Position$$
$$\exists SelectedTree, RestSeq, Transformed$$
$$\qquad Tree0 = Node/[T0|T0s]\land$$
$$\qquad select(Position, [T0|T0s], SelectedTree, RestSeq)\land$$
$$\qquad d\_zero(SelectedTree, Transformed)\land$$
$$\qquad select(Position, Seq, Transformed, RestSeq)\land$$
$$\qquad Tree = Node/Seq$$
$$\lor\quad Tree0 = \emptyset/[]\land$$
$$\qquad Tree = d/[]$$
$$).$$

Notice that this formalization does not mention any specific node labels except the three labels of leaf nodes that are involved in the transformation, and so the number of trees in the domain of the theory can be enlarged to any extent by the addition of new vocabulary (i.e. new node labels), and the definition of the transduction will remain correct.[8] It follows, as we would expect, that the gains in conciseness obtained by moving to this logical notation from the standard R-transducer notation can be arbitrarily large.[9]

7.2   Substitutions and adjunctions

Two types of applications of move-α are distinguished in *Barriers*: substitutions and adjunctions. A modest extension of the previous logical formulation of an R-transducer suffices to define substitutions. As the brief earlier discussion of substitution indicated, a substitution moves a constituent to an empty node, i.e. a linguistic category that dominates nothing and has no features — in particular, no index (cf. Chomsky, 1981, 46). A "trace" is left behind, but this is only an empty category with an index (cf. Chomsky, 1981, 23, 61). In Chomsky (1982) and in *Barriers*, traces really are empty, though they may of course have indices and other non-phonological features. Many of their particular properties are functionally determined according to their structural position. Empty noun phrases are assigned the feature *+pronominal* (Chomsky, 1986a, 16), and may be determined to have the features of *pro* or *PRO*. So a trace is an empty category that is not *+pronominal* and has an index.

A more surprising aspect of standard approaches to movement is that empty categories can move. An interplay of θ-theory and case theory forces a movement analysis of simple and exceptional passives like

John$_i$ was shot t$_i$.
John$_i$ was believed t$_i$ to be unsympathetic.

while a subject-controlled PRO analysis is motivated for

John wants PRO to win.

These same arguments motivate an analysis in which the controlled PRO has moved in structures like

John wants PRO$_i$ to be shot t$_i$.
John doesn't want PRO$_i$ to appear t$_i$ to be unsympathetic.

If we take the view that *PRO* is just a bare NP category with the features *+pronominal* and *+anaphoric*, then this movement involves nothing more than the movement of these features from one NP to another. That is, these features must be *removed* from one category, and given to the category that is the "landing site." In these cases the PRO gets a θ role in its original position, and must move (to a $\overline{\theta}$-position), not to be in a governed position that is assigned case, but on the contrary, to avoid being governed. Chomsky (1981, 330; 1986, 24) calls the features that remain with the trace category ϕ-features. These include person, number, gender, and case, but notably not the pronominal feature.

We also see the movement of empty categories in the derivation of certain relative clauses. It turns out that the treatment of relative clauses is considerably simplified by the assumption that relative clauses without wh-phrases contain empty +wh noun phrases. The notational convention is to indicate the position of such an empty "operator" with an "O". On this approach, we get parallel treatments for similar constructions like the following:

the linguists who$_i$ I mentioned t$_i$ disavow computational commitments
the linguists O$_i$ I mentioned t$_i$ disavow computational commitments

Once again, the indicated movement of the empty operator in the latter example is merely the movement of features from one empty node to another. Other examples are mentioned in Chomsky (1986a, 40; 1986b, 109).

In summary, we can describe substitutions as follows:

A node is *visible* to move-α iff it is maximal or minimal.

A *substitution* (i) replaces a constituent with a root *node* by the empty category *node$_i$*, where *node$_i$* is just the bare root with the ϕ features of *node* and an index i, and (ii) modifies an empty nonterminal leaf *node*1 by giving it the index i and all the features of *node*, and letting it dominate exactly the subtrees dominated by *node* (if any, and in order).

If we presume that the features given to the landing site *node*1 must be compatible with those already assigned, and that these features include those that define the syntactic category, then it follows that the root of the moved constituent and the landing site must both be of the same category. Since we will not treat syntactic category as a feature, however, this leaves open the possibility of substituting a constituent I into an empty C, unless that is explicitly ruled out by some other principle.

The extensions that we must make to the R-transducer are the following: any visible constituent (not just d) should be able to move into an "empty" position; the "empty" positions are not marked by $\emptyset$ but will be visible leaf nodes; the trace that is left behind is not some special symbol but is only the bare category with only its ϕ features and an index; and the resulting tree must be properly numbered, with identical occurrence numbers indicating adjunction structures. Since the occurrence numbers and indices may take any integer value, these extensions, strictly speaking, take us beyond the power of an R-transducer. In the logical specification, however, we can let our relations be parameterized by the moved category, adding an extra first argument to the tree-transforming relations to hold this parameter. Because our logical formulation is independent of the size of the domain of trees to which we apply the transformation, the formalization can remain essentially the same in other respects. To preserve the renumbering property, when part of an adjunction structure is moved, we renumber the segments in the moved constituent, passing a "renumbering" argument of the form $OldNumber/NewNumber$ in this case. One final, trivial addition: for the purposes of imposing special linguistic conditions on movements, it is useful to bring out the moved constituent and its "landing site" as separate arguments to the movement predicates.

The formalization is as follows:

$$substitute(Tree0, Tree, MRoot, Landing, Renumbering) \leftrightarrow \qquad (7.2.2)$$

$\exists Node, Seq0, Seq, Pos1, Selected1, RestSeq1$
$\quad Tree0 = Node/Seq0 \wedge$
$\quad Tree = Node/Seq \wedge$
$\quad select(Pos1, Seq0, Selected1, RestSeq1, Renumbering) \wedge$
$(\quad \exists Transformed$
$\qquad substitute(Selected1, Transformed, MRoot, Landing) \wedge$
$\qquad select(Pos1, Seq, Transformed, RestSeq1)$
$\vee \quad \exists Pos2, Selected2, RestSeq2, Moved$
$\qquad \exists Transformed1, Transformed2, Seq1$
$\qquad select(Pos2, RestSeq1, Selected2, RestSeq2) \wedge$
$\qquad zero\_cat(MRoot/Moved, Selected1, Transformed1, Renumbering) \wedge$
$\qquad cat\_zero(MRoot/Moved, Landing, Selected2, Transformed2) \wedge$
$\qquad select(Pos2, Seq1, Transformed2, RestSeq2) \wedge$
$\qquad select(Pos1, Seq, Transformed1, Seq1)$
$).$

The $MRoot$ and $Landing$ arguments can be used to impose the special linguistic requirement that the categories involved be visible, using the following relation:

$$subst\_conds(Moved, Landing) \leftrightarrow visible(Moved) \wedge \qquad (7.2.3)$$
$$visible(Landing)$$

$$visible(Node) \leftrightarrow maximal(Node) \vee minimal(Node). \qquad (7.2.4)$$

The predicate $subst\_conds$ will be used as a condition on the cases of $substitute$ that can count as instances of move-α.

The real work gets done by the following predicates, which are similar to $zero\_d$ and d_zero, except that the node dominating an empty trace is co-indexed with the moved constituent, and (all segments of) the root of a moved constituent are renumbered if necessary.[10]

$zero\_cat(Moved, Tree0, Tree, Renumbering) \leftrightarrow$ (7.2.5)

$\quad\quad\quad$ ($\quad\exists Node0, T0, T0s, Seq, Pos, Selected, RestSeq, Transformed$

$\quad\quad\quad\quad\quad\quad Tree0 = Node0/[T0|T0s] \wedge$

$\quad\quad\quad\quad\quad\quad select(Pos, [T0|T0s], Selected, RestSeq, Renumbering) \wedge$

$\quad\quad\quad\quad\quad\quad zero\_cat(Moved, Selected, Transformed, Renumbering) \wedge$

$\quad\quad\quad\quad\quad\quad select(Pos, Seq, Transformed, RestSeq) \wedge$

$\quad\quad\quad\quad\quad\quad Tree = Node0/Seq$

$\quad\quad\quad \vee \quad \exists L, C, N, F, Seq0, I, Node1, Node2, Seq2, Node$

$\quad\quad\quad\quad\quad\quad Tree0 = x(L, C, N, F)/Seq0 \wedge$

$\quad\quad\quad\quad\quad\quad feature(index : I, x(L, C, N, F), Node1) \wedge$

$\quad\quad\quad\quad\quad\quad renumber(Node1/Seq0, Node2/Seq2, Renumbering) \wedge$

$\quad\quad\quad\quad\quad\quad take\_features(Node1, Node) \wedge$

$\quad\quad\quad\quad\quad\quad Tree = Node/[] \wedge$

$\quad\quad\quad\quad\quad\quad Moved = Node2/Seq2$

$\quad\quad\quad$).

Like the simpler relations defined earlier, the axiom for *zero_cat* either transforms a subtree (the first disjunct), or else lets the current *Tree0* be the moved category (the second disjunct).

The axiom for placing the moved category back into the tree is defined as follows:

$cat\_zero(Moved, Landing, Tree0, Tree) \leftrightarrow$ (7.2.6)

$\quad\quad\quad$ ($\quad\exists Node, T0, T0s, Seq, Pos, Selected, RestSeq, Transformed$

$\quad\quad\quad\quad\quad\quad Tree0 = Node/[T0|T0s] \wedge$

$\quad\quad\quad\quad\quad\quad select(Pos, [T0|T0s], Selected, RestSeq) \wedge$

$\quad\quad\quad\quad\quad\quad cat\_zero(Moved, Landing, Selected, Transformed) \wedge$

$\quad\quad\quad\quad\quad\quad select(Pos, Seq, Transformed, RestSeq) \wedge$

$\quad\quad\quad\quad\quad\quad Tree = Node/Seq$

$\quad\quad\quad \vee \quad \exists I, Node0, Node1, Node2, Seq$

$\quad\quad\quad\quad\quad\quad Tree0 = Node0/[] \wedge$

$\quad\quad\quad\quad\quad\quad feature(index : I, Node0, Node1) \wedge$

$\quad\quad\quad\quad\quad\quad Moved = Node2/Seq \wedge$

$\quad\quad\quad\quad\quad\quad feature(index : I, Node2, Node2) \wedge$

$\quad\quad\quad\quad\quad\quad put\_features(Node1, Node2, Landing) \wedge$

$\quad\quad\quad\quad\quad\quad Tree = Landing/Seq$

$\quad\quad\quad$).

When the axiom for *cat_zero* applies to transform the current tree *Tree0*, an unexpanded node, we require that it be co-indexed with the moved category using the predicate *feature* that was defined in §6.2.

The predicate *take_features* relates node labels α, β where β is the result of removing all features except ϕ features from α:

$$take\_features(A, B) \leftrightarrow \exists L, C, N \qquad (7.2.7)$$
$$\begin{aligned}
(\quad & A = x(L, C, N, []) \wedge \\
& B = x(L, C, N, []) \\
\vee \quad & \exists E, F0, F \\
& A = x(L, C, N, [E|F0]) \wedge \\
& take\_features(x(L, C, N, F0), x(L, C, N, F)) \wedge \\
& (\quad phi(E) \wedge B = x(L, C, N, [E|F]) \\
& \vee \quad \neg phi(E) \wedge B = x(L, C, N, F) \\
&) \\
).
\end{aligned}$$

It simplifies the formalization to let the ϕ features be *all* the features that can be left behind on a trace, so we include the index and finite features:

$$phi(E) \leftrightarrow \exists Val (\quad E = person : Val \qquad (7.2.8)$$
$$\begin{aligned}
\vee \quad & E = number : Val \\
\vee \quad & E = case : Val \\
\vee \quad & E = wh : Val \\
\vee \quad & E = index : Val \\
\vee \quad & E = th : Val \\
\vee \quad & E = finite : Val \\
).
\end{aligned}$$

The predicate *put_features* relates node labels α, β, γ where γ is the result of giving α certain features of β. For example, we do not want to give the moved category the θ-marking features of the original site, which are represented by a θ-grid $th : Value$ as explained in §8.4 (Chomsky, 1986, 72). Let's call the features that are to be placed into the new position ψ-features:

$$put\_features(A, B, G) \leftrightarrow \exists L, C, N \qquad (7.2.9)$$
$$\begin{aligned}
(\quad & B = x(L, C, N, []) \wedge \\
& A = G \\
\vee \quad & \exists E, F, A1
\end{aligned}$$

$$B = x(L, C, N, [E|F]) \wedge$$
$$(\quad psi(E) \wedge$$
$$feature(E, A, A1) \wedge$$
$$put\_features(A1, x(L, C, N, F), G)$$
$$\vee \quad \neg psi(E) \wedge$$
$$put\_features(A, x(L, C, N, F), G)$$
$$)$$
$$)$$

$$psi(E) \leftrightarrow \exists Val (\quad E = person : Val \tag{7.2.10}$$
$$\vee \quad E = number : Val$$
$$\vee \quad E = case : Val$$
$$\vee \quad E = wh : Val$$
$$\vee \quad E = index : Val$$
$$\vee \quad E = pronominal : Val$$
$$\vee \quad E = anaphoric : Val$$
$$).$$

This completes the formalization of substitutions.

Turning now to adjunction (Chomsky, 1986a, 6), we can informally state the rule as follows:

> An *adjunction* replaces a visible constituent *node/seq* by the indexed empty category $node_i/[]$, and changes some subtree *tree*1 with root *node*1 to *node*1 /[$node_i$/seq, tree1] (left-adjunction) or to *node*1/[tree1, $node_i$/seq] (right-adjunction). Furthermore, if *node*1 is maximal then it must be a nonargument.[11]

Since adjunction to empty nodes is not explicitly ruled out in the barriers framework, this rule allows, for example, the adjunction of *cat/seq* to an unexpanded maximal projection *xp*/[] to produce *xp*/[cat/seq, xp/[]] or *xp*/[xp/[], cat/seq]. Perhaps this should be ruled out in some way. For example, Emonds (1985, §3.5) has suggested that adjunctions to empty nodes should be given a special treatment, namely, they should be substitutions. We do not make this assumption here.

The formalization of the adjunction relation is slightly more complex than substitution. We can use *zero_cat*, defined as above, but an additional complexity comes from the fact that the adjunction may be to the root node of the input tree, and from the fact that we allow both left and right adjunction. Our definition of *adjoin* has a disjunction on its right side. The first disjunct selects a subtree within which an adjunction is performed, and the second covers the case where the root is the lowest node dominating the adjunction (i.e. the lowest node dominating both the moved constituent and the landing site). In this latter case, in effect, we select a subtree from which a category is removed (or "zeroed") leaving a trace; we replace that subtree in its original position; and then we give the resulting tree to *adjoin_cat*. The *adjoin_cat* relation adjoins the removed constituent to some node that is distinct from its original site. This allows adjunction to the root. And, as in the case of substitutions, the root segments of moved constituents must sometimes be renumbered, and this renumbering is indicated by a *Renumbering* argument:[12]

$$adjoin(Tree0, Tree, MRoot, LRoot, Renumbering) \leftrightarrow \qquad\qquad (7.2.11)$$

$\exists Node, Seq0, Seq, Pos, Selected, RestSeq, Transformed$
$\quad Tree0 = Node/Seq0 \land$
$\quad Tree = Node/Seq \land$
$\quad select(Pos, Seq0, Selected, RestSeq) \land$
$\quad (\qquad adjoin(Selected, Transformed, MRoot, LRoot, Renumbering) \land$
$\qquad\quad select(Pos, Seq, Transformed, RestSeq)$
$\quad \lor \quad \exists Seq1, Moved$
$\qquad\qquad zero\_cat(MRoot/Moved, Selected, Transformed, Renumbering) \land$
$\qquad\qquad select(Pos, Seq1, Transformed, RestSeq) \land$
$\qquad\qquad adjoin\_cat(MRoot/Moved, LRoot, Node/Seq1, Node/Seq, Renumbering)$
$\quad).$

As in the case of substitution, we test later (in the definition of *moveA*) to ensure that the additional linguistic restrictions on adjunction, as formalized by *adjoin_conds*, are satisfied. The question of whether a node is in non-argument position is a question about the structural position of the node in the tree. We assume an axiomatization of a binary predicate *argument(Node, Tree)* which will hold when *Node* is in a structural position that can receive a θ-role (Chomsky, 1986a, 6; 1981, 47). As we will see below, Chomsky extends θ-marking to include marking of VP by I, but this is not intended to indicate that VP is to be regarded as an argument of the I that θ-marks it. Rather, this is a special case of θ-marking of a non-argument. Adjunction to VP is permitted. So we tentatively adopt the following axiomatization:

$$argument(Node, T) \leftrightarrow \exists C, N, F, Node0 \qquad\qquad (7.2.12)$$

$\qquad\qquad (\qquad Node = x(s(s(0)), C, N, F) \land$
$\qquad\qquad\quad (\ C = n \lor C = c \lor C = i \lor C = a\ ) \land$
$\qquad\qquad\quad directly\_th\_governs(Node0, Node, T)$
$\qquad\qquad \lor \quad specifier(Node, x(s(s(0)), i, N, F), T)$
$\qquad\qquad).$

This assumes that the arguments in a tree T are directly θ-marked categories other than VP or else they are specifiers of I. Notice that argumenthood is a relation between a node and the tree containing that node. It should hold of an NP or CP only if it is in an appropriate structural position (the sister of a θ-assigning category). Consequently, the conditions on adjunction must supply the tree as an argument:

$$adjoin\_conds(Moved, Landing, Tree) \leftrightarrow visible(Moved) \wedge \qquad\qquad (7.2.13)$$
$$visible(Landing) \wedge$$
$$\neg argument(Landing, Tree).$$

The $adjoin\_cat$ relation can be defined as follows:

$$adjoin\_cat(Moved, Landing, Tree0, Tree, Renumbering) \leftrightarrow \qquad\qquad (7.2.14)$$

$\exists L, C, N, F, Seq0, Seq$
$\quad Tree0 = x(L, C, N, F)/Seq0 \wedge$
$\quad Tree = x(L, C, N, F)/Seq \wedge$
$\quad (\quad \exists Pos, Selected, RestSeq, Transformed$
$\qquad select(Pos, Seq0, Selected, RestSeq) \wedge$
$\qquad adjoin\_cat(Moved, Landing, Selected, Transformed, Renumbering) \wedge$
$\qquad select(Pos, Seq, Transformed, RestSeq)$
$\quad \vee \quad \exists L1, C1, N1, F1, Seq1, N2$
$\qquad Moved = x(L1, C1, N1, F1)/Seq1 \wedge$
$\qquad newnumber(Renumbering, N2) \wedge$
$\qquad (\quad Seq = [x(L1, C1, N2, F1)/Seq1, Tree0]$
$\qquad \vee \quad Seq = [Tree0, x(L1, C1, N2, F1)/Seq1]$
$\qquad) \wedge$
$\qquad Landing = Tree0$
$\quad).$

An application of move-α is either a substitution or an adjunction, so we can easily define the corresponding relation $moveA$. To assure that the nodes of the output tree are appropriately numbered, we find a new number for renumbering in case that is needed with the predicate $new\_occurrence\_no$:

$$moveA(Tree0, Tree) \leftrightarrow \exists Moved, Landing, Renumbering \qquad\qquad (7.2.15)$$
$$new\_occurrence\_no(Renumbering) \wedge$$
$$(\quad substitute(Tree0, Tree, Moved, Landing, Renumbering) \wedge$$
$$subst\_conds(Moved, Landing)$$
$$\vee \quad adjoin(Tree0, Tree, Moved, Landing, Renumbering) \wedge$$

$$adjoin\_conds(Moved, Landing, Tree)$$
).

Now we are in a position to define a relation $moveAn$ which holds between two trees just in case the second tree is a result of applying move-α to the first tree n times ($n \geq 0$):

$$moveAn(Tree0, Tree) \leftrightarrow (\quad Tree = Tree0 \qquad\qquad (7.2.16)$$
$$\vee \quad \exists Tree1$$
$$moveA(Tree0, Tree1) \wedge$$
$$moveAn(Tree1, Tree)$$
$$).$$

It is interesting to note that even if we placed a finite bound on our node occurrence numbers and indices, in which case the set of node labels would be finite, the relation $moveAn$ could not be represented as an R-transduction. Consider the R-transducer defined above which substituted a leaf d for a leaf $\emptyset$. That transducer cannot be modified in such a way as to allow all substitutions of d for $\emptyset$ while blocking derivations in which the number of substitutions of d for 0 is not the same as the number of substitutions of t for d:

$$(subst, a/[b/[d/[], d/[]], b/[\emptyset/[], \emptyset/[]]]) \Rightarrow^* \quad a/[b/[t/[], t/[]], b/[d/[], d/[]]]$$
$$(subst, a/[b/[d/[], d/[]], b/[\emptyset/[], \emptyset/[]]]) \not\Rightarrow^* \quad a/[b/[d/[], t/[]], b/[d/[], d/[]]].$$

This is an easy and unsurprising consequence of the pumping lemma for (finite-state) R-transducers.[13] It may turn out, however, that one of the more constrained versions of move-α is an R-transduction.

7.3 Preliminary tests and discoveries

Our formalization of move-α is complete. Our axioms allow us to prove that the following two trees, in the order shown, are related by $substitute$, and hence also by $moveA$ and $moveAn$. In other words, the second tree is derived from the first by one substitution step (indicated by an arrow) in Figure 7.2. Here and throughout we show the node labels of the tree in enough detail to let the proof of the result go through once the abbreviations have been undone into the proper x notation. That is, when the terms t_1 and t_2 corresponding to these trees are used, we can actually deduce $moveA(t_1, t_2)$ from the axiomatization provided above.

The two trees of Figure 7.3 are related by two adjunction steps (and hence by $moveAn$ but not by $moveA$): It would now be a trivial matter to formalize a well-formedness

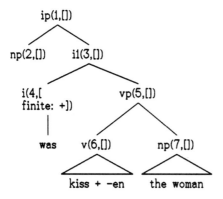

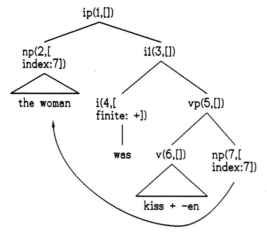

Figure 7.2
Trees related by *substitute* and *moveA*

condition like the following: for every SS structure *ss*, there is some D-structure *ds* such that *moveAn(ds, ss)*.

It should be clear that the nice examples displayed in these figures have been chosen from a proliferation of unwanted movements. For example, the fact that the quantified NPs adjoin to IP rather than to a higher CP accords with the suggestions of Chomsky (1986a, 5) and May (1985, 18), but this is not yet required by any of our principles. In fact, Chomsky (1986a, 32) suggests that, in the *Barriers* framework, the sort of movement illustrated by the last example should not be regarded as simply another instance of move-α, but should be treated as an application of a special rule which applies at LF and

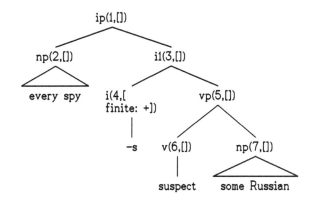

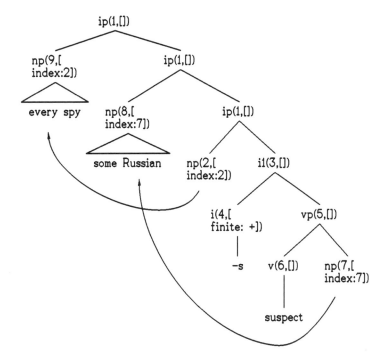

Figure 7.3
Trees related by *moveAn*

which is not subject to all of the restrictions that apply to move-α, such as subjacency.[14] It is important to keep in mind that the formalization does not know anything about move-α except what we have captured in the axioms, and so it does not yet know about subjacency and other restrictions. As we will see in §9, our formalization of subjacency is modular, leaving the axioms for *moveA* essentially untouched. Consequently, as this last example shows, if LF movement is not subject to subjacency, it still may be formalized using our relation *moveA*. We can get LF movement simply by using the *moveA* relation restricted with different conditions.

An automatic theorem prover is an excellent tool for proliferating unwanted and sometimes unanticipated consequences. Consider the trees in Figure 7.3 again. To establish that these trees are related by *moveAn*, we establish that there is an intermediate tree related to the first by adjunction of $np(7, \ldots)$ to the root, and then that this intermediate tree is related to the second displayed tree by adjunction of $np(2, \ldots)$ to the root of the intermediate tree. However, after the first step, the theorem prover reveals a number of other possible adjunction sites, and some of them are surprising. For example, the intermediate tree has two nodes with identical labels $ip(1, [])$. Nothing in the formalization blocks adjunction to the non-root $ip(1, [])$, even though this site is inside an adjunction structure — it is only one segment of the category, enclosed inside another segment of that category. Surprisingly, this sort of movement of part of an adjunction structure has been proposed in some theories, although it conflicts with the intuition that segment structure is unanalyzable. An example comes up in the discussion of Pollock (1989) in §12, and similar ideas appear in Chomsky (1989), Roberts (1991) and elsewhere. If this kind of movement is not excluded, then the derived tree in Figure 7.3 can be derived by first moving $np(7 \ldots)$ and then adjoining $np(2, \ldots)$ to the non-root segment of $ip(1, [])$.

Another surprising type of adjunction allowed by the proposed formalization which the theorem prover often finds involves adjoining to a particular category several times. For example, $np(2, \ldots)$ can be adjoined to $ip(1, [])$ in a first step, and then it can be adjoined to its immediate ancestor $ip(1, [])$ again leaving a trace and producing another segment, and so on. And of course, this kind of movement can be combined with previous one. For example, nothing blocks taking the tree of Figure 7.3 and performing another adjunction which moves only the second segment of $ip(1, [])$, adjoining it to the first segment. The existence of such derivations has computational and empirical consequences, as one would expect. They will be discussed in §14.

Chapter 8

Government and barriers

Les faits les plus innocents, les mieux liés à leurs causes
paraissent se subordonner à des relations souterraines
dont notre âme aurait fourni le tracé. — *Joë Bousquet*

When we introduced movements in §5, we considered first the view that they were restricted by relative clause boundaries, and then the view that they were restricted to stay within two "bounding nodes." We did not come to anything like an adequate account, but it is clear that there is some sort of locality restriction on movement relations. Another stricter locality condition on linguistic relations comes into play through the concept of government. This relation is a slight extension of the relation that holds between a head and its complements. Before formalizing government, we will introduce it in the context of case theory. As we will see, case is assigned only to governed categories. Clearly, the relation between nodes that can be related by movement is not so local as the relation between a node and those to which it can assign case, but Chomsky proposes to unify these two notions of locality with the notion of a barrier. He says,

> The intuitive idea is that certain categories in certain configurations are barriers to government and to movement (application of the general rule move-α)...We might...expect that one barrier suffices to block government, whereas more than one barrier inhibits movement, perhaps in a graded manner. (1986a, 1)

We briefly introduce case theory, θ-theory and government, and then formalize a preliminary notion of barrier that might play this role.

8.1   Introducing case theory and government

The effort to find a minimal set of basic universal principles of grammar has led to substantial changes in the formulation of grammatical principles. There has been a shift away from specific movement rules to the very general movement relations discussed in the previous section, because it appears that the specific restrictions on movement that used to be coded into a large number of fairly complex rules could be captured by independently motivated principles. The independent well-formedness principles that play this role have themselves undergone considerable modification, becoming progressively simpler and more descriptively adequate. For example, Chomsky and Lasnik (1977) proposed filters on S-structures like the following. No well-formed S-structure contains an overt, lexical NP followed by a tenseless VP:

$$* \; [NP_{+phonetic} \; to \; VP]$$

This rules out cases like the following:

Bill to win is exciting.
I tried Bill to win.
What I expect is Bill to win.

There are exceptions to this principle, as in

For Bill to win is exciting.
John expects Bill to win.

So Chomsky and Lasnik proposed that the filter be qualified as follows,

$$* \; [NP_{+phonetic} \; to \; VP] \; \text{unless} \; P\text{\_\_\_\_} \; \text{or} \; V\text{\_\_\_\_}$$

This inelegant filter has been replaced with a set of case assignment rules which have certain parameters of language-specific variation, together with a stronger case filter: a structure that contains an overt NP that has not been assigned case is not well-formed:[1]

$$* \; NP_{+phonetic, -case}$$

This rule is now called the *case filter*, and its application is usually extended to *chains*, i.e., to NPs and their coindexed traces: every NP chain must have a case marked NP position as its first element. Since *for* assigns case in English, we can account for the following contrast:

Bill to win is exciting.
For Bill to win is exciting.

In the second string, but not the first, *Bill* is assigned case.[2]

Turning to the case assignment rules, we will assume that case is always assigned under government. That is, a category can assign case only to categories that it governs. The various structures in which case assignment takes place in English then give us a first indication of the wanted notion of government. A verb assigns case to its direct

Figure 8.1
Case assignment to object

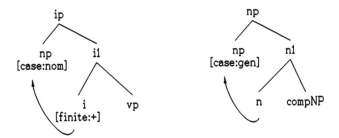

Figure 8.2
Case assignment to subject

object, and a preposition assigns accusative or oblique case to its object in the structures, as shown in Figure 8.1. Inflection assigns nominative case to its subject (i.e., the NP specifier of its maximal projection), and a noun can similarly assign genitive case to the NP specifier of its maximal projection, as in Figure 8.2. And finally, a verb that selects an IP complement can assign case to the subject of the embedded IP, as in

John expects Bill to win.

In this case, the embedded clause has no tense, and so it does not assign nominative case to its subject; that must be done by the higher verb. So we have case assignment in the

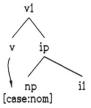

Figure 8.3
Case assignment to embedded subject

structure of Figure 8.3. The previous structure should be contrasted with the following, in which we would like to avoid case assignment across the CP and IP:

* I wonder [$_{cp}$how [$_{ip}$Bill to win]].

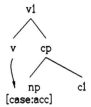

Figure 8.4
Case assignment to embedded specifier of CP

We find other examples where we want to allow government and case assignment across a CP, however. For example, Kayne's (1975, §5) arguments motivate the following analyses in French:

* Je crois [$_{cp}$ Jean être le plus intelligent de tous].   (a)
    (I believe Jean to be the most intelligent of all)

[Quel garçon]$_i$ crois-tu [$_{cp}$[$_{np}$t$_i$] [$_{c1}$t$_i$ être le plus intelligent de tous]]?   (b)
    (Which boy do you believe to be the most intelligent of all)

In (b), the wh-phrase is moved in two steps to sentence-initial position, leaving a trace in the position of the specifier of CP. Jean cannot receive case from the infinitive in (a), resulting in a violation of the case filter, but the specifier of CP can receive accusative case from the verb in (b). Thus we can use case theory and case assignment under government to account for the difference between (a) and (b) if we assume that the specifier of CP is governed by the verb.[3] Case theory requires movement in structures like b, just as it does in the more familiar English structures like

John$_i$ seems [$_{cp}$ t$_i$ to be intelligent].
* It seems [$_{cp}$John to be intelligent].

So Kayne's examples show another structure in which case assignment can occur, as shown in Figure 8.4. Clearly, defining a notion of government that holds in all of these configurations, and appropriately fails to hold in others, is a delicate matter.

It is worth mentioning one further government configuration that comes from binding theory. Binding theory requires that the empty NP PRO be ungoverned, that it have

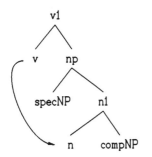
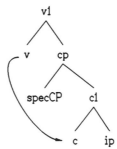

Figure 8.5
Government of heads of embedded NP and CP

no governing category. This feature of PRO is used in an analysis by Belletti and Rizzi (1981) of the possible positions of PRO and the Italian clitic pronoun *ne*. This clitic pronoun cannot occur in preverbal subject position, though PRO can:

Tre settimane passano rapidamente
    (Three weeks pass quickly)
Tre PRO passano rapidamente
    (Three PRO pass quickly)
* *Tre ne passano rapidamente*
    (Three (of them) pass quickly)

The clitic can occur in object position but PRO cannot:

* *Gianni trascorrerà tre PRO a Milano*
    (Gianni will spend three PRO in Milan)
Gianni ne trascorrerà tre a Milano
    (Gianni will spend three (of them) in Milan)

Belletti and Rizzi show that this asymmetry and a range of other data can be elegantly captured if we assume underlying structures like

$[_{ip}[_{np}$ *Tre PRO*] *passano rapidamente*]
* $[_{ip}$ *Gianni trascorrerà* $[_{np}$*tre PRO*] *a Milano*]

and if we assume that the latter is ruled out because the verb governs the head of the object NP. In the former structure, of course, PRO is ungoverned and the structure is grammatical. Other arguments also suggest that the head of a NP or CP can be governed from the outside, and so we have government in structures like the ones in Figure 8.5.

    Constraints on government come from other parts of the theory as well. Whereas case theory serves primarily to determine the distribution of NPs, *θ-theory* determines the arguments of the predicates.[4] A head assigns θ-roles to, or θ-marks, its arguments (the *agent, theme,...*), according to lexically specified requirements. In fact, every subcategorized position must be θ-marked. Furthermore, we impose the following constraint at all levels of representation:

> (θ-criterion) Every θ-role must be assigned to a chain, and each chain must have exactly one θ-role assignment.

Subcategorization and θ-marking of complements are also presumed to hold under government. We will not attempt to motivate θ-theory here, but it appears in the formal account of barriers and government which we will now develop. This notion of government, defined in terms of barriers, properly handles all of the structures we have considered, and the barriers will also play a role in bounding theory, as we will see in the next section.

8.2   Domination, c-command, and m-command

We must begin by defining a number of important, linguistically motivated relations between nodes in a tree. We will present many of the definitions as they appear in the text of *Barriers* to illustrate how direct our formalization is.

Following May (1985), Chomsky (1986a, 7) introduces a sense of *domination* that gives a special treatment to adjunction structures, which were mentioned in §6.4:

> α is dominated by β only if it is dominated by every segment of β.

In this definiens, "dominated" means the usual sense of domination, which we have formalized with the (irreflexive) relation *ancestor* in §4.2.1. We can formalize the new sense of domination for trees with segments very easily:

$$dominates(B, A, Tree) \leftrightarrow \qquad\qquad\qquad\qquad\qquad\qquad\qquad\qquad\qquad (8.2.1)$$

$$\forall Segment$$
$$Segment = B \rightarrow ancestor(Segment, A, Tree).$$

(Chomsky, 1986a, 8) uses this notion in place of the standard domination in the definition of c-command (Reinhart, 1976) and Aoun and Sportiche's (1983) variation on the idea for maximal rather than branching categories:

> α c-commands β only if α does not dominate β and every branching category (i.e. every category with at least two constituents) σ that dominates α dominates β.

α m-commands β only if α does not dominate β and every maximal category σ that dominates α dominates β.

$$c\_commands(A, B, Tree) \leftrightarrow \qquad\qquad\qquad\qquad\qquad\qquad (8.2.2)$$
$$\neg dominates(A, B, Tree) \wedge$$
$$\forall Sigma, T1, T2, Ts$$
$$(\ subtree(Sigma/[T1, T2|Ts], Tree) \wedge$$
$$dominates(Sigma, A, Sigma/[T1, T2|Ts])$$
$$\rightarrow dominates(Sigma, B, Sigma/[T1, T2|Ts])\ )$$

$$m\_commands(A, B, Tree) \leftrightarrow \qquad\qquad\qquad\qquad\qquad\qquad (8.2.3)$$
$$\neg dominates(A, B, Tree) \wedge$$
$$\forall Sigma$$
$$(\ dominates(Sigma, A, Tree) \wedge maximal(Sigma)$$
$$\rightarrow dominates(Sigma, B, Tree)\ ).$$

Note that this allows a node to m-command itself, and it allows the situation in which α m-commands β and α is dominated by β. Chomsky (1986a, 92n11) does not rule these cases out in the text, though he notes that the definitions could easily be modified to rule them out if necessary.

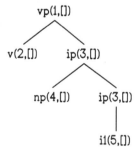

Figure 8.6
A tree with an adjunction

In treating adjunction structures, Chomsky (1986a, 9) also uses the related notion of exclusion: "α excludes β if no segment of α dominates β". We represent this as follows:

$$excludes(A, B, Tree) \leftrightarrow \neg \exists Segment \tag{8.2.4}$$
$$Segment = A \wedge$$
$$ancestor(Segment, B, Tree).$$

This definition gives the intended treatment to the example shown in Figure 8.6. Node $ip(3, [])$ does not exclude $np(4, [])$, but $np(4, [])$ excludes $ip(3, [])$. Node $v(2, [])$ excludes and is excluded by both $ip(3, [])$ and $np(4, [])$.

We also define a special notion of immediate domination between maximal projections, "so that σ immediately dominates δ in this sense even if a nonmaximal projection intervenes." (Chomsky, 1986a, 14-15)

$$imm\_dominates(S, D, Tree) \leftrightarrow maximal(S) \wedge \tag{8.2.5}$$
$$maximal(D) \wedge$$
$$dominates(S, D, Tree) \wedge$$
$$\neg \exists Max$$
$$maximal(Max) \wedge$$
$$ancestor(S, Max, Tree) \wedge$$
$$ancestor(Max, D, Tree).$$

8.3   Binding

Binding theory will not be developed here, but we will make use of some of the most basic concepts. In particular, the following notion is fundamental:

 α binds β if α c-commands β and α and β have the same index.

This notion is often restricted to "local binding:"

 α locally binds β iff α binds β, and there is no γ such that α binds γ and γ binds β. (cf. Chomsky, 1981, 59)

In the style that is by now familiar, we represent these notions as follows, adding a condition to make binding irreflexive:

$$binds(A, B, T) \leftrightarrow \neg A = B \wedge \tag{8.3.6}$$
$$\exists I \ feature(index : I, A, A) \wedge$$
$$feature(index : I, B, B) \wedge$$
$$c\_commands(A, B, T)$$

$$locally\_binds(A, B, T) \leftrightarrow binds(A, B, T) \wedge \tag{8.3.7}$$
$$\neg \exists G$$

$$binds(A, G, T) \land$$
$$binds(G, B, T).$$

Notice that the inequalities are necessary because every node c-commands itself. In Chapter 9 we will make use of the fact that move-α leaves a trail of traces that locally bind each other, and this allows us to read the derivational history from the structures that result.

8.4   Subcategorization and θ-marking

Since CP and IP appear to act as barriers only sometimes, as we noted above, Chomsky proposes an analysis that makes barrierhood a relational notion: a node can be a barrier either intrinsically or by standing in an appropriate relation to another node. In particular, a CP is not an intrinsic barrier but can "inherit" barrierhood from IP. As we will see, a node that is θ-marked by a lexical head cannot be an intrinsic barrier either, but can still inherit barrierhood. Our formalization of these notions can remain very close to the text of *Barriers*.

Chomsky (1986a, 13) says that "a zero-level category α *directly θ-marks β* only if β is the complement of α in the sense of X-bar theory," so for this notion we are not interested in the "external" θ-positions. The "internal" θ-positions are exactly the subcategorized positions, and since the θ-criterion applies at D-structure, these will be exactly the complements. But Chomsky identifies them as the *sister* nodes that are θ-marked, where "α and β are sisters if they are dominated by the same lexical projections:"

$$sisters(A, B, Tree) \leftrightarrow \forall S \; lexical(S) \rightarrow$$
$$(\; dominates(S, A, Tree) \leftrightarrow \; dominates(S, B, Tree) \;).$$

As Chomsky notes, according to this definition a VP is a sister of its subject, even though the VP but not the subject NP is dominated by I1. However, the head of the VP is not a sister of the subject, and so θ-marking in this case is indirect, mediated through the VP. This latter, indirect association is not relevant in the definition of a barrier.

We can now distinguish the θ-marked nodes that are sisters in this sense, where the θ-markers are heads or maximal projections (Chomsky, 1986a, 13). We need to make some assumptions about θ-role assignment here, but since these are not developed in *Barriers*, we will keep them to a minimum. It will be convenient to adopt an approach based on the suggestions of Stowell (1981, §6.1.4). We assume that θ-marking heads carry "θ-grids" which are an unordered set of roles, one for each subcategorized argument. Since the θ-criterion requires that each θ-role is assigned to exactly one argument, Stowell suggests that the assignment be regarded as a "slot" which can hold the index of the category or chain that plays the role. To implement this idea, we will use an ordered representation, but where the order indicates not the order of the arguments in the tree, but codes the role assigned. For the syntactic theories considered here, it actually does not matter what these roles are. We could say that the first is the external θ-role if there is one (typically the agent), the second is the theme, and so on. This matter deserves careful attention, but is not relevant to *Barriers*. (It comes up again in §13.) So for present purposes it suffices to represent θ-grids with terms of the form $th : [Index_1, \ldots, Index_n]$, where each $Index_i$ is the index of the appropriate argument in the tree. This notation suppresses the specification of the particular role that is assigned to each argument, as well as the subcategorization requirements on each argument. It would of course be a simple matter to encode additional information.

The particular case of θ-marking which is especially relevant to *Barriers* is "direct θ-marking":

α directly θ-marks β only if α and β are sisters. (Chomsky, 1986a, 14)

So, as mentioned above, a verb directly θ-marks its complements but not its external subject. Chomsky (1986a, 20,92n19,62) extends θ-marking to the category I, assuming that it θ-marks its complement VP.

With this notation for θ-grids, direct θ-marking can be defined as follows:

$directly\_th\_marks(A, B, Tree) \leftrightarrow sisters(A, B, Tree) \wedge$
$\exists Theta, I$
$feature(th : Theta, A, A) \wedge$
$feature(index : I, B, B) \wedge$
$member(I, Theta).$

One further special case of θ-marking is distinguished, direct θ-marking by a lexical category, which Chomsky (1986a, 15) calls θ-government:

α θ-governs β iff α is a zero-level category that θ-marks β, and α, β are sisters.

This idea is extended to specifiers and heads of the θ-governed categories in the following definition (Chomsky, 1986a, 24):[5]

α L-marks β iff α is a lexical category that θ-governs γ and $\beta = \gamma$, β is the head of γ, or β is the specifier of γ.

The formal rendering of these notions is transparent:

$th\_governs(A, B, Tree) \leftrightarrow minimal(A) \wedge$ (8.4.8)
$directly\_th\_marks(A, B, Tree)$

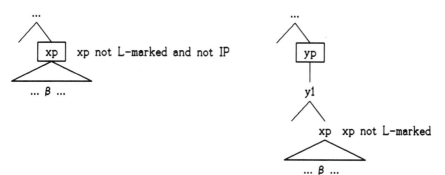

Figure 8.7
Barriers for β

$$l\_marks(A, B, Tree) \leftrightarrow lexical(A) \land \tag{8.4.9}$$
$$\exists G \ th\_governs(A, G, Tree)\land$$
$$(\quad B = G$$
$$\lor \quad head\_xp(B, G, Tree)$$
$$\lor \quad specifier(B, G, Tree)$$
$$).$$

These simple structural notions play a fundamental role in the theory of government. Chomsky (1986a, 15) suggests that θ-marking can be regarded as the "core case" of government.

8.5 Blocking categories, barriers, and government

We need to give special treatment to IP, so Chomsky (1986a, 14) defines barriers in terms of blocking categories (BCs) as follows:

> σ is a BC for β iff (σ is maximal and) σ is not L-marked and σ dominates β.

σ is a barrier for β iff either
(a) σ immediately dominates δ and δ is a BC for β, or
(b) σ is a BC for β and $\sigma \neq ip$.

In case (a) σ is a barrier by inheritance; in case (b) σ is an intrinsic barrier. Our formalization is again transparent:

156

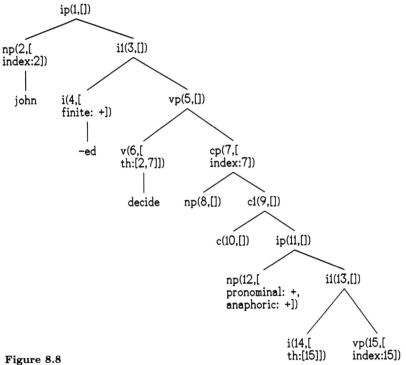

Figure 8.8
A tree with barriers

$$blocking\_cat(S, B, Tree) \leftrightarrow maximal(S) \land \qquad (8.5.10)$$
$$\neg \exists L \; l\_marks(L, S, Tree)$$
$$dominates(S, B, Tree)$$

$$barrier(S, B, Tree) \leftrightarrow (\quad \exists D \qquad\qquad\qquad (8.5.11)$$
$$imm\_dominates(S, D, Tree) \land$$
$$blocking\_cat(D, B, Tree)$$
$$\lor \quad blocking\_cat(S, B, Tree) \land$$
$$\neg \exists N, F \;\; S = x(s(s(0)), i, N, F)$$
$$).$$

The cases of inherent barriers and barriers by inheritance can be schematically depicted with the drawings in Figure 8.7. According to this definition, many nodes are barriers. Consider the following example from *Barriers* (Chomsky, 1986a, 11):

John decided [$_{cp}$e [$_{ip}$PRO to [$_{vp}$see the movie]]].

Part of this structure can be represented as in Figure 8.8, in which the PRO appears as an empty node that is labeled +*pronominal* and +*anaphoric*. We can now prove that $cp(7, \ldots)$ is a barrier by inheritance for $np(12, [])$ but is not a barrier for $np(8, [])$ because it is L-marked by $v(6, \ldots)$. We use this result to allow *decided* to govern the empty specifier of $cp(7, [])$ but not *PRO*.

A preliminary definition of *government* can now be formulated in terms of barriers and exclusion (Chomsky, 1986a, 9):

> α governs β iff α m-commands β and there is no σ, σ a barrier for β, such that σ excludes α.

Again, we follow the text closely:

$$governs(A, B, Tree) \leftrightarrow m\_commands(A, B, Tree) \land \tag{8.5.12}$$
$$\neg \exists S$$
$$barrier(S, B, Tree) \land$$
$$excludes(S, A, Tree).$$

8.6 Preliminary tests of the formalization

We now consider whether we can prove the mentioned results concerning the government of noun phrases in the tree of Figure 8.8. Consider, in the first place, the sisterhood relations. Traditionally, the relation consists in having a common parent, but *Barriers* gives it a much more liberal meaning. When Chomsky introduces this notion, he observes that a subject NP in a clause is not a sister to the main verb in its D-structure position: the verb but not the subject will be dominated by VP. (If the verb raises to I, it will then be in the position of a sister, but it will have lost its θ-marking capability, as discussed in §9.2.) Chomsky also observes that if the verb has a CP complement, the IP will be a sister to the verb. He suggests that this will not be a problem since if the verb assigns its θ-role to the IP rather than the CP, there will be a θ-criterion violation. However, notice that in Figure 8.8, not only $ip(11, \ldots)$ but all of the following are sisters of $v(6, \ldots)$:

$v(6, [th : [2, 7]])$
$cp(7, [index : 7])$
$np(8, [])$
$c1(9, [])$
$c(10, [])$
$ip(11, [])$
$np(12, [pronominal : +, anaphoric : +])$

$i1(13, [])$
$i(14, [th : [15]])$
$vp(15, [index : 15])$.

This sisterhood is used only in the definition of direct θ-marking. That is, it is used to pick out those θ-marking configurations where a head θ-marks its complements. The interesting point to notice is that it does this by picking out a superset of the head-complement relations. This produces computational difficulties for standard proof methods, as will be discussed in §15.

Now consider direct θ-marking in Figure 8.8. It is easy to prove that $cp(7, [index : 7])$ is the only node that stands in the *directly_th_marks* relation to $v(6, \ldots)$, and it is the only node that stands in the *th_governs* relation to $v(6, \ldots)$. The notion of L-marking is more liberal, however, and so we have the following nodes in the *l_marks* relation to this node:

$cp(7, [index : 7])$
$np(8, [])$
$c(10, [])$.

Now the crucial question is: can we prove that *decided* governs the empty specifier of CP but not PRO in Figure 8.8 (Chomsky's, 1986a, example (21))? Yes, we can prove that $v(6, \ldots)$ governs $np(8, [])$ but not $np(12, \ldots)$. Consider the latter result. Following our definitions of these notions, it is easy to show that $v(6, \ldots)$ m-commands $np(12, \ldots)$. The problem is that there is an intervening barrier, that is, there is a barrier σ for $np(12, \ldots)$ that excludes $v(6, \ldots)$, namely $cp(7, [])$ itself. This can be seen by noting that $cp(7, [])$ immediately dominates $ip(11, [])$ and this node is a blocking category for $np(12, \ldots)$, since $ip(11, [])$ is not l-marked and dominates $np(12, \ldots)$.

Although $v(6, \ldots)$ does not govern the PRO, $np(12, \ldots)$, it is interesting to observe that this position is governed. In fact, it is governed by $np(8, [])$, $c(10, [])$, $np(12, \ldots)$, $i1(13, [])$, $i(14, [])$, and $vp(15, [])$. Every one of these nodes m-commands $np(12, \ldots)$. (Remember that m-command is reflexive, as Chomsky, 1986a, 92n11, notes.) Furthermore, the barriers for $np(12, \ldots)$ in this tree are $ip(1, [])$, $vp(5, [])$, and $cp(7, \ldots)$. These barriers all dominate the m-commanders of $np(12, \ldots)$, and hence none of these m-commanders is excluded by a barrier. It follows, then, that these m-commanders all govern $np(12, \ldots)$. A glance back at the definitions quoted from *Barriers* shows that this result is not the fault of the formalization. We cannot simply say any more that PRO must be ungoverned; we need a more restrictive characterization of this idea from binding theory.[6]

Returning to the simpler case assignment principles with which we began the chapter, we can see that $i(4, [])$ governs $np(2, [])$ in the tree of Figure 8.8, and so nominative case can be assigned under government. *PRO* cannot be assigned case for the reasons just mentioned, but this does not violate the case filter since *PRO* is phonetically null. Checking the structures considered in our introduction to case theory is a good exercise, showing for example that the verb governs the embedded subject in

John expects Bill to win.

but not in

* *I wonder [$_{cp}$how [$_{ip}$Bill to win]].*

Chapter 9

Structure preservation, head movement, and bounding

The building material cannot be removed very far away from certain structural, harmonic-tonal and melodic prototypes, so that the listener can assume an active part in the process of musical realization.
— *Paul Hindemith*

In natural languages, categories cannot simply be moved anywhere. This fact is captured in our theory by the interaction of move-α with other grammatical principles. Some of these principles can be formalized straightforwardly as predicates that are satisfied by trees. Others are not typically expressed as simple well-formedness conditions on single trees. In this section, we consider two principles of the latter sort: the "structure preserving constraint" (SPC) and "subjacency." We then impose a special restriction on head movement, a refinement of SPC called the "head movement constraint."

9.1   The structure-preserving hypothesis

SPC says roughly that transformations can only create structures that are well-formed at D-structure.[1] Although no explicit formulation of the SPC is presented in *Barriers*, Chomsky (1986a, §2) indicates that it should be used to restrict applications of move-α, and so it is worth considering how it could be represented in such a way that it could properly restrict our relation *moveAn*.

Consider substitutions first. Emonds, who originally proposed and investigated the SPC, has recently proposed that a substitution is structure preserving just in case the moved constituent and the landing site are the same category (Emonds, 1985, §3.5). For example, the trees of Figure 9.1 are related by our *substitute*, but not by a structure preserving substitution. We will tentatively adopt this condition on substitutions of maximal projections.[2] Only minimal projections can substitute for minimal projections, and although we need not always assume identity of category, these movements will be subject to special restrictions introduced in §9.2.

Now consider adjunctions. Adjunction, as defined in *Barriers* and in §5 above, is already restricted in that the landing site must be a maximal projection that is not an argument. The moved constituent (like all categories related by move-α) must be either

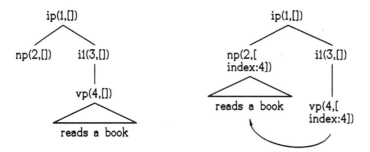

Figure 9.1
Non-structure preserving instance of *substitute*

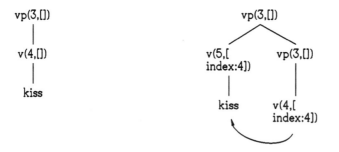

Figure 9.2
Non-structure preserving instance of *adjoin*

maximal or minimal, but it need not be the same category as the landing site. There
are some other adjunctions we want to rule out. For example, the trees in Figure 9.2 are
related by an adjunction step. To disallow cases like this, Chomsky (1986a, 73) proposes
that only maximal categories can adjoin to maximal categories. He suggests that this
restriction may follow from one or another binding principle, but does not develop an
account here, so we will impose this condition on adjunction explicitly.

Adding these restrictions to our formalization is trivial, since we need only make slight
extensions in *subst_conds* and *adjoin_conds*:

$$subst\_conds(Moved, Landing) \leftrightarrow \qquad\qquad\qquad (9.1.1)$$

$$(\quad \exists Cat, N, F, N1, F1$$
$$Landing = x(s(s(0)), Cat, N, F) \wedge$$
$$Moved = x(s(s(0)), Cat, N1, F1) \wedge$$

$$\lor \quad minimal(Moved) \land$$
$$\quad\quad minimal(Landing)$$
$$)$$

$$adjoin\_conds(Moved, Landing, Tree) \leftrightarrow \hspace{3cm} (9.1.2)$$
$$(\quad maximal(Moved) \land$$
$$\quad maximal(Landing) \land$$
$$\quad \neg argument(Landing, Tree)$$
$$\lor \quad minimal(Moved) \land$$
$$\quad\quad minimal(Landing)$$
$$).$$

These definitions obviously have the consequence that the previously displayed unwanted movements are not related by *moveA*.

9.2 Head movement

We must somehow account for the placement of verbs and inflection in our structures. *Barriers* departs from the previous affix-hopping and phrase-structure accounts, following Emonds (1976), Koopman (1984) and others in proposing a verb-raising analysis. Recent verb movement analyses of English suggest that the rule is subject to severe lexical restrictions: only *have* and *be* allow head movement in English, though perhaps all French verbs allow it. Thus we can get

Is he a warrior?

but not

Likes he battles?

In French, on the other hand, we get both

Est-il un guerrier?
Aime-t-il la bataille?

These facts are not mentioned in *Barriers*, and so of course we get no explanation of them.[3] For the moment, we will stick to the *Barriers* account, leaving aside the question of how the lexical restrictions on verb raising in English should be implemented.

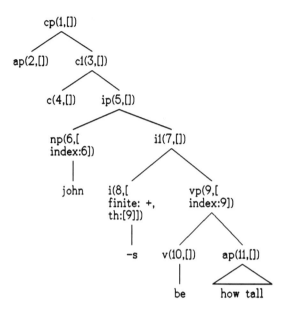

Figure 9.3
Structure before verb raising

Consider the example

How tall is John?

with the underlying structure shown in Figure 9.3.[4] Here, $v(10, \ldots)$ is to move to $i(8, \ldots)$, "amalgamating" or "incorporating" with it, and the resulting amalgamated element then moves to $c(4, [])$ (Chomsky, 1986a, 68f). Chomsky suggests that this raising of V to I is required by Lasnik's (1981, 162) principle:

> A morphologically realized affix must be a syntactic dependent at surface structure.

The formalization developed so far already allows this derivation.[5] Some elaboration of the theory of government (esp. in the definition of L-marking and the empty category principle) is required, as we will see in §10.2.

Chomsky (1986a, 71) suggests that head movement should be subject to the following special restriction:

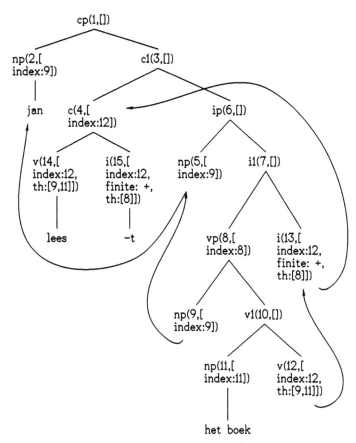

Figure 9.4
Head movement in Dutch

> *Head Movement Constraint (HMC):* Movement of a 0-level category β is restricted to the position of a head α that governs the maximal projection γ of β, where α θ-governs or L-marks γ if $\alpha \neq C$.

Chomsky does not mention the motivation for this proposal, but head movement and incorporation has gotten a lot of attention recently.[6] In Dutch, for example, the HMC properly forces V to move through I to get to verb second position in C, as shown in Figure 9.4,[7] to yield:

Jan leest het boek.
  (John reads the book.)

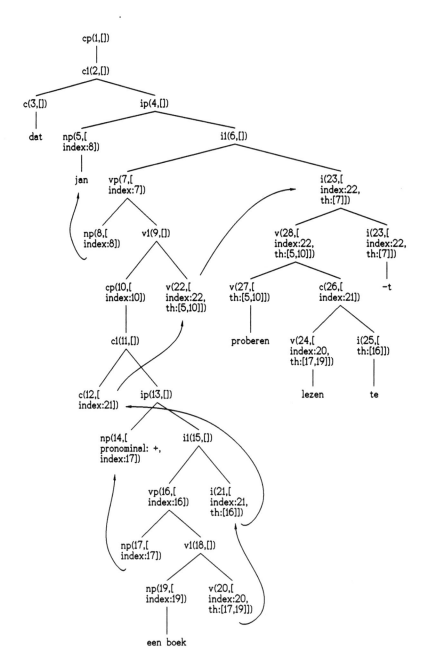

Figure 9.5
Crossing dependency created by 4 head movements

Head movements also are believed to be responsible for the crossing serial subject-verb dependencies in Dutch clauses like,

dat Jan PRO een boek probeert te lezen.
   (that John tries to read the book.)

with the structure shown in Figure 9.5. In this example, PRO (the *+pronominal* empty category) is the subject of *lezen*, and *Jan* is the subject of *probeert*. As mentioned in §5.1.1, structures of this sort have attracted particular attention from computational linguists because the derivation trees of context-free grammars cannot express these crossing relations.[8] Travis (1984, 131ff) discusses examples of similar movements of V to I and I to C in German, N to V in Mohawk, V to V in Japanese and P to V in Bahasa Indonesian, all falling into the same pattern in support of the HMC, though her formulation of the principle is slightly different. English appears to allow movement of V to I only with verbs *have* and *be*, movement of I to C, and no other type of head movement (but see §12 and footnote 5).

The HMC is easily incorporated into our formal definition of structure-preserving movements by modifying our definition of structure preserving movements. Since we need to test the relation between the original position and the landing site, we have to restore the original occurrence number to the moved category if it has been changed:

$$moveA(Tree0, Tree) \leftrightarrow \exists Moved, Landing, Renumbering \qquad (9.2.3)$$

$$new\_occurrence\_no(Renumbering) \wedge$$
$$(\quad substitute(Tree0, Tree, Moved, Landing, Renumbering) \wedge$$
$$subst\_conds(Moved, Landing)$$
$$\vee \quad adjoin(Tree0, Tree, Moved, Landing, Renumbering) \wedge$$
$$adjoin\_conds(Moved, Landing, Tree)$$
$$) \wedge$$
$$renumbering(Moved0, Moved, Renumbering) \wedge$$
$$hmc(Moved0, Landing, Tree).$$

Of course, maximal categories are exempted from the HMC:

$$hmc(Moved, Landing, Tree) \leftrightarrow \qquad (9.2.4)$$

$$(\quad maximal(Moved)$$
$$\vee \quad \exists Max, L, C, N, F, F1, G$$
$$head\_xp(Landing, Max, Tree) \wedge$$
$$Moved = x(L, C, N, F) \wedge$$
$$head\_xp(x(L, C, N, F1), G, Tree) \wedge$$
$$governs(Landing, G, Tree) \wedge$$

$$
\begin{array}{ll}
(& \exists N2, F2 \; Landing = x(0, c, N2, F2) \\
\vee & (\quad th\_governs(Landing, G, Tree) \\
& \vee \quad l\_marks(Landing, G, Tree) \\
&) \\
) &
\end{array}
$$

).

We will consider in §14 the idea that the HMC does not need to be included in the theory, because it actually follows from a stronger principle, namely, the formulation of the ECP that is developed in the next chapter.

In order to get an appropriate account of government, Chomsky (1986a, 68-72) suggests that the raising of V to I has special properties, over and above those it has as a case of head-movement. We will leave the motivation to the next chapter, but note here the idea that the verb and inflection can "amalgamate" in this process if I is an affix, forming an inflectional element which is lexical and has the index of the adjoined verb. It is natural to treat here the co-indexing of the adjoined category and the affix I, since it can be achieved by modifying $adjoin\_cat$, which was originally defined in §7.2. Keeping all of the indices straight gets rather complicated, but this suggestion, at least, can be handled:

$adjoin\_cat(Moved, Landing, Tree0, Tree, Renumbering) \leftrightarrow$ (9.2.5)

$\quad \exists L0, C0, N0, F0, Seq0$

$\quad\quad Tree0 = x(L0, C0, N0, F0)/Seq0 \wedge$

$\quad\quad (\quad \exists Seq, Pos, Selected, RestSeq, Transformed$

$\quad\quad\quad\quad select(Pos, Seq0, Selected, RestSeq) \wedge$

$\quad\quad\quad\quad adjoin\_cat(Moved, Landing, Selected, Transformed, Renumbering) \wedge$

$\quad\quad\quad\quad select(Pos, Seq, Transformed, RestSeq) \wedge$

$\quad\quad\quad\quad Tree = x(L0, C0, N0, F0)/Seq$

$\quad\quad \vee \quad \exists L, C, N, F, Seq, N2, Root, Tree1, Seq1$

$\quad\quad\quad\quad Moved = x(L, C, N, F)/Seq \wedge$

$\quad\quad\quad\quad amalgamate(x(L, C, N, F), Tree0, Root/Tree1) \wedge$

$\quad\quad\quad\quad newnumber(Renumbering, N2) \wedge$

$\quad\quad\quad\quad (\quad Seq = [x(L, C, N2, F)/Seq1, Root/Tree1]$

$\quad\quad\quad\quad \vee \quad Seq = [Root/Tree1, x(L, C, N2, F)/Seq1]$

$\quad\quad\quad\quad) \wedge$

$\quad\quad\quad\quad Tree = Root/Seq \wedge$

$\quad\quad\quad\quad Landing = Root$

$\quad\quad)$

$$amalgamate(MRoot, Tree0, Tree) \leftrightarrow \tag{9.2.6}$$
$$\begin{aligned}
(\quad & \exists L, N, F, I, Root0, Affix \\
& MRoot = x(L, v, N, F) \wedge \\
& member(index : I, F) \wedge \\
& Tree0 = Root0/[(-Affix)/[]] \wedge \\
& feature(index : I, Root0, Root) \wedge \\
& Tree = Root/[(-Affix)/[]] \\
\vee \quad & Tree0 = Tree \\
).\quad &
\end{aligned}$$

It is no wonder that it is in the context of discussing such delicate treatments of indices and movement that Chomsky (1982, 68) remarks, "An attempt at full-scale formalization of the relevant assumptions might be in order, given the level of complexity and the range of material that must be considered."

Since nothing has blocked movement to c, we can now prove that the tree in Figure 9.6 is related to the previous tree of Figure 9.3 by two head movements: an adjunction of V to I, and then a substitution of the resulting adjunction structure (which we can name with the expression "V+I") to C. Notice the indices associated with nodes 4, 8, 12. Also, we have indicated that VP is θ-marked by I in Figure 9.6, since θ-marking affects the determination of barrier relations, as we saw in the last chapter, and the barriers play a role in specifying the locality restrictions on movements, as we will now explain. It turns out that the movement relation just shown respects these locality restrictions.

9.3   The theory of bounding

The bounding principle, subjacency, is often expressed as a limitation on the scope of applications of move-α. An application of move-α satisfies subjacency if the movement takes place within a certain structurally defined domain, crossing a limited number of constituent boundaries of a certain kind. However, we need not regard it in this way. Successive applications of move-α can be regarded as producing a "chain" of co-indexed categories $(\alpha_1, \ldots, \alpha_n)$, where α_1 is the original D-structure constituent and $\alpha_2, \ldots, \alpha_n$ are co-indexed traces. In the limiting case, $n = 1$. Since a constituent co-indexed with a set of traces cannot occur in a tree except as the result of applying move-α, a chain provides a complete history of applications of move-α, and so bounding conditions can be stated as well-formedness conditions on chains in the output trees, rather than as a condition on the movement itself. In *Barriers*, Chomsky (1986, 93n25) does not commit himself to either one of these alternatives, but he uses the notion of a chain. He then defines the bounding condition on movement, *subjacency*, as follows:

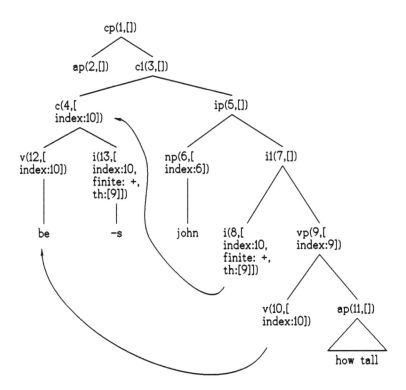

Figure 9.6
The tree of Figure 9.3 after head movements

> Every link (α_i, α_{i+1}) of a chain $(\alpha_1, \ldots, \alpha_n)$ is such that α_{i+1} is 1-subjacent
> to α_i. (Chomsky, 1986a, 30)

where,

> β is *n-subjacent* to α if and only if there are fewer than $n + 1$ barriers for β
> that exclude α.

The logical representation of these principles is a little tricky because of the need to, in effect, count the number of objects (barriers) satisfying a certain predicate.[9] A standard technique suffices: we need only represent the fact that the number of distinct objects satisfying the relevant predicate is less than the specified finite bound. Furthermore, since Chomsky holds that subjacency need not be respected by movements that occur at LF, we adopt subjacency as a condition on S-structures, rather than as an additional restriction on move-α. (It is clear that we could equally well formalize it as a condition on instances of *moveA*.)

In the formalization we make use of the fact that only nodes that have been involved in movements have indices:

$$subjacency(Tree) \leftrightarrow \qquad\qquad\qquad\qquad\qquad\qquad\qquad (9.3.7)$$

$$\forall A, B \; link(A, B, Tree) \rightarrow n\_subjacent(s(0), B, A, Tree, [])$$

$$n\_subjacent(N, Moved, Landing, Tree, L) \leftrightarrow \qquad\qquad\qquad (9.3.8)$$

$$\begin{aligned}
(\quad & \neg\exists Barrier \\
& barrier(Barrier, Moved, Tree)\wedge \\
& \neg member(Barrier, L)\wedge \\
& excludes(Barrier, Landing, Tree) \\
\vee \quad & \exists N1, Barrier \\
& N1 = s(N)\wedge \\
& barrier(Barrier, Moved, Tree)\wedge \\
& \neg member(Barrier, L)\wedge \\
& excludes(Barrier, Landing, Tree)\wedge \\
& n\_subjacent(N1, Moved, Landing, Tree, [Barrier|L]) \\
).
\end{aligned}$$

Notice how easily we could adjust the number of barriers that movements are allowed to cross in this formalization — we simply need to use some other number than $s(0)$. The only new predicate here that is tricky is *link*. We tentatively make use of the fact that every element of a chain except the first is a trace, and every element of the chain locally binds the next (Chomsky, 1981, 59). With these assumptions we can axiomatize *link* as follows:

$$link(A, B, Tree) \leftrightarrow locally\_binds(A, B, Tree) \wedge subtree(B/[], Tree). \qquad (9.3.9)$$

The predicate *locally_binds* was defined in §8.3.

Chomsky (1986a, 28) considers the following example, which the theory should certainly accommodate as a good structure:

Who did [$_{ip}$ john [$_{vp}$ see t]]?

The IP and VP boundaries indicated in this example are both barriers for the object of *see*, and so we cannot have a single wh-fronting movement without crossing more than one barrier. Chomsky suggests an alternative derivation, in which the embedded object is first adjoined to the VP and then substituted into the specifier of CP, as shown in

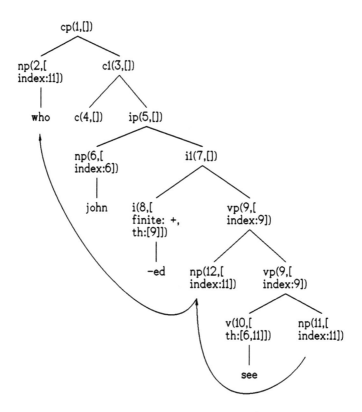

Figure 9.7
Two 0-subjacent movements

Figure 9.7. Chomsky suggests that this is the best case, in which even 0-subjacency is respected, but this is true only if we make a minor revision in the *Barriers* principles.

The problem is that there *is* a barrier for the object of *see* that excludes the VP, namely the VP itself. So although the adjunction to the VP would respect 1-subjacency, it is not a best case 0-subjacent movement unless we modify the *Barriers* definition of exclusion. Recall the previous definition: "α excludes β if no segment of α dominates β." (Chomsky, 1986a, 9) In our application of this definition to an example, we did not note the exclusion of every node by itself. We can easily eliminate self-exclusion, and reformalize the notion as follows:

$$excludes(A, B, Tree) \leftrightarrow \qquad\qquad\qquad\qquad\qquad\qquad\qquad (9.3.10)$$
$$\neg A = B \wedge$$
$$\neg \exists Segment$$
$$Segment = A \wedge ancestor(Segment, B, Tree).$$

Given this modification of our definition of *excludes*, the two movements shown in Figure 9.7 are provably 0-subjacent. Our formalization properly blocks the direct movement of $np(11, \ldots)$ to the specifier position of $cp(1, [])$ with the 1-subjacency restriction, although it is easy to prove that this movement respects 2-subjacency. Adjunction to $vp(9, \ldots)$ removes this barrier, allowing a 0-subjacent derivation.

After considering this example, Chomsky defines an additional, language-specific, "parametric" barrier for English: the deepest IP, if it is tensed. We will define this barrier precisely in the following section, but it should be noted that, with this addition, we have not succeeded in finding a 0-subjacent derivation of the example just displayed. As we will see, $ip(5, [])$ is an extra barrier for $np(12, \ldots)$ that excludes $np(2, \ldots)$. It then turns out that the derivation indicated in Figure 9.7, even with adjunction to $vp(9, \ldots)$, crosses 1 barrier, and so it respects 1-subjacency but not 0-subjacency.

9.4 Island constraints

The theory we have formulated so far is already remarkably powerful. It subsumes a number of the "island constraints." Consider some of the structures treated by Huang's (1982, §6.4) *condition on extraction domains* (CED) which blocks extractions from subjects, adjuncts and topics. Chomsky suggests that we should be able to account for the following examples:

* *The man who$_i$ [$_{ip}$[pictures of t$_i$] are on the table] arrived.*
* *The book that$_i$ [$_{ip}$[reading t$_i$] would be fun] was sold.*

We cannot yet prove these results from our theory.

Consider the first case, with extraction of *who* to the specifier position of a relative clause adjunct. The relevant part of the structure is shown in Figure 9.8.[10] We can show that the substitution of $np(15, \ldots)$ for $np(7, \ldots)$ is not 1-subjacent, since $np(11, \ldots)$ and $ip(10, [])$ are both barriers for $np(15, \ldots)$ that exclude $np(7, \ldots)$. The barrierhood of $ip(10, [])$ follows from the fact that $ip(10, [])$ immediately dominates $np(11, \ldots)$, and $np(11, \ldots)$ is a blocking category for $np(15, \ldots)$. And as Chomsky points out, the fact that $np(11, \ldots)$ is a blocking category for $np(15, \ldots)$ follows from the fact that $np(11, \ldots)$ dominates $np(15, \ldots)$ and is not L-marked.

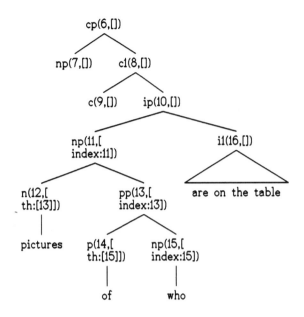

Figure 9.8
Structure blocking raising from a *picture* NP

However, there is an alternative derivation which is not yet blocked. The embedded NP, $np(15,\ldots)$, might first adjoin to the IP, and then substitute into the specifier of CP. The adjunction to IP is 1-subjacent. The only excluding barrier for this adjunction is $np(11,\ldots)$. (Node $pp(13,\ldots)$ would be a barrier for $np(15,\ldots)$ that excludes $ip(10,\ldots)$, except that it is L-marked by $n(12,\ldots)$.) The substitution for the specifier of CP is then 0-subjacent. How are we going to rule this out? Chomsky (1986a, 5, 32) proposes that a special restriction be placed on wh-phrases, requiring them to have "clausal scope," even in the intermediate steps of a derivation. Wh-phrases cannot be adjoined to IP. It would be nicer to get this restriction from independently motivated principles at LF, but since it is to apply to every movement, Chomsky stipulates this stronger restriction on valid movements.

It is a trivial matter to impose this additional condition on movements, although we are getting a rather inelegant collection of requirements. We can simply modify our definition of *adjoin_conds* to block the case where the moved category is an wh-phrase and the landing site is IP. The only trick is to identify exactly the moving wh-phrases, but these will always have a number of distinctive characteristics. We assume that they will be marked with an explicit $+wh$ feature.

$$adjoin\_conds(Moved, Landing, Tree) \leftrightarrow \qquad\qquad (9.4.11)$$

$$\begin{aligned}
(\quad & maximal(Moved)\wedge \\
& maximal(Landing)\wedge \\
& \neg argument(Landing, Tree)\wedge \\
& \neg wh\_ip\_violation(Moved, Landing) \\
\vee \quad & minimal(Moved)\wedge \\
& minimal(Landing) \\
)
\end{aligned}$$

$$wh\_ip\_violation(Moved, Landing) \leftrightarrow \exists N, F \qquad\qquad (9.4.12)$$

$$\begin{aligned}
& Landing = x(s(s(0)), i, N, F)\wedge \\
& feature(wh : +, Moved, Moved).
\end{aligned}$$

The following examples, covered by Huang's CED, are similarly accounted for:

* $[To\ whom]_i$ did $[_{ip}$ they leave $[_{xp}$ before speaking $t_i]]$?
* Who_i did $[_{ip}$ they leave $[_{xp}$ before speaking to $t_i]]$?

In these examples, the adjunct clauses XP, whatever their category, are blocking categories and hence intrinsic barriers, and the IPs inherit barrierhood.

9.5   A parametric intrinsic barrier and cumulative violations

There are other structures which require a complication of the account presented above. In the first place, the following sentences involve movements that cross one barrier:

Which car did John tell you how to fix t?
Which car did he wonder whether to fix t?

but so do the following:

??What did you wonder to whom John gave t t?
??To whom did you wonder what John gave t t?

The latter sentences seem less acceptable than the former. Chomsky (1986a, 37) proposes to account for this by assuming that there is a parametric selection of an extra intrinsic barrier: the deepest CP or IP can be an intrinsic barrier if it is tensed.[11] In at least some dialects of English, the most deeply embedded IP seems to act as an intrinsic barrier when it is tensed, and this accounts for the contrast just noted. On the basis of Rizzi's (1982) work on Italian and other languages, Chomsky suggests that the most embedded CP is an intrinsic barrier. These categories are extra barriers for movement, but not for government.

A second complication must be added to our account for the fact that structures involving two movements, each crossing a barrier, are unacceptable. Consider the following structure, involving five movements, each of which is allowed:

$* \ What_i \ did \ you \ [_{vp}t_i[_{vp}wonder \ who \ [_{vp}t_i[_{vp}said \ [_{cp}t_i \ that \ Bill \ [_{vp}t_i[_{vp} \ saw \ t_i]]]]]]] \ ?$

Starting from the original, deeply embedded site, the first adjunction to VP crosses no barriers; the substitution for the specifier of CP crosses the parametric tensed IP barrier; the adjunction to the intermediate VP crosses no barriers; the adjunction to the matrix VP then crosses one barrier (the intermediate CP, which is a barrier by inheritance); and finally, the substitution into the specifier position of the top CP crosses no barriers. We can exclude this sentence by modifying 1-subjacency to prohibit *chains* that cross more than one barrier: we make the violations of each movement cumulative (Chomsky, 1986a, 38).

Since the extra barriers, those subject to parametric variation, are not to affect government, we introduce them as nodes satisfying a new *extra_barrier* predicate. These nodes are counted by our revised definition of *n_subjacent*, as are barriers in previous links of the chain:

$n\_subjacent(N, Moved, Landing, Tree, L) \leftrightarrow$ (9.5.13)

$(\quad \neg \exists Barrier$

$\quad (\quad barrier(Barrier, Moved, Tree)$

$\quad \lor \quad extra\_barrier(Barrier, Moved, Tree)$

$\quad)\land$

$\quad \neg member(Barrier, L)\land$

$\quad excludes(Barrier, Landing, Tree)\land$

$\quad previously\_n\_subjacent(N, Landing, Tree)$

$\lor \quad \exists N1, Barrier$

$\quad N1 = s(N)\land$

$\quad barrier(Barrier, Moved, Tree)\land$

$\quad \neg member(Barrier, L)\land$

$\quad excludes(Barrier, Landing, Tree)\land$

$\quad n\_subjacent(N1, Moved, Landing, Tree, [Barrier|L])$

$).$

This definition works by, in effect, collecting a list of different barriers that intervene between the nodes *Moved* and *Landing*, and for each such barrier removing one from the number N. If there are no more intervening barriers, then the barriers between the Landing and a later landing site are counted, and so on through the chain of locally bound positions related by movement. If barriers remain in the chain when N has reached zero, the *n_subjacent* property does not hold.

The addition of the extra barrier is straightforward:

$$extra\_barrier(Barrier, A, Tree) \leftrightarrow \tag{9.5.14}$$

$$\begin{aligned}
(\quad & extra\_BC(Barrier, A, Tree) \\
\vee \quad & \exists D \\
& imm\_dominates(Barrier, D, Tree) \wedge \\
& extra\_BC(D, A, Tree) \\
)
\end{aligned}$$

$$extra\_BC(Barrier, A, Tree) \leftrightarrow \tag{9.5.15}$$

$$\begin{aligned}
\exists Cat&, N, F \\
& bounding\_parameter(Cat) \wedge \\
& Barrier = x(s(s(0)), Cat, N, F) \wedge \\
& dominates(Barrier, A, Tree) \wedge \\
& \neg \exists N1, F1 \; dominates(x(s(s(0)), Cat, N, F), \\
& \qquad\qquad\qquad x(s(s(0)), Cat, N1, F1), Tree) \wedge \\
& tensed(Barrier, Tree).
\end{aligned}$$

$$bounding\_parameter(X) \leftrightarrow X = i. \tag{9.5.16}$$

And finally, the definition of *previously_n_subjacent* takes the count of these barriers to earlier links in the chain, as discussed above:

$$previously\_n\_subjacent(N, Moved, Tree) \leftrightarrow \tag{9.5.17}$$

$$\begin{aligned}
(\quad & \exists Landing \\
& link(Landing, Moved, Tree) \wedge \\
& n\_subjacent(N, Moved, Landing, Tree, [\,]) \\
\vee \quad & \neg \exists Landing \\
& link(Landing, Moved, Tree) \\
).
\end{aligned}$$

In a tree respecting this cumulative version of n-subjacency, the movement from any node in a chain to the last node in that chain crosses no more than n barriers.

The only remaining predicate that is needed now is *tensed*. We assume a *finite* feature has the value + in all tensed IPs, as indicated in many of the trees displayed above. Then determining whether an IP or CP is tensed is fairly easy:

$$tensed(Cat, Tree) \leftrightarrow \exists Head, Seq, N, F \qquad\qquad (9.5.18)$$

$$head\_xp(Head, Cat/Seq, Tree) \land$$
$$(\quad Cat = x(s(s(0)), i, N, F) \land$$
$$feature(finite : +, Head, Head)$$
$$\lor\quad Cat = x(s(s(0)), c, N, F) \land$$
$$\exists IN, IF$$
$$sisters(Head, x(s(s(0)), i, IN, IF), Tree) \land$$
$$tensed(x(s(s(0)), i, IN, IF), Tree)$$
$$).$$

Notice that this test will work even if the tensed I has moved, as in Figure 9.6, since a trace of I will be left showing the features of the original.

These definitions allow us to prove that our example,

* *What$_i$ did you [$_{vp}t_i$ [$_{vp}$wonder who [$_{vp}t_i$ [$_{vp}$said [$_{cp}$ t_i that Bill [$_{vp}t_i$ [$_{vp}$ saw t_i]]]]]]?*

violates subjacency. Our implemented proof methods (described in Parts I and IV) find this proof easily, given the formal definitions provided here.

9.6   Some loose ends

We have accounted for some of the structures considered in §5, such as

Who$_i$ did you put t_i in the trunk?
The man who$_i$ you put t_i in the trunk is unhappy.

The violations of the complex NP constraint are covered

* *The man [who$_i$ the woman likes the book] reads t_i.*
* *What$_i$ did the man read [the book [about t_i]].*

We can similarly account for

* *What$_i$ do you wonder [$_{cp}$ how I fixed t_i]*
* *What$_i$ does [$_{np}$the man who$_j$ [$_{ip}t_j$ likes t_i]] read the book?*

Other cases will be ruled out in the next section by the ECP, such as

* *Who$_i$ do you think that t$_i$ saw Bill?*

Other structures must be ruled out by principles which are not presented in *Barriers*. For example, adjunction to VP has played a role in the account of wh-movement, but some principle must block the use of VP adjunction to derive structures like

* *John$_i$ [$_{vp}$t$_i$ [$_{vp}$ seems that it is [$_{vp}$t$_i$ [$_{vp}$ considered [$_{ip}$t$_i$ to be intelligent]]]]].*

Such movements from a non-argument position to an argument position are called "improper movements," and the usual idea is that they are to be excluded by some formulation of principle C of binding theory (Chomsky, 1981, §3.2.3; 1986a, 22,74,93n20). The idea is roughly this. Just as a *John* cannot be bound by *he* in

**he$_i$ said John$_i$ likes beer.*

so *he* cannot bind the trace in

**Who$_i$ did he$_i$ say t$_i$ likes beer?*

In general, a wh-trace cannot be bound by a constituent in argument position, "A-position," and a chain whose first element is in A-position, an A-chain, cannot include A-bar positions. So we can have

John$_i$ was arrested t$_i$

but not

John$_i$ was [t$_i$ [arrested t$_i$].

Adjunction to VP in NP-movement is ruled out. Formalizing an appropriate version of binding theory is beyond the scope of this work, but improper movements are mentioned again in §10.6.[12]

Another rather different kind of restriction on movements is considered by Chomsky (1986b, 143): the "last resort" principle is the idea that a movement cannot apply except to a structure that does not satisfy some well-formedness conditions. (Cf. also Chomsky (1988).) Such a restriction could be incorporated into our theory quite easily, but here we will attempt to formalize only the central ideas of *Barriers*.

Chapter 10

The empty category principle and minimality

An important source of restrictions on applications of move-α that can lead to well-formed structures comes from structural constraints on the occurrence of traces. Chomsky has pointed out that, for many speakers, there seems to be a contrast between the following two ungrammatical sentences, and that this contrast points to the very different fundamental principles that are violated in each case:[1]

* *What$_i$ [$_{ip}$do you wonder [$_{cp}$how [$_{ip}$John [$_{vp}$ fixed t$_i$]]]]?*
** *Who$_i$ do you wonder how [$_{ip}$t$_i$ fixed the car]?*

Assuming that the deepest tensed IP is an intrinsic barrier to movement, both of these structures are ruled out by subjacency. The latter structure seems worse, however, and we can account for this by noting that it violates not only subjacency but also the empty category principle (ECP), which will be the subject of this chapter. The trace in the embedded subject position in the latter sentence is not *properly governed*, as will become clear in this chapter.

10.1 Affect-α and the ECP as a filter at LF

The ECP restricts the positions in which traces can occur. Chomsky (1986a, 17) begins with the following formulation of the principle, based on Lasnik and Saito (1984):

(ECP) A nonpronominal empty category must be properly governed.

This formulation assumes that the only nonpronominal empty categories are traces. Chomsky (1986a, 16) stipulates that any empty category that is created at D-structure is marked +*pronominal*. Consequently, the only empty categories not so marked will be those produced by the action of move-α .[2] Chomsky (1986a, 16) accepts the view of

Lasnik and Saito that the ECP should really be expressed as a filter which applies at LF to eliminate $-\gamma$ constituents, where argument traces are assigned $+$ or $-\gamma$ at S-structure according to whether they are properly governed, and all other traces are assigned one of these features at LF.

LF-structures are related to S-structures by movements, insertions and deletions. Chomsky (1986a, 32,93n29) follows the analysis of Huang (1982) and of Lasnik and Saito (1984) in assuming that the movements that occur between S-structure and LF are not restricted by subjacency. However, this appears to be the only significant respect in which they differ from movements between D-structure and S-structure. LF-movements, like all the others we have considered, may adjoin non-wh constituents to IP (Chomsky, 1986a, 5), and they move wh-phrases to the specifier position of CP (Chomsky, 1986a, 50). Following Koopman and Sportiche (1982) and May (1985), Chomsky assumes that LF movements may also adjoin constituents (including wh-phrases) to VP (Chomsky, 1986a, 6). Since we represented subjacency as an S-structure constraint rather than as a constraint on move-α , we can simply regard movements that take place between S-structure and LF as additional instances of this relation, i.e., as instances of our *moveAn*.

Deletions play a crucial role in the Lasnik and Saito account of ECP effects (Lasnik and Saito, 1984, 1988; Chomsky, 1986a, 21,49). We must allow intermediate traces to be deleted in some cases to get the ECP to work properly. For this purpose, we formalize a deletion rule, and a new relation which associates trees that are related by 0 or more movements or deletions. The deletion rule is a transformation that removes an entire subtree, so it is naturally formalized as a tree transduction of the sort introduced in Chapter 7. In effect, we can think of the definition as going down every branch of the tree, removing exactly one subtree. Fortunately, deletion is a much simpler transduction than move-α :

$$deleteA(Tree0, Tree, DRoot) \leftrightarrow \qquad\qquad\qquad\qquad (10.1.1)$$

$$\exists Node, Seq0, Seq, Pos, Selected, RestSeq$$
$$Tree0 = Node/Seq0 \wedge$$
$$Tree = Node/Seq \wedge$$
$$select(Pos, Seq0, Selected, RestSeq) \wedge$$
$$(\quad \exists Transformed$$
$$\qquad deleteA(Selected, Transformed, DRoot) \wedge$$
$$\qquad select(Pos, Seq, Transformed, RestSeq)$$
$$\vee \quad RestSeq = Seq \wedge$$
$$\qquad \exists\ Seq1\ Selected = DRoot/Seq1$$
$$).$$

Deletion is a very powerful rule, and it must be constrained. Some sort of recoverability condition must apply, and so nothing with lexical content can be deleted. We tentatively

assume that this means that only empty categories and complementizers like the English
that can be deleted:

$$delete\_conds(A, Tree) \leftrightarrow (\quad subtree(A/[], Tree) \tag{10.1.2}$$
$$\lor \quad subtree(A/[that/[]], Tree)$$
$$).$$

We can now deploy this deletion in our account of affect-α, incorporating the definition
of *moveA* as it was last formulated in §9.2:

$$affectA(Tree0, Tree) \leftrightarrow \exists Moved, Landing, Renumbering \tag{10.1.3}$$
$$new\_occurrence\_no(Renumbering) \land$$
$$(\quad (\quad substitute(Tree0, Tree, Moved, Landing) \land$$
$$subst\_conds(Moved, Landing)$$
$$\lor \quad adjoin(Tree0, Tree, Moved, Landing) \land$$
$$adjoin\_conds(Moved, Landing, Tree)$$
$$) \land$$
$$renumbering(Moved0, Moved, Renumbering) \land$$
$$hmc(Moved0, Landing, Tree)$$
$$\lor \quad deleteA(Tree0, Tree, Moved) \land$$
$$delete\_conds(Moved, Tree0)$$
$$).$$

This axiom says that the *affectAn* relation holds between two trees just in case the trees
are related either by a movement or a deletion. The relation that holds between trees
related by zero or more of these steps can be represented with the following predicate:

$$affectAn(Tree0, Tree) \leftrightarrow (\quad Tree = Tree0 \tag{10.1.4}$$
$$\lor \quad \exists Tree1$$
$$affectA(Tree0, Tree1) \land$$
$$affectAn(Tree1, Tree)$$
$$).$$

To capture the ECP, then, what we have to formalize is just a relation that will map
S-structures into the corresponding structures with all argument traces labeled with
appropriate γ features, a relation that will map LF-structures into the corresponding
structures with all traces labeled with appropriate γ features, and a constraint that will
be satisfied by a tree just in case the tree contains no $-\gamma$ feature.

Let's begin by defining a relation that will map S-structures into structures in which
all argument traces are properly marked with a γ feature. Since this is a relation on

pairs of trees, where the nodes of the trees that are so related will in some cases have different labels, we use a tree transduction-like approach again. This time we can think of the definition as going down every branch of the tree, leaving everything untouched except the labels of nodes that are traces. We supply a third argument to this relation which will be the original tree being operated upon:

$$ss\_gamma(Tree0, Tree, T) \leftrightarrow \qquad\qquad (10.1.5)$$

$$
\begin{aligned}
&\exists Root0, Seq0, Root, Seq \; Tree0 = Root0/Seq0 \wedge Tree = Root/Seq\wedge \\
&(\quad \exists T0, Ts \\
&\qquad Seq0 = [T0|Ts]\wedge \\
&\qquad ss\_sub\_gamma([T0|Ts], Seq)\wedge \\
&\qquad Root0 = Root \\
&\vee\quad Seq0 = [\,] \wedge Seq0 = Seq\wedge \\
&\qquad \exists I \; feature(index : I, Root0, Root0)\wedge \\
&\qquad \neg feature(pronominal : +, Root0, Root0)\wedge \\
&\qquad argument(Root0, T)\wedge \\
&\qquad (\quad \exists A \; properly\_governs(A, Root0, T)\wedge \\
&\qquad\qquad feature(gamma : +, Root0, Root) \\
&\qquad \vee\quad \neg\exists A \; properly\_governs(A, Root0, T)\wedge \\
&\qquad\qquad feature(gamma : -, Root0, Root) \\
&\qquad) \\
&\vee\quad Seq0 = [\,] \wedge Seq0 = Seq\wedge \\
&\qquad (\quad \neg\exists I \; feature(index : I, Root0, Root0)\wedge \\
&\qquad \vee\quad \neg argument(Root0, T) \\
&\qquad \vee\quad \neg feature(pronominal : +, Root0, Root0) \\
&\qquad)\wedge \\
&\qquad Root0 = Root \\
&)
\end{aligned}
$$

$$ss\_sub\_gamma(Seq0, Seq, T) \leftrightarrow (\quad Seq0 = [\,] \wedge \qquad\qquad (10.1.6)$$

$$
\begin{aligned}
&\qquad\qquad\qquad\qquad\qquad\quad Seq = [\,] \\
&\qquad\qquad\qquad\qquad \vee\quad \exists A, As, B, Bs \\
&\qquad\qquad\qquad\qquad\qquad Seq0 = [A|As]\wedge \\
&\qquad\qquad\qquad\qquad\qquad ss\_gamma(A, B, T)\wedge \\
&\qquad\qquad\qquad\qquad\qquad ss\_sub\_gamma(As, Bs, T)\wedge \\
&\qquad\qquad\qquad\qquad\qquad Seq = [B|Bs] \\
&\qquad\qquad\qquad\qquad).
\end{aligned}
$$

The assignment of γ features at LF can be almost identical, except that we do not need to worry about traces that already have had their γ features assigned. (The definition of $lf\_gamma(Tree0, Tree, T)$ appears in Appendix B.) The filter itself is now easily defined. No category can be $-\gamma$:

$$ecp(Tree) \leftrightarrow \neg \exists L, C, N, F \tag{10.1.7}$$
$$subtree(x(L, C, N, F)/[], Tree) \wedge$$
$$member(gamma : -, F).$$

We can summarize the principles that have been developed up to this point and roughly indicate their interaction by defining a relation that holds of a triple of well-formed structures at the various levels of representation:

$$well\_formed(DS, SS, LF) \leftrightarrow \exists DS, SS, SS1, LF, LF1$$
$$(\quad xp(DS) \wedge$$
$$affectAn(DS, SS) \wedge$$
$$subjacency(SS) \wedge$$
$$ss\_gamma(SS, SS1) \wedge$$
$$affectAn(SS1, LF) \wedge$$
$$lf\_gamma(LF, LF1) \wedge$$
$$ecp(LF1)$$
$$).$$

Now we turn to the definition of proper government.

10.2   Proper government

As already noted, Chomsky begins with the Lasnik and Saito account:

> α *properly governs* β iff α θ-governs β or antecedent-governs β.

> α *antecedent-governs* β if (α, β) is a link of a chain and α governs β.

In logic:

$$properly\_governs(A, B, Tree) \leftrightarrow (\quad th\_governs(A, B, Tree) \tag{10.2.8}$$
$$\vee \quad ante\_governs(A, B, Tree)$$
$$)$$

$$ante\_governs(A, B, Tree) \leftrightarrow link(A, B, Tree) \wedge \tag{10.2.9}$$
$$governs(A, B, Tree).$$

We apply these definitions first to the following examples (Chomsky's (1986a) examples (22a) and (22b)):[3]

How$_i$ did John want [$_{cp}t_i$ [$_{ip}$ to fix the car t$_i$]] ?
* *How$_i$ did John know [which car]$_j$ [$_{ip}$ to [$_{vp}$fix t$_j$] t$_i$] ?*

In the former structure, the fronted wh-phrase does govern the intermediate trace. The indicated CP is L-marked by the verb, and so it is not a blocking category. And it does not inherit barrierhood because the only category that it immediately dominates is the IP which does not dominate the intermediate trace, which is in the position of the specifier of the CP. Consequently, this non-argument trace in the former structure is marked $+\gamma$ at LF. In the latter structure, though, the specifier of the CP is *which car*. The trace of the fronted wh-phrase is not θ-marked by the verb, since we are assuming that it comes from an adjunct position. It is not antecedent-governed either, because the CP inherits barrierhood from the blocking category IP. Consequently, this non-argument trace is not properly governed and is marked $-\gamma$ at LF.

These results can be demonstrated from the theory we have specified, but the relevant structures must actually be a little more complicated. Although the theory properly prevents CP from being a barrier to proper government in the first example, there is still a VP barrier here:

How$_i$ did John want [$_{cp}t_i$ [$_{ip}$ to fix the car t$_i$]] ?

The matrix VP is not L-marked and dominates the specifier of CP, and it excludes the landing site of the wh-phrase. We might consider the following structure instead (cf. Chomsky's (42)):

How$_i$ did John [$_{vp}t_i$ [$_{vp}$want [$_{cp}t_i$ [$_{ip}$ to fix the car t$_i$]] ?

In this case, all the traces are properly governed. We can prove that this tree is related to its D-structure by our *ecp_moveAn* relation.

So now let's consider Chomsky's (22b):

* *How$_i$ did John know [which car]$_j$ [$_{ip}$ to [$_{vp}$fix t$_j$] t$_i$] ?*

A movement from the embedded adjunct position to the specifier of the matrix CP would cross three barriers: the deepest CP is a barrier by inheritance, the matrix VP is an intrinsic barrier, and the matrix IP is a barrier by inheritance. So what intermediate sites are available for fronting *how* without violating subjacency? We cannot adjoin to the embedded CP since it is an argument. However, we can adjoin to the matrix VP:

* *How$_i$ did John [$_{vp}t_i$ [$_{vp}$know [which car]$_j$ [$_{ip}$ to [$_{vp}$fix t$_j$] t$_i$] ?*

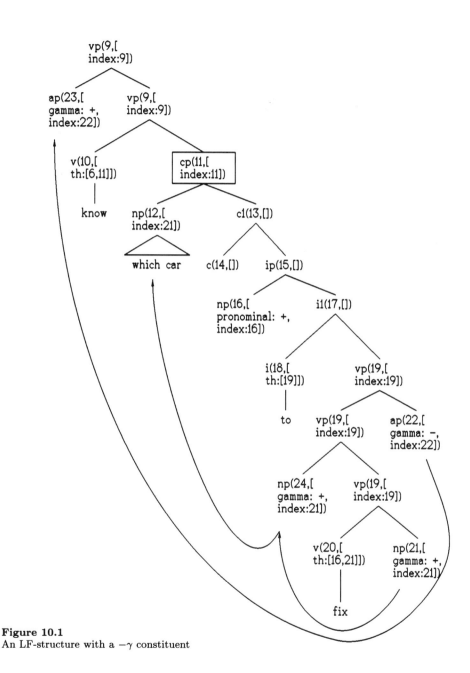

Figure 10.1
An LF-structure with a −γ constituent

In this structure, the adjunction of the adjunct wh-phrase to the VP crosses one barrier, the embedded CP. The second movement into the position of specifier of the matrix CP crosses no barriers, and so there is no subjacency violation. The embedded CP, on the other hand, prevents the intermediate trace from governing the original adjunct position, and so proper government does not hold, and the structure violates the ECP. When we are explicit about the structure, we can prove that it is not related to its D-structure by our *ecp_moveAn* relation. The relevant part of the structure is shown in Figure 10.1, with the relevant barrier for $ap(22, \ldots)$ highlighted.[4]

Returning to the examples mentioned at the beginning of this section, the situation should be clear:

* $What_i$ $[_{ip}do$ you $wonder$ $[_{cp}how$ $[_{ip}John$ $[_{vp}$ $fixed$ $t_i]]]]$?
* Who_i do you $wonder$ $[_{cp}how$ $[_{ip}t_i$ $fixed$ the $car]]$?

In the former structure, the trace is θ-governed by the verb, and so there is only a 1-subjacency violation, and that depends on the weak parametric barrier of the deepest tensed IP. In the latter structure, however, the embedded CP inherits barrierhood for the embedded subject from the embedded IP. The embedded trace is therefore not properly governed, and so we have an ECP violation that is notably more serious than the subjacency violation in the first structure.

10.3   Verb raising revisited

We noted in our earlier discussion of verb raising that a further elaboration of our account of government would be required in order to allow the trace of verb movement to be properly governed as required by the ECP. Actually, only a minor change is required: the amalgamation of verb and inflection changes I to an L-marker of VP. We can tell whether this amalgamation has occurred by checking to see whether I is co-indexed with a verb (as in Figure 9.6 of the previous chapter). We cover this possibility by redefining our unary *lexical* predicate of §6.4 as follows,

$$lexical(Node, Tree) \leftrightarrow \exists L, Cat, N, F \qquad (10.3.10)$$
$$Node = x(L, Cat, N, F) \wedge$$
$$(\quad member(Cat, [v, n, a, p])$$
$$\vee \quad Cat = i \wedge$$
$$\exists I, N1, F1, Sub$$
$$member(index : I, F) \wedge$$

$$subtree(x(0, v, N1, F1)/Sub, Tree) \wedge$$
$$member(index : I, F1)$$
).

To make this change consistently throughout the theory, we should change all uses of the earlier defined unary predicate *lexical* to this new binary predicate. The predicate was used in two places: in the definition of *sisters* and in the definition of *l_marks*, both in §8.3. The required change in these definitions is trivial.

Now let's reconsider the tree of Figure 9.6, shown in the previous chapter. When T is that tree, with our new definition of *lexical*, we can now prove

$$governs(x(0, i, 8, \ldots), x(0, v, 10, \ldots), T).$$

That is, we have government, and hence proper government, of the trace of the verb now that the verb has moved to a position where it L-marks its own maximal projection. Since we also have

$$governs(x(0, c, 4, \ldots), x(0, i, 8, \ldots), T),$$

there is no ECP violation in this tree.

10.4   Minimality

The theory formalized so far works quite well on a wide range of structures, but there is some evidence to support a minor change in our definition of the fundamental notion of a barrier. As Chomsky notes, this evidence supports the view that antecedent-government, as defined above, holds in some cases where it should be blocked. We briefly consider the evidence and then explore the consequences of the minor change in the theory.

Chomsky (1986a, 45) presents the following empirical evidence (from Torrego) to motivate a minimality condition in government. In Spanish, there is a contrast between the following sentences:

* [*De qué pintor*]$_i$ *me preguntaste si van a exponer* [*varios dibujos t*$_i$]?
   (by which painter did you ask me if they are going to exhibit several drawings?)
[*De cual de estas ediciones*]$_i$ *no sabes si hay* [*traducción francesa t*$_i$]?
   (of which of these editions don't you know if there is a French translation?)

The contrast can be attributed to the fact that in the latter case the trace is an NP complement and hence θ-governed. In the former case there is no θ-government, and so we can account for its unacceptability if it is not antecedent-governed. Unfortunately, we have antecedent-government in this structure. Assuming that the first movement is

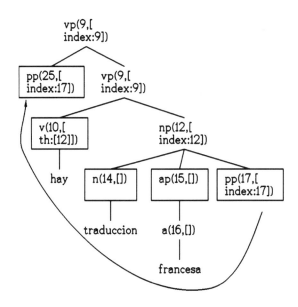

Figure 10.2
A structure with governors highlighted

adjunction to the embedded VP, above, the embedded PP is governed by the adjunction
site. Suppose that the structure of the relevant part of the second example is something
very roughly like Figure 10.2, in which we have highlighted all the nodes that govern
the embedded PP, $pp(17,\ldots)$. Since the trace category $pp(25,\ldots)$ governs $pp(17,\ldots)$,
antecedent-government holds according to the account we developed above. If we can
block the antecedent-government in this structure and in the similar structure for Torrego's second example, then we will be able to account for the contrast between the two
examples, because the trace of PP is also θ-governed in the second but not in the first
example.

Chomsky proposes the following modification:[5]

> σ is a barrier for β if σ is the immediate projection of δ, a zero level category
> distinct from β.

This passage seems to allow σ to be a barrier for β in the configuration

$$\ldots [_\sigma \ldots \delta \ldots] \ldots [\ldots \beta \ldots] \ldots$$

but the context indicates a more restrictive notion. What Chomsky intends is barrierhood
in the configuration where σ dominates both β and δ:

$$\ldots [_{\sigma} \ldots \delta \ldots \beta \ldots] \ldots$$

where σ can now be either a maximal or intermediate projection. Furthermore, IP and now also I1 are assumed to have the "defective" character noted above: they cannot be intrinsic barriers, but can pass barrierhood up to an immediately dominating maximal projection (Chomsky, 1986a, 48). Notice that this idea overlaps but does not subsume the previous definition of barrierhood, which, it will be recalled, applies in configurations

$$\ldots [_{\sigma} \ldots \beta \ldots] \ldots$$

where σ is a maximal projection that is either an intrinsic barrier (when σ is not IP and is not L-marked), or a barrier by inheritance (when σ immediately dominates a maximal projection that dominates β and is not L-marked).

We will formalize the idea that government is blocked not only by the barriers characterized earlier (in §8), but also by projections of distinct minimal categories. We cannot simply redefine *barrier*, since this new idea applies to government but not to movement, and so we will call barriers in the new sense *minimal barriers*: they include both the old barriers and the new ones added by the minimality condition. The notion can be formalized as follows:

$$
\begin{aligned}
minimal\_barrier(S, B, Tree) \leftrightarrow (\quad & barrier(S, B, Tree) \qquad\qquad (10.4.11)\\
\vee \quad & dominates(S, B, Tree) \wedge \\
& \exists D \\
& \quad parent(S, D, Tree) \wedge \\
& \quad minimal(D) \wedge \\
& \quad \neg \exists L, N, F \; D = x(L, i, N, F) \wedge \\
& \quad \neg D = B \\
). &
\end{aligned}
$$

Since this notion is relevant to proper government but not to movement (Chomsky, 1986a, 42), we can incorporate it without affecting our account of movement simply by modifying our account of government. Remember that the definition of government, specified in §8, is the following:

> α governs β iff α m-commands β and there is no σ, σ a barrier for β, such that σ excludes α.

We now introduce an alternative notion of government based on the minimality condition:

> α governs β iff α m-commands β and there is no σ, σ a minimal barrier for β, such that σ excludes α.

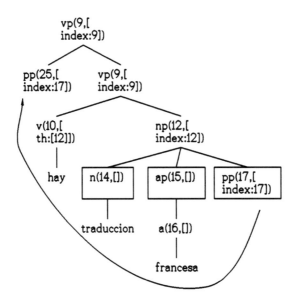

Figure 10.3
Figure 10.2 with minimal governors highlighted

The formalization is straightforward:

$$governs(A, B, Tree) \leftrightarrow m\_commands(A, B, Tree) \land \qquad (10.4.12)$$
$$\neg \exists S$$
$$minimal\_barrier(S, B, Tree) \land$$
$$excludes(S, A, Tree).$$

With these definitions, the nodes that minimally govern $pp(17, \ldots)$ are those highlighted in the Figure 10.3. The embedded PP is no longer governed by the landing site, and so we have an account of the contrast in Torrego's examples.

10.5   *that*-trace effects

One of the things that the ECP is sometimes thought to account for is the unacceptability of extraction from subjects of *that*-clauses:

Who$_i$ did you believe [$_{cp}$ t_i [$_{c1}$[$_{ip}$ t_i *would win*]]] *?*
* Who$_i$ did you believe [$_{cp}$ t_i [$_{c1}$ *that* [$_{ip}$ t_i *would win*]]] *?*

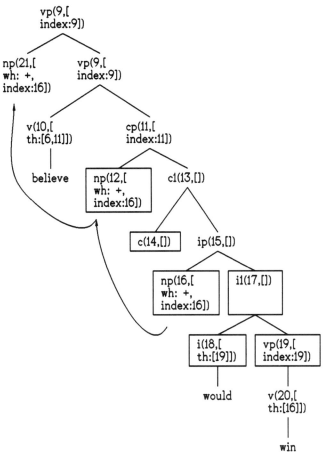

Figure 10.4
S-Structure with empty Comp

With the minimality condition, this contrast is accounted for if we assume that the minimal category whose projection intervenes cannot be a bare node with no features. We obtain this result if we modify our definition of minimal barrier as follows:[6]

$$minimal\_barrier(S, B, Tree) \leftrightarrow (\quad barrier(S, B, Tree) \qquad (10.5.13)$$

$$\lor \quad dominates(S, B, Tree) \land$$
$$\exists D$$
$$parent(S, D, Tree) \land$$
$$minimal(D) \land$$
$$\neg D = B \land$$
$$\exists L, C, N, F$$

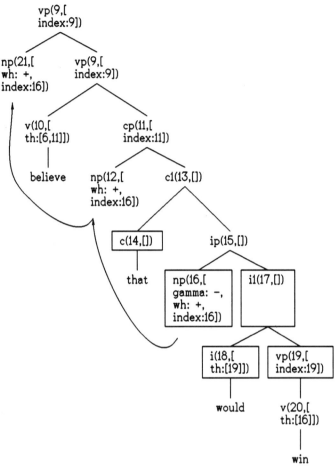

Figure 10.5
S-Structure with filled Comp

$$D = x(L, C, N, F) \wedge$$
$$\neg C = i \wedge$$
$$\neg(subtree(D/[], Tree) \wedge F = [])$$

).

Then the nodes that minimally govern the embedded trace category, $np(16, \ldots)$, are those highlighted in the Figure 10.4. In this structure, the trace category $np(16, \ldots)$ is properly governed by its antecedent $np(12, \ldots)$. If we let the complementizer be non-empty, though, it acts as a barrier to minimal government, so that the nodes minimally governing the embedded subject are those highlighted in Figure 10.5. The predicate *ss_gamma* marks the subject trace in this structure $-\gamma$, as indicated.

10.6 A-movement and agreement

Most of the previous discussion has concerned wh-movement to non-argument, i.e., Ā-positions. Now we turn to the NP-movement that occurs in raising and passive constructions. Chomsky notes that the formulation of the ECP and minimality noted above rules out the grammatical structure shown in Figure 10.6. The problem is that the matrix VP is a barrier for $np(9, \ldots)$, blocking antecedent-government. Although this VP is L-marked by I after V-raising, it is still a barrier by minimality since it is the immediate projection of V. This barrier cannot be avoided by adjunction to VP, since then we would have an "improper movement," a violation of the binding theory requirement that A-chains not include A-bar positions, as discussed at the end of §9.6. Chomsky's (1986a, 24-25) solution is to extend the "SPEC-head agreement" between I and its specifier to indices (Chomsky, 1986a, 74-75). Then, in the tree displayed in Figure 10.6, $i(4, \ldots)$ and $np(2, \ldots)$ would have the same index, and an extension of the notion of antecedent-government could plausibly allow this structure.

We have neglected agreement issues up to this point, but this aspect of the *Barriers* framework requires careful attention. In the first place, we assume that every category agrees with itself and with all of its projections (Chomsky, 1986a, 24). One natural perspective is that a lexical head, for example, has its features specified by the lexicon at the time of insertion, and these features, or perhaps only the agreement features, "percolate" up to the maximal projection of the category. The trees displayed in previous figures do not generally respect this idea, but we will assume henceforth that this percolation takes place at D-structure, at the time of lexical insertion. (Of course, we could easily formalize lexical insertion and this percolation from head to higher level projections. We have not done so just because these things have not been a focus of attention in *Barriers*.)

SPEC-head agreement is easily formalized transduction-style, adjusting the specifier and head features of every projection. To handle the case where there is more than one specifier, the addition of features to the specifiers is not done until "after" all agreement features have been added to the head. This is clearly essential, and has the consequence that all of the specifiers must agree with each other. It is convenient to assume that the features shared by this agreement step are exactly the ψ features, since this allows us to use the predicate *put_features*. If this assumption proves to be incorrect, a similar predicate could of course be defined to require sharing of some different set of features. The formalization appears in Appendix B. The basic idea is very simple, but the definition

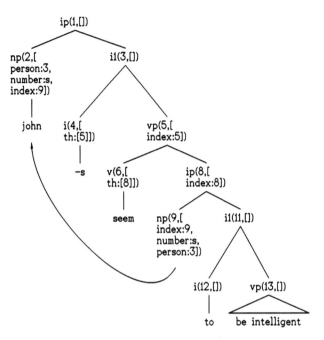

Figure 10.6
A structure with NP-movement

is complicated by the fact that there are a number of alternative phrase structures to be handled. For this reason, the definition of this relation is the longest definition in the whole theory, and its computational properties get some special attention in §14.

10.7   A modification in the ECP for raising and passive

Now we are in a position to implement Chomsky's use of agreement to get raising and passive constructions to satisfy the ECP, getting around the problem noted in connection with Figure 10.6. His idea is that after NP-movement and V-raising, if SPEC-head movement makes the I agree with its subject, then the subject will also be co-indexed with the verb, and we could extend the notion of a chain in such a way that these structures satisfy the ECP because the verb governs and binds the trace of NP. Chains were briefly introduced in §9.3 as sequences of co-indexed categories produced by movement. Chomsky (1986a, 75) proposes the notion of an "extended chain," defined as follows:

$\mathcal{C} = (\alpha_1, \ldots, \alpha_n, \beta)$ is an extended chain if $(\alpha_1, \ldots, \alpha_n)$ is a chain with index i and β has index i.

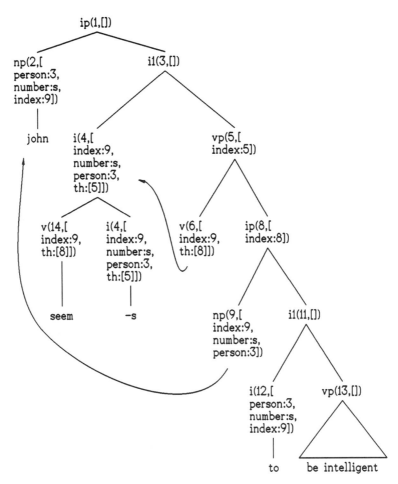

Figure 10.7
A tree after V-raising, NP-raising, and SPEC-head agreement

Figure 10.7 shows the tree of Figure 10.6 after V-movement and SPEC-head agreement. According to this definition of an extended chain,

$$(\ np(2, [index : 9]), np(9, [index : 9]), v(6, [index : 9]) \ )$$

is an extended chain in the tree of Figure 10.7. If we let the "links" of an extended chain $(\alpha_1, \ldots, \alpha_n, \beta)$ be either a pair (α_i, α_{i+1}) or the pair (β, α_n), then we have the desired result that the NP-trace $np(9, [index : 9])$ is antecedent-governed by the trace of the raised verb.[7]

Before formalizing this suggestion and exploring its consequences on a wider range of structures, we quickly consider passive constructions. Chomsky notes that the ECP as it is formulated at this point allows

$John_i$ was killed t_i.

since the trace is θ-governed by the verb. But it also allows the ungrammatical "super-raising" constructions of the sort pointed out by Lasnik (1985):

* $[A\ man]_i$ seems $[there\ to\ be\ killed\ t_i\ ]$.

Chomsky proposes to deal with this kind of construction by modifying the ECP so that θ-government does not suffice for proper government of verb complements. The problem here is that θ-government is licensing the trace, but the structure should be bad because the moved constituent is too far away. That is, perhaps the disjunctive formulation of the ECP should be replaced by a formulation in which only antecedent-governed traces are properly governed (Chomsky, 1986a, 76-79):

α properly governs β iff α antecedent-governs β.

Chomsky immediately observes that this proposal is based only on observations about extractions from V complements; the complements of P, A, and N call for further study.

We now consider the passive and super-raising examples to see that these proposals work at least on those cases. The S-structure of the passive might be something like that shown in Figure 10.8 (Chomsky, 1986a, 76-77).[8] Here, after SPEC-head feature sharing, the indices of the moved V and the moved NP are the same, and so if be is in the first segment of a VP adjunction structure, the NP-trace is antecedent-governed by the V-trace, as in the raising example we considered previously. The structure of the super-raising example, however, is something along the lines of Figure 10.9. In this case, the embedded verbs do not move to I since I contains the tenseless to, and so there is no V-trace in a position to antecedent-govern the embedded NP-trace.

Since it appears that these suggestions might be on the right track, let's formalize them. The required modifications in our principles are quite straightforward. Our new definition of proper government is wonderfully simple:

$$properly\_governs(A, B, Tree) \leftrightarrow ante\_governs(A, B, Tree). \qquad (10.7.14)$$

The definition of antecedent-government is complicated just by the fact that we need to use the extended notion of chain and link:

$$ante\_governs(A, B, Tree) \leftrightarrow ex\_link(A, B, Tree) \wedge \qquad (10.7.15)$$
$$governs(A, B, Tree).$$

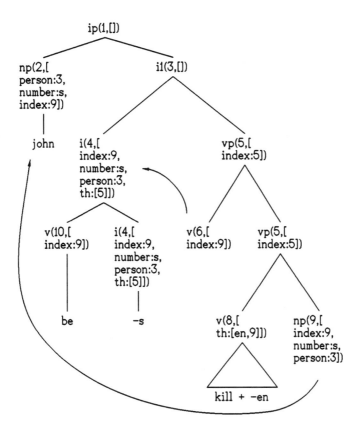

Figure 10.8
A passive structure

Chomsky's remarks suggest that we can add any co-indexed node to a chain produced by move-α to get an extended chain. This suggests that something as weak as the following can be proposed for *ex_link*:

$$ex\_link(A, B, Tree) \leftrightarrow (\quad link(A, B, Tree)$$
$$\lor \quad \exists I \ feature(index : I, A, A) \land$$
$$feature(index : I, B, B) \land$$
$$\neg A = B$$
$$).$$

Notice that an indexed node that is not linked to anything is the last node in a chain.

These modifications in our previous account of the ECP do, in fact, account for the passive and raising structures just considered. Applying *ss_gamma* to our first raising

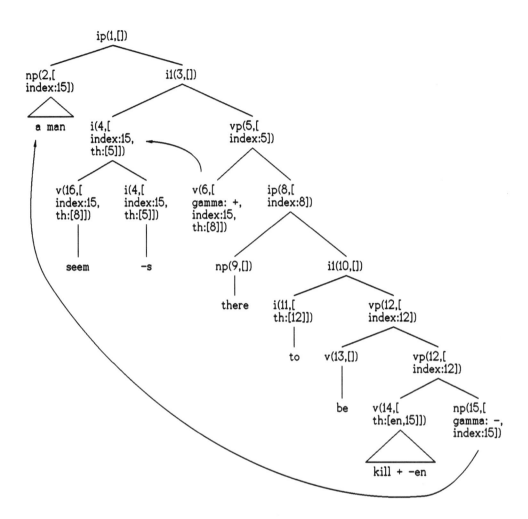

Figure 10.9
A super-raising structure

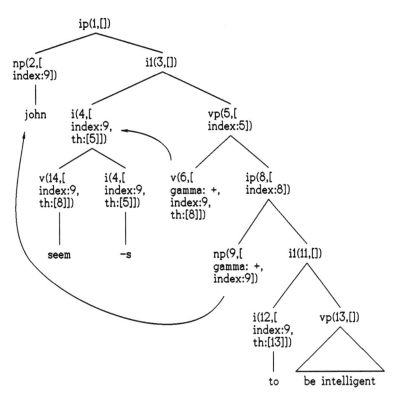

Figure 10.10
Raising and NP-movement

example, displayed in Figure 10.6, we get a $-\gamma$ trace. However, if we raise the verb to I (which we can do since we have not imposed any restrictions on V-raising in English, as discussed in §9.2), and then apply *spec_head* before applying *ss_gamma*, we get the tree shown in Figure 10.10 with properly governed traces. Since the trace of V is not in argument position, its trace is not marked by *ss_gamma*, but only by *lf_gamma*. Similarly, the simple passive shown in Figure 10.8 is allowed by the ECP, with *lf_gamma* labeling its traces $+\gamma$. The super-raising structure in Figure 10.9, on the other hand, gets a $-\gamma$ trace, as displayed.

10.8   Exploring some consequences of the ECP formalization

There has been a great deal of work on the ECP, and it is interesting to compare the *Barriers* account with the alternatives. Chomsky (1986a, 82) briefly mentions that his *Barriers* account does not explain the contrasts among the following examples:

* how raw did John [eat the meat t]?
how clean did John [pick the bone t]?
how angry did John [make his friends t]?

He suggests that proper government may require some special relation between verbs and the traces of the moved constituents in cases like these, suggesting a "conjunctive" formulation of the ECP. That is, the ECP would require that every trace be antecedent-governed *and* stand in some special local relation to a head governor. Conjunctive accounts of this kind have been developed by a number of linguists.[9]

The developments described in this chapter are presented very quickly, with only a few examples from *Barriers* to hint at the empirical motivation. Consequently it is natural to apply the proposed theory to some of the phenomena that are best known in the literature. We consider, in the first place, the original motivation for the disjunctive formulation of the ECP, with particular attention to whether that motivation has really been removed. The disjunctive accounts were formulated because of the need to account for subject/object asymmetries of the sort already discussed, but a few more examples may help round out the arguments. Subject/object asymmetries are clear in cases of the *that*-trace effect, and we have already discussed how the proposed minimality condition on government provides an account of the contrast between

Who did you believe would win?
* Who did you believe that would win?

To round out the consideration of these cases, though, it is important to see that we still allow:

What$_i$ did you believe that Bill [won t$_i$]?

Suppose that *what* first adjoins to the embedded VP, and then adjoins to the matrix VP, and finally is substituted into the specifier of the matrix CP. Part of the resulting structure is shown in Figure 10.11. Only one of the traces appears in an argument position, namely the trace $np(21,\ldots)$ in the original D-structure position of *what*. This trace is properly governed by the trace $np(22,\ldots)$ adjoined to the embedded VP, and so it is marked $+\gamma$. If we leave this chain untouched, trace $np(23,\ldots)$ will be marked

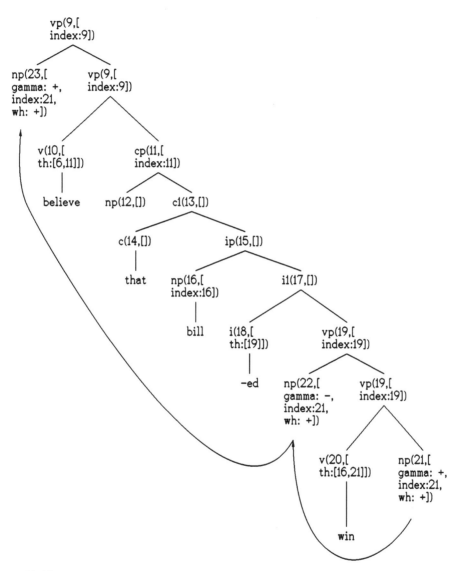

Figure 10.11
S-Structure with filled Comp and deletable $-\gamma$ trace

$+\gamma$ because it is governed by the specifier of CP, but trace $np(22, \ldots)$ is not properly governed and will be marked $-\gamma$. This trace would still be $-\gamma$ even if the movement had gone to the specifier position $np(12, [])$ instead of going directly to the matrix VP.

However, the offending trace is in a non-argument position, and so it is not required at LF by the projection principle or anything else. We can delete it without violating the recoverability principle since it has no content, and then there is no violation of the ECP at LF. That is, with our formalism, we begin with the D-structure of this tree, prove that it is related by two adjunction steps and one substitution step — three *affectA* steps altogether — to the tree that we see part of in Figure 10.11. Then we can apply *ss_gamma*, marking $np(21, \ldots) + \gamma$, delete $np(22, \ldots)$, and then apply *lf_gamma*, to end up with a tree containing only $+\gamma$ traces, a tree that satisfies the predicate *ecp*.[10]

In the remainder of this section we apply the formalism we have developed to two other interesting sorts of structures that are considered by Rizzi (1987; 1990, §1) in his arguments for an alternative account of the ECP. One of them is another of Huang's cases, which requires only a brief discussion:

* *How$_i$ [$_{ip}$do you [$_{vp}$ t$_i$ [$_{vp}$wonder [$_{cp}$[which problem]$_j$ [$_{ip}$PRO to [$_{vp}$ solve t$_j$ t$_i$]]]]]?*

In *Barriers*, this violates the ECP because the CP is a barrier to antecedent-government of the embedded adjunct trace. If the adjunct were first adjoined to the embedded VP,

* *How$_i$ [$_{ip}$do you [$_{vp}$ t$_i$ [$_{vp}$wonder [$_{cp}$[which problem]$_j$ [$_{ip}$PRO to [$_{vp}$ t$_i$ [$_{vp}$ solve t$_j$ t$_i$]]]]]]?*

the same barrier blocks antecedent-government of the empty category adjoined to VP. The following structure, with adjunctions to both the embedded VP and the embedded IP, does not violate the ECP, but violates the stipulation that wh-phrases should not adjoin to IP:

* *How$_i$ [$_{ip}$do you [$_{vp}$t$_i$[$_{vp}$wonder [$_{cp}$[which problem]$_j$ [$_{ip}$t$_i$[$_{ip}$ PRO to [$_{vp}$t$_i$[$_{vp}$ solve t$_j$t$_i$]]]]]]]?*

Thus the *Barriers* account can properly rule out this construction.

It is interesting to consider, at somewhat greater length, another kind of structure for which Rizzi (1987 ; 1990, §1.4) has proposed an ECP account: the pseudo-opacity phenomenon noted by Obenauer (1984) and others. In French the wh-quantifier *combien* can be fronted to produce structures like the following:

[Combien de livres]$_i$ a-t-il consulté t$_i$?
    (how many (of) books has he consulted?)
Combien$_i$ a-t-il consulté t$_i$ de livres?
    (how many has he consulted (of) books?)

This surprising ability for the quantifier to occur outside of the object NP is what Obenauer calls "quantification at a distance." French also allows adverbial quantifiers to precede the verb, and the same position can apparently hold a moved wh-quantifier:

Il a beaucoup consulté ces livres.
   (he has often consulted these books.)
Il a beaucoup$_i$ consulté t$_i$ de livres.
   (he has many consulted (of) books.)

Now, the interesting thing is that when the adverbial position is filled by an adverbial quantifier, extraction of *combien* is not possible. The adverbial introduces a "pseudo-opacity" that makes quantification at a distance impossible. Wh-fronting must move the whole object:

[Combien de livres]$_i$ a-t-il beaucoup consulté t$_i$?
   (how many (of) books has he often consulted?)
* *Combien$_i$ a-t-il beaucoup consulté t$_i$ de livres?*
   (how many has he often consulted (of) books?)

We first consider how these sentences could be analyzed in a *Barriers* framework.

The structure of phrases like *combien de livres* is not quite clear. One idea is to regard *combien de livres* as having the structure $[_{np}QP\ PP]$ (as in Obenauer, 1976, for example). These phrases seem rather like English partitives (i.e., NPs like *many of the books* in which it seems that *of* must be inserted between the quantifier and the head), where the preposition *de* must sometimes be inserted in French even when the quantifier is empty. But some explanation would need to be given of the apparent violation in the X-bar requirements. An alternative defended by Kayne (1983, §§1.5,2.9) is that *de* is not a preposition but part of a complex determiner. Yet another option is to regard *de* as a case marker. For the following argument, any of these analyses is acceptable, but we will follow Rizzi (1987; 1990) in making the arguable assumption that *combien de livres* is an NP and that *combien* can be regarded as a QP specifier.[11] We require, because of the minimality extension to the concept of barrier, only that in these NPs no 0-level category occurs as an immediate constituent.

Consider again the example

Combien a-t-il consulté de livres?

There is some debate about whether the *combien* has moved from the object NP, but we can follow Obenauer and others in assuming that it does. Then we want to see that we can allow

Combien$_i$ a-t-il t$_i$ consulté t$_i$ de livres?

in the *Barriers* framework. Since the intermediate trace is obviously properly governed, it is only the initial extraction from NP which could be a problem. Assuming the object

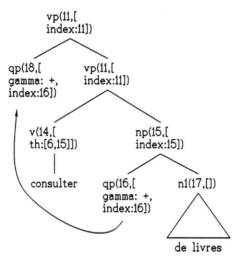

Figure 10.12
Wh-quantifier movement

NP has a $[_{np}QP\ N1]$ structure, the relevant part of this example is shown in Figure 10.12. Minimality aside, the NP node in this structure is L-marked, and so it is not a barrier to extraction of the QP. We properly predict that we could not have such an extraction from an NP that was not L-marked. (Cf., e.g., Kayne, 1983, §3.) When barrierhood is extended with the minimality condition, we still have no barrier to proper government, since even though the NP dominates the trace together with other material, NP is not the *immediate* projection of any 0-level category. Thus we can easily prove from our formalization of *Barriers* that this structure satisfies the ECP. Note that the trace is governed but not properly governed by the verb. In this respect, our analysis is essentially different from Kayne's (1983, §3): the trace is antecedent-governed on our analysis.

It is interesting to note that things are different in English and German. Similar extractions seem to be impossible:

[*How many letters*]$_i$ has he sent t$_i$ to you?
* [*How many*]$_i$ has he sent [t$_i$ *letters*] to you?
[*Wie viele Briefe*]$_i$ hat sie dir t$_i$ geschickt?
* [*Wie viele*]$_i$ hat sie dir [t$_i$ *Briefe*] geschickt?

Obenauer (1976) discusses these examples, and notes that there do seem to be English and German cases in which a QP can be fronted out of NP, as in

How many are left of those old containers?
Was sucht er für ein Werkzeug?

These examples suggest that the presence of the preposition is crucial. That is, it appears that extraction of QP is possible from $[_{np}QP\ PP]$ but not from $[_{np}QP\ N1]$. The matter is complicated, though, so we will not try to resolve these problems here.[12]

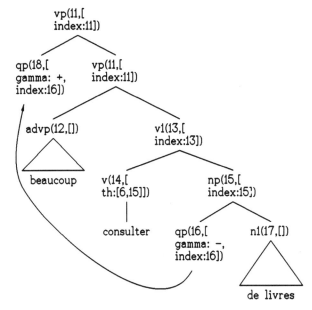

Figure 10.13
Movement blocked by quantification at a distance

In any case, we have seen that the *Barriers* framework can account fairly naturally for the basic paradigm:

$[Combien\ de\ livres]_i\ a$-$t$-$il\ consulté\ t_i$?
$Combien_i\ a$-t-$il\ consulté\ t_i\ de\ livres$?

So now let's return to the problem Rizzi raises: How can we account for

* $Combien_i\ a$-t-$il\ beaucoup\ consulté\ t_i\ de\ livres$?

The relevant structure is similar to the one we had before, but if *beaucoup* occurs as the specifier of VP, as shown in Figure 10.13, this difference matters. The *Barriers* account we have formalized rules this case out. Given the minimality extension to the notion of barrier, there is a barrier to the government of the embedded trace category $qp(16, [])$,

namely, $v1(13, [])$. This result is easily demonstrated from our formalization, though
Obenauer (1984) argues that it is inelegant to have the appropriate relation between
the trace and the moved constituent blocked by the presence of the adverbial, since the
relation between the adverbial position and the quantifier position is not established by
a movement, and this argument is endorsed by Koster (1987, 51-52) and others.

Barriers appears to be doing the right thing with these constructions, but when we
consider the range of cases in which minimality applies in this way, a number of serious
problems still remain, as Chomsky notes. In the first place, the minimality condition
predicts the following contrast

Who$_i$ did you t$_i$ see pictures of t$_i$?
* *Who$_i$ did you t$_i$ see his pictures of t$_i$?*

The situation here is much like the cases just discussed. The object NP is L-marked, but
when there is a specifier there must be an intermediate projection which the minimality
condition counts as a barrier. The problem is that the same logic rules out

Who$_i$ did you t$_i$ see three pictures of t$_i$?
Who$_i$ did you t$_i$ see more pictures of t$_i$?

Chomsky (1986a, p81) speculates that the latter examples may be better than the case
with *his* in specifier position because they are in some sense less "specific." The matter
is left unresolved.

In the second place, Chomsky (1986a, 87) attributes to Barss the observation that,
although minimality gives the structure in Figure 10.5 a $-\gamma$ constituent, the sentence

* *Who did you believe that would win*

is not ruled out. There is an alternative derivation in these cases which does not violate
the ECP: the embedded subject can be first adjoined to the embedded VP, *win*, then
substituted for specifier of the embedded CP, adjoined to the matrix VP, and finally
substituted for specifier of the matrix CP. In this derivation all of the traces are properly
governed, even with the minimality restriction. With our formalization and an automatic
theorem prover, it is easy to check in complete detail to see that this is, in fact, the case.

One final issue is worth noting. The extension of SPEC-head agreement to referential
indices has the effect of merging chains, and this has wide consequences. One problem is
that since SPEC-head agreement is mandatory, it will force some constituents to become
bound in domains where they should not have to be. Consider, for example, the condition
B contrast:

He$_i$ likes him$_i$.
[his$_i$ father]$_j$ likes him$_i$.

If *his* is the specifier of the subject NP, then SPEC-head agreement will give it the same index as the head, and if XPs have the indices of their heads, then $i = j$ and the latter construction would be incorrectly ruled out. In languages like Dutch, where head movement seems to move verbs to I and then into higher clauses (as discussed in §9.2), the effects of sharing indices will be drastic.

Part III

Variations and Elaborations

Chapter 11

Determiner phrases

In *Barriers*, Chomsky extends X-bar theory to the non-lexical categories I and C, and proposes that all specifiers and complements are maximal projections. Some adjustment is needed to fit this proposal with the most common specifiers of NP, the determiners. Here we consider the idea that determiners are actually the heads of phrases, determiner phrases (DPs), which have NP complements. We consider this elaboration of the *Barriers* framework and others in the next two chapters partly because they are interesting ideas, but mainly to illustrate the ease with which fundamental aspects of our theory can be modified and explored.

A considerable flexibility in our formalization has already been seen. For example, following Chomsky's development of the theory, we formalized adjunction and then modified it to allow amalgamation of a verb with its affix; we then modified slightly the definition of a lexical category to allow an amalgamation of verb with inflection to be an L-marker; we modified our first formulations of subjacency to allow it to be sensitive to parametric barriers; we modified our definition of government with a minimality condition and noted the consequences of this change for antecedent government. All of these changes were easy to make, and did not require any major overhaul of what had been done earlier, even though the changes to these fundamental notions have deep and widely various consequences. It is uncommon for a formalization to allow easy exploration of changes in fundamental ideas. McCarthy (1987) even suggests that the difficulty in maintaining flexibility in a formalization is the fundamental challenge of artificial intelligence. One reason that we are able to avoid the extensibility problem to a remarkable degree is that the theory we are formalizing is modular in structure. We have preserved this modularity in our formalization, staying close to the linguists' declarative principles rather than specializing the system for any particular application. Because so many of the basic concepts remain the same in many elaborations of *Barriers*-like frameworks, the formalization of

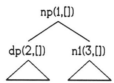

Figure 11.1
Jackendoff's NPs with DP specifiers

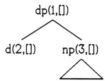

Figure 11.2
Abney's DPs with NP complements

those concepts can remain untouched. DPs by themselves require no revisions and only a very minimal elaboration, but at the end of this chapter we consider some ideas that would require major revisions. These drastic revisions will not be executed; other major revisions will be undertaken in the following two chapters.

11.1   Empirical motivations for a DP hypothesis

Different versions of the hypothesis that determiners are heads of phrases are proposed by Jackendoff (1977) and Abney (1986, 1987). Jackendoff proposes that DPs occur as specifiers of NP, as in Figure 11.1, while Abney proposes that NPs occur as complements of DPs, as in Figure 11.2. Both views have some appeal just because they simplify X-bar theory, but the apparent simplification could be an illusion if the facts call for introducing complications elsewhere in the theory. In recent work Stowell (1989, 1989a) has provided new and persuasive empirical support for Abney's DP proposal which favors it over Jackendoff's view and goes beyond the theory-internal motivation. Structures similar to Abney's have been used in various forms by many other researchers.[1] We will quite briefly show how these structures can be incorporated easily into the *Barriers* framework which we have formalized in previous chapters, with only a quick mention of some of the empirical motivations. (The reader is referred to the cited papers for careful discussion of the evidence.)

   One motivation for determiner phrases comes from the distribution of PRO. Stowell (1989) points out that the subject position in small clause complements appears to receive case from the matrix verb, and so PRO, which must occur in an ungoverned position, cannot occur there:

I consider [*John fascinating*].
Who_i did you hear [*t_i leave the room*].
* *Sam considers* [*PRO fascinating*].
* *Kevin heard* [*PRO read the lesson*].

The situation is similar in verbal complements like the following, in which PRO is again excluded:

John bought a shoe.
*John bought PRO's shoe.

Since these complements are θ-governed by the verb, a lexical category, the complements are L-marked and hence not barriers to government, and so these cases are properly handled in the *Barriers* framework. However, there is also evidence that in some similar constructions, PRO is allowed or even required:

John disapproves of [*the PRO hatred of oneself*].
John needs [*a PRO_i talking to t_i*].
Bill resented [*the PRO destruction of the city PRO to prove a point*].

Stowell suggests that in the first of these examples, PRO is needed as an antecedent of *oneself*; in the second, PRO is needed as the antecedent of the trace; and in the third, the first PRO is needed as the antecedent of the second. If the PRO in these cases occurs as a specifier of the NP, there is a problem, since these specifier positions are governed by the matrix verb.

This problem is avoided if we assume that PRO in the latter cases occurs as the specifier of an NP complement of DP, as shown in Figure 11.3, for example. In this position there is an additional maximal projection that intervenes between PRO (here treated as a +*pronominal* DP) and the verb. Although the DP complement is L-marked, its NP complement is not L-marked (even if it is θ-marked) since D itself is not a lexical category.

The DP structure is quite natural. DPs without complements are quite common, as in the case of demonstrative determiners,

That is not surprising,

but there are also cases of NPs that are not preceded by any overt determiners:

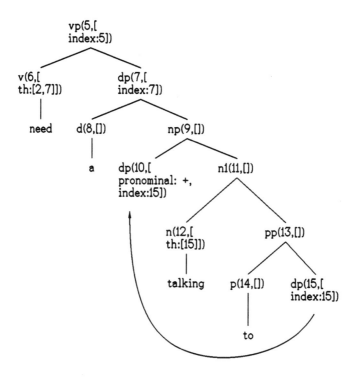

Figure 11.3
PRO inside complement DP protected from government by V

Empirical problems arise at every turn.
Trouble can arise.

One possibility here is that empty determiners can select NPs that are plural, mass, etc. Slightly more troubling are the cases of possessive NPs, which occur in a complementary distribution with determiners in English:

[John]'s worries are serious.
[The man]'s worries are serious.
[The man]'s the worries are serious.

Suppose that the DPs *John* or *the man*, with genitive case marking, appear as specifiers of null Ds. Then we need to require that a possessive specifier (or genitive case marked specifier) can only occur when D is null, or something to that effect. It is interesting to note that this stipulation is apparently not required in certain other languages, from Hungarian (Szabolcsi, 1987; 1990),

Csak te ismer-ed az én minden titk-om-at

   (only you know the 1st.person.Nom every secret)

to Bambara (Bird et al., 1977; Crook, 1990), where a low tone (indicated by underscore) indicates the definite article:

Kante ka wùlú tùn bɛ sàgá-ù faga.

   (Kanté Poss dog-Art Past Imcmp. sheep-Pl-Art kill

   (Kanté's dog was killing the sheep.)

   Another motivation for DP structures comes from its ability to account for certain extractions. Stowell (1989) points out that the DP hypothesis in a *Barriers*-like framework can account for contrasts like the following:

Who$_i$ did you sell [$_{dp}$ t$_i$ a [$_{np}$ picture of t$_i$]]?
* Who$_i$ did you sell [$_{dp}$ Mary's [$_{np}$ picture of t$_i$]]?

If *sell* selects DPs, a movement directly from the PP object position to the specifier of CP is not 1-subjacent. The indicated NPs are barriers for the object of PP since they are not L-marked, and the indicated DPs then are barriers for the object of PP by inheritance, even though they are L-marked. However, if the specifier of indicated DP is empty, as in the former example, the movement can proceed via that position. The trace left in this position will have to be deleted to avoid an ECP violation at LF.

11.2   The formalism and preliminary tests

To bring determiners into the X-bar system, we simply allow the use of *d* as a head in the notation *x*(*Level, Head, Number, Features*) that is introduced in §6.3. Remarkably, this step by itself suffices to incorporate DPs into the *Barriers* framework that has been formalized. No change in the earlier formalization is required, since determiners were never excluded from the X-bar system. Hence we can proceed immediately to check whether Stowell's analyses can be derived. Given the tree shown in Figure 11.3, we can prove that $dp(10,\ldots)$ is not governed by $v(6,\ldots)$. As discussed in §8.6, though, the *governs* relation that Chomsky defines is quite loose. In this tree, we can prove that $dp(10,\ldots)$ is governed by $dp(10,\ldots), n1(11,[]), n(12,\ldots)$ and $pp(13,[])$.

   Now consider the relevant part of the underlying structures of Stowell's examples of movement relations. One of these is displayed in Figure 11.4. Given this displayed tree, we can demonstrate, as Stowell suggests, that both $np(15,[])$ and $dp(11,\ldots)$ are barriers for $dp(21,\ldots)$. As noted above, $pp(19,\ldots)$ is also a barrier unless it is θ-marked by $n(18,\ldots)$, as indicated. Then movement to $dp(12,\ldots)$ crosses just one barrier, namely

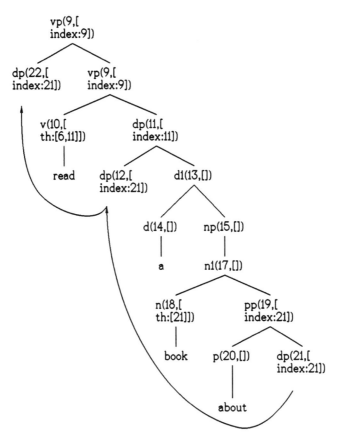

Figure 11.4
Grammatical movement out of DP

$np(15, [])$. Crossing one barrier is allowed by 1-subjacency. Further movement out of the displayed tree (e.g. by first adjoining to VP) is then a possibility, since $dp(11,\ldots)$ is not a barrier for $dp(12, [])$. We do not have any ECP violations either, since the resulting trace category $dp(12,\ldots)$ antecedent-governs $dp(21,\ldots)$.

Stowell's contrasting example is one in which the specifier of DP, $dp(12,\ldots)$, is not empty, but contains *Mary*, and receives a possessor θ-role and genitive case in that position. Substitution into $dp(12,\ldots)$ from $dp(21,\ldots)$ is of course blocked in this structure. Adjunction is not an option because $dp(12,\ldots)$ is an argument, having received a θ-role, and so fronting of $dp(21,\ldots)$ is blocked in this structure, according to the formalization of *Barriers*.

11.3   Subjacency and the strict cycle condition

Stowell (1989, 246) suggests that in the example,

Who_i did you sell [_dp Mary's [_np picture of t_i]]?

there is a preference to interpret "Mary" as the agent of the NP rather than as the possessor. The same preference plays a role in the following:

* *What_i did you present [_dp Mary's [_np theory of t_i]]?*
** *What_i did you read [_dp Mary's [_np book about t_i]]?*

The former example here seems slightly better than the latter, since the agent role for the genitive NP is more natural in that case. Stowell observes that accounting for this in the current framework leads to some surprising conclusions. Suppose we assume that possessor arguments are base generated in the specifier of DP, whereas NP subjects get to that position by movement. In the last section we saw that the unacceptability of the unpreferred readings is accounted for because these structures violate subjacency, since the specifier of DP is filled by the possessor and so the object must be fronted across the indicated NP and DP barriers. Then the problem is that the preferred readings violate subjacency in the same way: after the NP subject moves into the DP specifier position, there is still no way for the preferred readings to be derived except by crossing the same barriers. Stowell suggests that the contrast can be derived by assuming that the preferred readings are not derived by this subjacency violation, but rather by moving the object through the specifier of DP, and then moving the subject of the NP into the resulting trace position. This is a kind of movement we have not considered before, and have not ruled out. Stowell's idea is that it might be ruled out by some version of the "strict cycle condition" (SCC), and that the preference in these cases could be accounted for if SCC violations are less severe than 1-subjacency violations. It is worth a brief digression to see why this idea might be regarded as surprising, particularly because the SCC will be of some interest later.

   The sentence

* *What_i did you present [_dp Mary's [_np theory of t_i]]?*

might be derived from

* *did you present [_dp e [_np Mary theory of what]]?*

by substituting *what* for the empty specifier *e*, then adjoining it to VP, and then substituting into the specifier of CP; the subject *Mary* could then move into the specifier

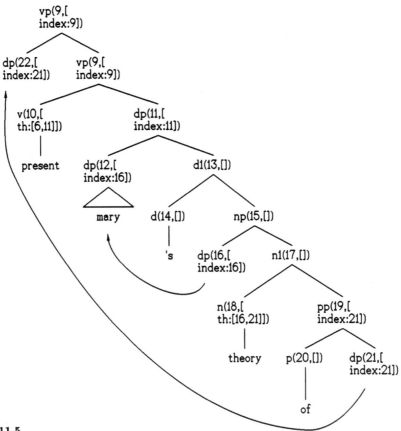

Figure 11.5
Derivation that violates subjacency

position which is now a trace of the fronted NP. This kind of movement has sometimes been ruled out by an ordering requirement called the "strict cycle condition" (SCC). If we define the *domain* of a movement as the minimal node that dominates both the original position and the landing site of the moved constituent, the SCC can be expressed as follows (Chomsky, 1973, 243):

> A movement in domain A cannot be followed by a movement in domain B if A properly includes B.

The idea is that we must do the most peripheral movements first, making small adjustments in structure out near the leaves before any of the larger movements. A sequence of movements respecting the SCC is said to be applied "successive cyclically." In the

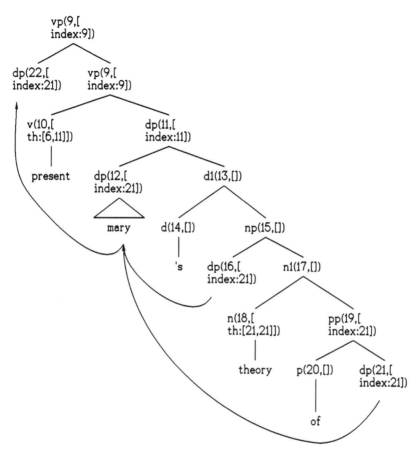

Figure 11.6
Derivation that substitutes into a trace

example we are interested in here, the movement of *what* out of the DP has a domain that properly includes the movement of *Mary* into the resulting trace, so this derivation violates the SCC. Stowell's idea is that the preference among the marginal readings noted at the end of the last section could be explained if subjacency violations are worse than SCC violations.[2]

This idea may seem simple, but it is not! We have not formalized the SCC, so it is no surprise that our formalization of movements allows the substitution of *Mary* into the position of the trace of *what*. Even though this is a possible movement, it produces a result that is ungrammatical even without the SCC. The problem is that this substitution causes the referential indices of the two chains to become identified. On the natural

representational characterization of chains, then, *Mary* and *what* become members of the
same chain, violating the θ-criterion and other requirements.[3] Since θ-criterion violations,
structures in which there are too many arguments or too few arguments, are typically
very bad, some adjustment in our framework would be required for SCC violations like
this one to become relatively mild violations.

A brief contemplation of what adjustments would be required shows that they are
not minor. One idea would be to let traces be left unindexed by movements, freely
indexing them later according to the restrictions of binding theory, etc. If subjacency
applies after trace indexing, then, we would not be able to draw the distinction Stowell
suggests. We could avoid this problem by letting subjacency be a condition on movements
instead of a condition on representations. We will not try to work out this alternative
sort of approach. In any case, the general point is interesting: the introduction of DPs
apparently does not require major changes in our theory, but a change which might have
seemed less substantial, wanting to allow SCC violations to be milder than subjacency
violations, has consequences that would require fundamental changes.

Chapter 12

Inflectional phrases and head movement

This score seeks to create the image of a tree or family tree. The deeper the line, the more slowly it moves, and vice versa. This results in three layers of movement, a mensuration canon in which each of the three layers presents the theme in a different tempo. — Arvo Pärt

The proposals about movements of verbs and other heads in *Barriers* are intriguing and suggestive, but they need further development. For example, we observed in §9.2 that, in English, verbs other than *have*, *be* and perhaps *do* cannot raise, and yet we saw in §10.5 that the special percolation of index that occurs when verbs raise to amalgamate with inflection is essential to the account of NP-raising constructions like

John seems to be intelligent.

Since many English verbs cannot raise to I and then to C as shown by

* Seems John to be intelligent?

there is an unresolved problem in the *Barriers* theory. These issues have been a focus of attention in recent research. We will briefly consider one of the prominent proposals, one advanced by Pollock (1989). Pollock provides a rich comparative study of verbs, inflection, negation and adverb placement in French and English, but we will restrict our attention to the modifications in the *Barriers* framework proposed to account for verb movement in English. Again, the reader is referred to Pollock (1989) for a careful discussion of the data, since only a brief review is presented before formalizing the central theoretical claims.[1]

12.1 Verb raising and affix lowering in English

Pollock (1989) proposes that inflectional phrases, IPs, have more structure than is usually assumed. In particular, he suggests that an English sentence may have projections of Tense (T), Negation (Neg), and Agreement (Agr) — all of these categories acting as heads in the X-bar system, and projecting to the phrasal level. A simple English sentence like

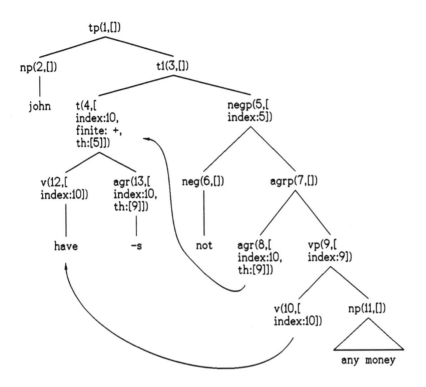

Figure 12.1
A simple tree with projections of T, Neg, and Agr

Hasn't John any money?

has a structure that is something like Figure 12.1.

The lexical restriction on raising V to I (or, more precisely, to Agr) that is evidenced in Modern English is explained by assuming that *have* and *be* are distinguished among Modern English verbs in that they do not assign θ-roles to the constituents that they subcategorize for, and that in sentences like the one in Figure 12.1, *have* is a raising verb. Pollock proposes that the subject NP in this sentence originates in the NP small clause $np(11, [])$, where it is θ-marked by a null preposition, and the NP *any money* is θ-marked by a null abstract predicate.[2] The special ability of *have* and *be* to raise then follows on the assumption that the amalgamated structure formed by V-raising to the Modern English Agr blocks the ability of (any element in the chain of) the verb to assign θ-roles. A verb with arguments needing θ-roles would be unable to assign those roles if it raised to Agr, and a θ-criterion violation would result.[3] How does the verb get the affix associated with Agr when raising to I would lead to a θ-criterion violation? Pollock proposes that this must be done by affix lowering, adjunction of Agr to V. If this movement leaves a trace at S-structure, that trace will violate the ECP unless it is deleted. Since it is in non-argument position and is not required by any other principles, this deletion would leave a structure fully compatible with all of the principles so far formalized. Another possibility is that the movement of Agr to V takes place at PF and the ECP does not apply there, and other accounts are also possible. Pollock (1989, 394) mentions some of these options, but does not explore them in detail.

The proposal that there are these two types of movement that can bring the agreement affix and the verb together suggests that the choice might be optional, and this is a serious consequence that Pollock rejects. Pollock argues, on the contrary, that verb raising is obligatory whenever it is possible. One argument for this view comes from adverb placement. Since *completely* is a VP adverb and not a sentential adverb, it can occur in VP-initial but not in pre-Agr position, as we see in structures like,

John completely lost his mind.
*John completely will lose his mind.

So if *be* and *have* did not have to raise to T, then some sort of special explanation would be required of the contrast between the following sentences ,

John is completely losing his mind.
* John completely is losing his mind.

Similarly, assuming that *do*-support would apply when the verbs do not raise to Agr, we would require an explanation of the unacceptability of

* I don't have sung.
* I don't be singing.
* I don't be happy.

Ungrammatical strings would also result if *do*-support did not apply in these cases. We could account for these facts if verb raising were obligatory whenever it were possible.

On the basis of verb raising in French, Pollock (1989, 392) argues that verb raising is always required in $+finite$ clauses, because $+finite$ (or $\pm past$) acts as an operator which must bind the trace of a verb:

$+finite$ must bind a variable $[_{v_i} e]$.

So then the proposed account for English is this: since raising a main verb other than *have* or *be* would lead to a θ-criterion violation, an auxiliary verb generated "beyond the VP boundary" can substitute for the main verb, raising to $+finite$ and leaving a trace, thereby rescuing the structure.

This idea raises a number of questions. Why can't such "substitution" of an auxiliary verb for the main verb take place in all cases, since as the last examples show, *do* cannot occur as an auxiliary verb with *have* or *be*? To account for this, Pollock suggests that the verb *do* is semantically empty, and can raise in place of a main verb only when it substitutes for a verb with a θ-grid. There may be some way to extend this account to explain examples like,

* John isn't happy, does he?
* John hasn't gone, does he?
* John wasn't kissed by Mary, did he?

but these sorts of cases will not be considered here. A second, even more basic question is how can the requirement for raising be reconciled with the fact that in sentences like

John left.
John leaves.

we want to say that the verb is properly inflected but does not, and cannot, move without producing a θ-criterion violation? Pollock's solution to this problem is to treat these cases in analogy with

John did leave.
John does leave.

by assuming that there is, in effect, a null verb *do* that raises to Agr and T, giving $+finite$ a verbal trace to bind, and then affix lowering moves Agr and T back down to the main verb. This null verb is not lexical, and so the ECP properly rules out

* John not left.
* John not leaves.

Preverbal VP-adverbs can occur, however, since they occur inside VP and their projections consequently do not intervene between the null verb and its trace.

12.2   Head movement and the structure of IP

We now formalize some of the main ideas in Pollock's account of English. Since no basic change in X-bar theory is proposed, no change in the *Barriers* X-bar theory is required to allow Figure 12.1 as a well formed maximal projection of T. However, the category that has been replaced, I, has some special properties in *Barriers*. In particular, as mentioned in §8.4, Chomsky wants to treat it as a "defective" category, one that is not a barrier merely in virtue of being a blocking category. It can only be a barrier "by inheritance." Pollock suggests that the "defective" distinction now be given to Agr, and so we can modify the definition of *barrier* as follows:

σ is a barrier for β iff either
(a) σ immediately dominates δ and δ is a BC for β, or
(b) σ is a BC for β and $\sigma \neq AgrP$.

$$barrier(S, B, Tree) \leftrightarrow (\qquad \exists D \qquad\qquad\qquad\qquad\qquad\qquad (12.2.1)$$
$$imm\_dominates(S, D, Tree) \wedge$$
$$blocking\_cat(D, B, Tree)$$
$$\vee \quad blocking\_cat(S, B, Tree) \wedge$$
$$\neg \exists N, F \ \ S = x(s(s(0)), agr, N, F)$$
$$).$$

Further adjustments are required. As indicated in Figure 12.1, Pollock wants to allow movement of the level 0 category V to Agr, but this violates the Head Movement Constraint (HMC) that was discussed in §9.2 and repeated here:

> *Head Movement Constraint (HMC):* Movement of a 0-level category β is restricted to the position of a head α that governs the maximal projection γ of β, where α θ-governs or L-marks γ if $\alpha \neq C$.

Pollock (1989, 383) accepts this constraint, and so a problem arises because although Agr governs the maximal projection of V, it does not θ-govern or L-mark it. Pollock suggests that the V in this case is to amalgamate with Agr to make it an L-marker, just as V amalgamated with I in the *Barriers* theory. Furthermore, if an amalgamated V-I constituent moves to T, it must also make T an L-marker.

In our formalization, the "amalgamation" property which triggers the lexical property in non-lexical categories is the percolation of the verbal index to the landing site. Consequently this amalgamation with Agr and T instead of with I requires a straightforward modification of *amalgamate*, previously defined in §9.2. Instead of amalgamating only when the moved constituent is itself a verb, we will amalgamate whenever the moved constituent already has the index of a verb. This requires that *amalgamate* be able to see the whole of the moved constituent, not merely its root. Adding the moved constituent as an argument to *amalgamate* requires a trivial change in *adjoin_cat*, and then the definition of *amalgamate* is easily formulated:

$$adjoin\_cat(Moved, Landing, Tree0, Tree, Renumbering) \leftrightarrow \qquad (12.2.2)$$

$\quad \exists L0, C0, N0, F0, Seq0$

$\quad\quad Tree0 = x(L0, C0, N0, F0)/Seq0 \wedge$

$\quad\quad (\quad \exists Seq, Pos, Selected, RestSeq, Transformed$

$\quad\quad\quad select(Pos, Seq0, Selected, RestSeq) \wedge$

$\quad\quad\quad adjoin\_cat(Moved, Landing, Selected, Transformed, Renumbering) \wedge$

$\quad\quad\quad select(Pos, Seq, Transformed, RestSeq) \wedge$

$\quad\quad\quad Tree = x(L0, C0, N0, F0)/Seq$

$\quad\quad \vee \quad \exists L, C, N, F, Seq, N2, Root, Tree1, Seq1$

$\quad\quad\quad Moved = x(L, C, N, F)/Seq \wedge$

$\quad\quad\quad amalgamate(Moved, Tree0, Root/Tree1) \wedge$

$\quad\quad\quad newnumber(Renumbering, N2) \wedge$

$\quad\quad\quad (\quad Seq = [x(L, C, N2, F)/Seq1, Root/Tree1]$

$\quad\quad\quad \vee \quad Seq = [Root/Tree1, x(L, C, N2, F)/Seq1]$

$\quad\quad\quad) \wedge$

$\quad\quad\quad Tree = Root/Seq \wedge$

$\quad\quad\quad Landing = Root$

$\quad)$

$$amalgamate(Moved, Tree0, Tree) \leftrightarrow \qquad (12.2.3)$$

$\quad\quad\quad\quad (\quad \exists MRoot, Seq, I, Seq0, L, N, F, Root0, Affix$

$\quad\quad\quad\quad\quad Moved = MRoot/Seq \wedge$

$\quad\quad\quad\quad\quad feature(index : I, MRoot, MRoot) \wedge$

$\quad\quad\quad\quad\quad subtree(x(L, v, N, F)/Seq0, Moved) \wedge$

$\quad\quad\quad\quad\quad member(index : I, F) \wedge$

$\quad\quad\quad\quad\quad Tree0 = Root0/[(-Affix)/[]] \wedge$

$\quad\quad\quad\quad\quad feature(index : I, Root0, Root) \wedge$

$\quad\quad\quad\quad\quad Tree = Root/[(-Affix)/[]]$

$\quad\quad\quad\quad \vee \quad Tree0 = Tree$

$\quad\quad\quad\quad).$

With these new definitions, we can adjoin V to Agr if Agr θ-marks the maximal projection of V, as in Figure 12.1.

Movement of the amalgamated Agr-V to T still cannot be achieved without violating the HMC. There are two problems. In the first place, if we assume that T θ-marks NegP, and that T becomes lexical when it amalgamates with V-I, then T L-marks NegP, but T still does not θ-govern or L-mark ArgP. In the second place, the movement would result in an ECP violation because NegP would be a minimal barrier intervening between the moved constituent and its trace. Pollock's suggestion is that Neg is to be regarded as "intrinsically inert" for government under minimality.[4] For this change to solve the first of the two mentioned problems, a substantial change in the HMC is obviously required. That is, Pollock might be interpreted as proposing a Weakened Head Movement Constraint, according to which movement of a 0-level category β is restricted to the position of a head α that governs the maximal projection γ of β under minimality. This constraint is too weak, however, and does not square with Pollock's concern about L-marking. Rejecting this idea, the only plausible alternative interpretation is unfortunately rather messy. We must assume that Neg is to be "inert" in the sense that its projections are never minimal barriers *and* in the sense that it is "transparent" to L-marking, where L-marking of such a "transparent" category penetrates to its complements.

In sum, then, we have two changes to make in the *Barriers* framework in order to allow movement of V-I across NegP to T. In the first place, we must redefine L-marking so that a category can be L-marked by being the complement of a "transparent" L-marked category, where the only such "transparent" category we require is Neg. In the second place, we must adjust the definition of minimal barriers so that projections of Neg are ruled out. We accordingly revise our definitions of *lexical* and *l_marks* from §10.3 and of *minimal_barrier* from §10.4:

$$lexical(Node, Tree) \leftrightarrow \exists L, Cat, N, F \qquad (12.2.4)$$

$$
\begin{aligned}
&Node = x(L, Cat, N, F) \wedge \\
&(\quad member(Cat, [v, n, a, p]) \\
&\vee \quad \neg member(Cat, [v, n, a, p]) \wedge \\
&\qquad \exists I, Root, Seq \\
&\qquad\quad member(index : I, F) \wedge \\
&\qquad\quad subtree(Root/Seq, Tree) \wedge \\
&\qquad\quad feature(index : I, Root, Root) \\
&)
\end{aligned}
$$

$$l\_marks(A, B, Tree) \leftrightarrow \exists G \quad lexical(A, Tree) \wedge \qquad (12.2.5)$$

$$
\begin{aligned}
&th\_governs(A, G, Tree) \wedge \\
&(\quad B = G \\
&\vee \quad head(B, G, Tree) \\
&\vee \quad specifier(B, G, Tree) \\
&\vee \quad \exists L, N, F \quad G = x(L, neg, N, F) \wedge \\
&\qquad\quad complement(B, G, Tree) \\
&)
\end{aligned}
$$

$minimal\_barrier(S, B, Tree) \leftrightarrow ($ $barrier(S, B, Tree)$ (12.2.6)

$\lor$ $dominates(S, B, Tree) \land$
$\exists D$
    $parent(S, D, Tree) \land$
    $minimal(D) \land$
    $\neg \exists L, N, F \quad D = x(L, agr, N, F) \land$
    $\neg \exists L, N, F \quad D = x(L, neg, N, F) \land$
    $\neg D = B$

$)$.

With these revised definitions, we can prove that the tree in Figure 12.1, once it has been modified to indicate that T θ-marks NegP and Agr θ-marks VP, can be generated by two head movements that respect the HMC, an adjunction of V to Agr, and a substitution of the resulting complex into the empty T.

It is easy now to formalize the variable-binding principle which makes these movements obligatory. The following suffices, for example:

$no\_vacuous\_ops(Tree) \leftrightarrow \neg \exists Root, Seq \ subtree(Root/Seq, Tree) \land$ (12.2.7)

$feature(finite : +, Root, Root) \land$
$\neg \exists N, F \ binds(Root, x(0, v, N, F), Tree)$

With this axiom, we can easily prove that the D-structure underlying the tree in Figure 12.1 is not well-formed — the verb must raise to Agr and then to T in order for the $+finite$ T to bind the trace of the verb.

Turning now to the examples,

John did leave.
John does leave.

Pollock's (1989, 399) proposal is this:[5]

> *Do* must be generated under Agr, from there it (or rather the amalgamated Agr + V) moves to [±Past] Tense, forming the constituent T_i shown in (83).
>
> *(83)* $[_{TP} John \ [_{T_i} [_{Agr_i} [_{V_i} \ Agr] \ T] [_{NegP} \ not \ ] [_{AgrP} \ e_i \ [_{VP} \ V]]]$
>
> [±Past] does bind a variable in that structure, e_i. The ECP is satisfied... the amalgamated *do*+Agr+T L-marking NegP.

When studied in detail, it is clear that the presented account cannot quite work. Consider, in the first place, the position of *do* under Agr. If *do* is to move, then it must satisfy the HMC, which requires that it move to the head of a category that governs its maximal projection. This cannot happen, even if we say that AgrP is its maximal projection, since we do not want to move *do* out of the AgrP, but only to adjoin with its head. The better assumption seems to be that *do* is base-generated in an adjunction structure with Agr, and so no movement is required to get it there, and there will be no trace of verb movement. This Agr+V structure could then move directly to Tense. However, this conflicts with the earlier statement of the constraint against Tense occurring as a vacuous operator. In that constraint, the bound variable is explicitly required to be the trace of a verb. (Our formulation mirrors Pollock's in imposing this requirement.) A change here seems to be the easiest way to make the account consistent. It may suffice to require just that the operator bind something. The prohibition against having a single variable bound by two operators will not allow Tense to bind a wh-trace that is already bound by a wh-phrase in the position of specifier of CP, for example, even if they somehow became co-indexed. So we tentatively reformulate *no_vacuous_ops* as follows:

$$no\_vacuous\_ops(Tree) \leftrightarrow \neg\exists Root, Seq \; subtree(Root/Seq, Tree) \wedge \qquad (12.2.8)$$
$$feature(finite: +, Root, Root)\wedge$$
$$\neg\exists B \; binds(Root, B, Tree).$$

Finally, we must further complicate our definition of *lexical*. Since the verb that confers lexicality on Agr and Tense will not always do so by moving to these categories, but can do so just by being carried along inside of Agr, the test for lexicality must be extended to allow this case. We also require at this point that only non-empty verbs can confer lexicality in L-marking:

$$lexical(Node, Tree) \leftrightarrow \exists L, C, N, F \qquad (12.2.9)$$
$$Node = x(L, C, N, F)\wedge$$
$$(\quad member(C, [v, n, a, p])$$
$$\vee \quad \exists Seq, N1, F1, Node1, Seq1, I, Seq2$$
$$subtree(Node/Seq, Tree)\wedge$$
$$(\quad imm\_dominates(Node, x(0, v, N1, F1), Node/Seq)\wedge$$
$$subtree(x(0, v, N1, F1)/Seq1, Node/Seq)$$
$$\vee \quad member(index: I, F)\wedge$$
$$subtree(Node1/Seq1, Tree)\wedge$$
$$feature(index: I, Node1, Node1)\wedge$$
$$imm\_dominates(Node1, x(0, v, N1, F1), Node1/Seq1)\wedge$$
$$subtree(x(0, v, N1, F1)/Seq2, Node1/Seq1)$$
$$)$$
$$).$$

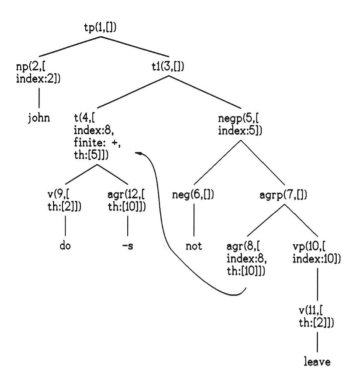

Figure 12.2
Raising *do*

With these new definitions, we can prove that the tree of Figure 12.2 can be formed by one head movement that satisfies the HMC and the constraint against vacuous +*finite*, leaving a trace that satisfies the ECP.[6]

The case that remains is the one that one might have expected to be the simplest. The sentence

John leaves.

is now analyzed as involving the raising of a null verb under Agr to T, and then lowering of the non-verbal parts of T and Agr to the main verb. As mentioned above, Pollock suggests that there are a number of ways to allow affix-lowering structures to satisfy the ECP. For example, affix-lowering could be regarded an instance of move-α , leaving traces at S-structure subject to the ECP unless they are deleted, and nothing blocks their deletion. However, the ECP is not the only problem! If affix-lowering is just another instance of move-α , then it is a very peculiar instance. It is peculiar because only one segment of the head category is to be moved, and also because such movement is blocked by the HMC. Pollock does not suggest a solution to these problems. For the moment, we adopt a simple solution to this problem. Let's simply exempt 0-level empty categories and affixes from the HMC. This can be done with the following reformulation of the principle from §9.2:

$$hmc(Moved, Landing, Tree) \leftrightarrow \qquad\qquad (12.2.10)$$

$$
\begin{aligned}
(\quad & maximal(Moved) \\
\vee\quad & \exists Seq\ subtree(Moved/Seq, Tree) \wedge \\
& (\ Seq = [] \wedge \exists Affix\ Seq = [-Affix/[]]\ ) \\
\vee\quad & \exists Max, C, N, F, F1, G \\
& head\_xp(Landing, Max, Tree) \wedge \\
& Moved = x(0, C, N, F) \wedge \\
& head\_xp(x(0, C, N, F1), G, Tree) \wedge \\
& governs(Landing, G, Tree) \wedge \\
& (\quad \exists N, F\ Landing = x(0, c, N, F) \\
& \vee\quad (\quad th\_governs(Landing, G, Tree) \\
& \qquad\ \vee\quad l\_marks(Landing, G, Tree) \\
& \qquad\ ) \\
&) \\
).\quad &
\end{aligned}
$$

It may be surprising, but this change in the HMC is all that is needed. Now we can derive the tree in Figure 12.3 by first raising the projection of Agr that includes the null verb, then lowering the Agr affix to the main V, then lowering the empty Tense (which might be regarded as a null affix) to the main V, then deleting the traces left by these lowering movements. When we say "derive" here, we mean, of course, that we can deduce that this tree is related to its underlying structure by $affectAn$, and that the tree satisfies the HMC and ECP conditions we have formalized.

12.3   Exploring some consequences of the formalization

We have modified a number of principles in order to admit the analyses of English that Pollock explicitly considers in his paper, but we have not carefully explored the interaction of these changes with other parts of the *Barriers* framework. In particular, it is worth considering whether Pollock's account fits with the *Barriers* proposals for allowing structures formed by NP-raising to satisfy the ECP. Let's consider again the examples mentioned at the beginning of this chapter,

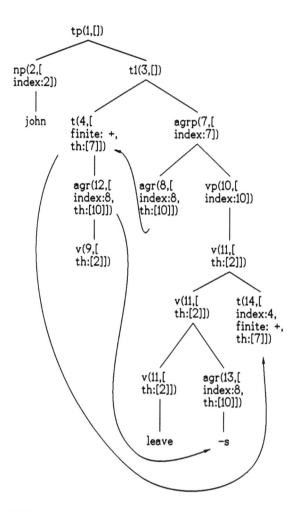

Figure 12.3
Raising Agr with null verb, lowering affixes, deleting traces

John seems to be intelligent.
* Seems John to be intelligent?

The first case is derived by raising a null verb, and then lowering the affixes, as has been discussed. We saw that after deleting the traces of the lowering, there was no ECP violation, but we did not consider the trace of the NP object that is left in these raising constructions. Remember, the *Barriers* story was that the object trace was properly governed after SPEC-head agreement, because then I and its head NP would be co-indexed, and then the trace of the verb properly governs the trace of the object. The similar story can be given in Pollock's framework, except that SPEC-head agreement now co-indexes T and its head NP, and T itself will not already have an index unless one has "percolated" up from Agr. If we assume this "percolation" happens (this percolation has *not* taken place in Figure 12.2 or Figure 12.3), then SPEC-head agreement could apply, allowing the raising constructions in the way Chomsky suggests.

The second, ill-formed example, which would have been derived in the *Barriers* framework by raising *seems* to I and then to C, cannot be derived in Pollock's approach, because raising *seems* out of VP would produce a θ-criterion violation. We have not formalized this aspect of Pollock's theory, but with this addition we would have a formal account of the contrast between these two structures.

Chapter 13

VP-internal subjects

In the last two chapters we explored the effects of a little tinkering with *Barriers* principles. In this chapter we will consider some fundamental changes. A number of linguists have proposed that subjects originate inside of VP. Recent work by Sportiche (1990) and Koopman and Sportiche (1990) adopts the VP-internal subject hypothesis and substantially simplifies the *Barriers* framework. This theory unifies the theories of movement and government more closely than ever, while avoiding many of the difficulties discussed in Part II. The ideas have been worked out and defended in some detail, but here a brief exploration will illustrate the flexibility and utility of our formalization even when faced with rather drastic revisions. As in previous chapters, our goal is to show how easily our formal theory can be modified and extended. For careful discussions of empirical motivations, the reader is referred to the cited sources.

Koopman and Sportiche (1990) point out that surface forms of I in English like *will* and *do* satisfy the familiar diagnostics of raising verbs, so it is reasonable to assume that a VP-internal subject raises to the position of specifier of IP in order to get case in English and similar languages, as in Figure 13.1, for example. Complex VPs with internal subject positions are already needed for small clauses.[1] Furthermore, there are other languages, such as Irish and Welsh, in which the structure [I NP VP] is well evidenced (Chung and McCloskey, 1987; Harlow, 1981), and so the assumption that English and other languages also have this structure would strengthen UG. We just need to explain why raising is not obligatory in languages like Italian, Welsh, Japanese, and Chinese. The beginnings of an account along these lines will be sketched and formalized.

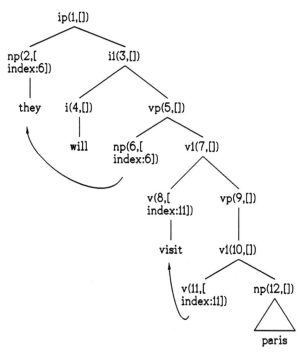

Figure 13.1
A structure with VP-internal subject

13.1 A restricted theory of movement and government

13.1.1 X-bar theory

The structural assumptions of *Barriers* are quite loose. Sportiche and Koopman propose tightening them up in various ways. Suppose all categories have an identical hierarchical structure, all of them allowing specifiers and always having intermediate projections. Furthermore, suppose that there is at most one specifier for each category.[2] A lexical category X that projects an external argument will have its internal arguments in a maximal projection XP, inside of an additional XP projection that has the external argument in specifier position, as shown in Figure 13.1 (but see footnote 1).

13.1.2 θ-theory, government, and barriers

Koopman and Sportiche point out that with the assumption that sentential subjects originate in VP, we can assume that all of a verb's θ-roles are assigned locally in VP.

There is no need to assume that external θ-roles can be assigned across an intermediate projection of I. However, since Sportiche does not rely on θ-government in the definition of L-marking, and since L-marking is the only thing that we have used θ-roles for, leaving them aside in this chapter will not hamper a comparison with the *Barriers* framework.

As for government, Chomsky defined this notion as an m-command relation that does not cross any barrier. Sportiche proposes a more restrictive notion: government is an i-command relation that does not cross an intervening barrier, where

> A i-commands B iff the first constituent dominating A dominates B.

In other words, A i-commands B iff everything that dominates A dominates B. This is easily formalized.

$$i\_commands(A, B, Tree) \leftrightarrow \qquad\qquad\qquad\qquad\qquad\qquad\qquad (13.1.1)$$
$$\forall Sigma$$
$$dominates(Sigma, A, Tree) \rightarrow dominates(Sigma, B, Tree).$$

Returning to government, then,

> A governs B iff
> > A i-commands B and
> > no barrier S for B intervenes between A and B, where
> S intervenes between A and B iff S excludes A and dominates B.

Notice that the domination condition in the definition of intervention is redundant in this context, since S will not be a barrier for B unless it dominates B. We accordingly formalize the idea as follows:

$$governs(A, B, Tree) \leftrightarrow i\_commands(A, B, Tree) \wedge \qquad\qquad\qquad (13.1.2)$$
$$\neg \exists S \;\; barrier(S, B, Tree) \wedge$$
$$excludes(S, A, Tree).$$

Sportiche proposes the following notion of a barrier:[3]

> Given some constituent B and some category Y such that B is not a projection of Y, YP is barrier for B iff some projection Yn of Y is not L-dependent and dominates B.

The requirement that B is not a projection of the head of Yn is slightly more restrictive than the condition that we had to add to Chomsky's formulation, i.e., that *excludes* is irreflexive (cf. §9.3). No auxiliary notion of a blocking category is needed, and no special status is given to IP.

Chomsky's account of lexical categories and L-marking can be kept with few modifications (§§6.4,8.4,10.3). We assume that all heads except C L-mark their complements, and we say that a category is L-dependent if it is L-marked or the specifier of an L-marked category. Furthermore, we assume that even C L-marks its complements if V+I raises into this position:

$$l\_marks(A, B, Tree) \leftrightarrow complement(B, A, Tree) \land \qquad (13.1.3)$$
$$\exists L, C, N, F$$
$$A = x(L, C, N, F) \land$$
$$(\quad \neg C = c$$
$$\lor \quad C = c \land$$
$$\exists I, N1, F1, Sub$$
$$member(index : I, F) \land$$
$$subtree(x(0, v, N1, F1)/Sub, Tree) \land$$
$$member(index : I, F1)$$
$$)$$

$$l\_dependent(B, Tree) \leftrightarrow (\quad \exists A \ l\_marks(A, B, Tree) \qquad (13.1.4)$$
$$\lor \quad \exists A, C$$
$$specifier(B, C, Tree) \land$$
$$l\_marks(A, C, Tree)$$
$$).$$

With these definitions, I always L-marks its complement VP, even when V has not raised into that position (cf. the definition of *lexical* in §10.3), but C is not an L-marker unless V+I lands there.

One more idea is useful for the definition of barriers. It is straightforward to define a relation $projection(A, B, Tree)$ that holds just in case A and B are projections of the same category in $Tree$. (A definition is presented in Appendix B.) Then we can define:

$$barrier(YP, B, Tree) \leftrightarrow maximal(YP) \land$$
$$\neg projection(YP, B, Tree) \land$$
$$\exists Yn$$
$$projection(YP, Yn, Tree) \land$$
$$\neg l\_dependent(Yn, Tree) \land$$
$$dominates(Yn, B, Tree).$$

13.1.3 Movement

The definition of substitution is unchanged from *Barriers*, as is the structure-preserving requirement that XPs can only substitute into other XPs of the same category, and so *subst_conds* is unchanged. As for adjunction, Sportiche proposes that maximal categories can adjoin only to VP, AP, and IP. As in *Barriers*, the idea is that somehow these categories that are never arguments do not block extraction. The following simplification of our earlier definition is straightforward:

$$adjoin\_conds(Moved, Landing) \leftrightarrow (\quad maximal(Moved) \wedge \qquad\qquad\qquad (13.1.5)$$

$$maximal(Landing) \wedge$$

$$nonargument(Landing)$$

$$\vee \quad minimal(Moved) \wedge$$

$$minimal(Landing)$$

$$)$$

$$nonargument(Node) \leftrightarrow \exists L, C, N, F \qquad\qquad\qquad\qquad\qquad (13.1.6)$$

$$Node = x(L, C, N, F) \wedge$$

$$(\ C = v \vee C = a \vee C = i \ ).$$

The Head Movement Constraint is dropped in favor of the more general Condition on Chain Links described below, and so we return to the definition of *moveAn* of §7.2, dropping the extra conditions imposed in §9.

13.1.4   A condition on chain links

Sportiche proposes the following Condition on Chain Links as an S-structure constraint:

(CCL): A trace must be governed by an antecedent in its chain.

That is, at S-structure, a trace must be governed by a category that binds it. As we will see, this condition provides a unified account of certain violations of subjacency, the head movement constraint, and the ECP. It is easily formalized, remembering that the traces are nonpronominal, indexed empty categories:

$$ccl(Tree) \leftrightarrow \neg \exists Node, I \qquad\qquad\qquad\qquad\qquad\qquad (13.1.7)$$

$$subtree(Node/[], Tree) \wedge$$

$$feature(index : I, Node, Node) \wedge$$

$$\neg feature(pronominal : +, Node, Node) \wedge$$

$$\neg \exists B \ binds(B, Node, Tree) \wedge$$

$$governs(B, Node, Tree).$$

With this restriction, movements out of an XP that is not L-dependent must either adjoin to XP, or move through the specifier of XP. This basic idea emerges very simply from the assumptions outlined above. While similar in spirit to the basic insights of *Barriers*, nothing so simple holds there. A quick survey of some consequences of this new idea is probably the best way to get an understanding of it.

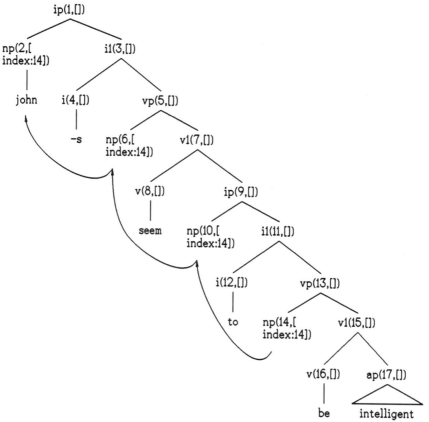

Figure 13.2
A tree after NP-raising (compare Figure 10.7)

13.2 Exploring some consequences of the formalization

13.2.1 VP-internal subjects and NP-movement

Let's consider the structure of Figure 13.1 first. Before moving, the VP-internal subject can get a θ-role (presumably compositionally from $vp(9, [])$), but it does not receive case, so it must move. It can move directly to the subject position, because $vp(5, [])$ is L-marked and not a barrier.

Consider now a traditional raising example like

John seems to be intelligent.

A structure for this sentence is displayed in Figure 13.2. Since neither of the verbs *seem* and *be* assign external θ-roles, they need not project extra VPs and their specifiers are empty, allowing an extraction that goes from specifier to specifier all of the way to the subject position.[4] Notice that no specifier of a containing XP can be skipped, because then XP would be a barrier in virtue of the fact that the intermediate containing projection X1 is not L-marked.

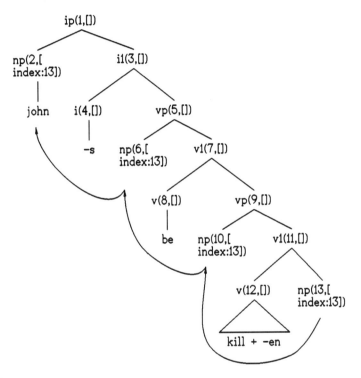

Figure 13.3
A passive structure (compare Figure 10.8)

The situation is essentially similar in passives. Since a passive verb does not assign an external θ role to an external argument, an object can move through specifier position to the matrix subject, as shown in Figure 13.3.

NP-movement out of VP led to major complications in the *Barriers* account because of the ECP, as discussed in §§10.5-10.7. It will be interesting to see whether this approach to movement, which easily allows movements out of VP, will have trouble blocking the bad structures that motivated the *Barriers* account.

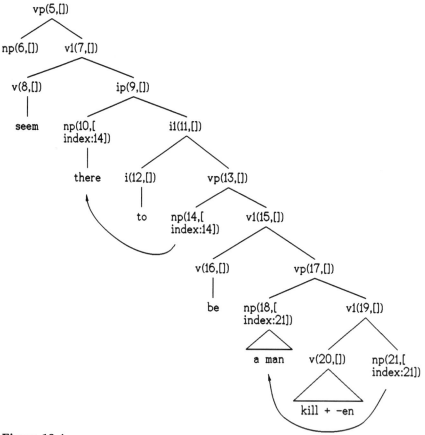

Figure 13.4
Before super-raising (compare Figure 10.9)

So let's consider, in the first place, ungrammatical super-raising examples like,

* [A man]ᵢ seems [there to be killed tᵢ].
* Johnᵢ is believed [that he likes tᵢ].

The former structure was ruled out in *Barriers* by assuming that the infinitival I in the embedded clause blocks raising of the verb. Since the verb cannot raise, its index will not be made identical to the subject by SPEC-head agreement, merging the chains of the subject and verb, and so the trace will not be antecedent-governed. In the present context, though, no merging of chains by SPEC-head agreement is required for the simple case, and so it does not need to be blocked in the super-raising examples. The structures of both examples are ruled out by the CCL: the specifier of the embedded IP is filled,

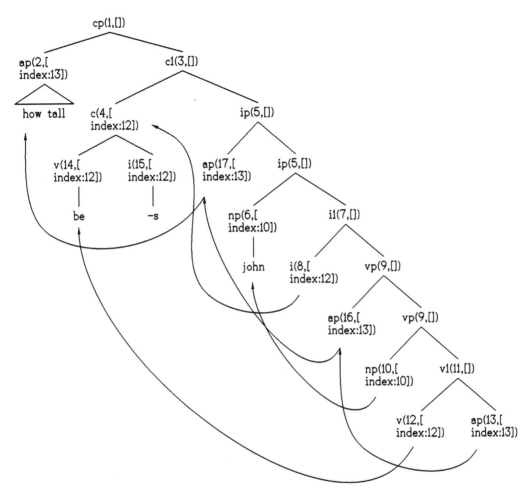

Figure 13.5
A tree after head movements (compare Figure 9.6)

and so extractions from IP are impossible without adjunction, but A-chains that include adjunction sites are ruled out as improper. Consider Figure 13.4, which shows the relevant part of the former example. Here, the embedded object has moved as far as it can without violating the CCL. If it moves to $np(6, [])$, the CCL will be violated: $ip(9, [])$ is a barrier because $i1(11, [])$ is not L-marked and dominates $np(14, \ldots)$. Node $vp(13, [])$ is also a barrier for $np(18, \ldots)$, and an adjunction to $vp(13, [])$ would produce an improper movement.

13.2.2   The head movement constraint

The earlier chapters displayed many structures with head movements which are allowed by the HMC: Figures 9.4-9.6, 10.7-10.10, and 12.1-12.3. Consider the structure of Figure 9.6, for example. In the present framework, the relevant structure is now the one shown in Figure 13.5.[5] The HMC serves to insure that head movement can only be to the next head position, as indicated by the movements of the verb; no head position can be skipped by these movements. The interesting point is that this is exactly what is required by the CCL. The structure preserving conditions on substitutions and adjunctions ensure that a head can only move to another head, and the CCL requires that the landing site governs the resulting trace. This is the HMC. So, for example, a movement directly from V to C is blocked, since IP is a barrier for V that excludes C.

Notice that when head movements are adjunctions, this framework must assume, as Chomsky and Pollock do, that amalgamation — sharing of indices — allows the category adjoined to to bind the trace of the moved head. This is not required for the first movement from V to I, but for the second movement of V+I to C. After the second movement, only the trace of I is left to bind and govern the original trace of V.

13.2.3   Subjacency effects

The structure in Figure 13.5 also shows a wh-movement that proceeds by adjunctions until a substitution into the specifier of CP can be done without violating the CCL. In the *Barriers* framework, wh-movement had to be constrained by subjacency and other principles. Let's consider some relevant examples in the present framework.

In the first place, let's reconsider Chomsky's "best case" wh-movement,

Who does John see?

Remember that Chomsky adjusts his framework so that this can be derived by crossing no barriers, but then later he adds the English parametric barrier and so one barrier is crossed. In the present framework, the sentence has the structure shown in Figure 13.6, and the CCL is satisfied. No barriers are crossed by any movement.

One kind of structure that contrasts with these good structures is exemplified by

* *The man who$_i$ [$_{ip}$[pictures of t$_i$] are on the table] arrived.*

To rule this out as a subjacency violation, Chomsky adds the stipulation that wh-phrases cannot adjoin to IP, as discussed in §9.4. In the present framework, the relevant structure is shown in Figure 13.7. Here, the CCL blocks the movement immediately. The NP projection of *pictures* is a specifier; it is not L-marked; and adjunction to NP is impossible.

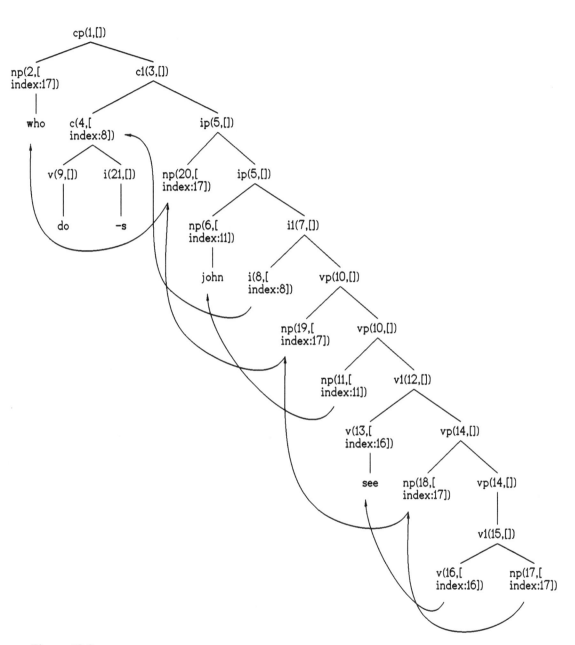

Figure 13.6
The best case again (compare Figure 9.7)

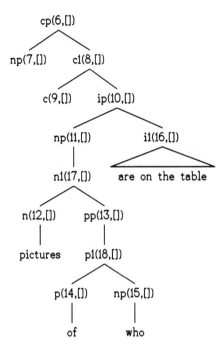

Figure 13.7
Structure blocking raising from a *picture* NP (compare Figure 9.8)

Therefore, *who* cannot get to the specifier of the relative clause CP without a CCL violation.

Chomsky proposes a parametric barrier to account for,

*What did you wonder to whom John gave t t?

On that account, the deepest tensed IP is a barrier in English, as discussed in §9.5. No such special device is required in the present theory. Since CP is always a barrier, the only way to extract from it is via the specifier position. In this example, the specifier of CP is filled by *to whom*, and so *what* cannot be fronted without a CCL violation. One other idea is that *to whom* might move into the trace of *what*. This would violate the SCC. We have not imposed the SCC, but as discussed in §11.3, if movement involves coindexing, the movement onto a trace merges two chains and results in violations of chain uniqueness properties, such as the θ-criterion.

Another construction discussed in §9.5 was the following:

* What$_i$ did you [$_{vp}t_i$ [$_{vp}$wonder who [$_{vp}t_i$ [$_{vp}$said [$_{cp}$ t$_i$ that Bill [$_{vp}t_i$ [$_{vp}$ saw t$_i$]]]]]] ?

In the *Barriers* analysis, each movement indicated here satisfies 1-subjacency. To account for the ungrammaticality of this structure, Chomsky proposes that subjacency applies cumulatively to chains. In the present context, we see that the extraction of *what* from the CP complement of *wonder* is blocked, since the specifier of CP is filled by *who*.

The easy account of these examples brings with it a difficulty in explaining the cases where extraction from a wh-CP is permitted, such as

Which car did John tell you how to fix t?
?? What do you wonder how John fixed t?

These extractions are not blocked in the *Barriers* framework, and that is why special restrictions are needed to account for the previous cases of ungrammatical wh-extraction. (The special parametric barrier accounts for the slight deviance of the second example here.) In the present framework, extractions from CPs with filled wh-specifiers are always blocked, and so we have the reverse problem.

The problem is that objects seem to have a special ability to escape wh-islands, as compared to subjects or adjuncts:

Which car did John tell you how to fix t?
* *Who do you wonder how fixed the car?*
* *How$_i$ do you know [when to resign t$_i$]?*

Sportiche suggests the following idea. In the first place, if the CCL is violated at S-structure, it will be violated at LF as well, since it is obvious that deletion of intermediate traces cannot provide an antecedent governor for a trace that lacks one at S-structure. So suppose that the CCL applies at LF, replacing the ECP. This by itself does not help with the problem of how objects can escape wh-islands. But suppose that an object trace may become a silent resumptive pronoun at LF, i.e., *pro*. Then object traces will not be subject to the CCL, and there will be no violation at LF. There is still a violation of the CCL at S-structure, but unlike other CCL violations, this S-structure violation is not compounded by a corresponding violation at LF. Sportiche (1988) considers how this sort of view could follow from a certain functional determination of empty categories, but we will set this matter aside.

13.3   Head government and *that*-trace effects

In §10.5 we discussed *that*-trace effects:

Who did you believe would win?
* *Who did you believe that would win?*

Chomsky uses the minimality condition with the ECP to account for this contrast. Sportiche suggests that the problem here is not a lack of antecedent government, but a lack of head government, as Stowell (1984, 1986) and others have argued. This residue of the ECP might be formulated roughly as follows:[6]

> (RECP) At S-structure, a trace category A must be governed by a head X such that there is no other head Y that i-commands A but not X.

The way that this is to account for the contrast shown in the last examples is this. In the former but not the latter case, the embedded head of C is empty, and so I can move to that position and head govern the specifier of IP. That is, since C is the only head that is not an L-marker, it does not head-govern the specifier of its complement. However, when V+I moves to C, C becomes an L-marker, and so we have head-government of the embedded subject position in just the right cases.

It is easy to formalize this idea:

$$recp(Tree) \leftrightarrow \neg \exists Node, I \qquad\qquad\qquad\qquad\qquad\qquad (13.3.8)$$
$$subtree(Node/[], Tree) \wedge$$
$$feature(index : I, Node, Node) \wedge$$
$$\neg feature(pronominal : +, Node, Node) \wedge$$
$$\neg \exists X \;\; head\_governs(X, Node, Tree)$$

$$head\_governs(X, Node, Tree) \leftrightarrow minimal(X) \wedge$$
$$governs(X, Node, Tree) \wedge$$
$$\neg \exists Y$$
$$minimal(Y) \wedge$$
$$i\_commands(Y, Node, Tree) \wedge$$
$$\neg i\_commands(Y, X, Tree).$$

With these axioms we can show that there is a grammatical structure for

Who did you believe would win?

Part of this structure is shown in Figure 13.8. After *who* moves out of $np(23, \ldots)$, the trace that remains in that position violates the RECP until $i(25, \ldots)$ moves to $c(21, \ldots)$.[7] Obviously, this way of saving the structure would not be possible if *that* were already in C. More precisely, substitution of I to C would then be impossible, and since adjunction would not result in amalgamation, the RECP violation would not be removed.

One nice feature of this account is that the following structure is properly allowed:

How$_i$ do you think (that) [John fixed the car t$_i$]?

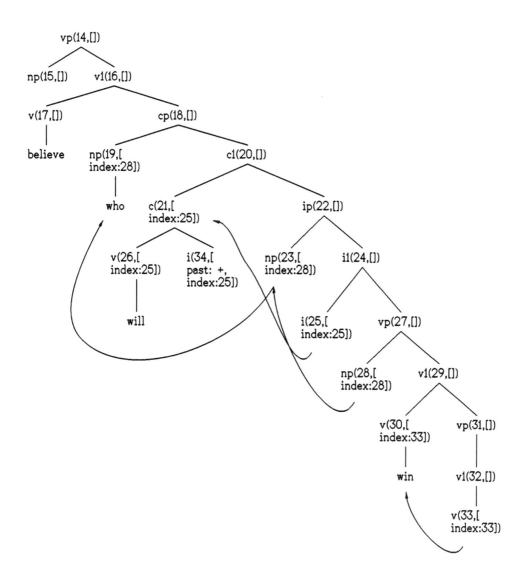

Figure 13.8
Grammatical structure after movement to C (compare Figure 10.4)

Extraction from adjunct position does not produce an RECP violation because the adjunct is head governed by the verb.[8] The relevant part of the structure is shown in Figure 13.9. Similarly,

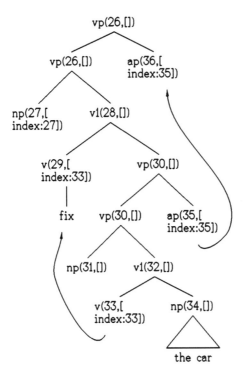

Figure 13.9
Adjunct extraction satisfies RECP (compare Figure 10.1)

[*Which car*]$_j$ *do you wonder how*$_i$ [*John fixed t*$_j$ *t*$_i$]?

is not an RECP violation, but just a mild CCL violation as discussed in the last section.

13.4 Movement, agreement, and case

One of Sportiche's (1988; 1990) most persuasive arguments for the highly restrictive approach to movement presented here comes from the pattern of object-participle agreement in French and other languages. The general idea can be quickly sketched. In French, there is sometimes agreement between a verb and a cliticized object:

Ils ont decrit cette robe a la femme dans la ville.
     (they described the dress to the woman in the city)
Ils l'ont decrit(e) a la femme dans la ville.
     (they it described to the woman in the city)

Ils lui ont decrit cette robe dans la ville.

(they to her described the dress in the city)

Ils y ont decrit cette robe a la femme.

(they there described the dress to the woman)

In the second example we see that an accusative clitic can optionally trigger agreement, but the other examples show that agreement is never triggered just by the accusative object in situ, nor is it triggered by dative or locative clitics. Following Kayne (1985), Sportiche suggests that object agreement might be treated as an instance of SPEC-head agreement.[9] Very roughly, the proposal is this. Clitics are treated as binding traces in the original object position, moving from the VP to adjoin to the aspectual element that is their host. How can this derivation proceed? To escape the VP by A-movement, these elements must move either by adjunction to the lower VP or by substitution into the specifier position of the lower VP. From there, they can adjoin to the higher VP (since objects cannot be allowed through the position of the external argument) and then adjoin to the aspectual verb. Agreement with the main verb is triggered when the object is in the specifier position of the lower VP. Agreement is optional because the object need not go through this position. Then we need to explain why datives and locatives cannot similarly trigger agreement. The simplest idea is that datives and locatives are PPs, and that the specifier of VP is restricted to NPs. Clearly, the account needs further elaboration (see Sportiche, 1990), but the general outline of this account seems to fit the facts remarkably well. Exactly the right consequences seem to follow from the options for movement that have been formalized.

Part IV

Computational Models

Chapter 14

Guided deductions from linguistic theory

> *The more of the details of our daily life we can hand over to*
> *the effortless custody of automatism, the more our higher powers*
> *of mind will be set free for their own proper work.*
> — *William James*

Let's call the formalization of *Barriers* presented in Part II *FB*. This theory, which includes both universal principles and language-specific parameters, contains only 84 first order sentences. These sentences are listed in Appendix B. In this chapter and the next we will consider how to reason from this theory, and of course these same methods could be applied to the theories discussed in Part III. As observed in Chapters 2 and 3, even very simple reasoning requires that we be able to deduce that *man* and *reads* denote different words, that n and v are different categories, and so on. To establish sentences like *man* $\neq$ *reads* and $n \neq v$, we will need to add to *FB* at least the standard axioms for equality (reflexivity, and the substitution principles for all predicates and function symbols), and we need the infinite syntactic equality theory SEQ_{FB}. Remember that this syntactic equality theory, as defined in §3.5.2, includes inequalities for all (non-Skolem) function symbols, and instances of the schema:

$$\neg X = \tau \qquad \textit{for all } \tau \textit{ containing } X. \tag{14.0.1}$$

In this chapter we explore two proof techniques which were introduced earlier: SEq resolution and SLDNF resolution. As discussed in §3, both of these proof methods "build in" the axioms defining syntactic equality, giving us (roughly) the consequences of these axioms without explicit representations of them. As we will see, SEq resolution then allows us to use *FB* in something quite close to its original form, so we can have confidence that our results do follow from the axioms we have formulated. SLDNF is much more tricky but potentially much more efficient. With appropriate user guidance, the complexity of finding a proof using either method can be avoided. Of course, the search problem has to be faced in parsing and other applications, but we leave this to the next chapter.

14.1   Representing FB for two proof methods

14.1.1   Representations for SEq-resolution

SEq resolution is just resolution with a special additional inference rule for equations that provides syntactic equality without the need to represent the axioms of SEQ_{FB}. The sentences of FB itself, though, must be represented in clausal form. There is some variation among algorithms for going from first order logic to clausal form, depending on how much redundancy is eliminated, etc. On any standard approach, though, some of our axioms will produce many clauses. With our standard conversion described in §3.1, the 84 first order sentences of FB yield 2882 clauses. This is a rather large set, and so it is worth looking at where this complexity comes from. It turns out that the problem comes from only a few axioms of the theory, and it is a nice surprise that the problematic axioms are not theoretically central or even tricky. The worst offenders are the definitions of ss_gamma, lf_gamma, $spec\_head$, and $agree$, all from §10.[1] With a standard algorithm for converting to clausal form, these sentences yield 110, 428, 652 and 782 clauses, respectively. The reason that these axioms yield so many clauses is, roughly, that they cover many different cases. They have large disjunctions on their right-hand sides which must be multiplied out in the conversion to conjunctive normal form. The theoretically central axioms of the *Barriers* theory do not have large disjunctions in them, and so their clausal forms are quite manageable.

There are three strategies that could be used to avoid the clausal form complexity of the problematic axioms. A first idea is simply to reformulate the problematic axioms, attempting to find a formulation that does not lead to such an explosion in the clausal form. Once we understand how this can be done, though, it is not hard to define a second less intrusive method for avoiding the complexity. A conversion to clausal form that avoids the potentially exponential complexity of the standard method is easily described.

With the standard conversion to clausal form, the formula

$$(p_1 \wedge q_1) \vee (p_2 \wedge q_2) \vee \ldots \vee (p_n \wedge q_n)$$

yields 2^n clauses. Plaisted and Greenbaum (1986) show that this explosion can be avoided just by introducing new predicates together with their definitions. For example, consider the case where $n = 2$:

$$(p_1 \wedge q_1) \vee (p_2 \wedge q_2).$$

If we define pr_1 to stand for this whole sentence, pr_2 for the subformula $p_1 \wedge q_1$, and pr_3 for the subformula $p_2 \wedge q_2$, we can express this proposition as follows:

$pr_1 \wedge$
$(pr_1 \rightarrow (pr_2 \vee pr_3)) \wedge$
$(pr_2 \rightarrow (p1 \wedge q1)) \wedge$
$(pr_3 \rightarrow (p2 \wedge q2)).$

Like the Skolem transformation that eliminates existentially quantified variables (as described in §3.1), this transformation preserves not logical equivalence but satisfiability. Furthermore, the transformation is intuitive. It is easy to see what the intended interpretation of the new predicates should be on the basis of the intended interpretation of the original predicates. When we convert this sentence with new predicates to clausal form in the standard way, we get 6 clauses, whereas the original sentence only gave us 4. The effect of this renaming, though, is that the disjunctions are never multiplied out, and so when we perform this same renaming step on instances of the formula where we have $n = 2, 3, 4, 5, 6, \ldots$ disjunctions, instead of getting $4, 8, 16, 32, 64, \ldots$ clauses, we get $6, 9, 12, 15, 18, \ldots$ clauses. Plaisted and Greenbaum define this renaming strategy precisely and prove that the complexity of the renamed clausal form is a polynomial function of the complexity of the original first order formula.

Rather than renaming all subformulas in this way, we have used a simple technique for estimating whether a renaming will actually reduce the size of the resulting clausal form, as suggested by Boy de la Tour (1990), in order to get even smaller clausal representations of our theories. With this method, the definitions of *ss_gamma*, *lf_gamma*, *spec_head* and *agree* yield only 37, 44, 45 and 40 clauses, respectively. For the whole theory of 84 first order sentences, we get 817 clauses. SEQ resolution can be applied directly to this formulation of the theory. Of course, if we begin our proof with steps that have the effect of replacing all of these new predicates with their definitions, the complexity of the clausal form has just been shifted into the search space of the theorem prover. However, we can often avoid or postpone the unpacking of these definitions, achieving proofs that are not only easier to find but much shorter than the shortest proofs from the standard clausal form.[2]

Guiding these proofs is straightforward. The user can determine every resolution step to be taken, or allow the simple parts of the problem to be handled by the system's blind but exhaustive search. Since we use the variant of resolution called "model elimination," as noted in §3, a considerable flexibility in choosing which subproblem to tackle at each step can be obtained without sacrificing completeness. That is, the proof method is complete even when a function deterministically selects the subproblem of the "center clause" or "goal" to be tackled at each step.[3] This is relevant in the present context because it allows us to guide a proof through a natural development. The same result is much more important in the next chapter, because the order of selection of subgoals can have a dramatic effect on the size of the search space.

14.1.2   Representations for SLDNF

There is another quite different response that can be made to the complexity of the standard clausal forms of our definitions, a response that abandons SEq resolution altogether. It is suggested by the observation that the sufficient conditions provided by the definitions of *ss_gamma*, *lf_gamma*, *spec_head* and *agree*, the ($\leftarrow$) parts of these definitions, yield only 6, 6, 4 and 5 clauses, respectively. Not all of these clauses are Horn, but most of them are. This suggests that programming with the completion of a "general program" formulation using SLDNF might be feasible, though it is hard to avoid the difficulties mentioned in §3.5.2.

As discussed in §3.5.2, the proof method SLDNF applies to "general logic programs," which are definite clause programs extended to allow negations to appear in the antecedents of the clauses. From a logical perspective, this appears to amount to allowing non-Horn clauses (disjunctions of literals containing more than one positive literal), but, in fact, SLDNF is so incomplete that this is a misleading way to look at it. The negations are handled with a special negation-as-failure proof rule. That is, the negation of a formula is taken to be refuted when an exhaustive search shows that there is no refutation of the unnegated formula. Let's quickly review again the difficulties this approach faces, with particular reference to the theory of Part II.

Consider first the definition of affect-α (definition 10.1.3 from §10.1), repeated here:

$$
\begin{aligned}
affectA(Tree0, Tree) \leftrightarrow\ &\exists Moved, Landing \\
&(\quad (\quad substitute(Tree0, Tree, Moved, Landing)\wedge \\
&\qquad\qquad subst\_conds(Moved, Landing) \\
&\quad \vee\quad adjoin(Tree0, Tree, Moved, Landing)\wedge \\
&\qquad\qquad adjoin\_conds(Moved, Landing, Tree) \\
&\quad)\wedge \\
&\quad hmc(Moved, Landing, Tree)\wedge \\
&\quad number\_tree(Tree) \\
&\quad \vee\quad deleteA(Tree0, Tree, Moved)\wedge \\
&\qquad\qquad delete\_conds(Moved, Tree0) \\
&\quad).
\end{aligned}
$$

The clausal form of the $\rightarrow$ part of this rule contains non-definite clauses. In a resolution system, this direction of the rule might be used to prove (roughly) that something is not a substitution, adjunction or deletion from the fact that it is not an application of affect-α. But if we can anticipate that this kind of reasoning will not be needed, we need not worry. In the course of derivations linguists typically do, it is unlikely that this will be needed. We will usually use the rule in the other direction, $\leftarrow$, and the clausal form of this part of the rule does contain only definite clauses. If we are going to use negation-as-failure soundly, though, it is crucial that we be sure about the fact that the $\rightarrow$ direction is not needed, and this crucial assurance is typically very hard to provide.

Another difficulty arises because of the fact that SLDNF cannot apply soundly when it would instantiate arguments. So, for example, if we want to prove that some node in a tree is not properly governed, as we need to do in assigning $-\gamma$-features (discussed in §10.1), we have to prove, for some particular node n and tree τ,

$$\neg \exists A \;\; properly\_governs(A, n, \tau).$$

This would be done ordinarily by refuting a (universally quantified) clause that says that node n is properly governed by something that is named by a Skolem function:

$$\leftarrow \neg properly\_governs(sk1, n, \tau).$$

(Remember that the $\leftarrow$ in general clause notation is, in effect, a negation sign, so the sentence to be refuted here is really a doubly negated literal, or equivalently, a positive literal.) Unfortunately, this subproblem could not be handled with SLDNF, because Skolem functions require more sophisticated equational reasoning. To handle this problem soundly in SLDNF, we must use the indirect strategy of first instantiating A with a variable-free term (or at least a term containing only variables that do not need to be instantiated further by the refutation). One standard way to do this is with a redundant condition. For example, since a node is properly governed in a tree just in case it is properly governed by the root of some subtree, we could define a new relation:

$$properly\_governed(B, T) \leftarrow subtree(A, T) \wedge properly\_governs(A, B, T),$$

and then refute instead:

$$\leftarrow \neg properly\_governed(n, \tau).$$

If the subproblems in the right-hand side of this new definition are taken from left-to-right, then A will be instantiated before the negation-as-failure rule is tried, and so there will be no problem. This approach requires:

(i) anticipating when this kind of instantiation is needed to avoid incompleteness;

(ii) making sure that the set of solutions of the new goal used to effect the instantiation is a superset (not necessarily proper) of the set of values the argument can have in solutions to the original problem; and

(iii) making sure that, with the redundant goals, the problem is not prohibitively complex.

With regard to the third worry, notice that the strategy suggested for the example above is needlessly inefficient. Every subtree of the tree is a solution to the redundant subgoal, and so to refute our new goal, every subtree is tested to see if it is a proper governor of node n. The redundant subgoals force us into generate-and-test inefficiencies that are potentially infeasible. One important point to notice here is that this complexity cannot be avoided by user guidance, since negation-as-failure draws a conclusion only when an exhaustive search for a refutation fails. This exhaustive search can be very costly even with the best user guidance, and even when there would be short direct refutations of the negative result from a first order formulation.

The use of SLDNF poses other problems as well. For example, when the antecedent of a conditional contains universal quantifiers, they must be carefully eliminated (Sato and Tamaki, 1984), and the resulting program can be quite inefficient. In sum, many difficult considerations are involved in formulating a general program for a particular SLDNF application, even after the axiomatic specification is provided. The problem of completely formalizing and justifying the transition from a first order specification to a feasible general program for a particular application is nontrivial and beyond the scope of the present effort. We have included a general program for guided derivations from FB using SLDNF in Appendix C, without attempting to guarantee that its calls to negation-as-failure are sound.

14.2 Theorems about particular structures

14.2.1 Some easy problems

A little experimentation with our proof systems shows that while some proofs are very easily obtained, others are very difficult. It turns out that some of the most difficult results to obtain from the clausal form of FB with SEq resolution are also hard or impossible to obtain from our general program with SLDNF resolution. We will consider a range of problems, beginning with some simple consequences of the theory FB, and proceeding towards some difficult and unsolved problems.

The basic properties of specified sequences and trees tend to be easily established with either of our proof methods. Beginning with some trivial cases, we see in Figures 14.1, 14.2, and 14.3 the SEq resolution refutation trees that establish $maximal(x(s(s(0)), n, 1, []))$, $member(b, [a, b])$ and $subtree(b/[c/[]], a/[b/[c/[]], d/[]])$. Notice that these proofs all use the trivial rule of syntactic identity. SLDNF finds the identical proofs using just

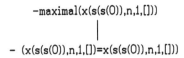

Figure 14.1

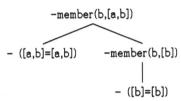

Figure 14.2

the Horn clause components of the clausal forms of our axiomatizations and the syntactic identity axiom.[4]

Going to slightly more complex results, the definition of *head_xp* has a disjunction on its right hand side, one that is large enough to be renamed with the strategy described in §14.1.1. When the renamed version of this definition is converted to clausal form, though, SEq resolution easily establishes the following result in 14 steps:

$$head\_xp(x(0, n, 4, []),$$
$$x(s(s(0)), n, 3, []),$$
$$x(s(s(0)), v, 1, [])/[$$
$$x(0, v, 2, [])/[],$$
$$x(s(s(0)), n, 3, [])/[$$
$$x(0, n, 4, [])/[john/[]]]]).$$

The tree of this proof is much too large to display on a page. Still, none of these results requires refuting a positive literal.

As discussed in §3 and Appendix A, results which do require refutations of positive literals are typically slightly more complex. For example, the following sentence is established with a 52-step proof:

$$cat\_zero(x(s(s(0)), n, 7, [index : 7])/['the\ woman'/[]],$$
$$x(s(s(0)), n, 2, [index : 7]),$$
$$x(s(s(0)), n, 2, [])/[],$$
$$x(s(s(0)), n, 2, [index : 7])/['the\ woman'/[]]).$$

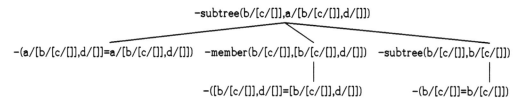

Figure 14.3

Refutations of positive literals are required in this proof to show that $x(s(s(0)), n, 2, [])$ has no index feature, and to show that $index : 7$ is not a ψ feature. This kind of reasoning is required in a number of places to establish results like the following:

$substitute(x(s(s(0)), i, 1, [])/[$
$\qquad x(s(s(0)), n, 2, [])/[],$
$\qquad x(s(0), i, 3, [])/[$
$\qquad\quad x(0, i, 4, [finite : +])/[was/[]],$
$\qquad\quad x(s(s(0)), v, 5, [])/[$
$\qquad\qquad x(0, v, 6, [])/['kiss + -en'/[]],$
$\qquad\qquad x(s(s(0)), n, 7, [])/['the\ woman'/[]]]]],$
$\qquad x(s(s(0)), i, 1, [])/[$
$\qquad\quad x(s(s(0)), n, 2, [index : 7])/['the\ woman'/[]],$
$\qquad\quad x(s(0), i, 3, [])/[$
$\qquad\qquad x(0, i, 4, [finite : +])/[was/[]],$
$\qquad\qquad x(s(s(0)), v, 5, [])/[$
$\qquad\qquad\quad x(0, v, 6, [])/['kiss + -en'/[]],$
$\qquad\qquad\quad x(s(s(0)), n, 7, [index : 7])/[]]]],$
$\qquad x(s(s(0)), n, 7, [index : 7]),$
$\qquad x(s(s(0)), n, 2, [index : 7]),$
$\qquad x/8\ ).$

This is established in 184 steps on our theorem prover, most of them being simple reasoning about equality as in the previously displayed examples. Soon after getting to proofs that are not conveniently presented on a page, we get to *results* like these which are not conveniently presented on a page. The graphical presentation in Figure 7.2 shows this result in a much more readable form!

14.2.2   Guiding deductions

The need for user guidance in direct applications of our theory FB is clear. The problem is to provide enough guidance for the proof system without requiring the user to see

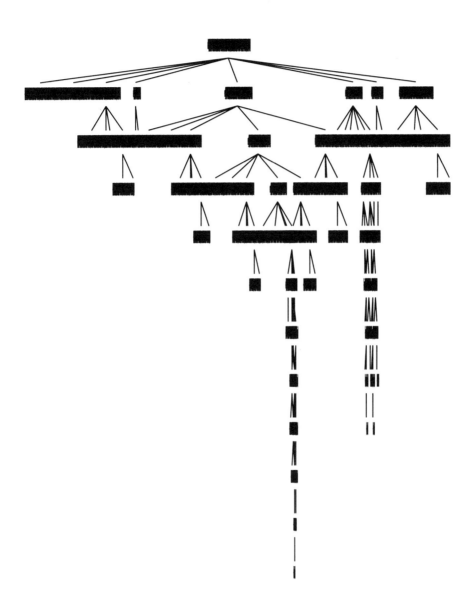

Figure 14.4
A proof of an instance of move-α, seen "from a distance"

unnecessary detail. Terms denoting large trees are very difficult to read in their text form, and a literal in a proof will often contain several function expressions that denote trees. Consequently, we do not want to have to look at even a single line of most interesting proofs. It is possible to provide two more practical viewpoints for our applications. One lets the user look at the structure of a proof "from a distance," in order to detect abnormal developments in the search for a proof. A simple proof of an instance of *moveA* is shown in Figure 14.4, reduced approximately 20 times. The two deep plunges correspond to the detachment of a node (i.e. a refutation of an instance of *zero_cat*) and the substitution of that node into another position (i.e. a refutation of an instance of *cat_zero*), respectively. Deeper plunges in the proof tree would indicate some kind of pathology (e.g. an error in the axioms) or a useless search. The user can move around in the tree display and expand any suspicious or otherwise interesting parts for closer inspection.

A second and much more useful view of proofs is provided by anticipating those points where guidance is required and providing for appropriate interactions at just those points. A graphical interface can present trees in their familiar form, and the wording of requests for guidance can be designed to yield a manageable system. The axioms that increase the search space most are those defining the complex recursive relations like *substitute* and *moveAn*. In these cases and in the demonstration of negative results, user guidance can be sought.

In the SLDNF system, where proofs involving equational reasoning are not required, the system can be used even by users who are unfamiliar with the underlying proof techniques. A snapshot from such a session (using the program "las.pl" of Appendix C) is shown in Figure 14.5. Here the system has been guided to display a tree, adjoin node 11 to node 9 on the left, substitute node 12 to node 2, and then display the result. For SEq reasoning, more extensive guidance is required: the user must be able to at least sketch the proof in order to give the system the needed guidance, and step-by-step guidance is required to get through the computationally explosive equational reasoning.

14.3   Induction and the non-well-foundedness of affect-α

The principles of grammar we have axiomatized should allow us to deduce that some strings are awkward at best. Consider the problem of showing that every derivation of a string violates subjacency (if it respects the other principles of the grammar). For example, it was suggested in §§9-10 that the following construction involves a subjacency violation:

?* What$_i$ does she wonder how John fixed t_i?

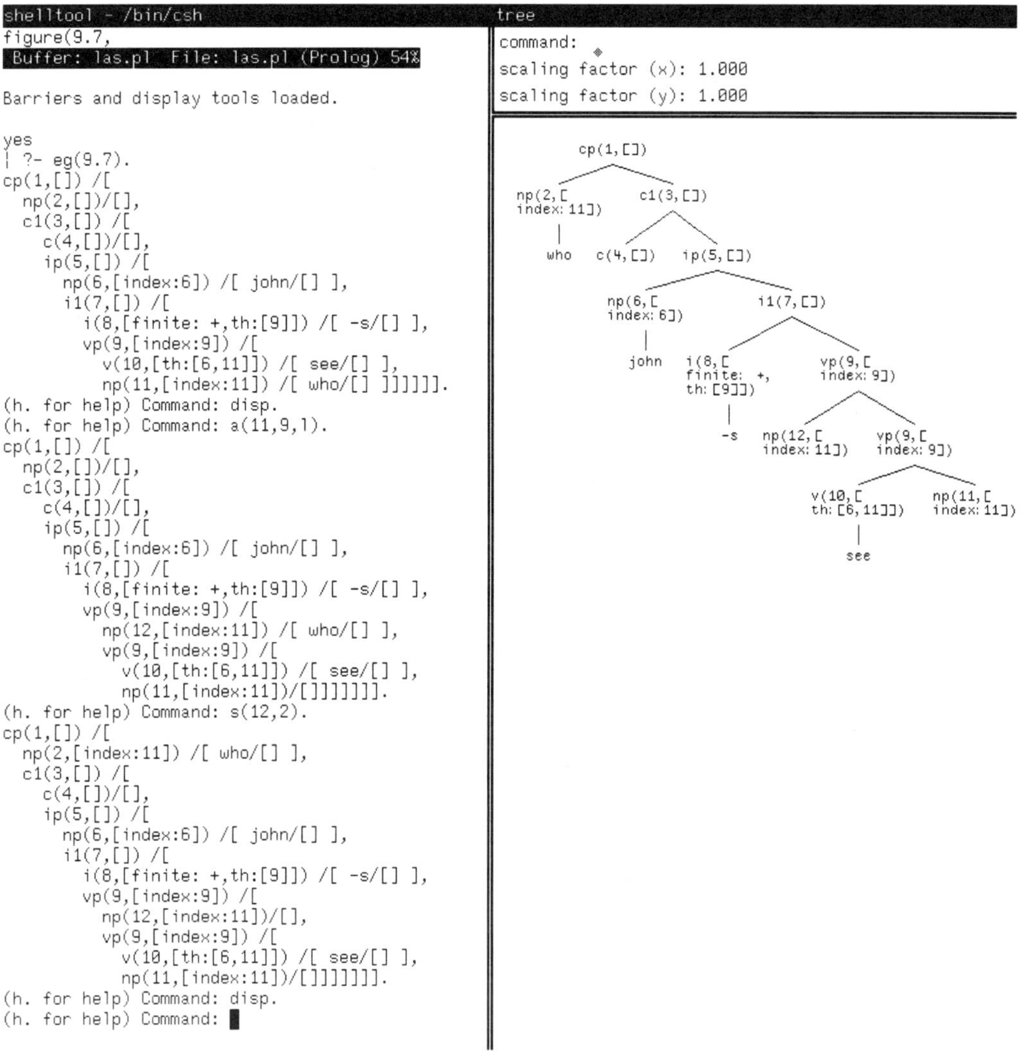

```
shelltool - /bin/csh                          tree
figure(9.7,                                   command:
 Buffer: las.pl  File: las.pl (Prolog) 54%    scaling factor (x): 1.000
                                              scaling factor (y): 1.000
Barriers and display tools loaded.

yes
| ?- eg(9.7).
cp(1,[]) /[
  np(2,[])/[],
  c1(3,[]) /[
    c(4,[])/[],
    ip(5,[]) /[
      np(6,[index:6]) /[ john/[] ],
      i1(7,[]) /[
        i(8,[finite: +,th:[9]]) /[ -s/[] ],
        vp(9,[index:9]) /[
          v(10,[th:[6,11]]) /[ see/[] ],
          np(11,[index:11]) /[ who/[] ]]]]]].
(h. for help) Command: disp.
(h. for help) Command: a(11,9,1).
cp(1,[]) /[
  np(2,[])/[],
  c1(3,[]) /[
    c(4,[])/[],
    ip(5,[]) /[
      np(6,[index:6]) /[ john/[] ],
      i1(7,[]) /[
        i(8,[finite: +,th:[9]]) /[ -s/[] ],
        vp(9,[index:9]) /[
          np(12,[index:11]) /[ who/[] ],
          vp(9,[index:9]) /[
            v(10,[th:[6,11]]) /[ see/[] ],
            np(11,[index:11])/[]]]]]]].
(h. for help) Command: s(12,2).
cp(1,[]) /[
  np(2,[index:11]) /[ who/[] ],
  c1(3,[]) /[
    c(4,[])/[],
    ip(5,[]) /[
      np(6,[index:6]) /[ john/[] ],
      i1(7,[]) /[
        i(8,[finite: +,th:[9]]) /[ -s/[] ],
        vp(9,[index:9]) /[
          np(12,[index:11])/[],
          vp(9,[index:9]) /[
            v(10,[th:[6,11]]) /[ see/[] ],
            np(11,[index:11])/[]]]]]]].
(h. for help) Command: disp.
(h. for help) Command: █
```

Tree display (right panel):

```
                          cp(1,[])
              np(2,[              c1(3,[])
              index: 11])
                 |
                who      c(4,[])    ip(5,[])

                       np(6,[              i1(7,[])
                       index: 6])
                          |
                        john      i(8,[              vp(9,[
                                  finite: +,         index: 9])
                                  th:[9]])
                                     |
                                    -s    np(12,[           vp(9,[
                                          index: 11])       index: 9])

                                                  v(10,[          np(11,[
                                                  th:[6,11]])     index: 11])
                                                     |
                                                    see
```

Figure 14.5
A snapshot of an interactive session

This sort of negative result is of special interest, because it is plausible that a parser should be able to notice when a structure involves a subjacency violation. People quickly notice the awkwardness that results from subjacency violations, and so a parsing model should quickly determine that this situation obtains (without external guidance, of course). Surprisingly, it is not easy to establish this sort of negative result with standard proof methods.

We formalize the claim first. Let τ be the term corresponding to the tree in Figure 14.6. Intuitively, we can see that *what* cannot be fronted without a 1-subjacency violation because the deepest tensed IP is a (parametric) barrier, and the embedded CP is also a barrier, no matter how the movement proceeds. We can formalize the claim that *what* cannot be moved to node 2 without a subjacency violation as follows:

$$\neg \exists T, F \; affectAn(\tau, T) \wedge$$
$$subjacency(T) \wedge$$
$$subtree(x(s(s(0)), n, 2, F)/[what/[]], T).$$

There is no difficulty in proving that the result of moving node 21 to node 2 in a single substitution step violates 1-subjacency, but to show that every sequence of movements and deletions that fronts the Wh-phrase yields a subjacency-violating structure requires a different approach, for reasons that are worth exploring.

Notice that there are infinitely many ways to front a Wh-phrase. In the first place, there are infinite sets of derivations which all yield structures of bounded complexity. An arbitrarily long derivation which does not increase complexity can be obtained simply by moving a constituent from a landing site back into one of its earlier positions, and back again. For example, in the structure of Figure 14.6, since substituting node 21 to node 2 directly produces a subjacency violation, we might consider a derivation that substitutes 21 to 2, 2 to 21, and 21 to 2 again. This "cycling derivation" produces exactly the same structure as the first derivation, and so of course it can fare no better with regard to the subjacency violation. A proof that proceeds by showing that each such derivation involves a subjacency violation will be unable to reach the desired conclusion in a finite number of steps. One response to this problem is to change the linguistic theory. Cycling derivations can be ruled out with some prohibition against "trace erasure" — perhaps some version of the SCC discussed in §11.3. But this response is inappropriate. What we have noted here is not a problem with the theory, but a problem with a particularly stupid proof strategy.

These observations show that, unlike the standard ordering on the natural numbers, $<$, the relation *affectAn* is neither connected nor well-founded, where

DEFINITION 48 Relation r is *connected* iff $\forall X, Y \; r(X, Y) \vee r(Y, X) \vee X = Y$.

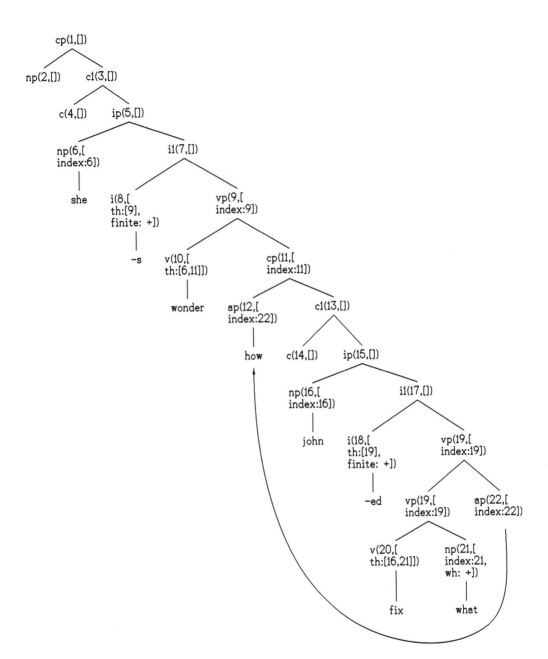

Figure 14.6
Structure underlying an unavoidable subjacency violation

DEFINITION 49 Relation r is *well-founded* iff in every nonempty set S there is some particular element $a \in S$ such that there is no $b \in S$, $\langle b, a \rangle \in r$.

Of course, every reflexive, transitive closure is reflexive and so cannot be well-founded. For example, the reflexive, transitive closure of the successor relation s on natural numbers $s^* = \leq$ is not well-founded, but the composition of $\leq$ with s, $s^+ = s \circ s^* = <$ is well-founded. In our formalization, $affectAn$ is the reflexive, transitive closure of $affectA$, but even $affectAn \circ affectA$ is not well-founded as the infinite derivations mentioned above show. The set containing only the result of substituting node 21 to node 2 is one that violates the condition for well-foundedness, since it is not $affectAn$-minimal.

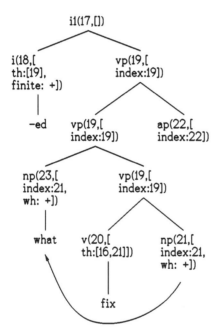

Figure 14.7
A first adjunction step

Before describing a proof strategy which can establish the desired results with finite number of steps, another interesting class of useless derivations allowed by the theory should be noted. Since $vp(19, \ldots)$ is a barrier for $np(21, \ldots)$ in the tree of Figure 14.6, the "best" derivations will adjoin node 21 to 19. Our formalization allows this to be done in either of two ways (even if we consider only left adjunctions) because the VP has 2 segments, with the relevant parts of the results shown in Figures 14.7 and 14.8.

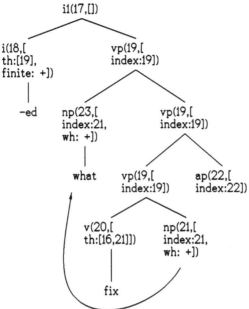

Figure 14.8
Another first adjunction step

Suppose we begin with the step that produces the structure of Figure 14.8. Our next step can adjoin the new node $np(23, \dots)$ to the VP again, and since the VP now has 3 segments, there are 3 possible ways to do this adjunction (even if we consider only left adjunctions). The NP can then adjoin again to produce 4 segments, and so on. Clearly, at every adjunction site, this kind of multiple adjunction is possible in the theory we have formalized, allowing the derivation of arbitrarily large structures.

It is interesting to note in this context a constraint on movements proposed in *Barriers* which we have not yet discussed. Chomsky (1986a, 39) considers the example

Who$_i$ did you wonder [$_{cp}$ what$_j$ John [$_{vp}$ gave t$_j$ to t$_i$]]?

which is much worse than

[to whom]$_i$ did you wonder [$_{cp}$ what$_j$ John [$_{vp}$ gave t$_j$ t$_i$]]?

He says,

> One possibility is a version of the earliest proposal concerning these struc-
> tures, namely, that double application of a rule to a given phrase is barred
> (Chomsky, 1964). This might follow, on our assumptions, from a condition

barring double adjunction of NP to VP, so that [the former example] would
be a much more severe violation of subjacency.

We could call this the "double adjunction condition" (DAC): at most one NP can adjoin
to any VP. This proposal endows multiple adjunction with empirical significance.[5] Some
careful empirical assessment is required to determine whether such a proposal can be
maintained when there are languages which seem to allow multiple-wh movements out of a
clause. For example, McDaniel (1989, 600) argues that in Romani there are constructions
like the following:[6]

Ko_1 kas_2 $[t_1$ $dikla$ $t_2]$?
   (what whom saw?)
Kaj_1 kas_2 $[misline$ so $[o$ $Demiri$ $dikhla$ t_2 $t_1]]$?
   (where do you think whom Demir saw?)

In the present context, though, the DAC is not needed. No empirical adjustment in
the theory should be required to show the impossibility of fronting *what* in Figure 14.6
without a subjacency violation.

So let's consider how the ungrammaticality of

$What_i$ *does she wonder how John fixed* t_i?

could be finitely established in the *Barriers* framework even though there are infinitely
many ways to move *what* to the front of the structure. The obvious alternative is to use
an inductive argument. As is often the case with inductive arguments, it turns out that it
is easier to demonstrate a slightly more general result than the one we need.[7] Remember
our intuitive explanation of the situation: *what* cannot be fronted without a 1-subjacency
violation because the deepest tensed IP is a (parametric) barrier, and the embedded CP
is also a barrier, no matter how the movement proceeds. So one idea is the following:
the initial structure has the property that it has no chain crossing the embedded CP and
IP that respects 1-subjacency, and for all trees this property is preserved by any single
movement or deletion. An inductive argument of the following form, then, demonstrates
our conclusion:

$$\chi(\tau) \tag{14.3.2}$$

$$(\forall T_0, T_1) \quad \chi(T_0) \to (affectA(T_0, T_1) \to \chi(T_1)) \tag{14.3.3}$$

$$[(\forall T_0, T_1) \quad \chi(T_0) \to (affectA(T_0, T_1) \to \chi(T_1))] \to \tag{14.3.4}$$
$$[(\forall T_0, T) \quad \chi(T_0) \to (affectAn(T_0, T) \to \chi(T))]$$

$$\overline{}$$

$$(\forall T)(affectAn(\tau, T) \to \chi(T)) \tag{14.3.5}$$

where τ is, as before, the term corresponding to the tree in Figure 14.6, and where χ is the property of a tree T_0 defined by the following open sentence:

$$\forall A, B \ \ binds(A, B, T_0) \rightarrow \neg(\quad \begin{aligned} &feature(wh : +, A, A) \wedge \\ &excludes(x(s(s(0)), c, 11, [index : 11]), A, T_0) \wedge \\ &dominates(x(s(s(0)), i, 15, []), B, T_0) \wedge \\ &subjacency(T_0) \end{aligned}$$
$$).$$

Premise 14.3.2 is easily established in this case, since the only binding relationship in the tree of Figure 14.6 is the one between nodes 12 and 22, and node 11 does not exclude node 12. Premise 14.3.3 is somewhat harder to establish, but follows because the only way a chain across the embedded CP and IP could avoid violating subjacency is by adjoining to one or the other, which is impossible because adjunction to arguments is ruled out, the CP is an argument, and Wh-phrases cannot adjoin to IP. (Remember that we are assuming the "cumulative" version of subjacency, formalized in §9.5.) Premise 14.3.4 is the most interesting. It is an instance of a schema of induction that holds for any property χ, saying that if χ is preserved by $affectA$, then it is preserved by $affectAn$. Since, under the intended interpretation, $affectAn$ is the reflexive transitive closure or "ancestral" of the relation $affectA$, this induction principle is an instance of what some logicians have called "ancestral induction" (e.g., Quine, 1969, §15) — the "ancestral" of a relation is just its reflexive, transitive closure. This kind of induction principle is sound for arbitrary relations r and their ancestrals r^*, unlike the more familiar induction principles: well-founded induction and mathematical induction.[8] The conclusion 14.3.5 entails the result we were after, since node 2 c-commands node 21 and would bind it if a constituent moved from 21 to 2 in any sequence of movements. So there is a proof of the desired result. It is implausible that that people use any such proof to notice an awkwardness in what they hear or read, and this motivates some proposals of the next chapter.

In these cases where we have used inductive reasoning, it is not clear that induction is *required*. Given the particular difficulties posed by mechanizing the induction principles, it would be nice if they could be avoided altogether. As one would expect, though, leaving out induction principles dramatically reduces the set of consequences of our theory, leaving us unnecessarily far from the goal of having a complete theory of the domain of syntactic structures.[9] Unfortunately, in our theory, no easily detectable syntactic property of a formula indicates that an induction principle will be required for its proof. That is, proving the independence of a given sentence from a theory like ours is usually a nontrivial business.[10] Thus it is no surprise that, for example, Boyer and Moore (1979, 89,146,163) adopt the straightforward strategy of attempting inductive proofs as a last resort, when their other proof strategies have all failed. Results like the one considered in this section appear to be unprovable from our axioms unless we use induction principles like 14.3.4. Other inductive arguments will be used in the next chapter.

14.4 General theorems of linguistic interest

14.4.1 The HMC does not follow from the ECP

In the last section, our quest for a simple negative result led to noticing the non-well-foundedness of affect-α and the discovery of induction principles that apply in any case. But we have not yet demonstrated any general result of particular linguistic interest. It would be a good experiment to see whether such results could be established with the techniques we have been using. As an example, let's consider the possibility, noted in §9.2, that the head movement constraint (HMC) follows from the empty category principle (ECP). We repeat both principles here for convenience:

> (HMC) Movement of a 0-level category β is restricted to the position of a head α that governs the maximal projection γ of β, where α θ-governs or L-marks γ if $\alpha \neq C$.

> (ECP) A nonpronominal empty category must be properly governed, where α *properly governs* β iff α antecedent governs β.

These principles are formalized in §9 and §10, respectively. Antecedent government is government by a binding category, where government is restricted by the minimality condition. Up to this point, we have been using the formalized theory $FB \cup SEQ_{FB}$, which contains all of these ideas. To be precise, the question we are now considering is whether $(FB \cup SEQ_{FB}) - HMC$ entails HMC. Equivalently, given a sound and complete proof method, the question is whether HMC can be derived from $(FB \cup SEQ_{FB}) - HMC$. If we remove the HMC from our conditions on acceptable movements (as formalized in the definition of $affectA$, axiom 10.1.3), does every movement that satisfies the ECP and other principles of the grammar also satisfy the HMC?

It is easy to see that the answer is: no. The easiest way to demonstrate the point is with the presentation of a counterexample to the claim. Consider the tree shown in Figure 14.9. Suppose that we substitute the affix $i(12, \ldots)$ to $i(6, \ldots)$, then left adjoin the verb $v(8, \ldots)$ to $i(6, \ldots)$. Then let's substitute $np(10, \ldots)$ to $np(4, \ldots)$ and apply SPEC-head agreement and γ-marking. The resulting structure, shown in Figure 14.10, is certainly deviant, but as the figure shows, there is no violation of the ECP or any other principle we have formalized. That is, this derivation and the resulting structure

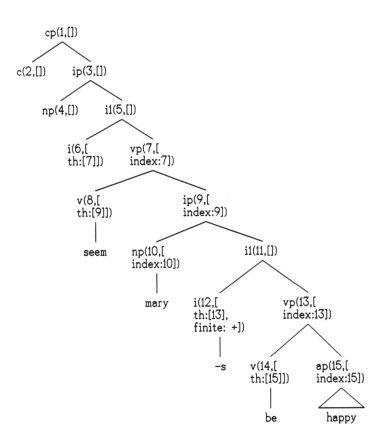

Figure 14.9
Structure underlying an HMC violation

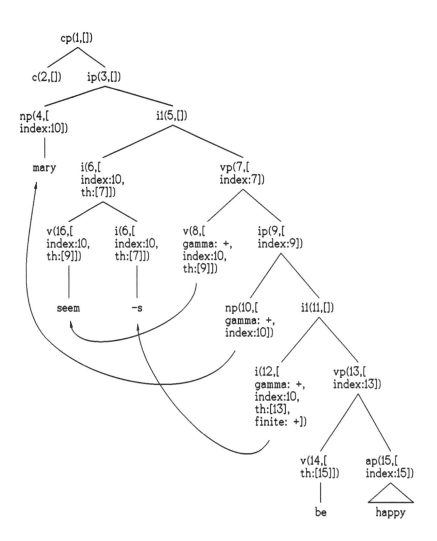

Figure 14.10
Structure derived with an HMC violation

is not ruled out by any principle of $(FB \cup SEQ_{FB}) - HMC$, even though the derivation involves the raising of $i(12, \ldots)$ to $i(6, \ldots)$ which violates the HMC because node 6 does not govern node 12.

This counterexample has a raising verb *seem* selecting a finite IP complement. Neither *seem* nor any other raising verb in English does this, but no principle in *Barriers* rules such a verb out. In fact, it is not clear how this kind of structure should be ruled out. It could be a lexical restriction on what types of complements raising verbs can select, or it might be a restriction on the selection of tensed IPs by C. However, it is clear that even with one of these restrictions, we would not be able to derive the HMC from the rest of $FB \cup SEQ_{FB}$. No general principle precludes the possibility that a trace in a head position X is locally bound by a governing head Y when Y is not the landing site for any movement from X. This can happen in many ways, within the constraints imposed by $FB \cup SEQ_{FB}$. For one thing, no formalized principle blocks the possibility that the governing head is just accidentally coindexed with the trace, though Chomsky (1986a, 75) observes the need for this. Another kind of derivation that is not ruled out moves the head first across the higher, governing head to an even higher position, and then back to the governing position, and then away again. Such a derivation violates the HMC (on a derivational interpretation), but can produce a representation that is identical to one produced by a derivation that respects the HMC.

Many linguists have argued that the HMC follows from the ECP in *Barriers* frameworks.[11] When the arguments offered by these linguists are considered carefully, it turns out that all of them neglect the many cases where a construction can be made to satisfy the ECP as a result of coindexing that is not the result of a single movement.

14.4.2   Barriers without subjacency entails the CED

Another proposition which might be subsumed by the principles of $FB \cup SEQ_{FB}$ is the condition on extraction domains (CED) of Huang (1982, §6.4). Strictly speaking, since many of Huang's background assumptions differ from those of *Barriers*, $FB \cup SEQ_{FB}$ and the CED are incomparable, but consider the following simple version of the idea:[12]

> (CED) Constituent A_i cannot be moved out of a constituent B that is not governed by a lexical category C or by a co-indexed category C_i.

As discussed in §9.4, Chomsky (1986a, §7) suggests that CED effects may follow from subjacency. After the ECP requirement of antecedent government (constrained by the minimality condition) is formalized in §10, we are in a position to see that the CED effects Chomsky considers lead not only to subjacency violations but also to ECP violations. For example, in Figure 9.8, if *who* is extracted from the subject *pictures of who*, the resulting trace will not be properly governed. The claim of this section is that the ECP alone suffices to cover CED effects, where these are characterized as indicated. But rather than just illustrating the claim for three or four structures, we attempt to establish the general result directly for all of the infinitely many structures in our domain. To be precise, $(FB \cup SEQ_{FB}) - subjacency$ entails CED. This result may be surprising, given that Chomsky relates CED effects to subjacency. It is no surprise that subjacency and the CED overlap; the surprise is that the CED, on a natural construal, is completely swallowed by the ECP. This result conflicts with Browning's (1989) suggestion that CED effects should not be lumped together with ECP effects. She classes *Barriers* together with Huang (1982) and Lasnik and Saito (1984) as avoiding this conflation, as opposed to approaches like Kayne's (1983) in which CED effects are subsumed by a generalization of the ECP. We consider Browning's argument in the next subsection, §14.4.3.

Considering the CED on its own terms, it is no surprise that it is respected in *Barriers* structures that satisfy the ECP, since L-marking plays such a crucial role in the definition of barriers for the ECP. Any phrase B other than IP that is not lexically governed will not be L-marked, and so will immediately constitute a barrier for both movements and the ECP. If B is not VP, the only way to move out of the constituent B without an ECP violation is by adjoining to it so that no link of the chain crosses B, in which case the coindexed adjoined category governs B. The case where B is a VP is an exception to this, because the V can raise to I, changing I to a lexical category, causing VP to be L-marked, and avoiding an ECP violation. The other special case arises when B is IP. Clearly, movement of a wh-NP subject of IP to a governing specifier of C is allowed, since then the IP is governed by the co-indexed moved category. Movement to a higher position that does not govern the IP is impossible because if the IP is not governed, the subject of IP will not be governed either.

An argument along these lines can be formalized, though we will provide only a sketch here. Given the peculiar consequence of raising V to I, the change of I into a lexical category, it is most convenient to reexpress the idea in terms of chains in a syntactic structure. If a constituent is extracted from any constituent Xn, the resulting structure will have a chain that crosses Xn, so we can say,

> (CED′) In a structure that satisfies the ECP, if A_i precedes C_i in a chain, and if Xn intervenes between A_i and C_i, then Xn is either governed by a lexical category or by some element of the chain B_i (possibly $B_i = A_i$).

For structures in which co-indexing occurs only as the result of movements and SPEC-head agreement, where links of an "extended chain" (as defined in §10.7) locally bind each other, this claim is easily formalized with the following conditional:[13]

$$(\; binds(A,C,T) \land$$

$$excludes(Xn,A,T) \land$$
$$dominates(Xn,C,T) \land$$
$$lf\_gamma(T,T1) \land$$
$$ecp(T1) \;) \;\; \rightarrow \exists B \; (\quad lexical(B) \land$$
$$governs(B,C,T)$$
$$\lor \quad binds(B,C,T) \land$$
$$governs(B,Xn,T)$$
$$).$$

(14.4.6)

The clausal form of the negation of this sentence is just 7 clauses. These clauses assert the existence of a counterexample, the existence of some A, C, Xn, T, T1 that make the antecedent true but the consequent false. We establish the claim by showing that this assumption of a counterexample, together with the axioms of $(FB \cup SEQ_{FB})$ − *subjacency*, leads to an explicit contradiction.

Assuming that an arbitrary tree T1 satisfies the ECP, we know that every empty category is antecedent governed in both T and T1, and so no link in the extended chain containing A and C has an intervening barrier. We then show by cases that we cannot avoid contradicting the assumption that the consequent of sentence 14.4.6 is false:

(a) If Xn is lexically governed, the consequent is trivially true.

(b) If Xn is not lexically governed, maximal, and not IP, it is a barrier for every category it dominates, and so no link can cross it. (It is crucial here to remember that in the *Barriers* system, NP raising across VP is allowed only when V raises to I, thus L-marking VP and voiding its barrierhood, as in Figure 10.7.) In this case, to satisfy the ECP, there must be an element of the chain adjoined to Xn. This element will govern Xn and bind C_i, and the consequent is true again.

(c) If Xn=IP and is not lexically governed, then it is not a blocking category. If it does not inherit barrierhood, it can be crossed by a link. Suppose that it is crossed by a link B_i, D_i. Then the ECP requires that B_i antecedent governs D_i, and so B_i governs Xn=IP, making the consequent true. Suppose on the other hand that Xn is not crossed by a link. Then some member B_i of the chain containing A_i, C_i must be adjoined to Xn, and Xn will be governed by that member of the chain, again making the consequent true.

(d) The only remaining case is where Xn is not lexically governed and not maximal. Then it is not a barrier because only maximal categories are barriers, and so it might be crossed by a link. However, it dominates C_i, and so its maximal projection XP dominates C_i. Now consider two subcases. First, suppose XP excludes A_i. Then one of the previous three cases applies to XP. If case (a) applies, that is, if XP is lexically governed, then Xn is lexically governed too, since government of XP goes through to all projections of the category. Similarly for cases (b) and (c). Finally, suppose that XP does not exclude A_i. Then either A_i is adjoined to XP, in which case it governs XP and the lower projections of X, or else XP dominates A_i. When XP dominates A_i and A_i governs C_i and Xn intervenes between A_i and C_i, then A_i itself governs Xn, and so again the consequent must be true.

14.4.3 Barriers without the ECP does not entail the CED

As we noted in the previous section, Chomsky initially relates the CED not to ECP effects but to subjacency, so the question naturally arises whether subjacency alone can completely account for the CED. In this section we will show that the answer is no. That is, $(FB \cup SEQ_{FB}) - ECP$ does not entail CED.

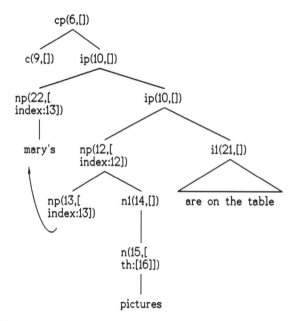

Figure 14.11
Violation of CED and ECP but not subjacency (compare Figure 9.8)

As in §14.4.1, this negative result is most easily established with a counterexample, and as in that section, once we find one counterexample it is clear that there is an abundance of CED violations which $(FB \cup SEQ_{FB}) - ECP$ does not rule out. In Figure 9.8, movement out of IP from within the NP specifier of IP is shown to violate 1-subjacency because both NP and IP are barriers. However, it is easy to construct cases where only one barrier is crossed, causing an ECP violation but not a subjacency violation. For example, we have not formalized any principles that block the occurrence of structures like Figure 14.11 in the syntax. The relevant point for present purposes, though, is just that we have identified a precise sense in which the ECP subsumes the CED, while subjacency does not.

As mentioned above, Browning (1989, 481, 482) suggests that Chomsky treats the CED "as a subcase of the Subjacency Condition," and that "distribution of NP-trace provides evidence that ECP effects and CED effects must derive from distinct sources." We have seen, though, that the CED does not really follow from subjacency in *Barriers*. Although some CED violations turn out to be subjacency violations, not all of them are. On the other hand, all CED violations are ECP violations.

Browning draws attention to some independently interesting facts which show that the ECP accounts for contrasts that the CED does not account for. She considers the following examples from Longobardi (1985):

Credo che Mario$_i$ non sia mai stato [tradito t$_i$ da sua moglie]
    (I) believe that Mario not has been [betrayed by his wife]
[Tradito t$_i$ da sua moglie]$_j$, credo che Mario$_i$ non sia mai stato t$_j$
    [betrayed by his wife], (I) believe that Mario not has ever been

In the first of these examples, we have a movement of *Mario* to the subject position of the embedded clause, with no CED violation. If the VP is then topicalized, which is also allowed by the CED, we end up with an empty category appearing in a position where it should not be allowed, according to certain versions of the ECP. The *Barriers* version of the ECP can allow this structure, though. If the verb *tradito* raises to I, it can L-mark VP, and by SPEC-head agreement antecedent govern the NP trace. In contrast, the *Barriers* ECP does not allow examples like Rizzi's (1982a) example,

* *[t$_i$ dormire]$_j$, Gianni$_i$ sembra t$_j$.*
    [to sleep], Gianni seems

Here, we simply do not have an antecedent governor for the NP-trace, even though both movements respect the CED, as in the previous case. Since the CED allows all of these structures, but the ECP does not, this establishes that CED$\neq$ECP, but it does not support the conclusion that CED and ECP effects must come from different sources. On the contrary, these observations are compatible with the view that the ECP is strictly more powerful, ruling out all CED violations and other things as well.

14.5   Decidability

In previous sections, we have presumed that $FB \cup SEQ_{FB}$ is consistent. When we are interested in proving that FB entails some formula, we consider whether $FB \cup SEQ_{FB}$, together with the negation of that formula, is unsatisfiable. It would be nice if we could guarantee that all such problems are decidable. Unfortunately, we have no such guarantee. Since our theory axiomatizes relations like the concatenation relation (consider *append*, or *select*) or similar tree composition relations (like *parent*), we have the power of arithmetic, along with the well known essential incompleteness of such systems. Thus we cannot guarantee the decidability of $FB \cup SEQ_{FB}$ using the fact that an axiomatizable and complete theory is decidable (our Theorem 1.1). In fact, as noted in §3, a theory like ours with the power of arithmetic is undecidable by Church's theorem.

We could still hope for some restricted but useful decidability results. For example, assuming FB is consistent, it would be nice to be able to decide the satisfiability of $FB \cup \neg \phi$ for certain classes of sentences ϕ. For parsing applications, for example, we might be interested in variable-free ϕ where ϕ asserts the existence of well-formed and transformationally related D-structure, S-structure, and LF-structure, where the S-structure has a certain string as its yield. Given the complexity of the theory, a brute force induction on the lengths of the proofs does not look like a promising strategy, but suppose that we could show that if there is any provable instance of the parsing problem for a string of length n, there is one whose terms are within some complexity bound $f(n)$. Then, if proofs of such instances of the parsing need never involve sentences with terms exceeding this bound, decidability would follow trivially. A sketch of a complexity bound on structural representations, Corollary 2, is presented in §15.4. It seems very likely that this result could be formalized and used to establish a decidability result for parsing and similar problems, but further research is needed.

14.6   Conclusions

The computational tools described in this section were used in the development of the formalization and in the proofs of results in previous chapters. The linguistic theory can be used quite directly, and consequently it is fairly easy to modify the theory and check the consequences. The prospects look very good for producing a tool that can be used by linguists who want to check the validity of their derivations without worrying about the details of resolution refutations. We now turn to the problem of designing more traditional, unguided natural language processors.

Chapter 15

Parsing as constraint satisfaction

All that happens at any point of this musical space has more than a local effect. It functions not only at its own point, but also in all other directions and planes, and is not without influence even at remote points.
— *Arnold Schönberg*

Linguists regard grammar as a representation of human knowledge of language, a representation which may be used in language understanding and other linguistic tasks. Our logical formalization is no more biased towards parsing or any other task than the informal theory, so how could it be used by a parser? Abstracting away from the peculiar limitations of the human parsing mechanism, some of which were observed in §5.1, we might assume that language understanding involves, among other things, computing the structures and relations defined by the grammar. Let's begin with this idea and consider how a system could compute the relations between phonetic forms, S-structures, D-structures and LF-structures defined by the grammar. Already, in taking this perspective, our approach to human language processing is different from most others. It is distinctive in its initial emphasis on the the language defined by the grammar. Rather than letting some peculiar limitations in human abilities or some short-term engineering goals guide our initial consideration of how the language might be processed, and then trying to extend the mechanism to the wide range of structures that people have no trouble with, we take the reverse approach. One way to express this perspective is this: the most peculiar and significant property of the human language processor is that it handles languages like English, Chinese, Bambara, Navajo, Warlpiri or any of the others that people have spoken. As for the facts about particular occasions of language understanding, a certain efficiency in processing can be observed. The human language processor handles a wide range of small structures very quickly. Humans probably do not pursue thousands of blind alleys before discovering an appropriate structure. Maybe the structure building is even largely deterministic. These assumptions by themselves set a very hard problem. Given any of the the readily comprehensible inputs, how can the structures defined by the grammar be computed in only some few steps?

The great advantage of the present approach is that we begin with a clear, though
still incomplete and controversial, account of some basic properties of human language.
Given our formalization of recent syntactic theory, a first idea might be that parsing
is done by deduction from this theory, in roughly the way it was done from the much
simpler theories in §§4-5. Unfortunately, nothing so easy will work. Efficiency is a serious
and immediate problem. Without external guidance of the sort used in the last chapter,
pointless search will consume excessive resources even in the simplest cases. We must have
either a much better deductive technique, or a different formulation of the problem, or
both. The elimination of unsuccessful search is exactly the focus of traditional constraint
satisfaction methods, and we draw on the insights from that work in this chapter. Details
of human performance such as the difficulty of center-embedding and garden-paths will
be left aside for the moment, since the language processing problem is already difficult
enough that we will not be able to solve it here. We take only the first steps toward
a mechanism that is "efficient" in the sense that something like the range of structures
that humans understand easily can be computed easily. It is crucial to distinguish this
informal sense of "efficient" from formal senses of the term, such as "computable in
polynomial time in the worst case." Ristad (1990) has argued persuasively that human
languages cannot be processed efficiently in that sense, no matter what grammar you
have for them.[1] After we have some ideas about how the problem can be solved quickly
on an appropriate range of structures, then it will be appropriate to attempt to explain
more of the details of human language processing.

15.1 A parsing problem

As discussed in §6, the problem of computing the syntactic structure of a phonetic form
τ could be regarded as the problem of finding a constructive proof of a sentence like:

$$\exists DS, SS, LF \quad xbar(DS) \wedge \tag{15.1.1}$$

$$lexical\_insertion(DS) \wedge$$
$$theta\_assignment(DS) \wedge$$
$$affect\text{-}\alpha(DS, SS) \wedge$$
$$subjacency(SS) \wedge$$
$$case\_theory(SS) \wedge$$
$$affect\text{-}\alpha(SS, LF) \wedge$$
$$binding(LF) \wedge$$
$$ecp(LF) \wedge$$
$$pf(SS, \tau).$$

Clearly, this is not a good characterization of the problem that people solve when they understand their language, since they are able to assign structure to and understand many things other than perfectly grammatical sentences. However, it is not clear how to characterize exactly which structures people formulate, especially when the structures are not "perfectly good." We get some rough indication from the fact that ECP violations are worse than subjacency violations (§10), subjacency violations are (perhaps) worse than SCC violations (§11.3), and so on. Transforming problem 15.1.2 into the one of appropriately optimizing the degree to which linguistic constraints (and perhaps other preferences) are satisfied is of considerable interest, but we will not pursue it here.[2] The simple problem 15.1.2 is close enough to the real one to serve in our preliminary study. A language understander who solves this problem will have a broad grasp of the language.

Unfortunately, since *Barriers* is incomplete, we are not yet in a position to tackle problem 15.1.2. We have not formalized enough of the theory, so rather than attempting to quickly fill in everything else about the language, we formulate a problem which is similar in form but restricted to those parts of *Barriers* that we have formalized:

$$\exists DS, SS, SS1, SS2, LF, LF2 \quad xp(DS) \ \wedge \qquad\qquad\qquad\qquad (15.1.2)$$

$$affectAn(DS, SS) \ \wedge$$
$$subjacency(SS) \ \wedge$$
$$yield(SS, \tau) \ \wedge$$
$$spec\_head(SS, SS1) \ \wedge$$
$$ss\_gamma(SS1, SS2) \ \wedge$$
$$affectAn(SS2, LF) \ \wedge$$
$$lf\_gamma(LF, LF1) \ \wedge$$
$$ecp(LF1)$$

This sentence uses only predicates defined in Part II. Instead of parsing a phonetic form, we parse the yield of an S-structure tree, where the yield is the string of leaves of the tree that have phonological features. This involves all the basic components of the formalized *Barriers* theory: X-bar theory is formalized in the definition of xp; the theory of movements and deletions is in $affectAn$; all movements are constrained by structure preservation, the HMC, and 1-subjacency; deletions are constrained by a tentative recoverability principle, and after γ-marking at S-structure and at LF, the ECP must be satisfied. Consider the computational difficulties in establishing instances of this sentence.

15.2   Parsing as constraint satisfaction

Suppose we adopt the approach to parsing considered in Part I, namely, we prove 15.1.2
indirectly, deducing a contradiction from the negation of the sentence to be proved, and
collecting substitutions to find the instance refuted. Negating sentence 15.1.2 and putting
it in clausal form, we have:

$$\{\neg xp(DS), \qquad\qquad\qquad\qquad\qquad\qquad\qquad\qquad\qquad\qquad (15.2.3)$$
$$\neg affectAn(DS, SS),$$
$$\neg subjacency(SS),$$
$$\neg spec\_head(SS, SS1),$$
$$\neg ss\_gamma(SS1, SS2),$$
$$\neg affectAn(SS2, LF),$$
$$\neg lf\_gamma(LF, LF1),$$
$$\neg ecp(LF1),$$
$$\neg yield(SS1, \tau)$$
$$\}$$

If we try to find a refutation by refuting the first literal first, then the second, and
so on, we engage in a hopelessly inefficient "generate-and-test" search.[3] Things are no
better if the literals are taken in reverse order. Using a more complex control strategy
to intermingle the steps involved in satisfying each constraint can help (Stabler, 1989a;
Johnson, 1989; Macias, 1990), but we still will be unable to avoid unnecessary complexity. It is valuable to see exactly what the problem is here. It is simply that there
are infinitely many ways to satisfy the *yield* constraint that could not be part of any
solution to the whole problem, and similarly for every other constraint. Each constraint,
taken by itself, fails to reflect the global requirements of the whole problem. The very
modularity that we have been seeking and praising in the formalization is what produces
these difficulties.

In this situation, the most direct strategies for avoiding the wasted search are what
Mackworth (1977; 1987) calls "consistency techniques." Consider the following trivial
problem, for example,

$$\exists X_1, X_2, X_3 \quad X_1 \in \{3, 4\} \wedge$$
$$X_2 \in \{3, 4\} \wedge$$
$$X_3 \in \{3, 2\} \wedge$$
$$X_1 > X_2 \wedge$$
$$X_2 > X_3$$

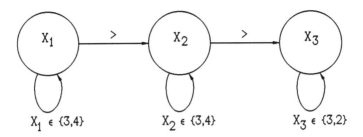

Figure 15.1
A trivial constraint satisfaction problem as a graph

This kind of problem is often represented with a graph like that shown in Figure 15.1 (from Stabler, 1990a). In this graph, each variable corresponds to a node, and the required properties and relations among these variables are indicated by arcs. In this simple problem, like the parsing problem, every subproblem has a solution that cannot be part of any complete solution. The obvious way to avoid wasted effort is to adopt a strategy that will avoid considering the values that cannot be part of any solution. Suppose that, rather than guessing solutions, we systematically modify the problem given on each individual arc to eliminate solutions than cannot be part of an overall solution to the problem. Once we bring the global constraints to bear on each individual constraint in the problem of Figure 15.1, each constraint is seen to have only one usable solution, and the solution to the whole problem is immediately determined. It is clear that this simple idea developed by Mackworth and others goes to the heart of the inefficiency problem that standard proof techniques face when given our parsing problem, and a feasible solution strategy must bring constraints from various levels of representation to bear on the construction of the representations at each particular level.

The parsing problem we are considering can be represented with a slightly more complex graph, shown in Figure 15.2, and the basic difficulty of avoiding spurious solutions to subproblems is exactly the same. Notice that lexical insertion and basic categorial structure are defined at D-structure (by xp), and we clearly do not want to just start generating trees that have the right yield without such basic lexical and structural constraints. However, because the relation between D-structure and S-structure is a rather complex, non-functional relation, it is not easy to see exactly which structural properties will carry over from one level to the next. With our formal representation, though, this question can be systematically attacked with methods that we know to be sound. We can establish as theorems the results that will tell us how to bring D-structure and LF constraints to bear at S-structure, and similarly for all the other levels of representation.

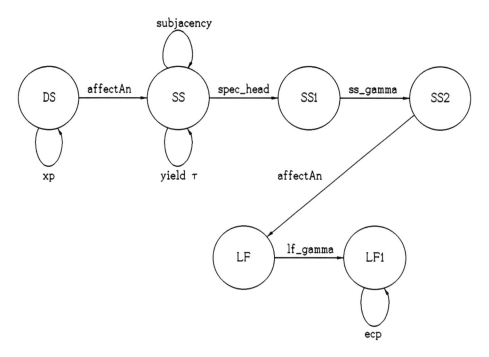

Figure 15.2
The parsing problem as a graph

15.3 Structure preservation theorems

In deciding what properties we would like to bring to bear when we start solving the parsing problem, it is helpful to think about how structures could be assigned to a simple example, like

the cat is on the mat.

In this case, with a parsing method that is (at least in part) bottom-up, it would be natural to begin by identifying *the* as a determiner and placing it into a tree structure under the category *d*, as in the parsers of Marcus (1980), Berwick and Weinberg (1984), Abney (1989; 1991), and others. Even this simple first step is not so easy to justify. In the first place, while the orthographic form *the* may be unambiguously a determiner, the overt leaves of S-structures are presumably not labelled with properly punctuated English text in any psychologically real S-structure, but with some phonological contents. This introduces a slight complication because the phonological form ðə is ambiguous. In fact, especially to a logically-minded listener, it is semantically and orthographically infinitely ambiguous: it might be the determiner, 'the'; it might be the name of the determiner, "the"; it might be the name of the name of the determiner; and so on. As far as its syntactically relevant features go, there is a two-way ambiguity: it is either a determiner or a name. For the moment, though, assume that the phonologically overt leaves at S-structure are orthographic forms and that *the* is unambiguously a determiner. Then the lexicon and X-bar theory will guarantee that it must be under d at D-structure.[4] With these axioms, we could try to establish the following simple structure-preservation result: if a lexical item has a parent of category C at D-structure, then it has a parent of category C at all levels of structure. Unfortunately, this result does not hold in the theories that we have formalized, because head movements are not required to be category-preserving. Again, let's simplify just for a moment and imagine that we have added an axiom saying that head movements of determiners can only be to determiner positions. The interesting question is then: how can we establish that if the parent of *the* is d at D-structure, then it must be d at S-structure as well? The argument will obviously have to turn on the particular character of the *affectAn* relation. The simplest idea would be just that, since no grammatical movement, deletion or insertion changes the category of the parent of *the*, any structure related to D-structure by any number of movements, deletions and insertions must be one where the parent of *the* has not changed. In fact, this form of inference is a sound inductive argument similar to the one described in §14.3.

The form of argument we need here can be schematized as follows (Stabler, 1990b):

$(\forall T_0)\quad d\_structure(T_0) \rightarrow \chi(T_0)$ \hfill (15.3.4)

$(\forall T_0, T_1)\quad \chi(T_0) \rightarrow (affectA(T_0, T_1) \rightarrow \chi(T_1))$ \hfill (15.3.5)

$[(\forall T_0, T_1)\quad \chi(T_0) \rightarrow (affectA(T_0, T_1) \rightarrow \chi(T_1))] \rightarrow$ \hfill (15.3.6)
$\qquad\qquad [(\forall T_0, T)\quad \chi(T_0) \rightarrow (affectAn(T_0, T) \rightarrow \chi(T))]$

$(\forall T_0, T)\quad d\_structure(T_0) \rightarrow (affectAn(T_0, T) \rightarrow \chi(T)).$ \hfill (15.3.7)

The first premise just says that some property χ holds of all D-structures. The second premise says that property χ is preserved by one movement or deletion. The third premise is the principle of induction discussed in §14.3. It says that, for any property χ, if χ is preserved by *affectA*, then it is preserved by *affectAn*.

As noted above, though, head movement by substitution does not always preserve the preterminal category. One property that is preserved by any number of movements and deletions is the basic X-bar structure of a tree. To formalize this idea, it is most convenient to introduce a modified version of our X-bar theory predicates in such a way that appropriate D-structure lexical insertion is not enforced. Suppose that we define new predicates $xp-li$, $x1-li$, and $x0-li$ just like $xp, x1$, and $x0$ except that the *lexicon* condition is removed from the definition of $x0$. That is, no requirements are imposed on subtrees rooted by minimal categories. Then, using an argument of the form described, we can establish:

THEOREM 9 $(\forall T_0, T)\quad xp - li(T0) \wedge affectAn(T_0, T) \rightarrow xp - li(T)$.

One other intuitive sort of result that we can establish, though we will not provide the full formalization here, is the following:

THEOREM 10 If T is at most n-branching for any $n > 1$, then for all T1 such that affectAn(T,T1), T1 is at most n-branching.

These results are limited, though, in that they tell us about simple properties of trees that are related by $affectAn$. We would also like to say things about how any trees related by $affectAn$ must be related. For example, consider any well-formed D-structure and any corresponding well-formed S-structure. For every nonempty XP with ψ-features F that occurs in the D-structure, there is a chain of NPs in the S-structure headed by a nonempty XP with ψ-features F. (The ψ-features are defined in §7.2.) The converse can be slightly strengthened: for each chain in the S-structure with an XP head (empty or not) with ψ-features F, there is an NP in the D-structure with those features. This latter result is clearly the sort of thing we would like to be able to establish for parsing purposes. With it, once an S-structure node is hypothesized, a corresponding D-structure commitment follows immediately. Part of this idea could be captured by a formula like the following:

THEOREM 11 $(\forall T_0, T)\quad affectAn(T_0, T) \rightarrow same\_xps(T_0, T)$,

where $same\_xps(T_0, T)$ holds just in case every XP with ψ-features F that occurs in $T0$ also occurs in T.

To establish this kind of result, we need a different kind of argument. The following form of argument will do the job:

$$(\forall T)\quad \chi(T, T) \tag{15.3.8}$$

$$(\forall T_0, T_1, T)\quad (\chi(T_0, T_1) \wedge affectA(T_1, T)) \rightarrow \chi(T_0, T) \tag{15.3.9}$$

$$\big[(\forall T_0, T_1, T)\quad \chi(T_0, T_0) \wedge ((\chi(T_0, T_1) \wedge affectA(T_1, T)) \rightarrow \chi(T_0, T))\big] \rightarrow \tag{15.3.10}$$
$$\big[(\forall T_0, T)\quad affectAn(T_0, T) \rightarrow \chi(T_0, T)\big]$$

$$\overline{\quad\quad\quad\quad\quad\quad\quad\quad\quad\quad\quad\quad\quad\quad\quad\quad}$$

$$(\forall T_0, T)\quad affectAn(T_0, T) \rightarrow \chi(T_0, T) \tag{15.3.11}$$

The key premise here is 15.3.10, which says that if a relation χ is reflexive and is preserved by $affectA$, then it is preserved by $affectAn$.[5]

This form of argument can establish Theorem 11, but for parsing purposes we would like a stronger result. We would like a 1-1 correspondence between chains at S-structure and D-structure categories. Unfortunately, as discussed in §11.3, nothing in our formalism blocks the merging of XP chains. Such merging would be blocked by an appropriate form of the θ-criterion, the SCC, and other principles, but since these are not part of our formal theory, we cannot yet guarantee that different D-structure XPs will always correspond to different S-structure chains. Once these principles are incorporated into the theory, though, the stronger result would follow by the same sort of inductive argument.

The ability to relate constituents of trees across the *affectAn* relation does allow us to establish further results which could be useful in parsing. Suppose that we strengthen *delete_conds* so that lexical categories cannot be deleted. (The case allowed in our formalization that we have to block is deletion of the trace of V+I.) Then we have the following results:

THEOREM 12 If Xn is governed by a lexical category in T, then for all T1 such that affectAn(T,T1), if Xn occurs in T1, Xn is governed in T1.

THEOREM 13 If Xn is not governed by any lexical category in T and Xn is not governed by I or C, then for all T1 such that affectAn(T,T1), Xn is not governed by any lexical category in T.

These results would mean that once we have determined that a constituent is governed in one tree, we do not need to repeat the test in any other trees that are related by *affectAn*.

Showing that properties are preserved across the relations *spec_head*, *ss_gamma*, and *lf_gamma* is typically much easier than showing that they are preserved across *affectAn*, since these relations simply change features in a fixed way. So the forms of argument we have outlined here will allow us to bring constraints from any part of the grammar to bear on the level we are constructing, at any point in parsing a string. Two sorts of results of this kind are especially valuable: bounds on structural complexity, and locality properties. These will be considered in the next two sections. The hope is that with results of this kind, we can guide the design of a reasonable parser, perhaps even a deductive parser that is sound and complete even without the use of inductive arguments.

A comparison with simple theories of arithmetic is again valuable. The standard Peano arithmetic with a second order induction axiom can be weakened simply by removing the induction axiom, but the result is a weak and uninteresting theory. This theory does not even entail the associativity of addition, and Mostowski, Robinson, and Tarski (1953, Theorem 11) show that it is decidable. With the addition of one simple axiom, though, we obtain Robinson's arithmetic Q from which most of the important results of elementary arithmetic can be established. Even though Robinson's arithmetic is much weaker than Peano arithmetic,[6] the theory is strong enough to represent many interesting relations. It is an open question whether there is an analogous first order axiomatization of our theory without induction principles that is strong enough to be used in parsing, but an affirmative answer appears very likely.

15.4 Structural complexity results

One of the most straightforward ways to significantly reduce the search problem for our parsing problem would be to impose some reasonable bound on the structural complexity of the trees that could be solutions to the problem. That is, if we had some measure of the complexity of our input and the complexity of trees, such that for inputs of complexity n we never need to consider trees with complexity greater than $f(n)$, then our search space would be finite and maybe even feasible.

Before we get carried away with these hopes, we should immediately note some well-known results. In the first place, even if all the syntactic structures are small — suppose each requires only 1 unit of memory — there is still a problem for any system which attempts to formulate all of the parse trees. We know, for example, that the number of attachment sites for k prepositional phrases in an English sentence is not polynomially bounded by k (Church and Patil, 1982), and since each prepositional phrase can be very short, it follows that the number of grammatical trees is not polynomially bounded by the length of the string. So even if we do not count the size of the trees, but only the number of trees, we do not have a linear bound on the size of the set of syntactic structures for n-word grammatical strings. Similar ambiguity is produced by other constructions, and these assessments are not particularly sensitive to controversial aspects of syntax.

One might respond here that we never need to formulate all of the trees explicitly. We could encode them all in a chart as Earley (1970) does, or use some other representation (e.g., Epstein, 1990). Then the processor might choose the appropriate structure from the exponentially many that are implicitly represented on the basis of a reasonable number of decisions. However, if the chosen structure is itself not of bounded size, the extraction process can still require an infeasible amount of space. That is, the extraction of a tree T from a reasonably sized representation of many trees is obviously infeasible if it involves formulating an "explicit" representation of T and T is infeasibly large. Of course, this point is irrelevant unless some particular trees are infeasibly large. Do the languages defined by linguistic theory ever associate phonological forms of "size" n with syntactic structures that are very large compared to n, for natural measures of size? The considerations that come up when we try to answer this question provide a perspective on linguistic theory that is worth having. Before tackling this problem, it is useful to see how size bounds can be provided for the structures defined by simpler grammars.

15.4.1   Size bounds for CFG derivation trees

It is no surprise that a study of the efficiency of context-free parsing methods will often begin with an upper bound on the size of context-free derivation trees. Obviously, if the trees are not bounded in size as a function of the length of the string to be parsed, there will be no bound on the complexity of an algorithm which computes an explicit representation of the largest tree.

Let the complexity of an input sequence be its length. Let the complexity of a tree be the sum of the complexities of its nodes, where the complexity of a node is 1 plus the length of its feature list. In the case of context-free grammars, there are no features, so we will simply count the nodes, including leaves.

With these measures it is easy to show that there is no bound on the size of context-free derivation trees:

THEOREM 14 There are context-free grammars for which there is no function f (on the integers) such that any derivation tree for a string of length n has at most $f(n)$ nodes.

Proof: This result follows immediately from the example of any grammar with infinitely ambiguous strings. Consider:

$S \rightarrow a$ *Grammar 1*
$S \rightarrow ES$
$E \rightarrow \epsilon$

This grammar defines a language containing only one string, but that string has arbitrarily large derivation trees. ∎

This result poses a problem for parsing ambiguous context-free languages. It is possible to efficiently *recognize* the strings of ambiguous CFGs using, for example, the Earley algorithm, but it is obviously not possible to output explicit representations of all of the derivation trees for a given string, since they can be arbitrarily large and infinite in number. We can, of course, represent even an infinite set of trees with a finite structure (polynomially bounded in size), like Earley's chart. But then the extraction of any particular tree from this chart may impose computational demands that are not bounded as a function of the length of the original input string.

Although Proposition 14 shows that there is no bound on the size of derivation trees in the general case, bounds can be obtained for some special cases. We might hope that although syntactic structures have empty categories, as do the structures of Grammar 1, some analogous special property of these structures will guarantee a feasible size bound.

DEFINITION 50 Grammar $G = \langle N, \Sigma, S, P \rangle$ is *cycle-free* iff there is no nonterminal category $A \in N$ such that $A \Rightarrow^+ A$ (that is, A can be derived from itself in one or more steps).

Notice that in *Grammar* 1 above, S is a cyclic category. Surprisingly, by imposing just the cycle-free property, the trees become not only bounded in size, but linearly bounded! For cycle-free grammars, there is a linear bound on the size of the derivation tree as a function of the length of the terminal string that is the yield of that tree.[7]

LEMMA 3 For any cycle-free context-free grammar G, there is a constant c_0 such that every derivation tree (from S or any other category) for the empty string has at most c_0 nodes.

Proof: Let p be 2 or the length of the longest righthand side of any production in G, whichever is greater. First consider the largest possible derivation of the empty string. The depth of this tree is at most $|N| - 1$, since this path cannot include any category more than once without violating the cycle-free property. At depth j, there are at most p^j nodes, so altogether a tree of this depth can have at most c_0 nodes where:

$$c_0 = \sum_{j=0}^{|N|-1} p^j = \frac{p^{|N|} - 1}{p - 1}. \quad \blacksquare$$

LEMMA 4 For any cycle-free context-free grammar G, every derivation tree of depth $j \geq 1$ for a single terminal or nonterminal, has at most $j((p-1)c_0 + 1)$ nodes, where p, c_0 are defined for G as in the proof of Lemma 3.

Proof: This result is established by an induction on j.

$(k = 1)$: In this case there are clearly at most $p + 1$ nodes, and the result holds.

Now assume for the induction that the result holds for trees up to some arbitrary depth $n > 0$. We show that it holds for trees of depth $n + 1$.

$(j = n + 1)$: The root of this tree has at most p daughters, one of which, p_a, is the ancestor of a. The other $p - 1$ daughters are the roots of trees with no yield, and so all of these subtrees taken together can contain at most $(p-1)c_0$ nodes. The subtree with root p_a itself has a depth of at most $j - 1$, so by the induction hypothesis, it has at most $(j-1)((p-1)c_0 + 1)$ nodes. Therefore the number of nodes in the whole tree is at most

$$1 + (j-1)((p-1)c_0 + 1) + (p-1)c_0 = j((p-1)c_0 + 1) \quad \blacksquare$$

THEOREM 15 For any cycle-free context-free grammar G, there is a constant c such that every derivation tree for a terminal string of length n has at most cn nodes.

Proof: We will actually show a stronger result. Let

$$c_1 = 2|N|((p-1)c_0 + 1) - c_0$$
$$c_2 = |N|((p-1)c_0 + 1) - c_0,$$

where $|N|$ is the size of the set of nonterminals in G, and c_0 and p are defined for G as in the proof of Lemma 3. We show that the number of nodes in a derivation tree for a string of length n is at most $c_1 n - c_2$. Letting $c = c_1$, the theorem follows.

The proof is by induction on the length of the terminal string n.

$(n = 1)$: In this case we need to show that the number of nodes in the tree is at most

$$c_1(1) - c_2 = |N|((p-1)c_0 + 1).$$

Since by reasoning analogous to the proof of 3, the depth of a derivation tree for one nonterminal is at most $|N|$, the result for this case follows from Lemma 4.

Now assume for the induction that the result holds for derivations of strings up to some arbitrary length $j > 0$. We show that it holds for strings of length $j + 1$.

$(n = j + 1)$: A derivation for a string of length $j + 1, j > 0$ has at least two terminals. Consider the largest subtree T that has at least two immediate subtrees with nonempty yields. The root of this subtree immediately dominates at most p daughters. Let $T_1, \ldots, T_r$ be the daughters that have nonempty yields of lengths $n_1, \ldots, n_r$, respectively, and let $T_{r+1}, \ldots, T_p$ be the other daughters. The size of the whole tree then is the size of the derivation of the root of T, plus the sizes of $T_1, \ldots, T_r$, plus the sizes of $T_{r+1}, \ldots, T_p$. By Lemma 4, the induction hypothesis, and Lemma 3, respectively, the number of nodes in this tree is at most:

$$(|N| - 1)((p-1)c_0 + 1) + \sum_{j=1}^{r}(c_1 n_j - c_2) + \sum_{j=r+1}^{p} c_0$$
$$=(|N| - 1)((p-1)c_0 + 1) + (c_1 n - r c_2) + (p - r)c_0$$
$$=(|N| - 1)((p-1)c_0 + 1) + c_1 n - r[|N|((p-1)c_0 + 1) - c_0] + (p - r)c_0$$
$$=(|N| - 1)((p-1)c_0 + 1) + c_1 n - r[|N|((p-1)c_0 + 1) - c_0] + p c_0 - r c_0$$
$$=(|N| - 1)((p-1)c_0 + 1) + c_1 n - r[|N|((p-1)c_0 + 1) - c_0 + c_0] + p c_0$$
$$=(|N| - 1)((p-1)c_0 + 1) + c_1 n - r[|N|((p-1)c_0 + 1)] + p c_0$$
$$=(|N| - 1)((p-1)c_0 + 1) - r[|N|((p-1)c_0 + 1)] + c_1 n + p c_0$$

Since $r \geq 2$, the number of nodes is at most

$$(|N| - 1)((p-1)c_0 + 1) - 2[|N|((p-1)c_0 + 1)] + c_1 n + pc_0$$
$$= -(|N| + 1)((p-1)c_0 + 1) + c_1 n + pc_0$$
$$= -|N|((p-1)c_0 + 1) - (p-1)c_0 - 1 + c_1 n + pc_0$$
$$= -|N|((p-1)c_0 + 1) - pc_0 - c_0 - 1 + c_1 n + pc_0$$
$$= -|N|((p-1)c_0 + 1) - c_0 - 1 + c_1 n$$
$$= c_1 n - [|N|((p-1)c_0 + 1) - c_0 - 1]$$

Relaxing (i.e. increasing) the upper bound to allow further simplification, the number of nodes is at most

$$c_1 n - [|N|((p-1)c_0 + 1) - c_0]$$
$$= c_1 n - c_2 \quad \blacksquare$$

The important idea here is that given a certain limit on bushiness (a limit on the "branching factor"), the thing that limits the size of these trees is their *depth*. In the case of cycle-free CFG derivation trees, the bushiness is limited by the lengths of the righthand sides of productions, while the depth is limited by the length of the terminal string. Without cycles, we cannot make the trees too deep without increasing the length of the terminal strings. As we have seen, though, the syntactic structures of recent theories involve intermediate adjunction sites, which are analogous to cycles. They increase the depth of the trees without increasing the yield. To prepare for that case, the following result is useful:

DEFINITION 51 A derivation tree has *k-bounded cycling* if for every category A, any subtree with root A that has a path containing more than k occurrences of A has a nonempty terminal string.

THEOREM 16 For any constant k and any context-free grammar G, there is a constant c such that every derivation tree with k-bounded cycling for a string of length n has at most cn nodes.

Proof: A straightforward extension of Lemma 3 shows that with k-bounded cycling, the largest possible empty tree has size

$$c_0 = \sum_{j=0}^{k|N|-1} p^j = \frac{p^{k|N|} - 1}{p - 1}.$$

Notice that k makes an exponential contribution to the size of this constant — if it were not constant with respect to n, we would lose our bound.

Next, we can establish by induction that every derivation tree of depth $j \geq 1$, for a single terminal or nonterminal, has at most $jk((p-1)c_0 + 1)$ nodes.

($j = 1$): In this case there are clearly at most $p + 1$ nodes, and the result holds.

Now assume for the induction that the result holds for trees up to some arbitrary depth $n > 0$. We show that it holds for trees of depth $n + 1$.

($j = n + 1$): The root of this tree has at most p daughters, one of which, p_a, is the ancestor of a. The other $p - 1$ daughters are the roots of trees with no yield, and so all of these subtrees taken together can contain at most $(p-1)c_0$ nodes. The subtree with root p_a itself has a depth of at most $jk - 1$, so by the induction hypothesis, it has at most $(jk - 1)((p-1)c_0 + 1)$ nodes. Therefore the number of nodes in the whole tree is at most:

$$1 + (jk - 1)((p-1)c_0 + 1) + (p-1)c_0 = jk((p-1)c_0 + 1)$$

Finally, letting

$$c_1 = 2|N|k((p-1)c_0 + 1) - c_0$$
$$c_2 = |N|k((p-1)c_0 + 1) - c_0,$$

the reasoning in the proof of 15 shows that a derivation tree for a string of length n is at most $c_1 n - c_2$. Letting $c = c_1$, the theorem follows. ∎

There is one other basic result that is worth noticing. Although for unrestricted context-free grammars there is no bound on the size of an arbitrary derivation tree as a function of the length of the terminal string, there is an upper bound on the size of the *smallest* derivation tree for a string. If this were not the case, general context-free parsers like Earley's could not be efficient.

COROLLARY 6 For any context-free grammar G, there is a constant c such that every string in the language of length n has some derivation tree with at most cn nodes.

Proof: Since a string that has any derivation will have a non-cycling (0-bounded cycling) derivation, this result follows immediately from the previous theorems. ∎

15.4.2   Size bounds for linguistic structures

Consider S-structures that are perfectly well-formed in the sense that they correspond to structures that are well-formed at all levels of representation. Because our formalization of *Barriers*, $FB \cup SEQ_{FB}$, is so incomplete, it is no surprise that we have:

THEOREM 17 $FB \cup SEQ_{FB}$ does not entail any bound on the size of a perfectly grammatical structural description as a function of the length of its yield.

THEOREM 18 If $FB \cup SEQ_{FB}$ entails the grammaticality of one structure for a certain yield, it entails the grammaticality of infinitely many structures for that yield.

These results follow immediately from the fact that the formalized theory does not block trees of arbitrary size with nothing but empty nodes. We will see what sort of linguistic assumptions would allow the demonstration of size bounds, and how such a demonstration uses inductive reasoning of the sort described in previous sections. This exercise will also provide an indication of some computationally relevant aspects of recent syntactic theory which are not yet well understood.[8]

Finding a bound on linguistic structure size requires attention to what linguistic theories say about the possibility of empty categories. Unfortunately, theories of empty categories are controversial, as is no surprise since our evidence for them is less direct than our evidence for overt constituents. Furthermore, it should be remembered that since we do not assume that every grammatical structure can be computed efficiently from the phonetic form (by humans or anything else), we have no immediate reason to expect that there should be a feasible bound on the complexity of syntactic structures. In advance of a careful consideration of linguistic facts, there is no reason to reject the idea that some grammatical structures are huge compared to their yields, and that these are just never computed in language understanding. This is what we say about deeply center-embedded structures and certain structures with many pronouns (cf. §5.1). Nevertheless, it is illuminating to see what sorts of properties theorists would have to confirm before we could have good bounds on the complexity of structural descriptions as a matter of universal grammar. These properties can be made explicit by introducing enough assumptions to establish a linear bound, as we do here. These are not proposed as principles, but as properties which might follow from principles of some grammar. Each of these properties is conjectured to hold universally, though many of them leave room for language-specific variation. We focus here on S-structure and D-structure.[9]

As in the case of context-free grammars, if linguistic theory is going to impose a linear bound on the size of S-structures, it needs to limit bushiness and depth as a function of the complexity of the phonological form (or of the string of morphemes in the yield of an S-structure). Linguists are not always careful to restrict their structures, but some restrictions are plausible and easily imposed. We will calculate the complexity of trees exactly as in the context-free case, and so the question of whether a node is just one segment of an adjunction structure is irrelevant to this measure of complexity. Adjunction structures will be counted just like any other nodes in the tree. Another complication is that in the theories we have formalized, each node specifies not only a syntactic category and bar level, but also various other features. So we begin with a proposal that will allow us to ignore the features:

(Proposal 1) In any language, there are only finitely many different sets of features and values that can label any node, apart from indices and occurrence numbers.

If this proposal is correct — a theory-internal question that is a matter of speculation at this point — then index values and node occurrence numbers aside, a linear bound on the number of nodes will imply a linear bound on the complexity of the tree. Since the set of index values is infinite, these values can make a significant contribution to the complexity of a tree. However, there is only one occurrence number per node, and the number of indices that can appear as values at each node is limited:

(Proposal 1a) In any language, there is a constant c_i, the *index constant*, such that no more than c_i occurrences of indices appear as feature values at any node, at any level of structure.

In our trees, index values appear only as values of the index feature and in θ-grids. In a formal system like ours, where feature values are copied into all of their positions, the coding of an index or occurrence number n is usually assumed to require $\log(n)$ symbols. So if the number of nodes in the tree with a yield of length n is bounded by a linear function cn, then the complexity of the tree is bounded by $cn\log(n)$.[10]

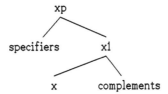

Figure 15.3
X-bar structure

Consider bushiness first. Given X-bar theory, the basic categorial structure is shown in 15.3 (where linear order is irrelevant). This structure can be altered by the presence of adjuncts, but only a single category is ever adjoined at a time, so a tree that is at most binary branching without its adjuncts is binary branching with its adjuncts. So we turn our attention to complements and specifiers. Some linguists assume that each XP has at most one specifier and one complement, but other linguists suppose that a V1 can immediately dominate the verb and all of its complements. The relevant question is whether there is a bound on the number of complements that can be selected by any category. It is plausible that there is a bound, perhaps in UG, perhaps in the lexicon. We can plausibly assume:

(**Proposal 2**) For any human language with a given lexicon, there is a constant $c_c > 0$, the *complement constant*, such that at most c_c constituents can occur as complements to any category.[11]

As for specifiers, these are commonly believed to be even more restricted in number than complements. No limit was imposed in §6, but in §13 the assumption of a single specifier position was made explicit, and was essential to capturing certain empirical phenomena. To be cautious, though, let's assume that the number of specifiers is bounded in any given language:

(**Proposal 3**) For any human language with a given lexicon, there is a constant $c_s > 0$, the *specifier constant*, such that at most c_s constituents can occur as complements to any category.

This completes the treatment of the maximal degree of branching. Unfortunately, the limits on depth are much more challenging.

In the first place, we should note that some versions of X-bar theory do not explicitly rule out structures like:

$np/[n1/[n/[man/[]]]]$

$np/[n1/[n1/[n/[man/[]]]]]$

$np/[n1/[n1/[n1/[n/[man/[]]]]]]$

$\dots$

This simple cycling of the category $n1$ increases the size of the tree without increasing the length of the yield. It is clearly inessential in the grammar, but it is rather tricky to rule it out without blocking analyses proposed by prominent theories. We do not want to reject all trees in which some category Xn immediately and exclusively dominates the same category Xn. The problem is that when a category Xn is an intermediate adjunction site, and the trace of the movement is later deleted, this will result in Xn immediately and exclusively dominating Xn. Trace deletion is essential in *Barriers* and certain other theories, so we aim for a linear bound on the number of nodes that does not depend on ruling it out. Consequently, we cautiously propose:

(**Proposal 4**) * Xn the only child of Xn at D-structure.

One other kind of cycling can probably be ruled out even more easily. It seems unlikely that we need empty adjunct modifier positions that are not traces of movement, regardless of the bar level of their attachment site. For example, we rule out:

$np/[d/[the], n1/[n1/[n/[man/[]]]$

$np/[d/[the], n1/[ap/[], n1/[n/[man/[]]]$

$np/[d/[the], n1/[ap/[], n1/[ap/[], n/[man/[]]]$

...

(Proposal 5) * XP an empty adjunct at D-structure.

So much for the easy restrictions. Now consider the size of the largest empty tree that can occur at S-structure. A few initial observations show that getting an uncontroversial bound of this sort in our linguistic framework is not going to be easy. Consider, to begin with, the variety of X-bar structural positions that can be empty. We have seen empty specifiers, both as the result of extraction and as the result of containing an unmoved empty element. For example, the specifiers of the indicated IPs are empty in

Who [$_{ip}t$ reads]?
He prefers [$_{ip}$ PRO to read]?

In Italian and certain other languages, specifiers of finite IPs can contain the non-trace empty element *pro* (e.g. Jaeggli and Safir, 1989). Other categories can also have empty specifiers.

Heads can be empty, too. Certain heads can be emptied by deletion. For example, the English complementizer *that* can be deleted in many contexts. Heads can be emptied by extraction, as discussed in §§9, 10, 12, and 13. And they can be empty even when they have not been moved or deleted. For example, it is often proposed that simple English declaratives are CPs with an empty C. With its impoverished inflectional system, English sentences often have phonologically empty inflection I. When determiners are brought into the X-bar system, empty Ds are often proposed, as discussed in §11. In §12 we discussed Pollock's proposal of an empty V and an empty P in English. Empty N is also proposed in certain theories (e.g. Emonds, 1985, 105ff).

Proposal 5 tells us that adjuncts can be empty by extraction, but must be overt otherwise, so the remaining X-bar structural positions are complements. We have seen many varieties of empty complements. Consider VP complements, for example. In English, a single complement can be extracted, but in other languages, more than one complement can be extracted, as discussed in §14.3. Many linguists suppose that the complements of VP can also be present and empty when there has been no extraction. English is not usually treated as allowing empty complements unless there has been movement, but other languages are more liberal about this. PRO cannot occur in verbal complement position, since it would be lexically governed there, but the empty NP *pro* can. Many languages are analyzed as allowing not only governed *pro* subjects, but also *pro* complements, and it is still unclear how constraints on the distribution of these empty categories should be represented. For example, Laka (1990; 1990a) proposes that Basque has structures like the following:[12]

zuk ni ekarri na-u-zu
    (you me brought me-have-you)
    (you have brought me)
pro pro ekarri na-u-zu
    ((you) (me) brought me-have-you)
pro pro pro eman d-i-da-zu
    ((you) (me) (it) given it-have-me-you)

This sort of syntactic expression of implicit arguments is controversial, but these views have some currency and so it would be nice to get a size bound that does not depend on ruling them out.[13]

In sum, we see that recent theories allow specifiers, heads, adjuncts and complements to be empty. In fact, these possibilities are allowed even in the few prominent accounts of English discussed in Parts II and III. Consequently, to obtain an S-structure size bound that most linguists can accept, we must exploit restrictions on where these empty categories can occur. In particular, we must show how occurrences of these empty categories are allowed as a function of overt category occurrences.

Let's begin by considering English VPs. Can they be completely empty? Yes, we have seen empty VPs in the theories of Parts II and III. For example, in *Barriers*, a verb in a VP can raise to I and then to C, leaving a structured VP with a V trace but no (phonological) yield, as in

Is it $[_{vp}[_v e]]$?
What$_i$ is$_j$ it $[_{vp} [_v e]_i [_{np} e]_j]$?

In the theory of Sportiche (1990) discussed in §13, the empty VPs in S-structures of sentences like this are even larger, because the subject originates there, as shown in Figure 15.4. (Cf. also Figure 13.6.) Do principles of universal grammar rule out the possibility of a structures like these where the verb and inflection are empty, the fronted wh-operator is empty, and the subject is the empty NP *pro*? Then we would have a completely empty, structured CP. To utter the question expressed by this clause would require the production of no phonological form at all. Something would have to signal that a question had been asked in this language — perhaps a raising of the eyebrows? And once we have completely empty CPs, these could be embedded in each other to produce arbitrarily large structures with no phonological content, and we would have no

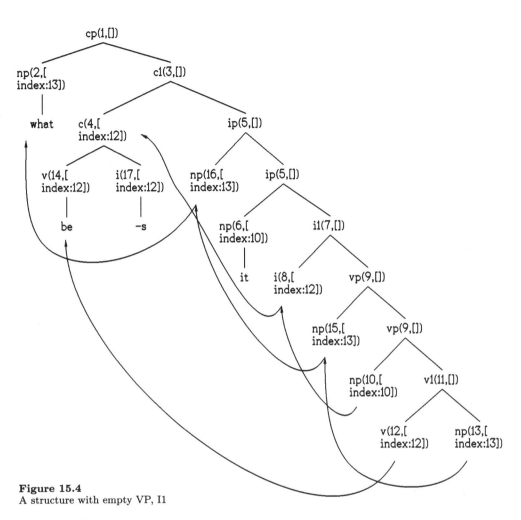

Figure 15.4
A structure with empty VP, I1

size bound for S-structures. But it is plausible that something has gone wrong here. No human languages would allow arbitrarily large S-structures. How are they ruled out?

One idea that seems to fit with recent work in syntax is something like the following: lexical heads are the canonical θ-assigners, and these must be overt. They must occur in structures with certain functional categories, but the real content of a phrase is lexical. In the theories discussed in Parts II and III, this classification of the categories does not quite work. For example, in *Barriers* the functional category I is a θ-assigner, and in §12 the English auxiliary verbs are not θ-assigners.[14] Perhaps in some sense that could be made precise, auxiliary verbs and inflection are not semantically significant. So consider the idea that semantically significant items with θ-grids cannot be null: most nouns, verbs, adjectives and adverbs are in this class. This allows functional heads, auxiliary verbs, and prepositions to be null in some cases.[15] For example, Pollock's (1986) null verb in English has no semantic content of its own, and the semantically empty copula is unexpressed in certain constructions of many languages.[16] One further complication is needed to allow for the ideas discussed in §13, where a single semantically significant, phonologically overt verb can license a number of heads, heads which will be associated by a V-chain at S-structure. In these theories, the empty heads licensed by an overt, semantically significant item must be "local" in a clear sense, so we propose the following:[17]

(Proposal 6) In any language, there is some constant $c_h \geq 0$, the *head constant*, such that the D-structure of a constituent that is well-formed at all levels of representation cannot contain more than $c_h(k + 1)$ phonologically empty heads, where k is the number of semantically significant, phonologically overt heads it contains.

This predicts that null verbs do not license multiple heads, but on the contrary they require some special licensing from phonologically overt elements. For example, we might say that an overt verb that assigns n θ-roles licenses exactly n heads.

This last proposal conflicts with Bouchard's (1982; 1983) appealing idea that grammars should not require any special principles for empty categories — their properties should be determined by the same principles that apply to all constituents. (Cf. also Chomsky, 1982, §5). The proposal here seems more general than certain "empty category principles," and perhaps less objectionable for that reason, but ultimately the proposal is exactly that there *is* something special about phonologically null categories. Human languages do not allow arbitrary words to be phonologically null, and the conjecture is that, in any language, the amount of formative structure is bounded as a linear function of the amount of semantically significant and phonologically overt structure.

To get a size bound on this approach, we now need to somehow restrict the size of the empty "functional skeletons" on which our semantically significant lexical categories hang. Abney (1986) and others have suggested that functional categories each select a unique complement: C selects IP, I selects VP, and D selects NP. Examples like the following suggest that these selections might not be mandatory, though:

$I \, [_{ip} \, do]$
$[_{dp} \, That] \, bothers \, me$

So perhaps a functional category can occur with no overt lexical category in it. In a DP that contains DPs, such as the left recursive structure of 11.5 or structures like

Mary's mother's father's sister's . . . brother's book is a thriller,

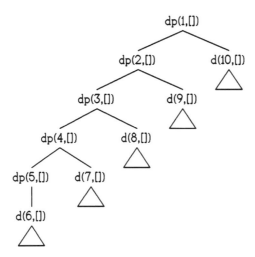

Figure 15.5
Recursion through DPs without lexical categories

could all of the lexical categories be absent or empty? We conjecture that this is not possible:

(**Proposal 7**) In any language, there is some constant $c_f \geq 0$, the *formative constant*, such that the D-structure of a constituent that is well-formed at all levels of representation cannot contain more than $c_f(k + 1)$ maximal categories where k is the number of semantically significant maximal lexical categories it contains.

This allows left recursion through DP of the sort in Figure 11.5 and the previous example, because in these cases every D selects a lexical complement NP. A DP can also occur with no lexical complement, but not recursively without bound. That is, we cannot have a DP like the one shown in Figure 15.5, no matter what determiners are inserted in nodes 6-10 (assuming that in English $c_f < 5$).

   Since we want a bound on depth as a function of the length of a sentence, and since adjunctions increase depth, we need some additional restrictions on movements and deletions. Ruling out spurious multiple adjunctions of the sort mentioned in §14.3 presumably does not have any untoward empirical consequences:

(**Proposal 8**) No constituent can adjoin to any category more than once.

We add to this constraint on representations an equally innocuous constraint on movements:

(**Proposal 9**) No constituent can adjoin to itself.

Unfortunately, for a linear bound on the number of nodes, we require some more controversial restrictions as well. In earlier transformational theories, versions of the wh-island constraint blocked long-distance movement of more than one wh-phrase. Given the additional restrictions on other movements, a raising constant would follow easily. In the *Barriers* framework, instead of the wh-island constraint, we have the cumulative version of 1-subjacency, the constraint against wh-adjunctions to IP, and parametric barriers. In §9.5 we discussed the example,

* *What$_i$ did you wonder [$_{cp}$who said that Bill saw t$_i$] ?*

We noted that, in English, because adjunction to IP is ruled out, once the specifier of the indicated CP is filled, that CP will be a barrier by inheritance for any other wh-phrases that move out of that CP. Since this barrier counts for both movement and government, such an extraction also produces an ECP violation — a failure of antecedent government. If more specifiers of CP were allowed, more wh-phrases could escape the clause, but there is no way that an unlimited number can get out in such a system. With a richer specification of clausal structure than *Barriers* provides — to rule out not only unlimited numbers of specifiers, but also such deviations as verbs taking both VP and NP complements at once — such a bound might be derived.[18]

When we consider movements other than wh-movement, matters are perhaps simpler, but still not settled. In the first place, it is crucial that if A moves to B (or to some position in B), and B moves out of C, this should count as just one extraction from C even though C now has two traces in it. In Figure 9.5 for example, the subject and the verb are shown moving out of $vp(7, \ldots)$. This counts as two extractions, even though the verb itself is a complex containing the verb and inflection from a lower clause, and the VP contains 4 head traces. In the second place though, we see in this same figure another loophole that must be closed. The figure was considered before the ECP was presented, and since amalgamation has not applied to all parts of the verbal complex, the ECP is violated: the traces at nodes 12 and 20 are $-\gamma$, not properly governed, in this tree. If amalgamation were formulated so that all parts of the complex adjunction structure had the same index, then there would be no ECP violations, but a problem relevant to current concerns comes up. Any element of this complex, after amalgamation, could move to any position where the whole structure could move. If this were allowed, the grammar would admit derivations with arbitrarily many extractions from a constituent. We might say that any movement of an adjunction structure must move the whole structure, but as already noted, this idea conflicts with Pollock's analysis of simple finite sentences in English, as discussed in §12.2, and with other similar proposals in the literature such as Roberts' (1991) "excorporation." Further research is needed here, but it is plausible that a more worked out account would allow us to deduce the following, applying to both head movements and phrasal movements:

(**Proposal 10**) In every language, there is some constant c_r, the *raising constant*, such that that no constituent in a well-formed structure at any level of representation has more than c_r constituents extracted from it.

We need a counterpart to this raising constraint to hold for lowering. Recall from §12.2 that Pollock (1989) and many others reject the HMC, arguing, for example, that heads can sometimes lower in the syntax, in violation of the original formulation of the HMC given in §9.2.[19] If lowering of empty categories is allowed without restriction at S-structure, then there is no bound on the size of an empty XP that has no embedded maximal projections. Any number of higher heads could lower to X, creating an adjunction structure with as many segments as there are heads in the whole tree. A similar idea is used by Lasnik and Saito (1984) and others to account for certain ECP effects, as noted in §10: they suppose that an XP can move to a lower position if it later raises back to a position where it can play an appropriate role in the chain. Certainly, nothing in any of the theories formalized in Parts II and III rule this out. But then, every XP can be an adjunction site for all the other XPs in the tree, so long as all traces are deleted except those required to leave appropriate chains in the structure. Structures produced by derivations like these will not respect a linear bound on the number of nodes, even with Proposals 4 and 9. The following constraint on movements would block such derivations:

(**Proposal 11**) In every language, there is some constant c_l, the *lowering constant*, such that no constituent can be an adjunction site more than c_l times for constituents that do not, in this adjoined position, govern their traces.

It would be nice if c_l were 0 for all languages, but this proposal allows a wider range of linguistic analyses, and any finite bound will suffice for present purposes. Notice that this is stated as a constraint on movements, not on representations, so that adjunctions by more than c_l higher constituents are ruled out even if all of their traces are deleted.

As for deletions, we generalize the tentative condition provided in §10.1, following Emonds (1985, §4.6):

(**Proposal 12**) Semantically significant, phonologically overt lexical constituents cannot be deleted.

This means that in VP-ellipsis constructions like:

John likes his Mother, and Max does too,

the VP in the coordinated clause is not deleted, but is simply empty.[20] Similarly, this
proposal does not allow "coordinate structure reduction" to derive constructions like the
following by somehow deleting and rearranging the structure:[21]

John and Mary like the beach.

Affect-α is sometimes supposed to involve insertions as well as movements and deletions. For example, expletives may be inserted rather late in the derivation of a structure.
We will simply assume that no completely empty structure is ever inserted, and that any
inserted material respects Proposal 7. We also assume that no other processes apply in
the syntax (reanalysis, reconstruction, etc.) in a way that will affect the ratio between
phonologically overt material and S-structure size.

With these proposals and some basic ideas from the theories discussed in Parts II and
III, we can obtain a linear bound on the number of nodes in S-structures very easily:

LEMMA 5 Given proposals 1-12, in any human language, there is a constant k such that
every well-formed D-structure has k-bounded cycling.

Proof: By Proposal 7, we can have c_f maximal categories in a constituent if we have
one semantically significant maximal lexical category XP. Imagine that we have c_f empty
functional categories YP embedded through the complement position or specifier position, with an empty XP in one of the complement or specifier positions. All of these YPs
must be different constituents, rather than segments of a single category, by Proposals
4 and 5. Adding one more empty XP, we can embed YP c_f more times. By Proposal
6, then, we can cycle through YP at most $k = c_h c_f$ times without introducing an overt
constituent. ∎

LEMMA 6 Given proposals 1-12, in any human language, there is a constant k such that
every well-formed S-structure has k-bounded cycling.

Proof: The only way affect-α can increase the number of cycles in a structure is by
deletion and adjunction. By Proposal 12, deletions alone cannot increase the cycling
beyond the bounds allowed by the formative constant c_f, as in the proof of Lemma 5.
Adjunction can take us beyond those bounds, but only by a constant amount, since
by Proposals 10 and 11, together with Proposals 8 and 9, the number of adjunctions
produced by raising is limited to c_r, and the number produced by lowering is limited
to c_l. ∎

THEOREM 19 Given Proposals 1-12, in any human language, there is a constant c such
that every well-formed S-structure for a sentence with n words has at most cn nodes.

Proof: Features and occurrence numbers aside, the S-structures of any given language are included in a set of derivation trees defined by a cyclic context-free grammar with productions whose righthand sides do not exceed the greatest of $c_c + 1, c_s + 1$, and 2. (The fact that the inclusion may be proper is irrelevant.) So the conclusion follows by Theorem 16 and Lemma 6. ∎

As suggested at the beginning of this section, the conjecture is that Proposals like 1-12 will follow from a more complete theory of the syntactic structure of human languages. A formalization of this theory would presumably allow a more rigorous deduction of a linear bound along the lines we have sketched here. In spite of our efforts to use assumptions that are widely accepted, Proposals 6, 7, 10, 11, and 12 are all controversial. Proposals 7 and 10 are especially in need of more careful assessment.

In spite of the fact that context-free grammars do not have an upper bound on derivation tree size as a function of the length of the terminal string, we were able to obtain an upper bound on the size of the smallest derivation tree in Corollary 6. That is, every string in a context-free language has some derivation tree of linear size. We can do a similar thing for $FB \cup SEQ_{FB}$. This theory does not provide an upper bound on S-structure size, but it is plausible that there is a linear bound on the size of some S-structure, since Theorem 19 immediately gives us the following Corollary:

COROLLARY 7 Suppose that the conditions formalized by $FB \cup SEQ_{FB}$ are consistent with a more complete theory that entails Proposals 1-12, as they appear to be, in the sense that if a string has structures that satisfy all the constraints of the more complete theory, some of these structures must also satisfy the constraints of the incomplete theory $FB \cup SEQ_{FB}$. Then there is a constant c such that any English sentence of length n with a well-formed S-structure has some S-structure SS that is well-formed according to $FB \cup SEQ_{FB}$, where SS has less than cn nodes.

Although the difficulties in finding reasonable bounds on data structure size (and other indicators of computational resource demands) arise in this framework because it is capable of defining infeasibly large structures, the problem does not stem from the formal framework, but from our ignorance about human languages. Switching to some more restrictive formal system does not decrease this ignorance, but merely imposes arbitrary restrictions that can make it much more difficult to state the facts about human languages. Avoiding such a pointless step, we can study human languages until we understand more clearly what sorts of structural relations are involved, and then, defining those relations in a suitably powerful formalism, the resource requirements of particular problems will follow from properties of human language rather than from arbitrary limitations of the formalism. So, for example, we have seen that assumptions about which movements are possible matter because adjunction increases the complexity of a tree. Since it is unfortunately not quite clear yet what sorts of adjunctions occur in human languages, there is some difficulty in being precise about an upper bound on structural complexity. The point to notice is that this is not a good reason to move to a theory in which there is just one level of structure and no movements at all. Our difficulties do not stem from the possibility of movements, but rather from our ignorance about which movement relations can occur in human languages. These difficulties about movements reappear in monostratal theories as, for example, difficulties in specifying which chains are well-formed.[22] It is hard to imagine that computational considerations would have any bearing on the decision between monostratal and movement theories (but see the discussion in §15.7, below).

15.5   Locality

After determining, in so far as possible, that we will be dealing with structures of reasonable size, it is natural to consider what information suffices to determine whether a particular constituent can appear in a given position in a complete well-formed structure. Ideally, the information needed at any point will be "local" in some sense.[23] Unfortunately, the most valuable locality conditions are only available if we venture onto shaky ground, as we did in the last section, going well beyond principles formalized in Parts II and III to new assumptions that call for more careful empirical assessment than can be provided here. Some few examples will suffice to indicate the sort of result which can be obtained.

Consider, to begin with, the definition of *m_commands* from §8.2, repeated here:

> α m-commands β only if α does not dominate β and every maximal category σ that dominates α dominates β.

We formalized this as a definition rather than merely a necessary condition:

$$m\_commands(A, B, Tree) \leftrightarrow \tag{15.5.12}$$
$$\neg dominates(A, B, Tree) \wedge$$
$$\forall Sigma$$
$$(\ dominates(Sigma, A, Tree) \wedge maximal(Sigma)$$
$$\rightarrow dominates(Sigma, B, Tree)\ ).$$

This formalization is elegant and transparent, and it is suitable for some deductions. For example, if we know that α m-commands β and want to deduce that every maximal category σ that dominates α dominates β, this axiom is fine. However, for parsing, this axiomatization presents unnecessary computational difficulty for standard search methods. To establish that α m-commands β, given that α does not dominate β, we do not really need to show that *every* maximal category in the tree that dominates α dominates β. It suffices to show that the *first* maximal category dominating α dominates β. This trivial observation could be expressed by saying that the "m-command domain" of a node n is just the subtree whose root is the least maximal projection dominating n. Though trivial, this result should be exploited in any reasonable language processing system that needs to test m-command relations.

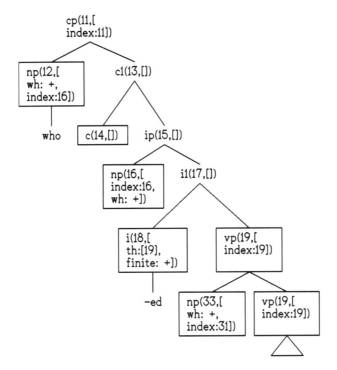

Figure 15.6
Proper government domain of node 33

It is more challenging to determine the amount of structure relevant to enforcing subjacency and the ECP. Consider again the ungrammatical structure mentioned in §15.4.2 and §9.5:[24]

* $What_i^1$ did you $[_{vp}t_i^{34}[_{vp}$wonder who $[_{vp}t_i^{33}[_{vp}$said $[_{cp}t_i^{22}$ that Bill $[_{vp}t_i^{32}[_{vp}$ saw $t_i^{31}]]]]]]]$?

We have added superscripts to the indicated traces for ease of reference. Suppose that we were interested in whether the trace noun phrase t_i^{33} is properly governed. (It is not.) Clearly, we should not have to show for each node in the tree that it is not a proper governor. If there is a proper governor for this position, it is "nearby" in the tree. In particular, it must be an m-commander that is not separated from the position by a barrier. Unfortunately, barrierhood is a relative notion, so the matter is a little complicated. The m-commanders of t_i^{33} include the specifier of the matrix CP, but the CP complement of *wonder* is a barrier by inheritance to everything dominated by IP. So using just these structural considerations, we limit ourselves to the highlighted nodes in Figure 15.6: the m-commanding nodes not excluded by $cp(11, \ldots)$. This highlighted domain, which is one potential characterization of what might be called the "proper government domain" of node 33, can be quickly checked for antecedent governors. It would be nice to know that there is a bound on the size of the proper government domain (so characterized) of any node in any tree that results from movements applied to well-formed D-structures. This requires reasoning about the sizes of structures, as was done in the last section, using principles that we have not formalized. We will not take up this question in detail, but we have considered enough other similar problems that we can imagine how this one could be approached.

This problem illustrates one of the simplest ideas about locality: in some cases the explicit representation of a relevant structural domain will always be bounded in size. In the *Barriers* framework, though, we would probably be interested in a slightly harder problem. In building an S-structure like this from left to right, we would probably not be interested in whether node 33 is properly governed, because it is not an argument trace. We would be interested in whether it is either properly governed at LF or else deletable. The relevant structural considerations for this problem are considerably harder to specify, because the intermediate traces play a number of roles. In $FB \cup SEQ_{FB}$, they play a role not only in the ECP but also in subjacency. In a more complete theory, they would be relevant to other things as well. For example, as we discussed in §11.3 and elsewhere, a trace position is typically not available as a substitution landing site because this would lead to θ-criterion violations. Ideally, though, we would like to deduce from all these principles together that only a bounded amount of structure is required to answer the more complicated question, whether nonargument traces at S-structure are either properly governed at LF or else deletable there.

Now let's turn to the relevant structural domain for questions about subjacency. Suppose, for example, that in building a tree from left to right,

* *What*$_i^1$ *did you* $[_{vp}t_i^{34}[_{vp}wonder\ who\ [_{vp}t_i^{33}[_{vp}said\ [_{cp}t_i^{22}\ that\ Bill\ [_{vp}t_i^{32}[_{vp}\ saw\ t_i^{31}]]]]]]]$?

we were interested in whether the indicated chain respects subjacency up to and including node 33. What are the relevant considerations? According to *Barriers*, we check to make sure that the links of the chain do not cross more than one barrier. This requires looking at the whole of the chain that has been built. Consequently, using our standard representation of the tree, the amount of relevant structure is not finitely bounded. There is a further complication. Proceeding from left to right, it is clear that the link from *what*$_i$ to t_i^{34} crosses no barriers, and that the link from t_i^{34} to t_i^{33} crosses a CP barrier, but we are not in a position to know at this point whether the embedded IP is also a parametric barrier. If this were the most embedded clause, as it would be if the sentence were,

* *What*$_i^1$ *did you* [$_{vp}t_i^{34}$ [$_{vp}$*wonder who* [$_{vp}t_i^{33}$ [$_{vp}$*said* t_i]]]]?

then because it is tensed, the IP would be a parametric barrier, and the link from t_i^{34} to t_i^{33} would cross 2 barriers, violating 1-subjacency. However, if the tree is built strictly from left to right, the verb will not be in the structure when t_i^{33} is built (unless the verb has raised to I), and we will not be able to tell whether the clause is the deepest tensed IP.

One other minor complication should be mentioned. In the *Barriers* framework formalized in Part II, intermediate traces can be deleted even at S-structure, but we can suppose that a parser can just ignore derivations that posit and delete a trace before S-structure. This idea might be added to the *Barriers* framework in something like the following form:

(Proposal 13) No trace deletion "in the syntax," before S-structure.

The justification for this proposal is that an intermediate trace, proposed and deleted before S-structure, does not appear in any level of representation to which any conditions apply, and is also irrelevant to all of the conditions on movement, with the possible exception of the HMC. In systems that allow "excorporation," the interaction of this proposal with the HMC would require further investigation (cf. Roberts, 1991). In any case, Proposal 13 would simplify the assessment of chains.

In summary, the linguistic principles relevant to locality are not yet well understood. Current research is addressing the relevant issues. Nevertheless, we can see, at least roughly, how structural complexity and locality issues could be tackled in a rigorous way once the requisite theoretic principles are formulated. As the more promising proposals emerge, they can be brought into the formalism fairly easily, as illustrated in Part II, and immediately brought to bear on issues relevant to parsing. We are not in the much more difficult position of developing a new theory of language.

15.6   Structural and locality theorem deployment

Suppose that we had established structure preservation, structural complexity, and locality results for a particular theory. How could such results be deployed in a deductive parsing strategy? There are two basic ideas here: the results can be used to guide the deduction of results from linguistic principles, or the results can be used to motivate reformulations of the problem. In computer scientists' jargon, we can prune the search or transform the program. Notice that the complexity and locality results discussed above are specific to the particular parsing problems we are considering. They follow from particular details of linguistic theory. In this respect, they contrast with the general methods for pruning search and for transforming problems, methods that are appropriate for all problems. It is to be expected that the specialized, linguistic results will be the more valuable. Dijkstra (1986) makes essentially this point in a discussion of general efficiency-enhancing program transformations. He points out that an efficient program can often be regarded as the successful exploitation of a mathematical theorem. Since very few useful theorems have been discovered by general automated mathematical discovery procedures (without user guidance), general program transformations or pruning methods seem unlikely to yield the best results for non-trivial problems:

> A number of so-called 'semantics-preserving program transformations' have been discovered. Each such transformation, when applicable and applied to program A generates a new program A' that, when executed, will produce the same result as the original program A, the difference being that the costs of execution of A and A' may differ greatly... The question now is: what are our chances of deriving an efficient program A' by applying mechanizable transformations from a finite library to the original program A? ... All our experience in mathematics tell us that... the derivation paths from A to A' — if, with a given library, they exist at all — can be expected to be long and difficult to find. (Dijkstra, 1986, 325-328)

An analogy with context-free parsing may be appropriate here: it is hard to imagine a general pruning or transformation technique that would yield an LR(k) parser (like the one in §4.4, for example) from a logical specification of a context-free grammar. The discovery and justification of this parsing method required detailed study of special properties of context-free derivations. It is for this reason that we have concentrated in the previous sections on sketching how specific, relevant theorems about natural language structures could be derived. Adding these theorems to our arsenal, we can do much better than general methods could without such problem-specific guidance.

In applications of *Barriers*-like frameworks, we have used both pruning and program transformation strategies. Since this work is still at a preliminary stage, the various techniques will just be surveyed. The detailed presentation of a particular approach to the parsing problem must be left to another place.

15.6.1   Pruning the search

General methods for avoiding useless search have been a major focus of research in automatic theorem proving. For example, the model elimination technique defined by Loveland and others is typically restricted with a number of general pruning rules which are guaranteed to preserve the completeness of the method.[25] Search can be further reduced by ordering subproblems in a way that is most appropriate for particular proofs. For example, we suggested in §3 that in SEq resolution, it is typically valuable to delay the evaluation of positive equations, and positive formulas generally. And in §14.1.1 we suggested that resolving on renamed literals should be postponed. It is in general better to do the easiest subproofs first, since their solution may help to further specify other parts of the problem. These strategies have been extensively studied and applied to great advantage both in SLD-resolution and in full first order resolution.[26]

However, it is no surprise that problem-specific methods can be even more useful. For example, with a structural complexity bound, we can restrict our search to trees within the bound without losing completeness. Metatheoretic techniques like those developed in §4 for SLD-resolution proofs can be extended to model elimination, allowing us to check properties not only of the derivation itself, including not only the size of its terms, but also restrictions on the course of the derivation. We can use conditional pruning rules of the form:

In any proof of ψ, subproofs of ϕ must meet conditions $p_1, p_2, \ldots, p_n$.

In fact, strategies of exactly this sort have been applied fruitfully on a wide variety of simpler constraint satisfaction problems.[27] Similar techniques for simple parsing problems were explored in Stabler (1988), and they provide one way to deploy our domain-specific results.

A proof method itself can also be modified for domain-specific efficiency with the addition of "derived rules," rules that are provably sound in the domain of interest. SEq resolution, briefly described in §3.4, is an example of this. That proof method adds a special rule on the basis of the axioms of syntactic equality. Similar rules could license, for example, a conclusion about all the nodes in a tree from properties of an appropriate subset of these nodes, based on a locality result of the kind described in §15.5.

15.6.2   Transforming the problem

Another strategy for improving efficiency will be to move from the specification to a more tractable representation in a series of justifiable steps, transforming the specification into a form that is more suitable for the particular problem at hand, given either of the specialized proof methods introduced in §4: SEq resolution or SLDNF resolution. In earlier sections of this chapter we argued that problem-specific, inductively justified transformations of the problem are likely to be the most valuable, but there are some completely general transformation strategies that are useful as well. We will briefly survey a range of these general methods. The proper orchestration of these techniques for logic-based parsing remains an open problem.

Adding useful lemmas.   If we simply wanted to modify our theory in such a way as to preserve logical equivalence but minimize the length of refutations, the most obvious modification is the addition of consequences. That is, if we modify a theory T by adding a consequence to get a larger theory T', it is obvious that we will make some refutations shorter and no sentence will have only longer refutations. However, the addition of a sentence has the potential of increasing the search space, and since search is a severe problem, this risk is serious. However, there are two sorts of additions that can be worthwhile. In the first place, it can be valuable to add sentences which play a valuable role as lemmas in large classes of refutations of interest. This practice is familiar in logic and mathematics. In the second place, while working on any particular problem, it can be valuable to add, on a temporary basis, particular lemmas about the structures involved. This strategy must be used with some care, but can be fruitfully applied. Since we have used a model elimination system, we have used the version of the latter strategy described by Loveland (1978, §3.6). When the available lemmas are carefully filtered to weed out some of the useless ones, this strategy does, in fact, shorten some proofs without making the search infeasible.

Alternative axiomatizations.   The linguistic theory is formulated as a series of definitions of structural relations, and so sometimes it can happen that two equivalent definitions can be provided for a relation, where one definition has some computational advantage over another. More generally, it can happen that there is a definition $\phi \leftrightarrow_{df} \psi$ and another definition $\phi \leftrightarrow_{df} \chi$, which are equivalent *in the presence of other independently motivated theoretical assumptions*. In such a case, we could include both definitions, but it is often computationally more valuable to use only the best definition for the particular application under development. Consider, for example, the definition of *m_commands* discussed above in §15.5. Rather than modifying the search strategy, we could try to reformulate the definition so as to avoid wasteful tests on irrelevant parts of the tree.

Transformations that preserve substitution equivalence. One general technique in logic programming is called "unfolding" or "partial evaluation".[28] Pereira and Shieber (1987), Johnson (1989; 1991), and others have shown that this technique can be usefully applied to language processing problems. The basic idea has a natural first order generalization, where it is more often called "reduction" (Bibel, 1987; Dreben and Goldfarb, 1979). A reduction is standardly defined as an effective function f such that, for some class of theories $\mathcal{T}$, for every $T \in \mathcal{T}$, T has a model iff $f(T)$ has a model. This satisfiability equivalence is a much weaker requirement than logical equivalence! In fact it is much too weak, so we have used two types of reduction which can be extended to preserve not only satisfiability but also "answer substitution equivalence" (cf. Maher, 1986). The first type, resolution reduction, performs a simple resolution step, adding the resolvent to the theory and discarding at least one of the parents. The second type, simple reduction, removes a clause from a theory. Thus, both types of reduction are such that $f(T)$ has the same number or fewer clauses than T. It is clear that for both of these types of reduction, if T is Horn, then $f(T)$ is also Horn. Some reductions of these types can increase the length of the shortest refutation of a theory. For example, a reduction that simply removes valuable lemmas preserves unsatisfiability and falls into our category of simple reductions, but it can obviously increase the length of the shortest refutation. We are not interested in reductions like this. Rather, we are interested in reductions f such that the shortest refutation of $f(T)$ has the same number or fewer steps than the shortest refutation of T. We call resolution reductions and simple reductions with this additional property "useful." Many applications of "unfolding" or "partial evaluation" in Horn clause theorem proving can be regarded as the application of useful resolution reductions on finite clausal form theories.

A simple example will illustrate the idea. Suppose a theory contains the clauses

$$\{answer(X), \neg q(X), \neg test(X)\}$$
$$\{q(a)\}$$

If we suppose that the predicate q is not used in any other clauses in the theory, then we can remove the two clauses shown and replace them by their resolvent $\{answer(a), \neg test(a)\}$. The resulting theory is obviously unsatisfiable just in case the original theory is. This basic idea can be generalized quite substantially.

There is one important kind of problem in parsing and similar tasks, though, that cannot be reduced in this way. This sort of problem is illustrated by a theory that includes a clausal form of the definition of natural numbers (displayed as Theory $Cl(NN)$ in §3.4 and repeated as the last 4 clauses here):

$\{p(X), \neg nn(X), \neg test(X)\}$
$\{\neg nn(A), A=0, A=s(f(A))\}$
$\{A \neq 0, nn(A)\}$
$\{\neg nn(A), nn(f(A)), A=0\}$
$\{\neg nn(A), B \neq s(A), nn(B)\}$

In this theory, we can of course still resolve the first with the third (or fourth or fifth) clause to produce a resolvent, but we cannot replace these two sentences by that resolvent, because they may be needed for other reductions. None of the well-known useful reductions can remove all occurrences of the predicate nn from this theory. Intuitively, the problem comes from the fact that nn is recursively defined and has an infinite extension, unlike the predicate q in our previous example. More precisely (in the terminology of Seki and Furukawa, 1987) the predicate nn cannot be unfolded into a finite disjunction of "primitive evaluable predicates." We can, so to speak, "partly unfold" a recursive predicate like this, without eliminating it entirely. This can be valuable, but notice that, unlike many of the situations in which unfolding is most valuable, the extension of the generator nn contains simple objects (i.e. numbers) rather than sequences of some objects. Consequently, a problem like the one shown will not always be more tractable when nn and $test$ are unfolded and their components are interleaved. For some tests, tests that depend only on part of the structure of the terms denoting the numbers (tests like "is less than 5"), unfolding and interleaving can be valuable. But for other tests that depend on more "global" properties of the numbers (like "is odd"), the strategy has no straightforward application. Unfortunately, many of the predicates in our formalization of syntax are like nn and unlike q, and so, although we can get some important gains from resolution reductions, they are not as substantial as one would like.

Data structure transformations. One of the most fruitful ways to achieve better performance is by an appropriate choice of data structures. A change in data structures obviously calls for subsequent reformulation of the axioms that apply to those structures. The introduction of difference lists in context-free parsing is a relevant example, and we showed in §4.1 that although neither logical equivalence nor substitution equivalence is preserved by this change, we can nevertheless provide a rigorous demonstration that the modification is justified and does not remove the relevant consequences. Difference lists could also be useful in our parsing problem, though their effects may be obtainable with an appropriate search strategy. Of more direct interest are the tree and feature structures that are the primary concern of the theories we have formalized. Now that we have a particular application of these theories in mind, it makes sense to look for representations of these objects that can be used more efficiently. The more efficient notations may not be so simple and intuitive for human contemplation, but the intuitive simplicity that is so important in the specification of a complex problem becomes irrelevant when the goal is efficiency. The separation of these two stages of the design process, specification and implementation, has this great advantage: we determine correctness for a simple and intuitive specification, and then establish the correctness of a more complex but efficient implementation with formal methods.

Computer scientists have long observed that there are many different ways to represent trees, and that the different representations can have significant effects on the efficiency of computations over them.[29] Nested functional structures of the sort used in our formalism are known to be less than ideal for many problems. For example, consider the problem of computing the least common ancestor of two nodes in a tree. With a nested structure like ours, the most straightforward approaches to this problem are infeasible. An interesting line of research has shown that a different notation allows for much more efficient processing. This notation is redundant but allows constant time access to any node, regardless of its depth in the tree, and fast access to arbitrarily distant ancestors of any node.[30] Special tree notations have also been used in natural language processing.[31] The selection of an optimal notation for parsing really depends on details of the grammar. For example, in the unlikely event that we decide that subjacency should be tested by actually looking back through the whole chain as discussed above in §15.4, it would make sense to consider tree representations in which all links in any path could be quickly accessed. With non-cumulative principles (such as the replacements for subjacency discussed in §13), access to all earlier links would not be necessary.

Another idea about tree representations is suggested by efficient implementations of deductive reasoning methods. As discussed in §3.2, each resolution step can involve the application of a substitution to a variable. Most implementations of resolution proof methods do not actually apply these substitutions. Instead, the literals in a resolvent are typically represented as a term plus a sequence of substitutions. In this representation, all resolvents share the structure of the original axioms and their ancestors, adding only a substitution of their own. In resolution-based automated reasoning about trees, such as we have done in this text, such structure sharing implementations have the effect that the trees in transformational derivations are handled with structure sharing. That is, derived trees are, in effect, denoted by terms corresponding to D-structure trees plus a sequence of movements.[32] This valuable structure sharing is not provided if trees are explicitly represented in axioms rather than being built up in the course of a proof.

Inside the nodes of our trees we find some structures that also deserve some attention. The node occurrence numbers in our specification are integers, but this clearly provides more structure than is needed. All we need is the association of segments of an adjunction structure, and this can be provided by a pointer rather than by identical structured contents. In a logic-based implementation, the appropriate sort of pointer can be introduced by having the occurrence number arguments of an adjunction structure instantiated to the same variable, and we can treat such pointers appropriately with standard metalogical operations that allow us to test "strict" or "syntactic identity" of variables, etc. The feature lists at each node call for similar treatment. The values of index features and θ-grids can be treated as pointers rather than integers. A more interesting challenge comes from the need to treat groups of features together. For example, the sharing of ψ and ϕ features that is accomplished in the formalization of movements in §7.2 is more appropriately done with pointers than by explicit copying. For one thing, when one of a number of agreeing nodes has any of its agreement features further specified, we want this additional specification to apply to all the nodes in the agreement relation, "percolating" through.[33]

15.7   Some psychological considerations

Given an appropriate initial representation of the parsing problem, the specialization of search and the transformation of the problem enhance efficiency by bringing constraints from various parts of the grammar to bear on all relevant structure-building operations. This is the basic strategy for handling any non-trivial constraint satisfaction problem. The strategy has a liability, though. Suppose that we show, using various principles from various levels of representation together with properties of affect-α, that S-structures have some property χ. Since in our framework S-structure is "closer" to PF than D-structures or LF, by checking for such derived properties at S-structure we can bring constraints from later levels of representation to bear earlier, avoiding wasteful search of alternatives that will never pan out. The liability of this approach, though, is that when we determine that an S-structure fails to have the derived property χ, we do not know which of the basic properties would fail if we pursued the derivation anyway. In other words, a derived property, in bringing together various basic constraints, may make the relative contributions of those basic constraints indistinguishable. This can be problematic if we want our computational model to preserve the linguists' hypotheses about the relative severity of various grammar violations. For example, if 1-subjacency violations are not as bad as ECP violations, as suggested at the beginning of §10, and we want our computational model to be sensitive to this difference, then we do not want to be checking derived properties in which these two constraints are merged and indistinguishable. This sort of consideration may provide some guidance about what sorts of properties should be derived for early enforcement.

Suppose that we take this guidance to heart. It might nevertheless be possible for the derived property approach to yield monostratal computational models, theories in which constraints at all levels of representation are brought to bear on a single representation, perhaps S-structure or some annotated or augmented version of S-structure. In such a model, D-structure is completely eliminated by providing the images of all D-structure constraints at S-structure. This idea raises another puzzle: if there is syntactic evidence for a separate level in the competence model, wouldn't this same evidence support a separate level in the performance model? For example, Burzio (1986, 305, 428, 436f) argues for a theory in which clitics must stand in a special relation to an argument position at D-structure. If they come to stand in the similar position at S-structure by movements, the resulting structure is unacceptable. The distinction between levels of representation thus plays a crucial role in his account. (Baker, 1988, 424-425) presents a similar form of argument based on head movements. In both cases one might reply that whatever constraints these theories apply at D-structure could simply be reformulated to have identical effects at S-structure? But even if this is possible, Baker (1988, 427) argues that the corresponding S-structure principles would be rather complex and arbitrary, hiding what is really a simple relation between D-structure and pure thematic relations. Do such arguments have any significance for processing models? It is plausible that they do. If D-structure is not formulated in language understanding and other linguistic tasks, it would be hard to explain the evidence for the competence theories. That is, why would a competence theory be so simplified by the assumption of a level of D-structure if no such level is ever computed in the exercise of linguistic abilities? Of all the ways a monostratal processor could be designed, why should it be designed to make it seem as if the more superficial structures came in regular ways from underlying structures with simple properties? One can imagine answers. For example, we could say that the competence model is explicitly represented, and that people somehow derive special modules for linguistic activities, modules in which levels of representation that are distinct and simple in the representation of competence are collapsed. But this theoretical option is not appealing. We may be driven to some such account, but it is not plausible at this point. It is much more natural to assume that parsing and other linguistic tasks involve the distinct levels of structure posited by the competence theory.

15.8   Conclusions and future directions

This chapter is the culmination of our project, launching an approach to the language processing problem which can be more directly and rigorously based on recent linguistic theory than has been possible before. The formal specification of linguistic theories allows us to explore their properties directly, with particular attention to those properties which are relevant to designing search strategies or reformulations that are efficient for

particular linguistic problems. Of course, the formalization does not add anything to
the theories. Anyone who understood them well enough might be able to draw the same
conclusions without the aid of the formalism, but the theories are rather complex. The
formalism is a valuable aid to specify unambiguously the theory about which claims are
being made, and the exercise of discovering a proof is a valuable check on whether we have
forgotten any cases that would be exceptions to our claims. Two kinds of claims about
a formalized theory are of interest. First, we want to claim that the formalism is faithful
to the linguists' intentions. The formal definitions are not always trivial, as we saw, for
example, in the definitions of *adjoin* and *amalgamate*. But it is much easier to formalize
these definitions in logic than it is to, say, directly produce rules defining LR(k,t) or
LRRL(k) parsers (with conflicts) that operate according to the linguistic theory.[34] Our
formal definitions correspond much more directly to the linguists' claims, and are much
more easily assessed. In Parts II and III, there were various key points where we were
unable to claim that our formalism was adequate in this respect, as in the definitions of
link and *argument*, and there are, no doubt, other places where we should have been
more careful. In any case, the modest achievement of having a system where such errors
might be explicit enough to be discoverable and correctable is worth noting. Progress
toward better formalizations can be expected. The second kind of claim that we make
about our formalization is much clearer: claims about consequences of the formal theory.
When we claim that some formal proposition follows from $FB \cup SEQ_{FB}$, this is a claim
with a definite truth value, a claim that can be checked with standard proof methods.

In this chapter, we also speculated about properties that more complete theories would
have, theories which could quite easily be formalized as elaborations of $FB \cup SEQ_{FB}$.
Given the structural complexity bounds defended in §15.4, it appears very likely that
decidability results for our parsing problems will be forthcoming, as suggested in §14.5.
And though it is likely that some instances of the parsing problem (adapted to the terms
of a more complete grammar) will have no feasible solution methods, many instances
of the problem can be efficiently computed. Aiming for a system that has reasonable
computational demands on small and typical problems, we have seen how the rather
extreme local ambiguities, the generate-and-test complexities, in standard searches for
proofs from the competence theory can be identified and eliminated with domain-specific
constraint satisfaction methods. The justification of these methods is based on particular
details of the adopted account of the language, as it should be. Finally, we noted very
briefly some empirical considerations that can guide us toward psychological models.

This new perspective on parsing as a constraint satisfaction problem is the computational image of the fundamental shift from construction-specific generative rules to the
highly general and interactive principles and parameters of syntactic theory. The development of a parser on the basis of results like those briefly surveyed here will be difficult,

but this approach has the potential of leading to a system that does justice to human language insofar as we understand it. The development of the computational theory can proceed in tandem with the development of linguistic theory. Computational models can be principled and open to careful assessment, not only with regard to resource demands and other computational properties, but also with regard to their appropriateness for languages with the properties of human languages.

Appendix A

Proving a negative result
from RT

This proof of a negative result, a refutation of a positive result, is discussed in §3.3. We will prove that RT entails that there is something which is not a sentence by refuting the claim that everything is a sentence, $\{s(A)\}$. The theory RT has infinitely many sentences, and hence infinitely many clauses in a standard clausal form, but the following refutation needs only the following:

8. $\{np(sk1(A)), append(sk3(A), [and|sk4(A)], A), \neg s(A)\}$
12. $\{append(sk1(A), sk2(A), A), append(sk3(A), [and|sk4(A)], A), \neg s(A)\}$
13. $\{\neg np(A), A = [lions]\}$
17. $\{A = [], A = [sk5(B, C, A)|sk6(B, C, A)], \neg append(A, C, B)\}$
19. $\{A = [], B = [sk5(B, C, A)|sk7(B, C, A)], \neg append(A, C, B)\}$
24. $\{A = B, B = [sk5(B, A, C)|sk7(B, A, C)], \neg append(C, A, B)\}$
25. $\{A = B, \neg append(C, A, B), append(sk6(B, A, C), A, sk7(B, A, C))\}$
32. $\{A = B, \neg[A|C] = [B|D]\}$
33. $\{A = B, \neg[C|A] = [D|B]\}$
34. $\{A = A\}$
35. $\{\neg A = B, \neg C = A, \neg D = B, C = D\}$
36. $\{append(A, B, C), \neg A = D, \neg B = E, \neg C = F, \neg append(D, E, F)\}$
37. $\{\neg and = sleep\}$
38. $\{\neg[] = [A|B]\}$
40. $\{\neg sleep = lions\}$

The Skolem functions all begin with sk, so they are easily recognized. It is not difficult to figure out which sentences of RT_0 these clauses are derived from. Notice that 32-33 tell us that the binary list constructor is a 1-1 function, 34 is the reflexive axiom for equality, 35-36 are substitution axioms, and 37-40 are some of the pairwise inequalies among the (non-Skolem) function symbols and constants in the language.

In the following refutation, every line except the first is a resolvent, and every resolvent has the previous line as one of its parents (it's "center parent"). The other parent (the "side parent") is always either an axiom or an earlier resolvent. All resolution steps are binary, there is no "factoring," and the last literal in the center parent is always the one resolved upon. The refutation has this simple structure because it was actually found by a model elimination theorem prover, though it is presented here as a standard resolution proof. The practical advantages of model elimination have been discussed by Stickel (1986), Loveland (1978) and others. Although resolution proofs may be shorter than the shortest model elimination proof, the search space for general resolution is vastly larger.

The following refutation $s(A)$ finds a particular instance A of a nonsentence. This can be collected out of the proof using the technique described in §3.2. This collection of the answer substitutions from such a complex proof is a tedious business, so it is fortunate that a computer can do the work for us. My computer says that the answer set for $\{s(A)\}$ in this refutation is

$\{s([sleep])\}.$

Just a little study of the proof reveals how this instance is shown to be different from every one of the infinitely many sentences in the extension of s under the intended interpretation.

$\{$ *for refutation*

$s(A)$

$\}$

$\{$ *R0 by 8*

$np(sk1(A)),$

$append(sk3(A), [and|sk4(A)], A)$

$\}$

$\{$ *R1 by 24*

$np(sk1(A)),$

$[and|sk4(A)] = A,$

$A = [sk5(A, [and|sk4(A)], sk3(A))|sk7(A, [and|sk4(A)], sk3(A))]$

$\}$

$\{$ *R2 by 33*

$np(sk1([A|B])),$

$[and|sk4([A|B])] = [A|B],$

$B = sk7([A|B], [and|sk4([A|B])], sk3([A|B]))$

$\}$

$\{$ *R3 by 36*

$np(sk1([A|B])),$

$[and|sk4([A|B])] = [A|B],$

$append(G, H, B),$

$\neg G = I,$

$\neg H = J,$

$\neg append(I, J, sk7([A|B], [and|sk4([A|B])], sk3([A|B])))$

$\}$

$\{$ *R4 by 25*

$np(sk1([A|B])),$

$[and|sk4([A|B])] = [A|B],$

$append(G, H, B),$

$\neg G = sk6([A|B], [and|sk4([A|B])], sk3([A|B])),$

$\neg H = [and|sk4([A|B])],$

$[and|sk4([A|B])] = [A|B],$

$\neg append(sk3([A|B]), [and|sk4([A|B])], [A|B])$

$\}$

$\{$ *R5 by R3*

$np(sk1([A|B])),$

$[and|sk4([A|B])] = [A|B],$

$append(G, H, B),$

$\neg G = sk6([A|B], [and|sk4([A|B])], sk3([A|B])),$

$\neg H = [and|sk4([A|B])],$

$[and|sk4([A|B])] = [A|B]$

$\}$

$\{$ $R6 \; by \; 32$
$np(sk1([A|B])),$
$[and|sk4([A|B])] = [A|B],$
$append(G, H, B),$
$\neg G = sk6([A|B], [and|sk4([A|B])], sk3([A|B])),$
$\neg H = [and|sk4([A|B])],$
$and = A,$
$\}$

$\{$ $R7 \; by \; 37$
$np(sk1([sleep|A])),$
$[and|sk4([sleep|A])] = [sleep|A],$
$append(F, G, A),$
$\neg F = sk6([sleep|A], [and|sk4([sleep|A])], sk3([sleep|A])),$
$\neg G = [and|sk4([sleep|A])]$
$\}$

$\{$ $R8 \; by \; 34$
$np(sk1([sleep|A])),$
$[and|sk4([sleep|A])] = [sleep|A],$
$append(F, [and|sk4([sleep|A])], A),$
$\neg F = sk6([sleep|A], [and|sk4([sleep|A])], sk3([sleep|A]))$
$\}$

$\{$ $R9 \; by \; 34$
$np(sk1([sleep|A])),$
$[and|sk4([sleep|A])] = [sleep|A],$
$append(sk6([sleep|A], [and|sk4([sleep|A])], sk3([sleep|A])),$
$\quad [and|sk4([sleep|A])], A)$
$\}$

$\{$ $R10 \; by \; 24$
$np(sk1([sleep|A])),$
$[and|sk4([sleep|A])] = [sleep|A],$
$[and|sk4([sleep|A])] = A,$
$A = [sk5(A, [and|sk4([sleep|A])]), sk6([sleep|A], [and|sk4([sleep|A])],$
$\quad sk3([sleep|A]))) | sk7(A, [and|sk4([sleep|A])]), sk6([sleep|A],$
$\quad [and|sk4([sleep|A])], sk3([sleep|A])))]$
$\}$

$\{$ $R11 \; by \; 38$
$np(sk1([sleep])),$
$[and|sk4([sleep])] = [sleep],$
$[and|sk4([sleep])] = []$
$\}$

$\{$ $R12 \; by \; 35$
$np(sk1([sleep])),$
$[and|sk4([sleep])] = [sleep],$
$\neg G = [],$
$\neg H = G,$
$H = [and|sk4([sleep])]$
$\}$

$\{$ $R13 \; by \; 38$
$np(sk1([sleep])),$
$[and|sk4([sleep])] = [sleep],$
$\neg G = [],$
$\neg [] = G,$
$\}$

$\{$
$np(sk1([sleep])),$ R14 by 34
$[and|sk4([sleep])] = [sleep],$
$\neg[] = []$
$\}$
$\{$ R15 by R8
$np(sk1([sleep])),$
$[and|sk4([sleep])] = [sleep]$
$\}$
$\{$ R16 by 32
$np(sk1([sleep])),$
$and = sleep$
$\}$
$\{$ R17 by 37
$np(sk1([sleep]))$
$\}$
$\{$ R18 by 13
$sk1([sleep]) = [lions]$
$\}$
$\{$ R19 by 35
$\neg D = [lions],$
$\neg E = D,$
$E = sk1([sleep])$
$\}$
$\{$ R20 by 36
$\neg D = [lions],$
$\neg E = D,$
$append(E, G, H),$
$\neg G = I,$
$\neg H = J,$
$\neg append(sk1([sleep]), I, J)$
$\}$
$\{$ R21 by 12
$\neg D = [lions],$
$\neg E = D,$
$append(E, G, H),$
$\neg G = sk2([sleep]),$
$\neg H = [sleep],$
$append(sk3([sleep]), [and|sk4([sleep])], [sleep]),$
$\neg s([sleep])$
$\}$
$\{$ R22 by R1
$\neg D = [lions],$
$\neg E = D,$
$append(E, G, H),$
$\neg G = sk2([sleep]),$
$\neg H = [sleep],$
$append(sk3([sleep]), [and|sk4([sleep])], [sleep])$
$\}$

{   *R*23 *by* 24
$\neg D = [lions]$,
$\neg E = D$,
$append(E, G, H)$,
$\neg G = sk2([sleep])$,
$\neg H = [sleep]$,
$[and|sk4([sleep])] = [sleep]$,
$[sleep] = [sk5([sleep], [and|sk4([sleep])], sk3([sleep]))|sk7([sleep],$
    $[and|sk4([sleep])], sk3([sleep]))]$
}
{   *R*24 *by* 33
$\neg D = [lions]$,
$\neg E = D$,
$append(E, G, H)$,
$\neg G = sk2([sleep])$,
$\neg H = [sleep]$,
$[and|sk4([sleep])] = [sleep]$,
$[] = sk7([sleep], [and|sk4([sleep])], sk3([sleep]))$
}
{   *R*25 *by* 36
$\neg D = [lions]$,
$\neg E = D$,
$append(E, G, H)$,
$\neg G = sk2([sleep])$,
$\neg H = [sleep]$,
$[and|sk4([sleep])] = [sleep]$,
$append(M, N, [])$,
$\neg M = O$,
$\neg N = P$,
$\neg append(O, P, sk7([sleep], [and|sk4([sleep])], sk3([sleep])))$
}
{   *R*26 *by* 25
$\neg D = [lions]$,
$\neg E = D$,
$append(E, G, H)$,
$\neg G = sk2([sleep])$,
$\neg H = [sleep]$,
$[and|sk4([sleep])] = [sleep]$,
$append(M, N, [])$,
$\neg M = sk6([sleep], [and|sk4([sleep])], sk3([sleep]))$,
$\neg N = [and|sk4([sleep])]$,
$[and|sk4([sleep])] = [sleep]$,
$\neg append(sk3([sleep]), [and|sk4([sleep])], [sleep])$
}
{   *R*27 *by* *R*11
$\neg D = [lions]$,
$\neg E = D$,
$append(E, G, H)$,
$\neg G = sk2([sleep])$,
$\neg H = [sleep]$,
$[and|sk4([sleep])] = [sleep]$,
$append(M, N, [])$,
$\neg M = sk6([sleep], [and|sk4([sleep])], sk3([sleep]))$,
$\neg N = [and|sk4([sleep])]$,
$[and|sk4([sleep])] = [sleep]$
}

$\{$ $R28$ by 32
$\neg D = [lions],$
$\neg E = D,$
$append(E, G, H),$
$\neg G = sk2([sleep]),$
$\neg H = [sleep],$
$[and|sk4([sleep])] = [sleep],$
$append(M, N, []),$
$\neg M = sk6([sleep], [and|sk4([sleep])], sk3([sleep])),$
$\neg N = [and|sk4([sleep])],$
$and = sleep$
$\}$
$\{$ $R29$ by 37
$\neg D = [lions],$
$\neg E = D,$
$append(E, G, H),$
$\neg G = sk2([sleep]),$
$\neg H = [sleep],$
$[and|sk4([sleep])] = [sleep],$
$append(M, N, []),$
$\neg M = sk6([sleep], [and|sk4([sleep])], sk3([sleep])),$
$\neg N = [and|sk4([sleep])]$
$\}$
$\{$ $R30$ by 34
$\neg D = [lions],$
$\neg E = D,$
$append(E, G, H),$
$\neg G = sk2([sleep]),$
$\neg H = [sleep],$
$[and|sk4([sleep])] = [sleep],$
$append(M, [and|sk4([sleep])], []),$
$\neg M = sk6([sleep], [and|sk4([sleep])], sk3([sleep]))$
$\}$
$\{$ $R31$ by 34
$\neg D = [lions],$
$\neg E = D,$
$append(E, G, H),$
$\neg G = sk2([sleep]),$
$\neg H = [sleep],$
$[and|sk4([sleep])] = [sleep],$
$append(sk6([sleep], [and|sk4([sleep])], sk3([sleep])),$
$\quad [and|sk4([sleep])], [])$
$\}$
$\{$ $R32$ by 24
$\neg D = [lions],$
$\neg E = D,$
$append(E, G, H),$
$\neg G = sk2([sleep]),$
$\neg H = [sleep],$
$[and|sk4([sleep])] = [sleep],$
$[and|sk4([sleep])] = [],$
$[] = [sk5([], [and|sk4([sleep])], sk6([sleep], [and|sk4([sleep])],$
$\quad sk3([sleep])))|sk7([], [and|sk4([sleep])], sk6([sleep], [and|$
$\quad sk4([sleep])], sk3([sleep])))]$
$\}$

```
{                           R33 by 38
¬D = [lions],
¬E = D,
append(E, G, H),
¬G = sk2([sleep]),
¬H = [sleep],
[and|sk4([sleep])] = [sleep],
[and|sk4([sleep])] = []
}
{                           R34 by 35
¬D = [lions],
¬E = D,
append(E, G, H),
¬G = sk2([sleep]),
¬H = [sleep],
[and|sk4([sleep])] = [sleep],
¬O = [],
¬P = O,
P = [and|sk4([sleep])]
}
{                           R35 by 38
¬D = [lions],
¬E = D,
append(E, G, H),
¬G = sk2([sleep]),
¬H = [sleep],
[and|sk4([sleep])] = [sleep],
¬O = [],
¬[] = O,
}
{                           R36 by 34
¬D = [lions],
¬E = D,
append(E, G, H),
¬G = sk2([sleep]),
¬H = [sleep],
[and|sk4([sleep])] = [sleep],
¬[] = []
}
{                           R37 by R16
¬D = [lions],
¬E = D,
append(E, G, H),
¬G = sk2([sleep]),
¬H = [sleep],
[and|sk4([sleep])] = [sleep]
}
{                           R38 by 32
¬D = [lions],
¬E = D,
append(E, G, H),
¬G = sk2([sleep]),
¬H = [sleep],
and = sleep
}
```

{   *R39 by 37*
$\neg D = [lions]$,
$\neg E = D$,
$append(E, G, H)$,
$\neg G = sk2([sleep])$,
$\neg H = [sleep]$
}
{   *R40 by 34*
$\neg D = [lions]$,
$\neg E = D$,
$append(E, G, [sleep])$,
$\neg G = sk2([sleep])$
}
{   *R41 by 34*
$\neg D = [lions]$,
$\neg E = D$,
$append(E, sk2([sleep]), [sleep])$
}
{   *R42 by 19*
$\neg D = [lions]$,
$\neg E = D$,
$E = []$,
$[sleep] = [sk5([sleep], sk2([sleep]), E) | sk7([sleep], sk2([sleep]), E)]$
}
{   *R43 by 32*
$\neg D = [lions]$,
$\neg E = D$,
$E = []$,
$sleep = sk5([sleep], sk2([sleep]), E)$
}
{   *R44 by 35*
$\neg D = [lions]$,
$\neg E = D$,
$E = []$,
$\neg sk5([sleep], sk2([sleep]), E) = J$,
$\neg K = J$,
$sleep = K$,
}
{   *R45 by 40*
$\neg D = [lions]$,
$\neg E = D$,
$E = []$,
$\neg sk5([sleep], sk2([sleep]), E) = J$,
$\neg lions = J$,
}
{   *R46 by 34*
$\neg D = [lions]$,
$\neg E = D$,
$E = []$,
$\neg sk5([sleep], sk2([sleep]), E) = lions$
}

$\{$ $R47$ by 35
$\neg D = [lions],$
$\neg E = D,$
$E = [],$
$\neg K = L,$
$\neg sk5([sleep], sk2([sleep]), E) = K,$
$\neg lions = L,$
$\}$

$\{$ $R48$ by $R6$
$\neg D = [lions],$
$\neg lions = D,$
$G = [],$
$\neg K = sk1([sleep]),$
$\neg sk5([sleep], sk2([sleep]), G) = K,$
$\}$

$\{$ $R48$ by 32
$\neg D = [lions],$
$\neg E = D,$
$E = [],$
$\neg K = L,$
$\neg sk5([sleep], sk2([sleep]), E) = K,$
$\neg [lions|N] = [L|O]$
$\}$

$\{$ $R49$ by 17
$\neg D = [lions],$
$\neg E = D,$
$E = [],$
$\neg K = sk5(L, M, [lions|N]),$
$\neg sk5([sleep], sk2([sleep]), E) = K,$
$[lions|N] = [],$
$\neg append([lions|N], M, L)$
$\}$

$\{$ $R50$ by $R7$
$\neg D = [lions],$
$\neg [lions|E] = D,$
$[lions|E] = [],$
$\neg K = sk5([sleep], sk2([sleep]), [lions|E]),$
$\neg sk5([sleep], sk2([sleep]), [lions|E]) = K,$
$[lions|E] = []$
$\}$

$\{$ $R51$ by 35
$\neg D = [lions],$
$\neg [lions|E] = D,$
$[lions|E] = [],$
$\neg K = sk5([sleep], sk2([sleep]), [lions|E]),$
$\neg sk5([sleep], sk2([sleep]), [lions|E]) = K,$
$\neg O = [],$
$\neg P = O,$
$P = [lions|E]$
$\}$

{   *R52 by 38*
$\neg D = [lions],$
$\neg [lions|E] = D,$
$[lions|E] = [],$
$\neg K = sk5([sleep], sk2([sleep]), [lions|E]),$
$\neg sk5([sleep], sk2([sleep]), [lions|E]) = K,$
$\neg O = [],$
$\neg [] = O,$
}
{   *R53 by 34*
$\neg D = [lions],$
$\neg [lions|E] = D,$
$[lions|E] = [],$
$\neg K = sk5([sleep], sk2([sleep]), [lions|E]),$
$\neg sk5([sleep], sk2([sleep]), [lions|E]) = K,$
$\neg [] = []$
}
{   *R54 by 34*
$\neg D = [lions],$
$\neg [lions|E] = D,$
$[lions|E] = [],$
$\neg K = sk5([sleep], sk2([sleep]), [lions|E]),$
$\neg sk5([sleep], sk2([sleep]), [lions|E]) = K,$
}
{   *R55 by 34*
$\neg D = [lions],$
$\neg [lions|E] = D,$
$[lions|E] = [],$
$\neg sk5([sleep], sk2([sleep]), [lions|E]) = sk5([sleep], sk2([sleep]), [lions|E])$
}
{   *R56 by R3*
$\neg D = [lions],$
$\neg [lions|E] = D,$
$[lions|E] = []$
}
{   *R57 by 35*
$\neg D = [lions],$
$\neg [lions|E] = D,$
$\neg I = [],$
$\neg J = I,$
$J = [lions|E]$
}
{   *R58 by 38*
$\neg D = [lions],$
$\neg [lions|E] = D,$
$\neg I = [],$
$\neg [] = I,$
}
{   *R59 by 34*
$\neg D = [lions],$
$\neg [lions|E] = D,$
$\neg [] = []$
}

$$\{ \qquad\qquad R60 \ by \ R8$$
$$\neg D = [lions],$$
$$\neg [lions|E] = D,$$
$$\}$$
$$\{ \qquad\qquad R61 \ by \ R3$$
$$\neg [lions] = [lions]$$
$$\}$$
$$\square \qquad\qquad R62 \ by \ 34$$

Appendix B

The first order formalization

A factor hindering the progress of AI seems to be that AI programs are not produced in a form suitable for easy comprehension by humans... Consequently the programs themselves are rarely published, but are only described, leading inevitably to vagueness and ambiguity... Programs need to be published. For this one requires a language with the simplicity and universality of the predicate calculus. The aim of programming should be towards an ideal of beauty and clarity.

— D.H.D. Warren

We present our formalizations in the notation that is accepted by our theorem prover. As in the text, each formula represents its universal closure.

B.1 The Barriers theory

We list here all of the sentences considered in Part II, together with others too insignificant, too tentative, or too familiar to deserve attention in the text. Example trees that can be used with this formalization are provided in Appendix C.

```
% File : las.fol
% Author  : Ed Stabler, Jr
% Updated :  June, 1991
% Purpose :  BARRIERS formalization
% There are 81 first order sentences in this file --
%    ignoring those that are commented out

%%%%% Section 4.2.1

subtree(Sub,Tree) <=>
    (    Sub = Tree
    or   some(Node,some(Seq,some(Sub1,
            Tree = Node/Seq and
            member(Sub1,Seq) and
            subtree(Sub,Sub1)
        )))
    ).

member(Element,L) <=>
    (    some(Seq1, L=[Element|Seq1] )
    or   some(Element1,some(Seq1,
            L=[Element1|Seq1] and
            member(Element,Seq1)
        ))
    ).

parent(Parent,Node,Tree) <=>
    some(Seq,some(Seq0,
```

```
          subtree(Parent/Seq,Tree) and
     member(Node/Seq0,Seq)
     )).

ancestor(Anc,Node,Tree) <=>
     (    parent(Anc,Node,Tree)
     or   some(Mid,
               parent(Anc,Mid,Tree) and
               ancestor(Mid,Node,Tree)
          )
     ).

%%%%% Section 6.4

feature(AV,Node0,Node) <=>
     some(Att,some(Val,some(L,some(C,some(F0,some(F,
          AV = Att:Val and
          Node0 = x(L,C,N,F0) and
          (    member(Att:Val,F0) and F = F0
          or   every(Val0, ~ member(Att:Val0,F0)) and F=[Att:Val|F0]
          ) and
          Node = x(L,C,N,F)
     )))))).

/*** this is revised to use lexical/2 in Section 10.2, below
lexical(Node) <=>
     some(L,some(Cat,some(N,some(F,
          Node=x(L,Cat,N,F) and
          member(Cat,[v,n,p,a])
     )))).
***/

maximal(Node) <=>
     some(Cat,some(N,some(F,
          Node=x(s(s(0)),Cat,N,F)
     ))).

minimal(Node) <=>
     some(C,some(N,some(F,
          Node=x(0,C,N,F)
     ))).

% These are English-specific parameter settings
head_spec(X) <=> X=0.
head_compl(X) <=> X=s(0).

separate(N,Head,List,Remainder) <=>
     (    N=0 and last(Head,List,Remainder)
     or   N=s(0)  and
          List=[Head|Remainder]
     ).

last(Element,List,Remainder) <=>
     (    some(E1,some(E2,some(Rest,some(Rem,
               List = [E1,E2|Rest]  and
               Remainder = [E1|Rem]  and
               last(Element,[E2|Rest],Rem)
          ))))
     or   List = [Element]  and
          Remainder = []
     ).
```

```
xps(L) <=>
    (    L   = []
    or   some(Tree,some(Seq,
             L = [Tree|Seq]   and
             xp(Tree)   and
             xps(Seq)
             ))
    ).

x0(X0) <=> some(Cat,some(N,some(F,some(Seq,
      X0=x(0,Cat,N,F)/Seq and
      (     Seq=[] and F=[]
      or    some(Word,
                  Seq=[Word/[]] and
                  lexicon(Word,Cat,F)
                  )
      ) )))).

x1(X1) <=>
    some(Cat,some(N,some(F,some(Subtrees,
      X1=x(s(0),Cat,N,F)/Subtrees and
      (    some(Position,some(N0,some(L,some(Remainder,
             head_compl(Position) and
             separate(Position,x(0,Cat,N0,F)/L,Subtrees,Remainder) and
             xps(Remainder) and
             x0(x(0,Cat,N0,F)/L)
          )))))
      or   some(L,some(XP,
             (   Subtrees = [x(s(0),Cat,N,F)/L,XP]
             or Subtrees = [XP,x(s(0),Cat,N,F)/L]
             )  and
             x1(x(s(0),Cat,N,F)/L) and
             xp(XP)
          ))
      ) ))).

xp(XP) <=>
    some(Cat,some(N,some(F,some(T,some(Ts,
    some(Pos,some(Nn,some(L,some(Rem,some(XP1,
      (     XP=x(s(s(0)),Cat,N,F)/[]
      or    XP = x(s(s(0)),Cat,N,F)/[T|Ts]   and
            head_spec(Pos) and
            separate(Pos,x(s(0),Cat,Nn,F)/L,[T|Ts],Rem) and
            xps(Rem)      and
            x1(x(s(0),Cat,Nn,F)/L)
      or    XP = x(s(s(0)),Cat,N,F)/[T|Ts]   and
            head_compl(Pos) and
            separate(Pos,x(0,Cat,Nn,F)/L,[T|Ts],Rem) and
            xps(Rem)      and
            x0(x(0,Cat,Nn,F)/L)
      or    XP = x(s(s(0)),Cat,N,F)/[T|Ts]   and
            (  [T|Ts] = [x(s(s(0)),Cat,N,F)/L,XP1]
            or [T|Ts] = [XP1,x(s(s(0)),Cat,N,F)/L]
            )  and
            xp(x(s(s(0)),Cat,N,F)/L) and
            xp(XP1)
      )
    )))))))))).
```

```
% we allow for the optionality of the intermediate projection, and for
```

```
%    the possibility of adjunctions in the following 4 definitions
head_xp(X,XP,Tree) <=>
    some(Cat,some(N0,some(F0,some(N2,some(F2,some(Seq1,
    some(N1,some(F1,some(Seq2,
      X=x(0,Cat,N0,F0) and
      XP=x(s(s(0)),Cat,N2,F2) and
      subtree(XP/Seq1,Tree) and
      (    member(x(s(0),Cat,N1,F1)/Seq2,Seq1)  and
           head_x1(X,x(s(0),Cat,N1,F1),x(s(0),Cat,N1,F1)/Seq2)
      or   member(X/Seq2,Seq1)
      or   member(x(s(s(0)),Cat,N2,F2)/Seq2,Seq1) and
           head_xp(X,x(s(s(0)),Cat,N2,F2),x(s(s(0)),Cat,N2,F2)/Seq2)
      ) )))))))))).

head_x1(X,X1,Tree) <=>
    some(Cat,some(N0,some(F0,some(N1,some(F1,some(Seq1,some(Seq2,
      X=x(0,Cat,N0,F0) and
      X1=x(s(0),Cat,N1,F1)/Seq1 and
      subtree(X1,Tree) and
      (    member(X/Seq2,Seq1)
      or   member(x(s(s(0)),Cat,N1,F1)/Seq2,Seq1) and
           head_x1(X,x(s(0),Cat,N1,F1),x(s(0),Cat,N1,F1)/Seq2)
      ) ))))))).

% three cases: complement of X, of X1, of XP
complement(Complement,Xn,Tree) <=>
    some(Cat,some(N,some(F,some(Node,some(Subtrees,some(Position,
    some(Remainder,some(Seq0,some(Seq,
          (    Xn=x(0,Cat,N,F) and
               subtree(Node/Subtrees,Tree) and
               head_compl(Position) and
               separate(Position,x(0,Cat,N,F)/Seq0,Subtrees,Remainder) and
               member(Complement/Seq,Remainder)
          or   Xn=x(s(0),Cat,N,F) and
               head_x1(Node,x(s(0),Cat,N,F),Tree) and
               complement(Complement,Node,Tree)
          or   Xn=x(s(s(0)),Cat,N,F) and
               head_xp(Node,x(s(s(0)),Cat,N,F),Tree) and
               complement(Complement,Node,Tree)
          )
    ))))))))).

% three cases: complement of X, of X1, of XP
specifier(Specifier,Xn,Tree) <=>
    some(Cat,some(N,some(F,some(N1,some(F1,some(T,some(Ts,
    some(Pos,some(Nn,some(Fn,some(Seq,some(Remainder,some(Seq1,
          (    Xn=x(0,Cat,N,F) and
               subtree(x(s(s(0)),Cat,N1,F1)/[T|Ts],Tree) and
               head_spec(Pos) and
               separate(Pos,x(s(0),Cat,Nn,Fn)/Seq,[T|Ts],Remainder) and
               member(Specifier/Seq1,Remainder) and
               head_x1(x(0,Cat,N,F),x(s(0),Cat,Nn,Fn),Tree)
          or   Xn=x(s(0),Cat,N,F) and
               subtree(x(s(s(0)),Cat,N1,F1)/[T|Ts],Tree) and
               head_spec(Pos) and
               separate(Pos,x(s(0),Cat,N,F)/Seq,[T|Ts],Remainder) and
               member(Specifier/Seq1,Remainder)
          or   Xn=x(s(s(0)),Cat,N,F) and
               subtree(x(s(s(0)),Cat,N,F)/[T|Ts],Tree) and
               head_spec(Pos) and
               separate(Pos,x(s(0),Cat,N1,F1)/Seq,[T|Ts],Remainder) and
```

```
          member(Specifier/Seq1,Remainder)
    )
))))))))))))).

%%%%% Section 7.1 %%% Movement definitions

select(Position,List,Selected,Remainder) <=>
    (    Position = s(0) and
         List = [Selected|Remainder]
    or   some(Head,some(Tail,some(Rest,some(Position1,
             List = [Head|Tail] and
             Remainder = [Head|Rest] and
             select(Position1,Tail,Selected,Rest) and
             Position=s(Position1)
         ))))
    ).

%%%%% Section 7.2 %%% Movement definitions

substitute(Tree0,Tree,MRoot,Landing,Renumbering) <=>
    some(Node,some(Seq0,some(Seq,some(Pos1,some(Selected1,some(RestSeq1,
        Tree0 = Node/Seq0  and
        Tree = Node/Seq   and
        select(Pos1,Seq0,Selected1,RestSeq1)  and
        (    some(Transformed,
               substitute(Selected1,Transformed,MRoot,Landing,Renumbering) and
               select(Pos1,Seq,Transformed,RestSeq1)
             )
        or   some(Pos2,some(Selected2,some(RestSeq2,some(Moved,
             some(Transformed1,some(Transformed2,some(Seq1,
                 select(Pos2,RestSeq1,Selected2,RestSeq2) and
                 zero_cat(MRoot/Moved,Selected1,Transformed1,Renumbering) and
                 cat_zero(MRoot/Moved,Landing,Selected2,Transformed2) and
                 select(Pos2,Seq1,Transformed2,RestSeq2) and
                 select(Pos1,Seq,Transformed1,Seq1)
             )))))))
        )
    )))))).

/*** modified in Section 9.1
subst_conds(Moved,Landing) <=> visible(Moved) and visible(Landing).
***/

visible(Node) <=> maximal(Node) or minimal(Node).

zero_cat(Moved,Tree0,Tree,Renumbering) <=>
    (    some(Node0,some(T0,some(T0s,some(Seq,some(Pos,some(Selected,
         some(RestSeq,some(Transformed,
             Tree0 = Node0/[T0|T0s]  and
             select(Pos,[T0|T0s],Selected,RestSeq)  and
             zero_cat(Moved,Selected,Transformed,Renumbering) and
             select(Pos,Seq,Transformed,RestSeq) and
             Tree = Node0/Seq
         ))))))))
    or   some(L,some(C,some(N,some(F,some(Seq0,some(I,
         some(Node1,some(Node2,some(Seq2,some(Node,
             Tree0 = x(L,C,N,F)/Seq0  and
             feature(index:I,x(L,C,N,F),Node1)   and
             renumber(Node1/Seq0,Node2/Seq2,Renumbering) and
             take_features(Node1,Node)  and
             Tree = Node/[]   and
```

```
            Moved = Node1/Seq0 and
            (I=N or x=x)
      )))))))))
  ).

cat_zero(Moved,Landing,Tree0,Tree)  <=>
    (     some(Node,some(T0,some(T0s,some(Seq,some(Pos,some(Selected,
          some(RestSeq,some(Transformed,
              Tree0 = Node/[T0|T0s]  and
              select(Pos,[T0|T0s],Selected,RestSeq) and
              cat_zero(Moved,Landing,Selected,Transformed) and
              select(Pos, Seq, Transformed, RestSeq)  and
              Tree = Node/Seq
          ))))))))
    or    some(I,some(Node0,some(Node1,some(Node2,some(Seq,
              Tree0 = Node0/[]  and
              feature(index:I,Node0,Node1)  and
              Moved = Node2/Seq  and
              feature(index:I,Node2,Node2)  and
              put_features(Node1,Node2,Landing)  and
              Tree = Landing/Seq
          )))))
    ).

take_features(A,B)  <=> some(L,some(C,some(N,
    (     A = x(L,C,N,[]) and
          B = x(L,C,N,[])
    or    some(E,some(F0,some(F,
              A = x(L,C,N,[E|F0]) and
              take_features(x(L,C,N,F0),x(L,C,N,F)) and
              (     phi(E)   and B = x(L,C,N,[E|F])
              or  ~ phi(E) and B = x(L,C,N,F)
              )
          )))
    )  ))).

phi(E)   <=> some(Val,
    (     E = person:Val
    or    E = number:Val
    or    E = gender:Val
    or    E = case:Val
    or    E = wh:Val
    or    E = index:Val
    or    E = theta:Val
    or    E = th:Val
    or    E = finite:Val
    )  ).

put_features(A,B,G)  <=> some(L,some(C,some(N,
    (     B = x(L,C,N,[]) and
          A = G
    or    some(E,some(F,some(A1,
              B = x(L,C,N,[E|F]) and
              (   psi(E)   and
                  feature(E,A,A1) and
                  put_features(A1,x(L,C,N,F),G)
              or  ~ psi(E) and
                  put_features(A,x(L,C,N,F),G)
              )
          )))
    )  ))).
```

```
psi(E) <=> some(Val,
    (      E = person:Val
    or     E = number:Val
    or     E = gender:Val
    or     E = case:Val
    or     E = wh:Val
    or     E = theta:Val
    or     E = pronominal:Val
    or     E = anaphoric:Val
    ) ).

adjoin(Tree0,Tree,MRoot,LRoot,Renumbering) <=>
  some(Node,some(Seq0,some(Seq,some(Pos,some(Selected,
  some(RestSeq,some(Transformed,
   Tree0 = Node/Seq0  and
   Tree = Node/Seq  and
   select(Pos,Seq0,Selected,RestSeq)  and
   (    adjoin(Selected,Transformed,MRoot,LRoot,Renumbering)  and
        select(Pos,Seq,Transformed,RestSeq)
   or   some(Seq1,some(Moved,some(Landing,
            zero_cat(MRoot/Moved,Selected,Transformed,Renumbering) and
            select(Pos,Seq1,Transformed,RestSeq) and
            adjoin_cat(MRoot/Moved,LRoot/Landing,Node/Seq1,Node/Seq,Renumbering)
            )))
   )
  ))))))).

argument(Node,T) <=> some(C,some(N,some(F,some(Node0,
    (      Node=x(s(s(0)),C,N,F) and
           (C=n or C=c or C=i or C=a) and        % VPs are not args
           directly_th_governs(Node0,Node,T)
    or     specifier(Node,x(s(s(0)),i,N,F),T)
    ) )))).

/*** revised in Section 9.1
adjoin_conds(Moved,Landing,Tree) <=>
        visible(Moved) and
        visible(Landing) and
        ~ argument(Landing,Tree).
***/

/*** revised in Section 9.2, below
adjoin_cat(Moved,Landing,Tree0,Tree,Renumbering) <=>
    some(L,some(C,some(N,some(F,some(Seq0,some(Seq,
        Tree0 = x(L,C,N,F)/Seq0  and
        Tree = x(L,C,N,F)/Seq  and
        (    some(Pos,some(Selected,some(RestSeq,some(Transformed,
                select(Pos,Seq0,Selected,RestSeq) and
                adjoin_cat(Moved,Landing,Selected,Transformed,Renumbering) and
                select(Pos,Seq,Transformed,RestSeq)
             ))))
        or   some(L1,some(C1,some(N1,some(F1,some(Seq1,some(N2,
                Moved=x(L1,C1,N1,F1)/Seq1 and
                newnumber(Renumbering,N2) and
                (    Seq = [x(L1,C1,N2,F1)/Seq1,Tree0]
                or   Seq = [Tree0,x(L1,C1,N2,F1)/Seq1]
                )
             )))))) and
             Landing=Tree0
        )
```

```
     )))))).
***/

/*** revised in Section 9.2, below, then replaced by affectA in 10.1
moveA(Tree0,Tree) <=> some(Moved,some(Landing,some(Renumbering,
    new_occurrence_number(Tree0,Renumbering) and
    (     substitute(Tree0,Tree,Moved,Landing,Renumbering) and
          subst_conds(Moved,Landing)
    or    adjoin(Tree0,Tree,Moved,Landing,Renumbering) and
          adjoin_conds(Moved,Landing,Tree)
    )
    ))).
***/

/*** replaced by affectAn in Section 10.1, below
moveAn(Tree0,Tree) <=>
    (     Tree = Tree0
    or    some(Tree1,
              moveA(Tree0,Tree1)  and
              moveAn(Tree1,Tree)
          )
    ).
***/

%%% renumbering predicates: these can be axiomatized, but in
%%%    most proofs it makes more sense to do the numbering with
%%%    special non-logical methods. It is a simple matter to
%%%    allow a special trivial clause for each of these predicates
%%%    to trigger an appropriate procedure.

new_occurrence_no(Tree,Renumbering) <=>
    some(N1,some(OldNo,
      maxno(s(0),Tree,N1) and
      Renumbering = OldNo/s(N1)  )).

maxnode(NO,Node,N) <=>
    (   some(L,some(C,some(F, Node=x(L,C,N,F) and gt(s(N),NO) )))
    or  ~ some(L,some(C,some(No,some(F, Node=x(L,C,No,F) )))) and
        NO=N
    ).

maxno(NO,Tree,N) <=> some(Root,some(Seq,some(N1,
        Tree = Root/Seq and maxnode(NO,Root,N1) and maxnos(Seq,N1,N)  ))).

maxnos(T0,NO,N) <=>
    (   T0=[] and NO=N
    or  some(T,some(Ts,some(N1,
            T0=[T|Ts] and maxno(NO,T,N1) and maxnos(Ts,N1,N)
            )))
    ).

gt(N,NO) <=>
    some(N1, N=s(N1) and ( NO=0 or some(N2, NO=s(N2) and gt(N1,N2) ))).

% If no renumbering at root of moved category was needed, use NO;
%    otherwise, use NO+1
newnumber(Renumbering,NewNumber) <=>
    (   some(NO, Renumbering = x/NO  and NewNumber=NO)
    or  ~some(NO,Renumbering=x/NO) and
        some(OldNo,some(NO, Renumbering = OldNo/NO and NewNumber=s(NO)))
    ).
```

```
% if there is an adjunction structure at the root, renumber it
renumber(Tree0,Tree,Renumbering) <=>
   some(L,some(C,some(N,some(F,some(Seq0,
      Tree0=x(L,C,N,F)/Seq0 and
      (   some(L1,some(C1,some(F1,some(Seq1,some(No,some(Seq,
            member(x(L1,C1,N,F1)/Seq1,Seq0) and
            Renumbering = N/No  and
            renumber_trees(Seq0,Seq,N/No) and
            Tree=x(L,C,No,F)/Seq
            ))))))
      or   ~some(L1,some(C1,some(F1,some(Seq1,
               member(x(L1,C1,N,F1)/Seq1,Seq0) )))) and
            Renumbering = x/N and
            Tree=Tree0
      )
   ))))).

renumber_tree(Tree0,Tree,Renumbering) <=>
   some(L,some(C,some(N,some(F,some(Seq0,
      Tree0=x(L,C,N,F)/Seq0 and
      (   some(No,
            Renumbering = N/No and
            renumber_trees(Seq0,Seq,Renumbering) and
            Tree=x(L,C,No,F)/Seq
            )
      or  ~some(No, Renumbering = N/No ) and
            Tree=Tree0
      ) ))))).

renumber_trees(Seq0,Seq,Renumbering) <=>
   (   Seq0=[] and
       Seq=[]
   or  some(T0,some(T0s,some(T,some(Ts,
          Seq0=[T0|T0s] and
          renumber_tree(T0,T,Renumbering) and
          renumber_trees(T0s,Ts,Renumbering) and
          Seq=[T|Ts]
       ))))
   ).


%%%%% Section 8.2

dominates(B,A,Tree) <=>
   every(Segment, (Segment = B) => ancestor(Segment,A,Tree) ).

c_commands(A,B,Tree) <=>
   ~ dominates(A,B,Tree) and
   every(Sigma,every(T1,every(T2,every(Ts,
   subtree(Sigma/[T1,T2|Ts],Tree) and
   dominates(Sigma,A,Sigma/[T1,T2|Ts])
     => dominates(Sigma,B,Sigma/[T1,T2|Ts])
   )))).

m_commands(A,B,Tree) <=>
   ~ dominates(A,B,Tree) and
   every(Sigma,
      ( dominates(Sigma,A,Tree) and maximal(Sigma) )
      => dominates(Sigma,B,Tree)  ).

/*** revised in Section 9.3, below
```

```
excludes(A,B,Tree) <=>
    ~ some(Segment,
          Segment = A and
          ancestor(Segment,B,Tree)
       ).
***/

imm_dominates(S,D,Tree) <=>
    maximal(S) and
    maximal(D) and
    dominates(S,D,Tree) and
    ~ some(Max,
          maximal(Max) and
          ancestor(S,Max,Tree) and
          ancestor(Max,D,Tree)
       ).

%%%%%% Section 8.3

binds(A,B,T) <=>
    ~ A=B and
    some(I,
        feature(index:I,A,A) and
        feature(index:I,B,B)
       ) and
    c_commands(A,B,T).

locally_binds(A,B,T) <=>
    some(G,
       binds(A,G,T) and
       binds(G,B,T)
      ).

%%%%%% Section 8.4

/*** this is revised to use lexical/2 in Section 10.2, below
sisters(A,B,Tree) <=>
    every(S, lexical(S) => ( dominates(S,A,Tree) <=> dominates(S,B,Tree) )).
***/

directly_th_marks(A,B,Tree) <=>
    sisters(A,B,Tree) and
    some(Theta,some(I,
         feature(th:Theta,A,A) and
         feature(index:I,B,B) and
         member(I,Theta)
        )).

th_governs(A,B,Tree) <=>
    minimal(A) and
    directly_th_marks(A,B,Tree).

/*** revised in Section 10.2, below
l_marks(A,B,Tree) <=>
    lexical(A) and
    some(G,
        th_governs(A,G,Tree) and
        (    B=G
        or   head_xp(B,G,Tree)
        or   specifier(B,G,Tree)
        ) ).
```

```
***/

%%%%% Section 8.5

blocking_cat(S,B,Tree) <=>
    maximal(S) and
    ~some(L,
        l_marks(L,S,Tree) and
        dominates(S,B,Tree)
    ).

barrier(S,B,Tree) <=>
    (   some(D,
            imm_dominates(S,D,Tree) and
            blocking_cat(D,B,Tree)
        )
    or  blocking_cat(S,B,Tree) and
        ~some(N,some(F, S=x(s(s(0)),i,N,F) ))
    ).

/*** revised in Section 10.3
governs(A,B,Tree) <=>
    m_commands(A,B,Tree) and
    ~some(S,
        barrier(S,B,Tree) and
        excludes(S,A,Tree)
    ).
***/

%%%%% Section 9.1

subst_conds(Moved,Landing) <=>
    some(Cat,some(N,some(F,some(N1,some(F1,
        (   Landing=x(s(s(0)),Cat,N,F) and
            Moved=x(s(s(0)),Cat,N1,F1)
        or  minimal(Moved) and
            minimal(Landing)
        )
    ))))).

/*** revised in Section 9.4
adjoin_conds(Moved,Landing,Tree) <=>
        (   maximal(Moved) and
            maximal(Landing) and
            ~ argument(Landing,Tree)
        or  minimal(Moved) and
            minimal(Landing)
        ).
***/

%%%%% Section 9.2

/*** replaced by affectA in Section 10.1 below
moveA(Tree0,Tree) <=> some(Moved,some(Landing,some(Renumbering,
    new_occurrence_number(Tree0,Renumbering) and
    (   substitute(Tree0,Tree,Moved,Landing,Renumbering) and
        subst_conds(Moved,Landing)
    or  adjoin(Tree0,Tree,Moved,Landing,Renumbering) and
        adjoin_conds(Moved,Landing,Tree)
    ) and
    renumbering(Moved0,Moved,Renumbering) and
```

```
      hmc(Moved0,Landing,Tree)
      ))).
***/

renumbering(Moved0,Moved,Renumbering) <=>
    some(L,some(C,some(N,some(F,some(N1,
        Moved0=x(L,C,N,F) and
        (   some(N1, Renumbering = x/N1 and Moved0=Moved )
        or some(N1, Renumbering=N/N1 and Moved=x(L,C,N1,F) )
        ) )))))).

hmc(Moved,Landing,Tree) <=>
        (       maximal(Moved)
        or      some(Max,some(L,some(C,some(N,some(F,some(F1,some(G,
                    head_xp(Landing,Max,Tree)   and
                    Moved=x(L,C,N,F)   and
                    head_xp(x(L,C,N,F1),G,Tree)   and
                    governs(Landing,G,Tree)   and
                    (       some(N2,some(F2, Landing = x(0,c,N2,F2)))
                    or      (       th_governs(Landing,G,Tree)
                            or      l_marks(Landing,G,Tree)
                            )
                    )
                )))))))
        ).

adjoin_cat(Moved,Landing,Tree0,Tree,Renumbering) <=>
    some(L0,some(C0,some(N0,some(F0,some(Seq0,
        Tree0 = x(L0,C0,N0,F0)/Seq0 and
        (   some(Seq,some(Pos,some(Selected,some(RestSeq,some(Transformed,
                select(Pos,Seq0,Selected,RestSeq) and
                adjoin_cat(Moved,Landing,Selected,Transformed,Renumbering) and
                select(Pos,Seq,Transformed,RestSeq)   and
                Tree = x(L0,C0,N0,F0)/Seq
                )))))
        or some(L,some(C,some(N,some(F,some(Seq,some(N2,some(Root,
            some(Tree1,some(Seq1,
                Moved=x(L,C,N,F)/Seq   and
                amalgamate(x(L,C,N,F),Tree0,Root,Tree1)   and
                newnumber(Renumbering,N2) and
                (       Seq  =  [x(L,C,N2,F)/Seq1,Tree1]
                or      Seq  =  [Tree1,x(L,C,N2,F)/Seq1]
                ) and
                Tree = Root/Seq   and
                Landing = Tree1
                )))))))))
        )
    ))))).

amalgamate(MRoot,Tree0,Root,Tree) <=>
    (       some(L,some(N,some(F,some(I,some(Root0,some(Affix,
            MRoot = x(L,v,N,F) and
            member(index:I,F) and
            Tree0 = Root0/[(-Affix)/[]] and
            feature(index:I,Root0,Root) and
            Tree = Root/[(-Affix)/[]]
            ))))))
    or     ~some(L,some(N,some(F,some(Affix,
            MRoot = x(L,v,N,F) and
            Tree0 = Root/[(-Affix)/[]] and
            Tree0 = Tree
```

```
        ))))
    ).

%%%%% Section 9.3

subjacency(Tree) <=>
    every(A,every(B,
        link(A,B,Tree) => n_subjacent(s(0),B,A,Tree,[])
    )).

/*** revised in Section 9.5, below
n_subjacent(N,Moved,Landing,Tree,L) <=>
    (   ~some(Barrier,
            barrier(Barrier,Moved,Tree) and
            ~member(Barrier,L) and
            excludes(Barrier,Landing,Tree)
        )
    or  some(N1,some(Barrier,
            N1=s(N) and
            barrier(Barrier,Moved,Tree) and
            ~ member(Barrier,L) and
            excludes(Barrier,Landing,Tree) and
            n_subjacent(N1,Moved,Landing,Tree,[Barrier|L])
        ))
    ).
***/

link(A,B,Tree) <=> locally_binds(A,B,Tree) and subtree(B/[],Tree).

excludes(A,B,Tree) <=>
    ~ A = B and
    ~ some(Segment,
        Segment = A and
        ancestor(Segment,B,Tree)
    ).

%%%%% Section 9.4

adjoin_conds(Moved,Landing,Tree) <=>
    (   maximal(Moved) and
        maximal(Landing) and
        ~ argument(Landing,Tree) and
        ~ wh_ip_violation(Moved,Landing)
    or  minimal(Moved) and
        minimal(Landing)
    ).

wh_ip_violation(Moved,Landing) <=>
    some(N,some(F,
        Landing=x(s(s(0)),i,N,F) and
        feature(wh:'+',Moved,Moved)
    )).

%%%%% Section 9.5

n_subjacent(N,Moved,Landing,Tree,L) <=>
    (   ~some(Barrier,
            (   barrier(Barrier,Moved,Tree)
            or  extra_barrier(Barrier,Moved,Tree)
            ) and
            ~member(Barrier,L) and
```

```
            excludes(Barrier,Landing,Tree)
          ) and
          previously_n_subjacent(N,Landing,Tree,[])
    or  some(N1,some(Barrier,
            N1=s(N) and
            (     barrier(Barrier,Moved,Tree)
            or    extra_barrier(Barrier,Moved,Tree)
            ) and
            ~ member(Barrier,L) and
            excludes(Barrier,Landing,Tree) and
            n_subjacent(N1,Moved,Landing,Tree,[Barrier|L])
      ))
    ).

extra_barrier(Barrier,A,Tree)  <=>
    (    extra_BC(Barrier,A,Tree)
    or   some(D,
            imm_dominates(Barrier,D,Tree) and
            extra_BC(D,A,Tree)
         )
    ).

extra_BC(Barrier,A,Tree) <=>
    some(Cat,some(N,some(F,
        bounding_parameter(Cat) and
        Barrier=x(s(s(0)),Cat,N,F) and
        dominates(Barrier,A,Tree) and
        ~ some(N1,some(F1,
            dominates(x(s(s(0)),Cat,N,F),x(s(s(0)),Cat,N1,F1),Tree)
            ))
     ))) and
    tensed(Barrier,Tree).

% This is an English-specific parameter setting
bounding_parameter(X) <=> X=i.

previously_n_subjacent(N,Moved,Tree,L) <=>
    (    some(Landing,
            link(Landing,Moved,Tree) and
            n_subjacent(N,Moved,Landing,Tree,L)
         )
    or   ~some(Landing,link(Landing,Moved,Tree))
    ).

tensed(Cat,Tree) <=> some(Head,some(Seq,some(N,some(F,
    head_xp(Head,Cat/Seq,Tree) and
    (    Cat = x(s(s(0)),i,N,F) and
         feature(finite:'+',Head,Head)
    or   Cat = x(s(s(0)),c,N,F)   and
         some(IN,some(IF,
            sisters(Head,x(s(s(0)),i,IN,IF),Tree) and
            tensed(x(s(s(0)),i,IN,IF),Tree)
         ))
    )
    )))).

%%%%% Section 10.1

deleteA(Tree0,Tree,DRoot) <=>
    some(Node,some(Seq0,some(Seq,some(Pos,some(Selected,some(RestSeq,
        Tree0 = Node/Seq0  and
```

```
            Tree = Node/Seq  and
            select(Pos,Seq0,Selected,RestSeq)  and
            (    some(Transformed,
                     deleteA(Selected,Transformed,DRoot)  and
                     select(Pos,Seq,Transformed,RestSeq)
                )
            or   RestSeq=Seq and
                     some(Seq1, Selected=DRoot/Seq1)
            )
            )))))).

delete_conds(A,Tree)<=>
        (    subtree(A,Tree)
        or   subtree(A/[that/[]],Tree)
        ).

affectA(Tree0,Tree)<=> some(Moved,some(Landing,some(Renumbering,
        (    new_occurrence_number(Tree0,Renumbering) and
             (          substitute(Tree0,Tree,Moved,Landing,Renumbering) and
                        subst_conds(Moved,Landing)
             or         adjoin(Tree0,Tree,Moved,Landing,Renumbering) and
                        adjoin_conds(Moved,Landing,Tree)
             ) and
             renumbering(Moved0,Moved,Renumbering) and
             hmc(Moved0,Landing,Tree)
        or   deleteA(Tree0,Tree,Moved) and
             delete_conds(Moved,Tree0)
        ) ))).

affectAn(Tree0,Tree) <=>
        (    Tree = Tree0
        or   some(Tree1,
                affectA(Tree0,Tree1)  and
                affectAn(Tree1,Tree)
             )
        ).

ss_gamma(Tree0,Tree,T) <=>
        some(Root0,some(Seq0,some(Root,some(Seq,
             Tree0 = Root0/Seq0 and
             Tree = Root/Seq and
             (    some(T0,some(Ts,
                      Seq0 = [T0|Ts] and
                      ss_sub_gamma([T0|Ts],Seq)
                  )) and
                  Root0=Root
             or   Seq0=[] and Seq0=Seq and
                  some(I,feature(index:I,Root0,Root0)) and
                  ~ feature(pronominal: '+',Root0,Root0) and
                  argument(Root0,T) and
                  (     some(A,properly_governs(A,Root0,T)) and
                        feature(gamma: '+',Root0,Root)
                  or    ~some(A,properly_governs(A,Root0,T)) and
                        feature(gamma: '-',Root0,Root)
                  )
             or   Seq0=[] and Seq0=Seq and
                  (    ~some(I,feature(index:I,Root0,Root0))
                  or   feature(pronominal: '+',Root0,Root0)
                  or   ~ argument(Root0,T)
                  ) and
                  Root0 = Root
```

```
        )
    )))).
ss_sub_gamma(Seq0,Seq,T) <=>
    (      Seq0 = [] and
           Seq = []
    or     some(A,some(As,some(B,some(Bs,
              Seq0 = [A|As] and
              ss_gamma(A,B,T) and
              ss_sub_gamma(As,Bs,T) and
              Seq = [B|Bs]
           ))))
    ).

lf_gamma(Tree0,Tree,T) <=>
    some(Root0,some(Seq0,some(Root,some(Seq,
        Tree0 = Root0/Seq0 and
        Tree = Root/Seq and
        (      some(T0,some(Ts,
                  Seq0 = [T0|Ts] and
                  lf_sub_gamma([T0|Ts],Seq)
                  )) and
               Root0=Root
        or     Seq0=[] and Seq0=Seq and
               some(Value, feature(gamma:Value,Root0,Root0)) and
               Root0=Root
        or     Seq0=[] and Seq0=Seq and
               some(I,feature(index:I,Root0,Root0)) and
               ~ feature(pronominal: '+',Root0,Root0) and
               ~ some(Value, feature(gamma:Value,Root0,Root0)) and
               (      some(A,properly_governs(A,Root0,T)) and
                      feature(gamma: '+',Root0,Root)
               or     ~some(A,properly_governs(A,Root0,T)) and
                      feature(gamma: '-',Root0,Root)
               )
        or     Seq0=[] and Seq0=Seq and
               (  ~some(I,feature(index:I,Root0,Root0)) or
                  feature(pronominal: '+',Root0,Root0)
               ) and
               Root0 = Root
        )
    )))).

lf_sub_gamma(Seq0,Seq,T) <=>
    (      Seq0 = [] and
           Seq = []
    or     some(A,some(As,some(B,some(Bs,
              Seq0 = [A|As] and
              lf_gamma(A,B,T) and
              lf_sub_gamma(As,Bs,T) and
              Seq = [B|Bs]
           ))))
    ).

%%%%% Section 10.2

/*** revised in Section 10.5, below
properly_governs(A,B,Tree) <=>
    (      th_governs(A,B,Tree)
    or     ante_governs(A,B,Tree)
    ).
```

```
***/

/*** revised in Section 10.5, below
ante_governs(A,B,Tree) <=>
    link(A,B,Tree) and
    governs(A,B,Tree).
***/

%%%%% Section 10.3

lexical(Node,Tree) <=>
    some(L,some(Cat,some(N,some(F,
        Node=x(L,Cat,N,F) and
        (     member(Cat,[v,n,a,p])
        or    Cat=i and
              some(I,some(N1,some(F1,some(Sub,
                  member(index:I,F) and
                  subtree(x(0,v,N1,F1)/Sub,Tree) and
                  member(index:I,F1)
              ))))
        )
    )))).

l_marks(A,B,Tree) <=>
    lexical(A,Tree) and
    some(G,
        th_governs(A,G,Tree) and
        (     B=G
        or    head_xp(B,G,Tree)
        or    specifier(B,G,Tree)
        )
    ).

sisters(A,B,Tree) <=>
    every(S, lexical(S,Tree) =>
            ( dominates(S,A,Tree) <=> dominates(S,B,Tree) )).

%%%%% Section 10.4

/*** revised in Section 10.5, below
minimal_barrier(S,B,Tree) <=>
    (     barrier(S,B,Tree)
    or    dominates(S,B,Tree) and
          some(D,
              parent(S,D,Tree) and
              minimal(D)   and
              ~ some(L,some(N,some(F, D=x(L,i,N,F) ))) and
              ~ D=B
          )
    ).
***/

governs(A,B,Tree) <=>
    m_commands(A,B,Tree) and
    ~some(S,
        minimal_barrier(S,B,Tree) and
        excludes(S,A,Tree)
    ).

%%%%% Section 10.5
```

```
minimal_barrier(S,B,Tree) <=>
    (   barrier(S,B,Tree)
    or  dominates(S,B,Tree) and
        some(D,
            parent(S,D,Tree) and
            minimal(D)  and
            ~ D=B and
            some(L,some(C,some(N,some(F,
                D=x(L,C,N,F) and
                ~C=i and
                ~ (F=[] and subtree(D/[],Tree))
            ))))
        )
    ).


%%%%% Section 10.6

% This definition has a disjunct for each of the following cases:
% 1. XP0 parent of a sequence of specifiers and an X1;
% 2. XP has no specifiers and is a parent of X and complements;
% 3. XP is empty;
% 4. XP is an adjunction structure
spec_head(XP0,XP) <=>
        some(C,some(N,some(F,some(Seq0,some(Pos,some(N1,some(F1,some(Seq1,
        some(Specs0,some(Pos1,some(Seq1,some(Head0,some(Comps0,
        some(N2,some(F2,some(Head,some(Specs1,some(Specs,some(Comps,
        some(Seq2,some(Seq,some(Adjunct0,some(Adjunct,
    (   XP0= x(s(s(0)),C,N,F)/Seq0 and
        select(Pos,Seq0,x(s(0),C,N1,F1)/Seq1,Specs0) and
        select(Pos1,Seq1,x(0,C,N2,F2)/Head0,Comps0) and
        agree(Specs0,Head0,Head,Specs1) and
        spec_heads(Specs1,Specs) and
        spec_heads(Comps0,Comps) and
        select(Pos1,Seq2,Head,Comps) and
        select(Pos,Seq,x(s(0),C,N1,F1)/Seq2,Specs) and
        XP=x(s(s(0)),C,N,F)/Seq
    or  XP0=x(s(s(0)),C,N,F)/Seq0 and
        ~ member(x(s(0),C,N1,F1)/Seq1,Seq0) and
        select(Pos1,Seq0,x(0,C,N2,F2)/Head,Comps0) and
        spec_heads(Comps0,Comps) and
        select(Pos1,Seq,Head,Comps) and
        XP=x(s(s(0)),C,N,F)/Seq
    or  XP0=x(s(s(0)),C,N,F)/[] and
        XP=x(s(s(0)),C,N,F)/[]
    or  XP0=x(s(s(0)),C,N,F)/Seq0  and
        select(Pos,Seq0,x(s(s(0)),C,N,F)/Seq1,Adjunct0) and
        spec_head(x(s(s(0)),C,N,F)/Seq1,x(s(s(0)),C,N,F)/Seq2) and
        spec_head(Adjunct0,Adjunct) and
        select(Pos,Seq,x(s(s(0)),C,N,F)/Seq2,Adjunct) and
        XP=x(s(s(0)),C,N,F)/Seq
    ) )))))))))))))))))))))))).


spec_heads(Seq0,Seq) <=>
        (   Seq0 = [] and  Seq = []
        or  some(T,some(Ts,some(A,some(As,
                    Seq0 = [T|Ts] and
                    spec_head(T,A) and
                    spec_heads(Ts,As) and
                    Seq = [A|As]
            ))))
        ).
```

```
agree(Seq0,X0,X,Seq) <=>
    some(Root0,some(Root,some(Ts,some(As,some(Head0,some(SeqH,
    some(Head,some(Head1,
      (   Seq0 = [] and
          Seq = [] and
          X0 = X
      or  (    Seq0 = [Root0/Seq|Ts] and
               Seq = [Root/Seq|As] and
               X0 = Head0/SeqH and
               X = Head/SeqH
          or       Seq0 = [Root0/Seq|Ts] and
               Seq = [Root/Seq|As] and
               X0 = Head0 and
               X = Head
          or       Seq0 = [Root0|Ts] and
               Seq = [Root|As] and
               X0 = Head0/Seq and
               X = Head/Seq
          or       Seq0 = [Root0|Ts] and
               Seq = [Root|As] and
               X0 = Head0 and
               X = Head
          ) and
          put_features(Head0,Root0,Head1) and
          agree(Ts,Head1,Head,As) and
          put_features(Root0,Head0,Root)
      ) )))))))).

%%%%% Section 10.7

properly_governs(A,B,Tree) <=> ante_governs(A,B,Tree).

ante_governs(A,B,Tree) <=>
        ex_link(A,B,Tree)   and
        governs(A,B,Tree).

ex_link(A,B,Tree) <=>
        (    link(A,B,Tree)
        or   some(I,
                feature(index:I,A,A) and
                feature(index:I,B,B)
                ) and
             ~ A = B
        ).
```

B.2   Inflectional phrases and head movement

```
% File : ip.fol
% Authors : E Stabler, Jr
% Updated : March, 1991
% Purpose : axioms inspired by Pollock (1989)

barrier(S,B,Tree) <=>
    (   some(D,
            imm_dominates(S,D,Tree)  and
            blocking_cat(D,B,Tree)
            )
    or  blocking_cat(S,B,Tree)  and
        ~some(N,some(F, S=x(s(s(0)),agr,N,F) ))
    ).

adjoin_cat(Moved,Landing,Tree0,Tree) <=>
    some(L0,some(C0,some(N0,some(F0,some(Seq0,
        Tree0 = x(L0,C0,N0,F0)/Seq0  and
        (   some(Seq,some(Pos,some(Selected,some(RestSeq,some(Transformed,
                select(Pos,Seq0,Selected,RestSeq) and
                adjoin_cat(Moved,Landing,Selected,Transformed) and
                select(Pos,Seq,Transformed,RestSeq)  and
                Tree = x(L0,C0,N0,F0)/Seq
            )))))
        or  some(L,some(C,some(N,some(F,some(Seq,some(N1,
                some(Root,some(Tree1,some(Seq1,
                    Moved=x(L,C,N,F)/Seq  and
                    ~N0=N  and
                    amalgamate(Moved,Tree0,Root/Tree1)  and
                    (     Seq  = [x(L,C,N1,F)/Seq1,Root/Tree1]
                    or    Seq  = [Root/Tree1,x(L,C,N1,F)/Seq1]
                    ) and
                    Tree = Root/Seq  and
                    Landing = Root
                )))))))))
        ) )))).

amalgamate(Moved,Tree0,Tree) <=>
    (   some(MRoot,some(Seq,some(I,some(Seq0,some(L,some(N,some(F,
        some(Root0,some(Root,some(Affix,
            Moved = MRoot/Seq  and
            feature(index:I,MRoot,MRoot)  and
            subtree(x(L,v,N,F)/Seq0,Moved)  and
            member(index:I,F)  and
            Tree0 = Root0/[(-Affix)/[]]  and
            feature(index:I,Root0,Root)  and
            Tree = Root/[(-Affix)/[]]
        )))))))))
    or  Tree0 = Tree
    ).

lexical(Node,Tree) <=> some(L,some(Cat,some(N,some(F,
    Node = x(L,Cat,N,F)  and
    (     member(Cat,[v,n,a,p])
    or    ~ member(Cat,[v,n,a,p]) and
        some(I,some(Root,some(Seq,
            member(index:I,F)  and
            subtree(Root/Seq,Tree)  and
            feature(index:I,Root,Root)
```

```
                        )))
                ) )))).

l_marks(A,B,Tree) <=>
     lexical(A,Tree)   and
     some(G,
          th_governs(A,G,Tree) and
          (      B = G
          or     head(B,G,Tree)
          or     specifier(B,G,Tree)
          or     some(L,some(N,some(F,
                   G = x(L,neg,N,F) and
                   complement(B,G,Tree)
                   )))
          ) ).

minimal_barrier(S,B,Tree) <=>
     (      barrier(S,B,Tree)
     or     dominates(S,B,Tree)   and
            some(D,
                 parent(S,D,Tree)   and
                 minimal(D)   and
                 ~ some(L,some(N,some(F, D = x(L,agr,N,F) ))) and
                 ~ some(L,some(N,some(F, D = x(L,neg,N,F) ))) and
                 ~ D = B
            )
     ).

/***
no_vacuous_ops(Tree) <=>
     ~some(Root,some(Seq,
          subtree(Root/Seq,Tree)   and
          feature(finite: '+',Root,Root)   and
          ~some(N,some(F, binds(Root,x(0,v,N,F),Tree) )) )).
***/

no_vacuous_ops(Tree) <=>
     ~some(Root,some(Seq,
          subtree(Root/Seq,Tree)   and
          feature(finite: '+',Root,Root)   and
          ~some(B, binds(Root,B,Tree) ) )).

lexical(Node,Tree) <=> some(L,some(C,some(N,some(F,
     Node = x(L,C,N,F)   and
     (      member(C,[v,n,a,p])
     or     some(Seq,some(N1,some(F1,some(Node1,some(Seq1,some(I,some(Seq2,
                 subtree(Node/Seq,Tree) and
                 (  imm_dominates(Node,x(0,v,N1,F1),Node/Seq) and
                    subtree(x(0,v,N1,F1)/Seq1,Node/Seq)
                 or member(index:I,F) and
                    subtree(Node1/Seq1,Tree) and
                    feature(index:I,Node1,Node1) and
                    imm_dominates(Node1,x(0,v,N1,F1),Node1/Seq1) and
                    subtree(x(0,v,N1,F1)/Seq2,Node1/Seq1)
                 ) )))))))
     ) )))).

hmc(Moved,Landing,Tree) <=>
     (      maximal(Moved)
     or     some(Seq,
                 subtree(Moved/Seq,Tree) and
```

```
              ( Seq=[] and some(Affix, Seq=[-Affix/[]] )) )
or      some(Max,some(C,some(N,some(F,some(F1,some(G,
             head_xp(Landing,Max,Tree)   and
             Moved=x(0,C,N,F)   and
             head_xp(x(0,C,N,F1),G,Tree)   and
             governs(Landing,G,Tree)   and
             (    some(N,some(F, Landing = x(0,c,N,F) ))
             or  (    th_governs(Landing,G,Tree)
                  or  l_marks(Landing,G,Tree)
                  )
             ) ))))))
   ).
```

B.3 VP-internal subjects

```
% File: vp.fol
% Author: Ed Stabler, Jr
% Date: May 1991
% Subject: axioms inspired by Sportiche and Koopman

i_commands(A,B,Tree) <=>
   every(Sigma,  dominates(Sigma,A,Tree) => dominates(Sigma,B,Tree) ).

governs(A,B,Tree) <=>
   i_commands(A,B,Tree)  and
   ~some(S,
      barrier(S,B,Tree)  and
      excludes(S,A,Tree)
   ).

l_marks(A,B,Tree) <=>
   complement(B,A,Tree) and
   some(L,some(C,some(N,some(F,
   A = x(L,C,N,F) and
   (   ~ C=c
   or    C=c and
         some(I,some(N1,some(F1,some(Sub,
         member(index:I,F) and
         subtree(x(0,v,N1,F1)/Sub,Tree) and
         member(index:I,F1)
   )))))))))).

l_dependent(B,Tree) <=>
   (   some(A, l_marks(A,B,Tree) )
   or  some(A,some(C,
         specifier(B,C,Tree) and
         l_marks(A,C,Tree)
         ))
   ).

barrier(YP,B,Tree) <=>
   maximal(YP) and
   ~ projection(YP,B,Tree)  and
   some(Yn,
      projection(YP,Yn,Tree)  and
      ~ l_dependent(Yn,Tree) and
      dominates(Yn,B,Tree)
      ).

projection(Node0,Node,Tree) <=>
 some(C,some(N,some(F,some(N1,some(F1,some(T,some(Ts,some(Pos,
 some(Seq0,some(Seq,
   (   Node0=Node
   or    Node0=x(0,C,N,F) and
         Node=x(s(0),C,N1,F1) and
         head_x1(Node0,Node,Tree)
   or    Node0=x(s(0),C,N1,F1) and
         Node=x(0,C,N,F) and
         head_x1(Node,Node0,Tree)
   or    Node0=x(0,C,N,F) and
         Node=x(s(s(0)),C,N1,F1) and
         head_xp(Node0,Node,Tree)
   or    Node0=x(s(s(0)),C,N1,F1) and
```

```
          Node= x(0,C,N,F) and
          head_xp(Node,Node0,Tree)
     or   Node0=x(s(0),C,N1,F1) and
          Node=x(s(s(0)),C,N,F) and
          subtree(Node/[T|Ts],Tree) and
          head_spec(Pos) and
          separate(Pos,Node0/Seq0,[T|Ts],Seq)
     or   Node0=x(s(s(0)),C,N,F) and
          Node=x(s(0),C,N1,F1) and
          subtree(Node0/[T|Ts],Tree) and
          head_spec(Pos) and
          separate(Pos,x(s(0),C,N1,F1)/Seq0,[T|Ts],Seq)
     )
  ))))))))))).

adjoin_conds(Moved,Landing) <=>
    (   maximal(Moved) and
        maximal(Landing) and
        nonargument(Landing)
    or  minimal(Moved) and
        minimal(Landing)
    ).

nonargument(Node) <=> some(L,some(C,some(N,some(F,
     Node=x(L,C,N,F) and
     ( C=v or  C=a or  C=i ) )))).

ccl(Tree) <=> ~some(Node,some(I,
     subtree(Node/[],Tree) and
     feature(index: I,Node,Node) and
     ~ feature(pronominal: +,Node,Node) and
     ~ some(B,
        binds(B,Node,Tree) and
        governs(B,Node,Tree)
        ) )).
```

Appendix C

A guided proof system

*It is perhaps surprising to notice that even in the rarefied language
of purely recursive programs there is a sharp contrast between programs
written for maximal clarity and those written for tolerable efficiency.*
— *R.M. Burstall and J. Darlington*

We present Prolog implementations here that depart as little from the first order formalizations as possible. In consequence, they are still quite inefficient, but usable on small trees. As noted in §13, much greater efficiency can be obtained if one is willing to move further from the first order formalization.

We present Barriers theory first, followed by the variations on it. The user guidance system is also rather minimal, but provides an indication of how one might proceed towards a useful research tool.

C.1 The Barriers theory

The notation is that of Edinburgh Prolog. This implementation was developed in Quintus Prolog 2.4.2. The utility programs for collecting input (guidance from the user) and for displaying trees have no particular theoretical interest, and so we do not show them here, though they are used in the definition of *affectA*. Their names provide a rough indication of what they do.[1]

```
% File : las.pl
% Authors : E Stabler, Jr
% Updated : January, 1991
% Purpose : a guided derivation system for BARRIERS

eg(X) :- figure(X,T),pp_term(T),affectAn(T,_),fail.

%%%%%% Section 4.2
% To be usable at all, basic predicates on nodes and trees must be "hacked"
%    for Prolog, since they are used so frequently in proofs.
% The relations defined by linguists can then be kept closer to their
%    original forms.

subtree(Tree,Tree).
subtree(Sub,_/Seq) :- member(Sub1,Seq),subtree(Sub,Sub1).
```

```prolog
member(Element,[Element|_]).
member(Element,[_|Seq]) :- member(Element,Seq).

% This is inefficient when Parent is unspecified
parent(Parent,Node,Tree) :-
    subtree(Parent/Seq,Tree),
    member(Node/_,Seq).

ancestor(Anc,Node,Root/Seq) :-
    var(Anc), nonvar(Node),!,
    path(Node,Root/Seq,[],Path),
    member(Anc,Path).

% This is inefficent when first arg of parent is unspecified!!
ancestor(Anc,Node,Tree) :- parent(Anc,Node,Tree).
ancestor(Anc,Node,Tree) :- parent(Anc,Mid,Tree),ancestor(Mid,Node,Tree).

% path(Node,Root/Seq,Path): Path is nodes from Node to Root (excluding Node)
path(Node,Node/_,P,P).
path(Node,Root/Seq,P0,P) :- member(Tree,Seq),path(Node,Tree,[Root|P0],P).

%%%%% Section 6.3

feature(Attribute:Value,x(L,C,N,F0),x(L,C,N,F)) :-
    (    member(Attribute:Value,F0),F=F0
    ;    \+member(Attribute:_,F0),F=[Attribute:Value|F0]
    ).

%% lexical/1 replaced by lexical/2 in Section 10.3

maximal(x(s(s(0)),_C,_N,_F)).
minimal(x(0,_C,_N,_F)).

% language-specific parameter settings
head_spec(0).        % head follows specifiers
head_compl(s(0)).    % head precedes complements

separate(0,Head,List,Remainder) :- last(Head,List,Remainder).
separate(s(0),Head,[Head|Remainder],Remainder).

last(E,[E1,E2|Rest],[E1|Remainder]) :- last(E,[E2|Rest],Remainder).
last(E,[E],[]).

xps([]).
xps([Tree|Seq]) :- xp(Tree),xps(Seq).

x0(x(0,_C,_N,[])/[]).
x0(x(0,C,_N,F)/[Word/[]]) :- lexicon(Word,C,F).

lexicon(john,n,[]).
lexicon(-s,i,[]).
lexicon(read,v,[]).
lexicon(with,p,[]).
lexicon(mary,n,[]).

x1(x(s(0),Cat,_N,_F)/Subtrees) :-
    head_compl(Position),
    separate(Position,x(0,Cat,N0,F0)/L,Subtrees,Remainder),
    xps(Remainder),
    x0(x(0,Cat,N0,F0)/L).
x1(x(s(0),Cat,N,F)/[x(s(0),Cat,N,F)/L,XP]) :-
```

```
    x1(x(s(0),Cat,N,F)/L),
    xp(XP).
x1(x(s(0),Cat,N,F)/[XP,x(s(0),Cat,N,F)/L]) :-
    x1(x(s(0),Cat,N,F)/L),
    xp(XP).

xp(x(s(s(0)),_,_,_)/[]).
xp(x(s(s(0)),Cat,_,_)/[T|Ts]) :-
    head_spec(Pos),
    separate(Pos,x(s(0),Cat,Nn,Fn)/L,[T|Ts],Rem),
    xps(Rem),
    x1(x(s(0),Cat,Nn,Fn)/L).
xp(x(s(s(0)),Cat,_,_)/[T|Ts]) :-
    head_compl(Pos),
    separate(Pos,x(0,Cat,Nn,Fn)/L,[T|Ts],Rem),
    xps(Rem),
    x0(x(0,Cat,Nn,Fn)/L).
xp(x(s(s(0)),Cat,N,F)/[x(s(s(0)),Cat,N,F)/L,XP1]) :-
    xp(x(s(s(0)),Cat,N,F)/L),
    xp(XP1).
xp(x(s(s(0)),Cat,N,F)/[XP1,x(s(s(0)),Cat,N,F)/L]) :-
    xp(x(s(s(0)),Cat,N,F)/L),
    xp(XP1).

head_xp(x(0,Cat,N0,F0),x(s(s(0)),Cat,N2,F2),Tree) :-
    subtree(x(s(s(0)),Cat,N2,F2)/Seq1,Tree),
    (    member(x(s(0),Cat,N1,F1)/Seq0,Seq1),
         head_x1(x(0,Cat,N0,F0),x(s(0),Cat,N1,F1),x(s(0),Cat,N1,F1)/Seq0)
    ;    member(x(0,Cat,N0,F0)/_,Seq1)
    ;    member(x(s(s(0)),Cat,N2,F2)/L,Seq1),
         head_xp(x(0,Cat,N0,F0),x(s(s(0)),Cat,N2,F2),x(s(s(0)),Cat,N2,F2)/L)
    ).

head_x1(x(0,Cat,N0,F0),x(s(0),Cat,N1,F1),Tree) :-
    subtree(x(s(0),Cat,N1,F1)/Seq1,Tree),
    (    member(x(0,Cat,N0,F0)/_,Seq1)
    ;    member(x(s(0),Cat,N1,F1)/L,Seq1),
         head_x1(x(0,Cat,N0,F0),x(s(0),Cat,N1,F1),x(s(0),Cat,N1,F1)/L)
    ).

% three cases: complement of X, of X1, of XP
complement(Complement,x(0,Cat,N,F),Tree) :-
    subtree(_/Subtrees,Tree),
    head_compl(Position),
    separate(Position,x(0,Cat,N,F)/_,Subtrees,Remainder),
    member(Complement/_,Remainder).
complement(Complement,x(s(0),Cat,N,F),Tree) :-
    head_x1(X,x(s(0),Cat,N,F),Tree),
    complement(Complement,X,Tree).
complement(Complement,x(s(s(0)),Cat,N,F),Tree) :-
    head_xp(X,x(s(s(0)),Cat,N,F),Tree),
    complement(Complement,X,Tree).

% three cases: complement of X, of X1, of XP
specifier(Specifier,x(s(s(0)),Cat,N,F),Tree) :-
    subtree(x(s(s(0)),Cat,N,F)/[T|Ts],Tree),
    head_spec(Pos),
    separate(Pos,x(s(0),Cat,_,_)/_,[T|Ts],Remainder),
    member(Specifier/_,Remainder).
specifier(Specifier,x(s(0),Cat,N,F),Tree) :-
    subtree(x(s(s(0)),Cat,_,_)/[T|Ts],Tree),
```

```
      head_spec(Pos),
      separate(Pos,x(s(0),Cat,N,F)/_,[T|Ts],Remainder),
      member(Specifier/_,Remainder).
specifier(Specifier,x(0,Cat,N,F),Tree) :-
      subtree(x(s(s(0)),Cat,_,_)/[T|Ts],Tree),
      head_spec(Pos),
      separate(Pos,x(s(0),Cat,Nn,Fn)/_,[T|Ts],Remainder),
      member(Specifier/_,Remainder),
      head_x1(x(0,Cat,N,F),x(s(0),Cat,Nn,Fn),Tree).


figure(6-3, ip/[np/[john/[]],i1/[vp/[reads/[]]]] ).
figure(6.10,
 x(s(s(0)),i,1,[]) /[
  x(s(s(0)),n,2,[]) /[
    x(0,n,5,[]) /[ john/[] ]],
  x(s(0),i,3,[]) /[
    x(0,i,6,[])/[(-s)/[]],
    x(s(s(0)),v,4,[]) /[
      x(0,v,7,[]) /[ read/[] ]]]] ).

figure(6-11,
 x(s(s(0)),i,1,[]) /[
  x(s(s(0)),n,2,[]) /[
    x(0,n,5,[]) /[ john/[] ]],
  x(s(0),i,3,[]) /[
    x(0,i,6,[])/[(-s)/[]],
    x(s(s(0)),v,4,[]) /[
      x(0,v,8,[]) /[ read/[] ],
      x(s(s(0)),p,9,[])/[
        x(0,p,12,[])/[with/[]],
        x(s(s(0)),n,10,[]) /[
          x(0,n,11,[]) /[ mary/[] ]]]]]] ).

figure(6-12,
 x(s(s(0)),i,1,[]) /[
  x(s(s(0)),n,2,[]) /[
    x(0,n,5,[]) /[ john/[] ]],
  x(s(0),i,3,[]) /[
    x(0,i,6,[])/[(-s)/[]],
    x(s(s(0)),v,4,[]) /[
      x(s(0),v,7,[]) /[
      x(s(0),v,7,[]) /[
        x(0,v,8,[]) /[ read/[] ]],
        x(s(s(0)),p,9,[])/[
          x(0,p,12,[])/[with/[]],
          x(s(s(0)),n,10,[]) /[
            x(0,n,11,[]) /[ mary/[] ]]]]]]] ).

figure(6-13,
 x(s(s(0)),i,1,[]) /[
  x(s(s(0)),n,2,[]) /[
    x(0,n,5,[]) /[ john/[] ]],
  x(s(0),i,3,[]) /[
    x(0,i,6,[])/[(-s)/[]],
    x(s(s(0)),v,4,[]) /[
      x(s(s(0)),v,4,[]) /[
        x(0,v,8,[]) /[ read/[] ]],
        x(s(s(0)),p,9,[])/[
          x(0,p,12,[])/[with/[]],
          x(s(s(0)),n,10,[]) /[
            x(0,n,11,[]) /[ mary/[] ]]]]]] ).
```

```
%%%%% Section 7.2 %%% Movement definitions

substitute(Node/Seq0,Node/Seq,MRoot,Landing,Renumbering) :-
    select(Position1,Seq0,Selected1,RestSeq1),
    (    substitute(Selected1,Transformed,MRoot,Landing,Renumbering),
        select(Position1,Seq,Transformed,RestSeq1)
    ;    select(Position2,RestSeq1,Selected2,RestSeq2),
        zero_cat(MRoot/Moved,Selected1,Transformed1,Renumbering),
        cat_zero(MRoot/Moved,Landing,Selected2,Transformed2),
        select(Position2,Seq1,Transformed2,RestSeq2),
        select(Position1,Seq,Transformed1,Seq1)
    ).

zero_cat(Moved,Node/[T0|T0s],Node/Seq,Renumbering) :-
        select(Position,[T0|T0s],Selected,RestSeq),
        zero_cat(Moved,Selected,Transformed,Renumbering),
        select(Position,Seq,Transformed,RestSeq).

zero_cat(Node2/Seq2,x(L,C,N,F)/Seq,Node/[],Renumbering):-
        feature(index:I,x(L,C,N,F),Node1),
    renumber(Node1/Seq,Node2/Seq2,Renumbering),
        take_features(Node1,Node),
        ( I=N ; x=x ).

visible(Node) :- ( maximal(Node) ; minimal(Node) ).

take_features(x(L,C,N,[]),x(L,C,N,[])).
take_features(x(L,C,N,[H|F0]),x(L,C,N,[H|F])) :-
    phi(H),
    take_features(x(L,C,N,F0),x(L,C,N,F)).
take_features(x(L,C,N,[H|F0]),x(L,C,N,F)) :-
    \+ phi(H),
    take_features(x(L,C,N,F0),x(L,C,N,F)).

phi(person:_).
phi(number:_).
phi(case:_).
phi(wh:_).
phi(index:_).
phi(th:_).
phi(finite:_).

cat_zero(Moved,Landing,Node/[T0|T0s],Node/Seq) :-
    select(Position,[T0|T0s],Selected,RestSeq),
    cat_zero(Moved,Landing,Selected,Transformed),
    select(Position,Seq,Transformed, RestSeq).

cat_zero(Node2/Seq,Node,Node0/[],Node/Seq) :-
    feature(index:I,Node0,Node1),
    feature(index:I,Node2,Node2),
    put_features(Node1,Node2,Node).

% put_features(A,B,C) = C is the result of giving all features of B to A
put_features(x(L,C,N,F),x(_,_,_,[]),x(L,C,N,F)).
put_features(Node0,x(_,_,_,[H|F0]),Node) :-
    psi(H),
    feature(H,Node0,Node1),
    put_features(Node1,x(_,_,_,F0),Node).
put_features(Node0,x(_,_,_,[H|F0]),Node) :-
    \+psi(H),
```

```
        put_features(Node0,x(_,_,_,F0),Node).

psi(pronominal:_).
psi(person:_).
psi(number:_).
psi(case:_).
psi(wh:_).
psi(index:_).

%%% subst_conds/2 modified in Section 9.1

adjoin(Node/Seq0,Node/Seq,MRoot,LRoot,Dir,Renumbering) :-
    select(Position,Seq0,Selected,RestSeq),
    (      adjoin(Selected,Transformed,MRoot,LRoot,Dir,Renumbering),
        select(Position,Seq,Transformed,RestSeq)
    ;   zero_cat(MRoot/Moved,Selected,Transformed,Renumbering),
        select(Position,Seq1,Transformed,RestSeq),
        adjoin_cat(MRoot/Moved,LRoot,Node/Seq1,Node/Seq,Dir,Renumbering)
    ).

%%% adjoin_conds/3 modified in Section 9.1

argument(x(s(s(0)),C,N,F),T) :-
    (C=n ; C=c ; C=i ; C=a),          % VPs are not args
    directly_th_marks(_,x(s(s(0)),C,N,F),T).
argument(Node,T) :-
    specifier(Node,x(0,i,_,_),T).

%%% adjoin_cat/4 modified in Section 9.2

%%% moveA/2 revised in Section 9.2, replaced by affectA/2 in Section 10.1

new_occurrence_no(Root/Seq,_/N) :-
    maxnode(1,Root,N0), maxnos(Seq,N0,N1), N is N1+1.

%%% moveAn/2 replaced by affectAn in Section 10.1

select(s(0),[Head|Tail],Head,Tail).
select(s(s(Position)),[Head|Tail],Element,[Head|Rest]) :-
    select(s(Position),Tail,Element,Rest).

% if there is an adjunction structure at the root, renumber it
renumber(x(L,C,N,F)/Seq,x(L,C,N,F)/Seq,x/_) :-
    \+ member(x(_,_,N,_)/_ , Seq), !.
renumber(x(L,C,N,F)/Seq0,x(L,C,No,F)/Seq,N/No) :-
    renumber_trees(Seq0,Seq,N/No).

renumber_tree(x(L,C,N,F)/Seq0,x(L,C,No,F)/Seq,N/No) :- !,
    renumber_trees(Seq0,Seq,N/No).
renumber_tree(T,T,_).

renumber_trees([],[],_).
renumber_trees([T0|T0s],[T|Ts],Substitution) :-
    renumber_tree(T0,T,Substitution),
    renumber_trees(T0s,Ts,Substitution).

maxno(N0,Root/Seq,N) :- maxnode(N0,Root,N1),maxnos(Seq,N1,N).
maxnos([],N,N).
maxnos([T|Ts],N0,N) :- maxno(N0,T,N1),maxnos(Ts,N1,N).
maxnode(N,x(_,_,X,_),N) :- var(X),!.
maxnode(N0,x(_,_,N,_),N) :- N>=N0,!.
```

```
maxnode(N0,Abbrev,N) :- Abbrev=..[_,N1,_],(integer(N1),N1>=N0,N=N1;N=N0),!.
maxnode(N,_,N).

figure(7-1,
 x(s(s(0)),i,1,[]) /[
  x(s(s(0)),n,2,[])/[],
  x(s(0),i,3,[]) /[
    x(0,i,4,[finite: +]) /[ was/[] ],
    x(s(s(0)),v,5,[]) /[
      x(0,v,6,[]) /[ 'kiss + -en'/[] ],
      x(s(s(0)),n,7,[]) /['the woman'/[] ]]]]
 ).

figure(7-2,
 x(s(s(0)),i,1,[]) /[
  x(s(s(0)),n,2,[]) /[ 'every spy'/[] ],
  x(s(0),i,3,[]) /[
    x(0,i,4,[finite:'+'])/[(-s)/[]],
    x(s(s(0)),v,5,[]) /[
      x(0,v,6,[]) /[ suspect/[] ],
      x(s(s(0)),n,7,[]) /[ 'some Russian'/[] ]]]]
 ).

%%%%% Section 8.2

dominates(B,A,Tree) :-
    A=x(_,_,_,_),    % blocks probs with multiple ident leaves
    subtree(B/Seq,Tree),
    subtree(A/_,B/Seq),
    \+exists_non_dominating_segment(B,A,Tree).

exists_non_dominating_segment(B,A,Tree) :-
    subtree(B/Seq,Tree),
    \+subtree(A/_,xxx/Seq),!.

c_commands(A,B,Tree) :-
    subtree(A/_,Tree),
    subtree(B/_,Tree),
    \+dominates(A,B,Tree),
    \+distinguishing_branching_cat(_,A,B,Tree).

distinguishing_branching_cat(S,A,B,Tree) :-
    subtree(S/[T1,T2|Ts],Tree),
    dominates(S,A,S/[T1,T2|Ts]),
    \+dominates(S,B,S/[T1,T2|Ts]).

m_commands(A,B,Tree) :-
    subtree(B/_,Tree),
    subtree(A/_,Tree),
    \+dominates(A,B,Tree),
    \+distinguishing_maximal_cat(_,A,B,Tree).

distinguishing_maximal_cat(S,A,B,Tree) :-
    dominates(S,A,Tree),
    maximal(S),
    \+dominates(S,B,Tree).

% excludes/3 revised in Section 9.3, below

imm_dominates(x(s(s(0)),C,N,F),x(s(s(0)),C1,N1,F1),Tree) :-
    nonvar(N),nonvar(N1),!,
```

```
    subtree(x(s(s(0)),C,N,F)/Seq,Tree),
    path(x(s(s(0)),C1,N1,F1),x(s(s(0)),C,N,F)/Seq,[],Path),
    \+exists_intervening_max_in_path(Path),
    \+exists_non_dominating_segment(
        x(s(s(0)),C,N,F),x(s(s(0)),C1,N1,F1),Tree).

imm_dominates(x(s(s(0)),C,N,F),x(s(s(0)),C1,N1,F1),Tree) :-
    nonvar(N),var(N1),!,
    subtree(x(s(s(0)),C,N,F)/Seq,Tree),
    path_to_leaf(x(s(s(0)),C,N,F)/Seq,[],Path0),
    trim_to_max(Path0,[x(s(s(0)),C1,N1,F1),Next|Path]),
    \+exists_intervening_max_in_path([Next|Path]),
    \+exists_non_dominating_segment(
        x(s(s(0)),C,N,F),x(s(s(0)),C1,N1,F1),Tree).

imm_dominates(x(s(s(0)),C,N,F),x(s(s(0)),C1,N1,F1),Tree) :-
    var(N),nonvar(N1),!,
    path(x(s(s(0)),C1,N1,F1),Tree,[],Path0),
    trim_to_first_max(Path0,[x(s(s(0)),C,N,F)|_]),
    subtree(x(s(s(0)),C,N,F)/Seq,Tree),
    \+exists_intervening_max(
        x(s(s(0)),C,N,F),x(s(s(0)),C1,N1,F1),x(s(s(0)),C,N,F)/Seq),
    \+exists_non_dominating_segment(
        x(s(s(0)),C,N,F),x(s(s(0)),C1,N1,F1),Tree).

imm_dominates(x(s(s(0)),C,N,F),x(s(s(0)),C1,N1,F1),Tree) :-
    subtree(x(s(s(0)),C,N,F)/Seq,Tree),
    subtree(x(s(s(0)),C1,N1,F1)/_,x(s(s(0)),C,N,F)/Seq),
    \+x(s(s(0)),C1,N1,F1)=x(s(s(0)),C,N,F),
    \+exists_intervening_max(
        x(s(s(0)),C,N,F),x(s(s(0)),C1,N1,F1),x(s(s(0)),C,N,F)/Seq),
    \+exists_non_dominating_segment(
        x(s(s(0)),C,N,F),x(s(s(0)),C1,N1,F1),Tree).

% path_to_leaf(Root/Seq,Path): Path is nodes from Node to terminal Leaf
%    (including Leaf) Fails when leaf is nonterminal.
path_to_leaf(Root/Seq,P0,P) :-
    member(Tree,Seq),
    path_to_leaf(Tree,[Root|P0],P).
path_to_leaf(Node,P,[Node/[]|P]).

% remove some initial segment up to a maximal node
trim_to_max([Node|Rest],[Node|Rest]) :-
    maximal(Node).
trim_to_max([_Node|Rest],Path) :-
    trim_to_max(Rest,Path).

trim_to_first_max([Node|Rest],[Node|Rest]) :-
    maximal(Node), !.
trim_to_first_max([_Node|Rest],Path) :-
    trim_to_first_max(Rest,Path).

% We know that last element of Path is a maximal ancestor;
% we test for an *intervening* maximal node
exists_intervening_max_in_path([Node,Next|Rest]) :-
    (    maximal(Node)
    ;    exists_intervening_max_in_path([Next|Rest])
    ), !.

exists_intervening_max(S,D,Tree) :-
    subtree(S/Seq,Tree),
```

```
        path(D,S/Seq,[],Path),
        exists_intervening_max_in_path(Path).

%%%%% Section 8.3

binds(A,B,T) :-
        subtree(A/_,T),
        feature(index:I,A,A),
        subtree(B/_,T),
        \+ A=B,
        feature(index:I,B,B),
        c_commands(A,B,T).

locally_binds(A,B,T) :-
        binds(A,B,T),
        \+ intervening_binder(_,A,B,T).

intervening_binder(G,A,B,T) :-
        binds(A,G,T),
        binds(G,B,T).

%%%%% Section 8.4

sisters(A,B,Tree) :-
        subtree(A/_,Tree),
        subtree(B/_,Tree),
        \+distinguishing_lex_proj(_,A,B,Tree),
        \+distinguishing_lex_proj(_,B,A,Tree).

% distinguishing_lex_proj/3 is revised in Section 10.2

directly_th_marks(A,B,Tree) :-
        subtree(B/_,Tree),     % redundant -- reduces search
        feature(index:I,B,B),
        subtree(A/_,Tree),     % redundant -- reduces search
        feature(th:Theta,A,A),
        member(I,Theta),
        sisters(A,B,Tree).

th_governs(A,B,Tree) :-
        minimal(A),
        directly_th_marks(A,B,Tree).

% l_marks/3 revised in Section 10.3, below

%%%%% Section 8.5

blocking_cat(S,B,Tree) :-
        dominates(S,B,Tree) ,
        maximal(S),
        \+l_marks(_,S,Tree).

barrier(S,B,Tree) :-
        (    imm_dominates(S,D,Tree),
             blocking_cat(D,B,Tree)
        ;    blocking_cat(S,B,Tree),
             \+S=x(s(s(0)),i,_N,_F)
        ).

governs(A,B,Tree) :-
        m_commands(A,B,Tree),
```

```
        \+intervening_barrier(_,A,B,Tree).

/*** revised in Section 10.3
intervening_barrier(S,A,B,Tree) :-
    barrier(S,B,Tree),
    excludes(S,A,Tree).
***/

figure(8-8,
 x(s(s(0)),i,1,[]) /[
  x(s(s(0)),n,2,[index:2]) /[ john/[] ],
  x(s(0),i,3,[]) /[
    x(0,i,4,[finite: +]) /[ (-ed)/[] ],
    x(s(s(0)),v,5,[]) /[
      x(0,v,6,[th:[2,7]]) /[ decide/[] ],
      x(s(s(0)),c,7,[index:7]) /[
        x(s(s(0)),n,8,[])/[],
        x(s(0),c,9,[]) /[
          x(0,c,10,[])/[],
          x(s(s(0)),i,11,[]) /[
            x(s(s(0)),n,12,[pronominal: +,anaphoric: +])/[],
            x(s(0),i,13,[]) /[
              x(0,i,14,[th:[15]])/[],
              x(s(s(0)),v,15,[index:15]) /[
                x(0,v,16,[th:[12,17]]) /[ see/[] ],
                x(s(s(0)),n,17,[index:17]) /[
                  'the movie'/[] ]]]]]]]]]    ).

figure(8-9,
 x(s(s(0)),c,1,[]) /[
  x(s(s(0)),n,2,[])/[],
  x(s(0),c,3,[]) /[
    x(0,c,4,[])/[],
    x(s(s(0)),i,5,[]) /[
      x(s(s(0)),n,6,[index:6]) /[ you/[] ],
      x(s(0),i,7,[]) /[
        x(0,i,8,[th:[9]]) /[ (-ed)/[] ],
        x(s(s(0)),v,9,[index:9]) /[
          x(0,v,10,[th:[6,11]]) /[ believe/[] ],
          x(s(s(0)),c,11,[index:11]) /[
            x(s(s(0)),n,12,[])/[],
            x(s(0),c,13,[]) /[
              x(0,c,14,[]) /[ that/[] ],
              x(s(s(0)),i,15,[]) /[
                x(s(s(0)),n,16,[index:16]) /[ who/[] ],
                x(s(0),i,17,[]) /[
                  x(0,i,18,[th:[19]]) /[ would/[] ],
                  x(s(s(0)),v,19,[index:19]) /[
                    x(0,v,20,[th:[16]]) /[ win/[] ]]]]]]]]]]]]
    ).


%%%%% Section 9.1

subst_conds(x(0,_,_,_),x(0,_,_,_)).
subst_conds(x(s(s(0)),C,_,_),x(s(s(0)),C,_,_)).

%%% adjoin_conds/3 revised in Section 9.4

%%%%% Section 9.2
```

```
%% moveA replaced by affectA in Section 10

hmc(Moved,_,_) :- maximal(Moved).
hmc(x(L,C,N,_),Landing,Tree) :-
    head_xp(Landing,_,Tree),
    head_xp(x(L,C,N,_),G,Tree),
    governs(Landing,G,Tree),
    (    Landing=x(0,c,_,_)
    ;    (    th_governs(Landing,G,Tree)
         ;    l_marks(Landing,G,Tree)
         )
    ).

adjoin_cat(Moved,Landing,Node/Seq0,Node/Seq,Dir,Renumbering) :-
    select(Position,Seq0,Selected,RestSeq),
    adjoin_cat(Moved,Landing,Selected,Transformed,Dir,Renumbering),
    select(Position,Seq,Transformed,RestSeq).

adjoin_cat(x(L,C,N,F)/Moved,Root,x(L0,C0,N0,F0)/Seq0,Root/Seq,Dir,Reno) :-
    amalgamate(x(L,C,N,F),x(L0,C0,N0,F0)/Seq0,Root/Tree),
    newnumber(Reno,N2),
    (    Dir=l,
         Seq = [x(L,C,N2,F)/Moved,Root/Tree]
    ;    Dir=r,
         Seq = [Root/Tree,x(L,C,N2,F)/Moved]
    ).

% If no renumbering at root of moved category was needed, use N0;
%  otherwise, use N0+1
newnumber(x/N0,N0) :- !.
newnumber(_/N0,N) :- N is N0+1.

amalgamate(x(_,v,_,F),Root0/[(-Affix)/[]],Root/[(-Affix)/[]]) :- !,
    member(index:I,F),
    feature(index:I,Root0,Root).
amalgamate(_,Root/Tree,Root/Tree).

figure(9-3,
 x(s(s(0)),c,1,[]) /[
  x(s(s(0)),a,2,[])/[],
  x(s(0),c,3,[]) /[
    x(0,c,4,[])/[],
    x(s(0)),i,5,[]) /[
      x(s(s(0)),n,6,[index:6]) /[ john/[] ],
      x(s(0),i,7,[]) /[
        x(0,i,8,[finite: +,th:[9]]) /[(-s)/[]],
        x(s(s(0)),v,9,[index:9]) /[
          x(0,v,10,[]) /[ be/[] ],
          x(s(s(0)),a,11,[]) /['how tall'/[]]]]]]]]
    ).

figure(9-4,
 x(s(s(0)),c,1,[]) /[
  x(s(s(0)),n,2,[])/[],
  x(s(0),c,3,[]) /[
    x(0,c,4,[])/[],
    x(s(s(0)),i,6,[]) /[
      x(s(s(0)),n,5,[])/[],
      x(s(0),i,7,[]) /[
        x(s(s(0)),v,8,[index:8]) /[
          x(s(s(0)),n,9,[index:9]) /[ jan/[] ],
```

```
              x(s(0),v,10,[]) /[
                  x(s(s(0)),n,11,[index:11]) /[ 'het boek'/[] ],
                  x(0,v,12,[th:[9,11]]) /[ lees/[] ]]],
            x(0,i,13,[finite:'+',th:[8]]) /[ (-t)/[] ]]]]]
   ).

figure(9-5,
 x(s(s(0)),c,1,[]) /[
  x(s(0),c,2,[]) /[
    x(0,c,3,[]) /[ dat/[] ],
    x(s(s(0)),i,4,[]) /[
      x(s(s(0)),n,5,[])/[],
      x(s(0),i,6,[]) /[
        x(s(s(0)),v,7,[index:7]) /[
          x(s(s(0)),n,8,[]) /[ jan/[] ],
          x(s(0),v,9,[]) /[
            x(s(s(0)),c,10,[index:10]) /[
              x(s(0),c,11,[]) /[
                x(0,c,12,[])/[],
                x(s(s(0)),i,13,[]) /[
                  x(s(s(0)),n,14,[])/[],
                  x(s(0),i,15,[]) /[
                    x(s(s(0)),v,16,[index:16]) /[
                      x(s(s(0)),n,17,[pronominal: +,index:17])/[],
                      x(s(0),v,18,[]) /[
                        x(s(s(0)),n,19,[index:19]) /[ 'een boek'/[] ],
                        x(0,v,20,[th:[17,19]]) /[ lezen/[] ]]],
                      x(0,i,21,[th:[16]]) /[ te/[] ]]]]],
                  x(0,v,22,[th:[5,10]]) /[ proberen/[] ]]],
              x(0,i,23,[th:[7]]) /[(-t)/[]]]]]] ).

figure(9-6,T) :- figure(9-3,T).

%%%%% Section 9.3

subjacency(Tree) :-
    \+ bad_link(_,_,Tree).

link(A,B,Tree) :- locally_binds(A,B,Tree), subtree(B/[],Tree).

/*** revised in Section 9.5, below
bad_link(A,B,Tree) :-
    link(A,B,Tree),
    \+ n_subjacent(s(0),B,A,Tree,[]).

n_subjacent(_,Moved,Landing,Tree,L) :-
    \+ new_excluding_barrier(_,Moved,Landing,Tree,L).
n_subjacent(s(N),Moved,Landing,Tree,L) :-
    new_excluding_barrier(Barrier,Moved,Landing,Tree,L),
    n_subjacent(N,Moved,Landing,Tree,[Barrier|L]).

new_excluding_barrier(Barrier,Moved,Landing,Tree,L) :-
    barrier(Barrier,Moved,Tree),
    \+member(Barrier,L),
    excludes(Barrier,Landing,Tree).
***/

excludes(A,B,Tree) :-
    subtree(B/_,Tree),
    subtree(A/_,Tree),
    \+A=B,
```

```
    \+exists_dominating_segment(A,B,Tree).

exists_dominating_segment(A,B,Tree) :-
    \+A=B,
    subtree(A/Seq,Tree),
    subtree(B/_,xxx/Seq).

figure(9-7,
 x(s(s(0)),c,1,[]) /[
  x(s(s(0)),n,2,[])/[],
  x(s(0),c,3,[]) /[
    x(0,c,4,[])/[],
    x(s(s(0)),i,5,[]) /[
      x(s(s(0)),n,6,[index:6]) /[ john/[] ],
      x(s(0),i,7,[]) /[
        x(0,i,8,[finite:'+',th:[9]])/[(-s)/[]],
        x(s(s(0)),v,9,[index:9]) /[
          x(0,v,10,[th:[6,11]]) /[ see/[] ],
          x(s(s(0)),n,11,[index:11]) /[ who/[] ]]]]]]
 ).

%%%%% Section 9.4

figure(9-8,
 x(s(s(0)),c,6,[]) /[
  x(s(s(0)),n,7,[])/[],
  x(s(0),c,8,[]) /[
    x(0,c,9,[])/[],
    x(s(s(0)),i,10,[]) /[
      x(s(s(0)),n,11,[index:11]) /[
        x(0,n,12,[th:[13]]) /[ pictures/[] ],
        x(s(s(0)),p,13,[index:13]) /[
          x(0,p,14,[th:[15]]) /[ of/[] ],
          x(s(s(0)),n,15,[index:15]) /[ who/[] ]]],
      x(s(0),i,16,[]) /['are on the table'/[] ]]]]
 ).

adjoin_conds(Moved,Landing,Tree) :-
    (    maximal(Moved),
         maximal(Landing),
         \+ argument(Landing,Tree)
    ;    minimal(Moved),
         minimal(Landing)
    ),
    \+ wh_ip_violation(Moved,Landing).

wh_ip_violation(x(_,_,_,F),x(s(s(0)),i,_,_)) :- member(wh:'+',F).

%%%%% Section 9.5

figure(9-9,
 x(s(s(0)),c,1,[]) /[
  x(s(s(0)),n,2,[])/[],
  x(s(0),c,3,[]) /[
    x(0,c,4,[])/[],
    x(s(s(0)),i,5,[]) /[
      x(s(s(0)),n,6,[index:6]) /[ you/[] ],
      x(s(0),i,7,[]) /[
        x(0,i,8,[th:[9],finite:'+']) /[ (-ed)/[] ],
        x(s(s(0)),v,9,[index:9]) /[
          x(0,v,10,[th:[6,11]]) /[ wonder/[] ],
```

```
       x(s(s(0)),c,11,[index:11]) /[
         x(s(s(0)),n,12,[])/[],
         x(s(0),c,13,[]) /[
           x(0,c,14,[])/[],
           x(s(s(0)),i,15,[]) /[
             x(s(s(0)),n,16,[index:16,wh:'+'])/[who/[]],
             x(s(0),i,17,[]) /[
               x(0,i,18,[th:[19],finite: '+']) /[ (-ed)/[] ],
                 x(s(s(0)),v,19,[index:19]) /[
                   x(0,v,20,[th:[16,21]]) /[ say/[] ],
  x(s(s(0)),c,21,[index:21]) /[
   x(s(s(0)),n,22,[])/[],
   x(s(0),c,23,[]) /[
    x(0,c,24,[])/[that/[]],
    x(s(s(0)),i,25,[]) /[
      x(s(s(0)),n,26,[index:26]) /[ bill/[] ],
      x(s(0),i,27,[]) /[
        x(0,i,28,[th:[29],finite:'+']) /[ (-ed)/[] ],
        x(s(s(0)),v,29,[index:29]) /[
          x(0,v,30,[th:[26,31]]) /[ see/[] ],
          x(s(s(0)),n,31,[index:31,wh:'+']) /[ what/[] ]]]]]]]]]]]]]]]
  ).

% for cumulative subjacency, go to deepest link and work back from there
bad_link(A,B,Tree) :-
    binds(_,B,Tree),
    \+binds(B,_,Tree),
    link(A,B,Tree),
    \+ n_subjacent(s(0),B,A,Tree,[]).


n_subjacent(N,Moved,Landing,Tree,L) :-
    \+ new_excluding_barrier(_,Moved,Landing,Tree,L),
    previously_n_subjacent(N,Landing,Tree,L).
n_subjacent(s(N),Moved,Landing,Tree,L) :-
    new_excluding_barrier(Barrier,Moved,Landing,Tree,L),
    n_subjacent(N,Moved,Landing,Tree,[Barrier|L]).

previously_n_subjacent(N,Moved,Tree,L) :-
    link(Landing,Moved,Tree),
    n_subjacent(N,Moved,Landing,Tree,L).
previously_n_subjacent(_N,NotMoved,Tree,_L) :-
    \+ link(_,NotMoved,Tree).


new_excluding_barrier(Barrier,Moved,Landing,Tree,L) :-
    (    barrier(Barrier,Moved,Tree)
    ;    extra_barrier(Barrier,Moved,Tree)
    ),
    \+member(Barrier,L),
    excludes(Barrier,Landing,Tree).

extra_barrier(S,B,Tree) :-
    (    imm_dominates(S,D,Tree),
        extra_BC(D,B,Tree)
    ;    extra_BC(S,B,Tree)
    ).

extra_BC(x(s(s(0)),Cat,N,F),B,Tree) :-
    bounding_parameter(Cat) ,
    dominates(x(s(s(0)),Cat,N,F),B,Tree) ,
    \+dominates(x(s(s(0)),Cat,N,F),x(s(s(0)),Cat,_,_),Tree),
    tensed(x(s(s(0)),Cat,N,F),Tree).
```

```
bounding_parameter(i).

tensed(x(s(s(0)),i,N,F),Tree) :-
    head_xp(Head,x(s(s(0)),i,N,F),Tree),
    feature(finite:'+',Head,Head).
tensed(x(s(s(0)),c,N,F),Tree) :-
    head_xp(Head,x(s(s(0)),c,N,F),Tree),
    sisters(Head,x(s(s(0)),i,N,F),Tree),
    tensed(x(s(s(0)),i,N,F),Tree).


%%%%% Section 10.1

deleteA(Node/Seq0,Node/Seq,DRoot) :-
    select(Pos,Seq0,Selected,RestSeq),
    (    deleteA(Selected,Transformed,DRoot),
        select(Pos,Seq,Transformed,RestSeq)
    ;    RestSeq=Seq,
        Selected=DRoot/_
    ).

delete_conds(A,Tree) :-
    (    subtree(A/[],Tree)
    ;    subtree(A/[that],Tree)
    ).

affectA(Tree0,Tree) :-
    guidance(Type,Moved,Landing,Dir),
    (    (    Type=sub,
            new_occurrence_no(Tree0,Renumbering),
            renumbering(Moved,Moved1,Renumbering),
            substitute(Tree0,Tree,Moved1,Landing,Renumbering),
            subst_conds(Moved,Landing)
        ;    Type=ad,
            new_occurrence_no(Tree0,Renumbering),
            renumbering(Moved,Moved1,Renumbering),
            adjoin(Tree0,Tree,Moved1,Landing,Dir,Renumbering),
            adjoin_conds(Moved,Landing,Tree)
        ),
        hmc(Moved,Landing,Tree),
        pp_term(Tree)
    ;    Type=d,
        deleteA(Tree0,Tree,Moved),
        delete_conds(Moved,Tree0),
        pp_term(Tree)
    ;    Type=sh,
        spec_head(Tree0,Tree),
        pp_term(Tree)
    ;    Type=ss_gamma,
        ss_gamma(Tree0,Tree,Tree0),
        pp_term(Tree)
    ;    Type=lf_gamma,
        lf_gamma(Tree0,Tree,Tree0),
        pp_term(Tree)
    ;    Type=s,
        ( subjacency(Tree0) -> write(yes) ; write(no)),nl,
        Tree=Tree0
    ;    Type=ecp,
        ( ecp(Tree0) -> write(yes) ; write(no) ),nl,
        Tree=Tree0
    ;    Type=xp,
```

```
        ( xp(Tree0) -> write(yes) ; write(no) ),nl,
        Tree0=Tree
    ;   Type=nvo,
        ( predicate_property(no_vacuous_ops(Tree0),_) ->
          ( no_vacuous_ops(Tree0) -> write(yes) ; write(no) )
        ; write('no_vacuous_ops(Tree0) is not defined')
        ),nl,
        Tree=Tree0
    ;   Type=disp,
        uglify(PT,Tree0),
        dd(PT),
        Tree=Tree0
    ;   Type=gbhelp,
        gbhelp,
        Tree=Tree0,
        pp_term(Tree)
    ;   Type=disp(A,B,C),
        show(A,B,C,Tree0,Answers),
        uglify(Answers,PT,Tree0),
        dd(PT),
        Tree=Tree0
    ;   Type=disp(A,B),
        show(A,B,Tree0,Answers),
        uglify(Answers,PT,Tree0),
        dd(PT),
        Tree=Tree0
    ;   Type=show(A,B,C),
        show(A,B,C,Tree0,Answers),
        Tree=Tree0
    ;   Type=show(A,B),
        show(A,B,Tree0,Answers),
        Tree=Tree0
    ;   Type=w,
        Tree=Tree0,
        write('asserting: current_tree(Tree).'),nl,
        retractall(current_tree(_)),
        assert(current_tree(Tree))
    ;   write('failing...'),nl,fail
    ).

renumbering(Moved,Moved,x/_).
renumbering(x(_,_,OldNo,_),x(_,_,NewNo,_),OldNo/NewNo).

affectAn(Tree,Tree).
affectAn(Tree0,Tree) :-
    affectA(Tree0,Tree1),
    affectAn(Tree1,Tree).

ss_gamma(Root/[T0|Ts],Root/Seq,T) :-
    ss_sub_gamma([T0|Ts],Seq,T).
ss_gamma(Leaf0/[],Leaf/[],T) :-
    feature(index:_,Leaf0,Leaf0),
    \+ feature(pronominal: '+',Leaf0,Leaf0),
    argument(Leaf0,T),
    (   properly_governs(_,Leaf0,T),
        feature(gamma:'+',Leaf0,Leaf)
    ;   \+ properly_governs(_,Leaf0,T),
        feature(gamma:'-',Leaf0,Leaf)
    ).
ss_gamma(Leaf/[],Leaf/[],T) :- \+ argument(Leaf,T).
ss_gamma(Leaf/[],Leaf/[],_) :- \+ feature(index:_,Leaf,Leaf).
```

```
ss_gamma(Leaf/[],Leaf/[],_) :- feature(pronominal:'+',Leaf,Leaf).

ss_sub_gamma([],[],_).
ss_sub_gamma([A|As],[B|Bs],T) :- ss_gamma(A,B,T),ss_sub_gamma(As,Bs,T).

lf_gamma(Root/[T0|T0s],Root/Seq,T) :-
    lf_sub_gamma([T0|T0s],Seq,T).
lf_gamma(Leaf0/[],Leaf/[],T) :-
    feature(index:_,Leaf0,Leaf0),
    \+ feature(pronominal: '+',Leaf0,Leaf0),
    feature(gamma:Val,Leaf0,Leaf),
    (    Leaf0=Leaf
    ;    (     properly_governs(_,Leaf0,T),
               Val='+'
         ;     \+ properly_governs(_,Leaf0,T),
               Val='-'
         )
    ).
lf_gamma(Leaf/[],Leaf/[],_) :- \+ feature(index:_,Leaf,Leaf).
lf_gamma(Leaf/[],Leaf/[],_) :- feature(pronominal:'+',Leaf,Leaf).

lf_sub_gamma([],[],_).
lf_sub_gamma([A|As],[B|Bs],T) :- lf_gamma(A,B,T),lf_sub_gamma(As,Bs,T).

ecp(Tree) :- \+ non_gamma(_,Tree).

non_gamma(x(L,C,N,F),Tree) :-
    subtree(x(L,C,N,F)/[],Tree),
    member(gamma:'-',F).

/*** properly_governs/3 is revised in Section 10.5, below
properly_governs(A,B,Tree):-
    (    th_governs(A,B,Tree)
    ;    ante_governs(A,B,Tree)
    ).
***/

/*** ante_governs/3 is revised in Section 10.5, below
ante_governs(A,B,Tree):-
    link(A,B,Tree),
    governs(A,B,Tree).
***/

figure(10-1,
 x(s(s(0)),c,1,[]) /[
  x(s(s(0)),a,2,[])/[],
  x(s(0),c,3,[]) /[
   x(0,c,4,[])/[],
   x(s(s(0)),i,5,[]) /[
    x(s(s(0)),n,6,[index:6]) /[ john/[] ],
    x(s(0),i,7,[]) /[
     x(0,i,8,[finite: +,th:[9]]) /[ (-ed)/[] ],
     x(s(s(0)),v,9,[index:9]) /[
      x(0,v,10,[th:[6,11]]) /[ know/[] ],
      x(s(s(0)),c,11,[index:11]) /[
       x(s(s(0)),n,12,[])/[],
       x(s(0),c,13,[]) /[
        x(0,c,14,[])/[],
        x(s(s(0)),i,15,[]) /[
         x(s(s(0)),n,16,[pronominal: +,index:16])/[],
         x(s(0),i,17,[]) /[
```

```
                      x(0,i,18,[th:[19]]) /[ to/[] ],
                      x(s(s(0)),v,19,[index:19]) /[
                        x(s(s(0)),v,19,[index:19]) /[
                          x(0,v,20,[th:[16,21]]) /[ fix/[] ],
                          x(s(s(0)),n,21,[index:21]) /['which car'/[] ]],
                        x(s(s(0)),a,22,[]) /[ how/[] ]]]]]]]]]]
   ).

%%%%% Section 10.3

lexical(x(_,Cat,_,F),Tree) :-
   (      member(Cat,[v,n,a,p])
   ;      Cat=i,
          member(index:I,F),
          subtree(x(0,v,_,F1)/_,Tree),
          member(index:I,F1)
   ).

l_marks(A,B,Tree) :-
    th_governs(A,G,Tree),
    lexical(A,Tree),
    (     B=G
    ;     head_xp(B,G,Tree)
    ;     head_xp(G,HG,Tree), specifier(B,HG,Tree)
    ).

distinguishing_lex_proj(x(L,C,N,F),A,B,Tree) :-
    dominates(x(L,C,N,F),A,Tree),
    lexical(x(L,C,N,F),Tree),
    \+dominates(x(L,C,N,F),B,Tree).

%%%%% Section 10.4

figure(10-2,
 x(s(s(0)),c,1,[]) /[
   x(0,c,4,[])/[si/[]],
   x(s(s(0)),i,5,[]) /[
     x(s(s(0)),n,6,[index:6,pronominal:'+',anaphor:'-']) /[],
     x(s(0),i,7,[]) /[
       x(0,i,8,[finite:'+',th:[9]])/[],
       x(s(s(0)),v,9,[index:9]) /[
   x(0,v,10,[th:[12]]) /[ hay/[] ],
   x(s(s(0)),n,12,[index:12]) /[
     x(0,n,14,[]) /[ traduccion/[] ],
     x(s(s(0)),a,15,[]) /[
       x(0,a,16,[]) /[ francesa/[] ]],
     x(s(s(0)),p,17,[index:17])/['de que pintor']]]]]]]
   ).

/*** revised in Section 10.5
minimal_barrier(S,B,Tree) :-
   (      barrier(S,B,Tree)
   ;      dominates(S,B,Tree),
          parent(S,D,Tree),
          minimal(D),
          \+D=x(0,i,_N,_F),
          \+D=B
   ).
***/

intervening_barrier(S,A,B,Tree) :-
```

```
      minimal_barrier(S,B,Tree),
      excludes(S,A,Tree).

figure(10-3,T) :- figure(10-2,T).

%%%%% Section 10.5

minimal_barrier(S,B,Tree) :-
      (    barrier(S,B,Tree)
      ;    dominates(S,B,Tree),
           parent(S,D,Tree),
           minimal(D),
           \+D=B,
           \+D=x(0,i,_N,_F),
           (    \+ D=x(_,_,_,[])
           ;    \+ subtree(D/[],Tree)
           )
      ).

figure(10-4,
 x(s(s(0)),c,1,[]) /[
  x(s(s(0)),n,2,[])/[],
  x(s(0),c,3,[]) /[
   x(0,c,4,[])/[],
   x(s(s(0)),i,5,[]) /[
    x(s(s(0)),n,6,[index:6]) /[ he/[] ],
    x(s(0),i,7,[]) /[
     x(0,i,8,[th:[9]]) /[(-s)/[]],
     x(s(s(0)),v,9,[index:9]) /[
      x(0,v,10,[th:[6,11]]) /[ believe/[] ],
      x(s(s(0)),c,11,[index:11]) /[
       x(s(s(0)),n,12,[])/[],
       x(s(0),c,13,[]) /[
        x(0,c,14,[]) /[],
        x(s(s(0)),i,15,[]) /[
         x(s(s(0)),n,16,[wh: +,index:16]) /[ who/[] ],
         x(s(0),i,17,[]) /[
          x(0,i,18,[th:[19]]) /[
           would/[]],
          x(s(s(0)),v,19,[index:19]) /[
           x(0,v,20,[th:[16]]) /[ win/[] ]]]]]]]]]]]
  ).

figure(10-5,
 x(s(s(0)),c,1,[]) /[
  x(s(s(0)),n,2,[])/[],
  x(s(0),c,3,[]) /[
   x(0,c,4,[])/[],
   x(s(s(0)),i,5,[]) /[
    x(s(s(0)),n,6,[index:6]) /[ he/[] ],
    x(s(0),i,7,[]) /[
     x(0,i,8,[th:[9]]) /[(-s)/[]],
     x(s(s(0)),v,9,[index:9]) /[
      x(0,v,10,[th:[6,11]]) /[ believe/[] ],
      x(s(s(0)),c,11,[index:11]) /[
       x(s(s(0)),n,12,[])/[],
       x(s(0),c,13,[]) /[
        x(0,c,14,[]) /[ that/[] ],
        x(s(s(0)),i,15,[]) /[
         x(s(s(0)),n,16,[wh: +,index:16]) /[ who/[] ],
         x(s(0),i,17,[]) /[
```

```
                    x(0,i,18,[th:[19]]) /[
                      would/[]],
                    x(s(s(0)),v,19,[index:19]) /[
                      x(0,v,20,[th:[16]]) /[ win/[] ]]]]]]]]]]]
    ).

%%%%% Section 10.6

figure(10-6,
  x(s(s(0)),i,1,[]) /[
    x(s(s(0)),n,2,[])/[],
    x(s(0),i,3,[]) /[
      x(0,i,4,[th:[5]]) /[(-s)/[]],
      x(s(s(0)),v,5,[index:5]) /[
        x(0,v,6,[th:[8]]) /[ seem/[] ],
        x(s(s(0)),i,8,[index:8]) /[
          x(s(s(0)),n,9,[index:9,number:s,person:3]) /[ john/[] ],
          x(s(0),i,11,[]) /[
            x(0,i,12,[]) /[ to/[] ],
            x(s(s(0)),v,13,[]) /['be intelligent'/[]]]]]]]]
    ).

figure(10-7,T) :- figure(10-6,T).

figure(10-8,
  x(s(s(0)),i,1,[]) /[
    x(s(s(0)),n,2,[])/[],
    x(s(0),i,3,[]) /[
      x(0,i,4,[th:[5]]) /[(-s)/[]],
      x(s(s(0)),v,5,[index:5]) /[
        x(0,v,6,[]) /[ be/[] ],
        x(s(s(0)),v,5,[index:5]) /[
          x(0,v,8,[th:[en,9]]) /['kill + -en'/[] ],
          x(s(s(0)),n,9,[index:9,number:s,person:3]) /[ john/[] ]]]]]]
    ).

% XPs with specifiers and complements:
spec_head(x(s(s(0)),C,N,F)/Seq0,x(s(s(0)),C,N,F)/Seq) :-
    select(PosSpec,Seq0,x(s(0),C,N1,F1)/Seq1,Specifiers0),
    select(PosHead,Seq1,x(0,C,_N2,_F2)/Head0,Complements0),
    agree(Specifiers0,x(0,C,_N2,_F2)/Head0,Head,Specifiers1),
    spec_heads(Specifiers1,Specifiers),
    spec_heads(Complements0,Complements),
    select(PosHead,Seq2,Head,Complements),
    select(PosSpec,Seq,x(s(0),C,N1,F1)/Seq2,Specifiers).
% XPs without specifiers but with complements:
spec_head(x(s(s(0)),C,N,F)/Seq0,x(s(s(0)),C,N,F)/Seq) :-
    \+ member(x(s(0),C,_N1,_F1)/_Seq1,Seq0),
    select(PosHead,Seq0,x(0,C,_N2,_F2)/Head,Complements0),
    spec_heads(Complements0,Complements),
    select(PosHead,Seq,x(0,C,_N2,_F2)/Head,Complements).
% empty XPs:
spec_head(x(s(s(0)),C,N,F)/[],x(s(s(0)),C,N,F)/[]).
% XP adjunction structures:
spec_head(x(s(s(0)),C,N,F)/Seq0,x(s(s(0)),C,N,F)/Seq) :-
    select(Pos,Seq0,x(s(s(0)),C,N,F)/Seq1,Adjunct0),
    spec_head(x(s(s(0)),C,N,F)/Seq1,x(s(s(0)),C,N,F)/Seq2),
    spec_head(Adjunct0,Adjunct),
    select(Pos,Seq,x(s(s(0)),C,N,F)/Seq2,Adjunct).
% EXTRA CASE FOR CONVENIENCE: XPs with unspecified heads:
spec_head(x(s(s(0)),C,N,F)/[Word/[]],x(s(s(0)),C,N,F)/[Word/[]]).
```

```
agree([],Node,Node,[]).
agree([Root0/Seq|Ts],Head0/SeqH,Head/SeqH,[Root/Seq|As]) :-
    put_features(Head0,Root0,Head1),
    agree(Ts,Head1,Head,As),
    put_features(Root0,Head0,Root).
agree([Root0/Seq|Ts],Head0,Head,[Root/Seq|As]) :-
    put_features(Head0,Root0,Head1),
    agree(Ts,Head1,Head,As),
    put_features(Root0,Head0,Root).

spec_heads([],[]).
spec_heads([T|Ts],[A|As]) :- spec_head(T,A), spec_heads(Ts,As).

%%%%%% Section 10.7

properly_governs(A,B,Tree):- ante_governs(A,B,Tree).

ante_governs(A,B,Tree):- ex_link(A,B,Tree),governs(A,B,Tree).

ex_link(A,B,Tree) :- link(A,B,Tree).
ex_link(A,B,Tree) :-
    subtree(A/_,Tree),subtree(B/_,Tree),
    \+ A=B,
    feature(index:I,B,B),
    feature(index:I,A,A).

figure(10-9,
 x(s(s(0)),i,1,[]) /[
  x(s(s(0)),n,2,[]) /[],
  x(s(0),i,3,[]) /[
    x(0,i,4,[th:[5]]) /[ (-s)/[] ],
    x(s(s(0)),v,5,[index:5]) /[
      x(0,v,6,[th:[8]])/[seem/[] ],
      x(s(s(0)),i,8,[index:8]) /[
        x(s(s(0)),n,9,[]) /[ there/[] ],
        x(s(0),i,10,[]) /[
          x(0,i,11,[th:[12]]) /[ to/[] ],
          x(s(s(0)),v,12,[index:12]) /[
            x(0,v,13,[]) /[ be/[] ],
            x(s(s(0)),v,12,[index:12]) /[
              x(0,v,14,[th:[en,15]]) /['kill + -en'/[] ],
              x(s(s(0)),n,15,[index:15])/['a man'/[] ]
                ]]]]]]]]
    ).

figure(10-10,
 x(s(s(0)),i,1,[]) /[
  x(s(s(0)),n,2,[]) /[],
  x(s(0),i,3,[]) /[
    x(0,i,4,[index:9,th:[5]]) /[ (-s)/[] ],
    x(s(s(0)),v,5,[index:5]) /[
      x(0,v,6,[index:9,th:[8]])/[seem/[] ],
      x(s(s(0)),i,8,[index:8]) /[
        x(s(s(0)),n,9,[index:9])/[john/[] ],
        x(s(0),i,11,[]) /[
          x(0,i,12,[th:[13]]) /[ to/[] ],
          x(s(s(0)),v,13,[]) /['be intelligent'/[] ]]]]]]
    ).

figure(10-11,
```

```
x(s(s(0)),c,1,[]) /[
 x(s(s(0)),n,2,[])/[],
 x(s(0),c,3,[]) /[
   x(0,c,4,[])/[],
   x(s(s(0)),i,5,[]) /[
     x(s(s(0)),n,6,[index:6]) /[ you/[] ],
     x(s(0),i,7,[]) /[
       x(0,i,8,[th:[9]]) /[(-ed)/[]],
  x(s(s(0)),v,9,[index:9]) /[
   x(0,v,10,[th:[6,11]]) /[ believe/[] ],
   x(s(s(0)),c,11,[index:11]) /[
     x(s(s(0)),n,12,[])/[],
     x(s(0),c,13,[]) /[
       x(0,c,14,[]) /[ that/[] ],
       x(s(s(0)),i,15,[]) /[
         x(s(s(0)),n,16,[index:16]) /[ bill/[] ],
         x(s(0),i,17,[]) /[
           x(0,i,18,[th:[19]]) /[ (-ed)/[] ],
           x(s(s(0)),v,19,[index:19]) /[
              x(0,v,20,[th:[16,21]]) /[ win/[] ],
              x(s(s(0)),n,21,[index:21,wh: +])/[what/[]]
              ]]]]]]]]]  ).

figure(10-12,
 x(s(s(0)),c,1,[]) /[
 x(s(s(0)),q,2,[])/[],
 x(s(0),c,3,[]) /[
   x(0,c,4,[])/[],
   x(s(s(0)),i,5,[]) /[
     x(s(s(0)),n,6,[index:6]) /[ il/[] ],
     x(s(0),i,7,[]) /[
       x(0,i,8,[th:[9]]) /[(-s)/[]],
  x(s(s(0)),v,9,[index:9]) /[
   x(0,v,10,[th:[11]]) /[ avoir/[] ],
   x(s(s(0)),v,11,[index:11]) /[
     x(0,v,14,[th:[6,15]]) /[ consulter/[] ],
     x(s(s(0)),n,15,[index:15]) /[
       x(s(s(0)),q,16,[])/[combien/[]],
       x(s(0),n,17,[]) /['de livres'/[] ] ]]]]]]]
 ).

figure(10-13,
 x(s(s(0)),c,1,[]) /[
 x(s(s(0)),q,2,[])/[],
 x(s(0),c,3,[]) /[
   x(0,c,4,[])/[],
   x(s(s(0)),i,5,[]) /[
     x(s(s(0)),n,6,[index:6]) /[ il/[] ],
     x(s(0),i,7,[]) /[
       x(0,i,8,[th:[9]]) /[(-s)/[]],
  x(s(s(0)),v,9,[index:9]) /[
   x(0,v,10,[th:[11]]) /[ avoir/[] ],
   x(s(s(0)),v,11,[index:11]) /[
   x(s(s(0)),adv,12,[]) /['beaucoup'/[]],
    x(s(0),v,13,[index:13]) /[
     x(0,v,14,[th:[6,15]]) /[ consulter/[] ],
     x(s(s(0)),n,15,[index:15]) /[
       x(s(s(0)),q,16,[])/[combien/[]],
       x(s(0),n,17,[]) /['de livres'/[] ] ]]]]]]]]
 ).
```

```
%%%%% Section 14.2

figure(14-1,
 x(s(s(0)),c,1,[]) /[
  x(s(s(0)),n,2,[])/[],
  x(s(0),c,3,[]) /[
   x(0,c,4,[])/[],
   x(s(s(0)),i,5,[]) /[
     x(s(s(0)),n,6,[index:6]) /[ she/[] ],
     x(s(0),i,7,[]) /[
       x(0,i,8,[th:[9],finite:'+']) /[ (-s)/[] ],
       x(s(s(0)),v,9,[index:9]) /[
        x(0,v,10,[th:[6,11]]) /[ wonder/[] ],
        x(s(s(0)),c,11,[index:11]) /[
         x(s(s(0)),a,12,[])/[],
         x(s(0),c,13,[]) /[
          x(0,c,14,[])/[],
          x(s(s(0)),i,15,[]) /[
           x(s(s(0)),n,16,[index:16])/[john/[]],
           x(s(0),i,17,[]) /[
            x(0,i,18,[th:[19],finite: '+']) /[ (-ed)/[] ],
            x(s(s(0)),v,19,[index:19]) /[
             x(s(s(0)),v,19,[index:19]) /[
              x(0,v,20,[th:[16,21]]) /[ fix/[] ],
              x(s(s(0)),n,21,[index:21,wh:'+']) /[ what/[] ]],
             x(s(s(0)),a,22,[]) /[ how/[] ]]]]]]]]]]]
 ).

figure(14-9,
 x(s(s(0)),c,1,[]) /[
  x(0,c,2,[])/[],
  x(s(s(0)),i,3,[]) /[
   x(s(s(0)),n,4,[])/[],
   x(s(0),i,5,[]) /[
    x(0,i,6,[th:[7]])/[],
    x(s(s(0)),v,7,[index:7]) /[
     x(0,v,8,[th:[9]]) /[ seem/[] ],
     x(s(s(0)),i,9,[index:9]) /[
      x(s(s(0)),n,10,[index:10]) /[ mary/[] ],
      x(s(0),i,11,[]) /[
       x(0,i,12,[th:[13],finite: +]) /[ (-s)/[] ],
       x(s(s(0)),v,13,[index:13]) /[
        x(0,v,14,[th:[15]]) /[ be/[] ],
        x(s(s(0)),a,15,[index:15]) /[happy/[] ]]]]]]]]]
 ).

figure(14-10,
 x(s(s(0)),c,6,[]) /[
   x(0,c,9,[])/[],
   x(s(s(0)),i,10,[]) /[
    x(s(s(0)),n,12,[index:12]) /[
    x(s(s(0)),n,13,[])/[ 'mary''s'/[]],
    x(s(0),n,14,[]) /[
     x(0,n,15,[th:[16]]) /[ pictures/[] ]]],
    x(s(0),i,21,[]) /['are on the table'/[] ]]]
 ).
```

C.2   Determiner phrases

```
% File: dp.pl
% Author:  Ed Stabler, Jr
% Date: May 1991
% Subject: structures for chapter 11

figure(11-3,
x(s(s(0)),i,1,[]) /[
  x(s(s(0)),n,2,[index:2]) /[ john/[] ],
  x(s(0),i,3,[]) /[
    x(0,i,4,[th:[5],finite: +]) /[ -s/[] ],
    x(s(s(0)),v,5,[index:5]) /[
      x(0,v,6,[th:[2,7]]) /[ need/[] ],
      x(s(s(0)),d,7,[index:7]) /[
        x(0,d,8,[]) /[ a/[] ],
        x(s(s(0)),d,9,[]) /[
          x(s(s(0)),d,10,[])/[],
          x(s(0),n,11,[]) /[
            x(0,n,12,[th:[15]]) /[ talking/[] ],
            x(s(s(0)),p,13,[]) /[
              x(0,p,14,[]) /[ to/[] ],
              x(s(s(0)),d,15,[index:15,pronominal: +])/[]]]]]]]]]
  ).

figure(11-4,
 x(s(s(0)),c,1,[]) /[
  x(s(s(0)),d,2,[])/[],
  x(s(0),c,3,[]) /[
    x(0,c,4,[])/[],
    x(s(s(0)),i,5,[]) /[
      x(s(s(0)),d,6,[index:6]) /[' you '/[] ],
      x(s(0),i,7,[]) /[
        x(0,i,8,[th:[9]]) /[ (-s)/[] ],
        x(s(s(0)),v,9,[index:9]) /[
          x(0,v,10,[th:[6,11]]) /[ read/[] ],
          x(s(s(0)),d,11,[index:11]) /[
            x(s(s(0)),d,12,[])/[],
            x(s(0),d,13,[]) /[
              x(0,d,14,[]) /[ a/[] ],
              x(s(s(0)),n,15,[]) /[
                x(s(0),n,17,[]) /[
                  x(0,n,18,[th:[21]]) /[ book/[] ],
                  x(s(s(0)),p,19,[index:21]) /[
                    x(0,p,20,[]) /[ about/[] ],
                    x(s(s(0)),d,21,[index:21])/['what'/[]
                    ]]]]]]]]]]]
  ).

% *What$_i$ did you present $[_{dp}\ e\ [_{np}$Mary\ theory of $t_i\ ]]$?
figure(11-5,
 x(s(s(0)),c,1,[]) /[
  x(s(s(0)),d,2,[])/[],
  x(s(0),c,3,[]) /[
    x(0,c,4,[])/[],
    x(s(s(0)),i,5,[]) /[
      x(s(s(0)),d,6,[index:6]) /[' you '/[] ],
      x(s(0),i,7,[]) /[
        x(0,i,8,[th:[9]]) /[ (-ed)/[] ],
        x(s(s(0)),v,9,[index:9]) /[
```

```
          x(0,v,10,[th:[6,11]]) /[ present/[] ],
          x(s(s(0)),d,11,[index:11]) /[
            x(s(s(0)),d,12,[])/[],
            x(s(0),d,13,[]) /[
              x(0,d,14,[]) /[ '''s'/[] ],
              x(s(s(0)),n,15,[]) /[
                x(s(s(0)),d,16,[index:16]) /[' mary '/[] ],
                x(s(0),n,17,[]) /[
                  x(0,n,18,[th:[16,21]]) /[ theory/[] ],
                  x(s(s(0)),p,19,[index:21]) /[
                    x(0,p,20,[]) /[ of/[] ],
                    x(s(s(0)),d,21,[index:21])/[what/[]
                    ]]]]]]]]]]]
).
```

```
% this is identical to 11.5, except we must leave index of mary a variable!
figure(11-6,
 x(s(s(0)),c,1,[]) /[
  x(s(s(0)),d,2,[])/[],
  x(s(0),c,3,[]) /[
    x(0,c,4,[])/[],
    x(s(s(0)),i,5,[]) /[
      x(s(s(0)),d,6,[index:6]) /[' you '/[] ],
      x(s(0),i,7,[]) /[
        x(0,i,8,[th:[9]]) /[ (-ed)/[] ],
        x(s(s(0)),v,9,[index:9]) /[
          x(0,v,10,[th:[6,11]]) /[ present/[] ],
          x(s(s(0)),d,11,[index:11]) /[
            x(s(s(0)),d,12,[])/[],
            x(s(0),d,13,[]) /[
              x(0,d,14,[]) /[ '''s'/[] ],
              x(s(s(0)),n,15,[]) /[
                x(s(s(0)),d,16,[index:A]) /[' mary '/[] ],
                x(s(0),n,17,[]) /[
                  x(0,n,18,[th:[A,21]]) /[ theory/[] ],
                  x(s(s(0)),p,19,[index:21]) /[
                    x(0,p,20,[]) /[ of/[] ],
                    x(s(s(0)),d,21,[index:21])/[what/[]
                    ]]]]]]]]]]]
).
```

C.3   Inflectional phrases and head movement

```
% File :  ip.pl
% Authors :  E Stabler, Jr
% Updated :  March, 1991
% Purpose :  a guided derivation system based on Pollock (1989)

% in this tree, we left adjoin V10 to I8, then V-I to T4
figure(12-1,
 x(s(s(0)),t,1,[]) /[
  x(s(s(0)),n,2,[]) /[ john/[] ],
  x(s(0),t,3,[]) /[
    x(0,t,4,[finite:'+',th:[5]])/[],
      x(s(s(0)),neg,5,[index:5]) /[
      x(0,neg,6,[]) /[ not/[] ],
      x(s(s(0)),agr,7,[]) /[
        x(0,agr,8,[th:[9]]) /[(-s)/[]],
        x(s(s(0)),v,9,[index:9]) /[
          x(0,v,10,[]) /[ have/[] ],
          x(s(s(0)),n,11,[]) /['any money'/[]]]]]]]]
 ).

barrier(S,B,Tree) :-
    (   imm_dominates(S,D,Tree),
        blocking_cat(D,B,Tree)
    ;   blocking_cat(S,B,Tree),
        \+S=x(s(s(0)),agr,_N,_F)
    ).

adjoin_cat(Moved,Landing,Node/Seq0,Node/Seq,Dir,Renumbering) :-
    select(Position,Seq0,Selected,RestSeq),
    adjoin_cat(Moved,Landing,Selected,Transformed,Dir,Renumbering),
    select(Position,Seq,Transformed,RestSeq).

adjoin_cat(x(L,C,N,F)/Moved,Root,x(L0,C0,N0,F0)/Seq0,Root/Seq,Dir,Reno) :-
    amalgamate(x(L,C,N,F)/Moved,x(L0,C0,N0,F0)/Seq0,Root/Tree),
    newnumber(Reno,N2),
    (   Dir=l,
        Seq = [x(L,C,N2,F)/Moved,Root/Tree]
    ;   Dir=r,
        Seq = [Root/Tree,x(L,C,N2,F)/Moved]
    ).

amalgamate(MRoot/Moved,Root0/[(-Affix)/[]],Root/[(-Affix)/[]]) :- !,
    feature(index:I,MRoot,MRoot),
    subtree(x(0,v,_,F)/_,MRoot/Moved),
    member(index:I,F),!,
    feature(index:I,Root0,Root).
amalgamate(_/_,Root/Tree,Root/Tree).

lexical(x(L,C,N,F),Tree) :-
    (   member(C,[v,n,a,p])
    ;   \+ member(C,[v,n,a,p]),
        subtree(x(L,C,N,F)/Seq,Tree),
        (   imm_dominates(x(L,C,N,F),x(0,v,N1,F1),x(L,C,N,F)/Seq),
            subtree(x(0,v,N1,F1)/_,x(L,C,N,F)/Seq)
        ;   \+imm_dominates(x(L,C,N,F),x(0,v,_,_),x(L,C,N,F)/Seq),
            member(index:I,F),
            subtree(Node1/Seq1,Tree),
            feature(index:I,Node1,Node1),
```

```
                    imm_dominates(Node1,x(0,v,N1,F1),Node1/Seq1),
                    subtree(x(0,v,N1,F1)/_,x(L,C,N,F)/Seq)
        )
    ).

l_marks(A,B,Tree) :-
    th_governs(A,G,Tree),
    lexical(A,Tree),
    (   B=G
    ;   head(B,G,Tree)
    ;   head(HG,G,Tree), specifier(B,HG,Tree)
    ;   G=x(s(s(0)),neg,_,_),
        head(HG,G,Tree),
        complement(B,HG,Tree)
    ).

minimal_barrier(S,B,Tree) :-
    (   barrier(S,B,Tree)
    ;   dominates(S,B,Tree),
        \+D=x(_L,agr,_N,_F),
        \+D=x(_L,neg,_N,_F),
        parent(S,D,Tree),
        minimal(D),
        \+D=B,
        (   \+ D=x(_,_,_,[])
        ;   \+ subtree(D,Tree)
        )
    ).

no_vacuous_ops(Tree) :- \+ exists_vacuous_op(Tree).

/*** revised
exists_vacuous_op(Tree) :-
    subtree(A/_,Tree),
    feature(finite:'+',A,A),
    \+ binds(A,x(0,v,_,_),Tree).
***/

exists_vacuous_op(Tree) :-
    subtree(A/_,Tree),
    feature(finite:'+',A,A),
    \+ binds(A,_,Tree).

figure(12-2,
 x(s(s(0)),t,1,[]) /[
  x(s(s(0)),n,2,[index:2]) /[ john/[] ],
  x(s(0),t,3,[]) /[
    x(0,t,4,[finite:'+',th:[5]])/[],
    x(s(s(0)),neg,5,[index:5]) /[
     x(0,neg,6,[]) /[ not/[] ],
     x(s(s(0)),agr,7,[]) /[
       x(0,agr,8,[th:[10]]) /[
          x(0,v,9,[th:[2]])/[do/[]],
          x(0,agr,8,[th:[10]]) /[(-s)/[]]],
       x(s(s(0)),v,10,[index:10]) /[
          x(0,v,11,[th:[2]]) /[leave/[]] ]]]]]
 ).

figure(12-3,
 x(s(s(0)),t,1,[]) /[
  x(s(s(0)),n,2,[index:2]) /[ john/[] ],
```

```
x(s(0),t,3,[]) /[
  x(0,t,4,[finite:'+',th:[7]])/[],
    x(s(s(0)),agr,7,[index:7]) /[
      x(0,agr,8,[th:[10]]) /[
          x(0,v,9,[th:[2]])/[],
          x(0,agr,8,[th:[10]]) /[(-s)/[]]],
      x(s(s(0)),v,10,[index:10]) /[
        x(0,v,11,[th:[2]]) /[leave/[]] ]]]]
).

hmc(Moved,_,_) :- maximal(Moved),!.
hmc(x(0,C,N,F),_,Tree) :-
    \+ (subtree(x(0,C,N,F)/Seq,Tree),
         \+  (    Seq=[]
             ;    Seq=[(-_)/[]]
             )
       ),!.
hmc(x(0,C,N,_),Landing,Tree) :-
    head_xp(Landing,_,Tree),
    head_xp(x(0,C,N,_),G,Tree),
    governs(Landing,G,Tree),
    (   Landing=x(0,c,_,_)
    ;   (    th_governs(Landing,G,Tree)
        ;    l_marks(Landing,G,Tree)
        )
    ).
```

C.4   VP-internal subjects

```
% File: vp.pl
% Author:  Ed Stabler, Jr
% Date: May 1991
% Subject: axioms inspired by Sportiche and Koopman

% sportiche ms, pp10,20
figure(13-1,
 x(s(s(0)),i,1,[]) /[
  x(s(s(0)),n,2,[])/[],
  x(s(0),i,3,[]) /[
    x(0,i,4,[]) /[ will/[] ],
      x(s(s(0)),v,5,[]) /[
        x(s(s(0)),n,6,[]) /[ they/[] ],
        x(s(0),v,7,[])/[
          x(0,v,8,[]) /[],
          x(s(s(0)),v,9,[]) /[
            x(s(0),v,10,[]) /[
              x(0,v,11,[]) /[ visit/[] ],
              x(s(s(0)),n,12,[]) /['paris'/[] ]]]]]]]
  ).

%%%%% Section 13.1

i_commands(A,B,Tree) :-
    \+ intervening_dominator(A,_,B,Tree).

intervening_dominator(A,S,B,Tree) :-
    dominates(S,A,Tree),
    \+dominates(S,B,Tree).

governs(A,B,Tree) :-
    i_commands(A,B,Tree),
    \+ intervening_barrier(A,_,B,Tree).

intervening_barrier(A,S,B,Tree) :-
    barrier(S,B,Tree),
    excludes(S,A,Tree).

l_marks(x(L,C,N,F),B,Tree) :-
    complement(B,x(L,C,N,F),Tree),
    (     \+ C=c
    ;     C=c,
%     (    imm_dominates(x(L,C,N,F),x(0,v,_,F),Tree)
%     ;
          member(index:I,F),
          subtree(x(0,v,_,F1)/_,Tree),
          member(index:I,F1)
%     )
    ).

l_dependent(B,Tree) :- l_marks(_,B,Tree).
l_dependent(B,Tree) :- specifier(B,C,Tree),l_marks(_,C,Tree).

projection(x(L,C,N,F),x(L,C,N,F),_).
projection(x(0,C,N,F),x(s(0),C,N1,F1),Tree) :-
    head_x1(x(0,C,N,F),x(s(0),C,N1,F1),Tree).
projection(x(s(0),C,N1,F1),x(0,C,N,F),Tree) :-
    head_x1(x(0,C,N,F),x(s(0),C,N1,F1),Tree).
```

```
projection(x(0,C,N,F),x(s(s(0)),C,N1,F1),Tree) :-
    head_xp(x(0,C,N,F),x(s(s(0)),C,N1,F1),Tree).
projection(x(s(s(0)),C,N1,F1),x(0,C,N,F),Tree) :-
    head_xp(x(0,C,N,F),x(s(s(0)),C,N1,F1),Tree).
projection(x(s(0),C,N1,F1),x(s(s(0)),C,N,F),Tree) :-
    subtree(x(s(s(0)),C,N,F)/[T|Ts],Tree),
    head_spec(Pos),
    separate(Pos,x(s(0),C,N1,F1)/_,[T|Ts],_).
projection(x(s(s(0)),C,N,F),x(s(0),C,N1,F1),Tree) :-
    subtree(x(s(s(0)),C,N,F)/[T|Ts],Tree),
    head_spec(Pos),
    separate(Pos,x(s(0),C,N1,F1)/_,[T|Ts],_).

barrier(YP,B,Tree) :-
    maximal(YP),
    subtree(YP/_,Tree),           %redundant, for negation
    subtree(B/_,Tree),            %redundant
    \+ projection(YP,B,Tree),
    projection(Yn,YP,Tree),
    dominates(Yn,B,Tree),
    \+ l_dependent(Yn,Tree).

subst_conds(x(0,_,_,_),x(0,_,_,_)).
subst_conds(x(s(s(0)),C,_,_),x(s(s(0)),C,_,_)).

adjoin_conds(x(0,_,_,_),x(0,_,_,_)).
adjoin_conds(x(s(s(0)),_,_,_),x(s(s(0)),C,_,_)) :- (C=v ; C=a ; C=i).

ccl(Tree):- \+ ccl_violation(_,Tree).

ccl_violation(x(L,C,N,F),Tree) :-
    subtree(x(L,C,N,F)/[],Tree),
    member(index:_,F),
    \+ member(pronominal:'+',F),
    \+ ante_governs(_,x(L,C,N,F),Tree).

ante_governs(Binder,x(L,C,N,F),Tree) :-
    binds(Binder,x(L,C,N,F),Tree),
    governs(Binder,x(L,C,N,F),Tree).

% we add CCL, remove the HMC, subjacency, ECP, etc
affectA(Tree0,Tree) :-
    guidance(Type,Moved,Landing,Dir),
    (   (    Type=sub,
             new_occurrence_no(Tree0,Renumbering),
             renumbering(Moved,Moved1,Renumbering),
             substitute(Tree0,Tree,Moved1,Landing,Renumbering),
             subst_conds(Moved,Landing)
        ;    Type=ad,
             new_occurrence_no(Tree0,Renumbering),
             renumbering(Moved,Moved1,Renumbering),
             adjoin(Tree0,Tree,Moved1,Landing,Dir,Renumbering),
             adjoin_conds(Moved,Landing)
        ),
        pp_term(Tree)
    ;   Type=d,
        deleteA(Tree0,Tree,Moved),
        delete_conds(Moved,Tree0),
        pp_term(Tree)
    ;   Type=sh,
        spec_head(Tree0,Tree),
```

```
          pp_term(Tree)
    ;     Type=xp,
          ( xp(Tree0) -> write(yes) ; write(no) ),nl,
          Tree0=Tree
    ;     Type=ccl,
          ( ccl(Tree0) -> write(yes) ; write(no) ),nl,
          Tree=Tree0
    ;     Type=recp,
          ( recp(Tree0) -> write(yes) ; write(no) ),nl,
          Tree=Tree0
    ;     Type=disp,
          uglify(PT,Tree0),
          dd(PT),
          Tree=Tree0
    ;     Type=gbhelp,
          gbhelp,
          Tree=Tree0,
          pp_term(Tree)
    ;     Type=disp(A,B,C),
          show(A,B,C,Tree0,Answers),
          uglify(Answers,PT,Tree0),
          dd(PT),
          Tree=Tree0
    ;     Type=disp(A,B),
          show(A,B,Tree0,Answers),
          uglify(Answers,PT,Tree0),
          dd(PT),
          Tree=Tree0
    ;     Type=show(A,B,C),
          show(A,B,C,Tree0,Answers),
          Tree=Tree0
    ;     Type=show(A,B),
          show(A,B,Tree0,Answers),
          Tree=Tree0
    ;     Type=w,
          Tree=Tree0,
          write('asserting: current_tree(Tree).'),nl,
          retractall(current_tree(_)),
          assert(current_tree(Tree))
    ;     write('failing...'),nl,fail
    ).

%%%%% Section 13.2

figure(13-2,
 x(s(s(0)),i,1,[]) /[
  x(s(s(0)),n,2,[])/[],
  x(s(0),i,3,[]) /[
   x(0,i,4,[]) /[ -s/[] ],
   x(s(s(0)),v,5,[]) /[
    x(s(s(0)),n,6,[])/[],
    x(s(0),v,7,[]) /[
     x(0,v,8,[]) /[ seem/[] ],
     x(s(s(0)),i,9,[]) /[
      x(s(s(0)),n,10,[])/[],
      x(s(0),i,11,[]) /[
       x(0,i,12,[]) /[ to/[] ],
       x(s(s(0)),v,13,[]) /[
        x(s(s(0)),n,14,[]) /[ john/[] ],
        x(s(0),v,15,[]) /[
         x(0,v,16,[]) /[ be/[] ],
```

```
              x(s(s(0)),a,17,[]) /[intelligent/[] ]]]]]]]]]
   ).

figure(13-3,
 x(s(s(0)),i,1,[]) /[
  x(s(s(0)),n,2,[])/[],
  x(s(0),i,3,[]) /[
   x(0,i,4,[]) /[ (-s)/[] ],
   x(s(s(0)),v,5,[]) /[
    x(s(s(0)),n,6,[])/[],
    x(s(0),v,7,[]) /[
     x(0,v,8,[]) /[ be/[] ],
     x(s(s(0)),v,9,[]) /[
      x(s(s(0)),n,10,[])/[],
      x(s(0),v,11,[]) /[
       x(0,v,12,[]) /['kill + -en'/[] ],
       x(s(s(0)),n,13,[]) /[ john/[] ]]]]]]]
   ).

figure(13-4,
 x(s(s(0)),i,1,[]) /[
  x(s(s(0)),n,2,[]) /[],
  x(s(0),i,3,[]) /[
   x(0,i,4,[]) /[ (-s)/[] ],
   x(s(s(0)),v,5,[]) /[
   x(s(s(0)),n,6,[]) /[],
    x(s(0),v,7,[]) /[
     x(0,v,8,[])/[seem/[] ],
     x(s(s(0)),i,9,[]) /[
      x(s(s(0)),n,10,[]) /[],
      x(s(0),i,11,[]) /[
       x(0,i,12,[]) /[ to/[] ],
       x(s(s(0)),v,13,[]) /[
        x(s(s(0)),n,14,[]) /[ there/[] ],
        x(s(0),v,15,[]) /[
         x(0,v,16,[]) /[ be/[] ],
         x(s(s(0)),v,17,[]) /[
          x(s(s(0)),n,18,[]) /[],
          x(s(0),v,19,[]) /[
           x(0,v,20,[]) /['kill + -en'/[] ],
           x(s(s(0)),n,21,[])/['a man'/[] ]]]]]]]]]]]
   ).

figure(13-5,
 x(s(s(0)),c,1,[]) /[
  x(s(s(0)),a,2,[])/[],
  x(s(0),c,3,[]) /[
   x(0,c,4,[])/[],
   x(s(s(0)),i,5,[]) /[
    x(s(s(0)),n,6,[]) /[],
    x(s(0),i,7,[]) /[
     x(0,i,8,[]) /[(-s)/[]],
     x(s(s(0)),v,9,[]) /[
     x(s(s(0)),n,10,[]) /[ john/[] ],
     x(s(0),v,11,[]) /[
      x(0,v,12,[]) /[ be/[] ],
      x(s(s(0)),a,13,[]) /['how tall'/[]]]]]]]]]
   ).

figure(13-6,
 x(s(s(0)),c,1,[]) /[
```

```
   x(s(s(0)),n,2,[])/[],
  x(s(0),c,3,[]) /[
    x(0,c,4,[])/[],
    x(s(s(0)),i,5,[]) /[
      x(s(s(0)),n,6,[]) /[],
      x(s(0),i,7,[]) /[
        x(0,i,8,[])/[
            x(0,v,9,[])/[do/[]],
            x(0,i,8,[])/[(-s)/[]] ],
        x(s(s(0)),v,10,[]) /[
         x(s(s(0)),n,11,[])/[john/[] ],
        x(s(0),v,12,[]) /[
         x(0,v,13,[]) /[],
         x(s(s(0)),v,14,[]) /[
          x(s(0),v,15,[]) /[
           x(0,v,16,[]) /[ see/[] ],
           x(s(s(0)),n,17,[]) /[ who/[] ]]]]]]]]]
    ).

figure(13-7,
 x(s(s(0)),c,6,[]) /[
  x(s(s(0)),n,7,[])/[],
  x(s(0),c,8,[]) /[
    x(0,c,9,[])/[],
    x(s(s(0)),i,10,[]) /[
      x(s(s(0)),n,11,[]) /[
      x(s(0),n,17,[]) /[
        x(0,n,12,[]) /[ pictures/[] ],
        x(s(s(0)),p,13,[]) /[
        x(s(0),p,18,[]) /[
          x(0,p,14,[]) /[ of/[] ],
          x(s(s(0)),n,15,[]) /[ who/[] ]]]],
      x(s(0),i,16,[]) /['are on the table'/[] ]]]]
  ).

%%%%% Section 13.3

recp(Tree) :- \+ recp_violation(_,Tree).

recp_violation(Node,Tree) :-
    subtree(Node/[],Tree),
    feature(index: _,Node,Node),
    \+ feature(pronominal: +,Node,Node),
    \+ head_governs(_,Node,Tree).

head_governs(x(0,C,N,F),Node,Tree) :-
    subtree(x(0,C,N,F)/_,Tree),          % redundant
    \+ head_intervenes(x(0,C,N,F),_,Node,Tree),
    governs(x(0,C,N,F),Node,Tree).

head_intervenes(X,x(0,C,N,F),Node,Tree) :-
    i_commands(x(0,C,N,F),Node,Tree),
    \+ i_commands(x(0,C,N,F),X,Tree).
end{verbatim}
\begin{verbatim}
figure(13-8,
 x(s(s(0)),c,1,[]) /[
  x(s(s(0)),n,2,[])/[],
  x(s(0),c,3,[]) /[
    x(0,c,4,[])/[],
    x(s(s(0)),i,5,[]) /[
```

```
        x(s(s(0)),n,6,[]) /[],
        x(s(0),i,7,[]) /[
          x(0,i,8,[]) /[
              x(0,v,9,[])/[do/[]],
              x(0,i,8,[]) /[(-ed)/[]]],
          x(s(s(0)),v,10,[]) /[
        x(s(s(0)),n,11,[]) /[ he/[] ],
          x(s(0),v,12,[]) /[
            x(0,v,13,[]) /[],
          x(s(s(0)),v,14,[]) /[
        x(s(s(0)),n,15,[]) /[],
          x(s(0),v,16,[]) /[
            x(0,v,17,[]) /[ believe/[] ],
            x(s(s(0)),c,18,[]) /[
              x(s(s(0)),n,19,[])/[],
              x(s(0),c,20,[]) /[
                x(0,c,21,[]) /[],
                x(s(s(0)),i,22,[]) /[
                  x(s(s(0)),n,23,[]) /[],
                  x(s(0),i,24,[]) /[
                    x(0,i,25,[past: '+',index:V]) /[
                    x(0,v,26,[index:V])/[will/[]],
                    x(0,i,25,[past: '+',index:V]) /[] ],
                  x(s(s(0)),v,27,[]) /[
            x(s(s(0)),n,28,[])/[ who/[]],
                  x(s(0),v,29,[]) /[
                  x(0,v,30,[]) /[],
                  x(s(s(0)),v,31,[]) /[
                  x(s(0),v,32,[]) /[
                    x(0,v,33,[]) /[ win/[] ]]]]]]]]]]]]]]]]
  ).

figure(13-9,
  x(s(s(0)),c,1,[]) /[
   x(s(s(0)),a,2,[])/[],
   x(s(0),c,3,[]) /[
     x(0,c,4,[])/[],
     x(s(s(0)),i,5,[]) /[
       x(s(s(0)),n,6,[]) /[],
       x(s(0),i,7,[]) /[
        x(0,i,8,[]) /[
            x(0,v,9,[])/[do/[]],
            x(0,i,8,[]) /[ (-s)/[] ]],
        x(s(s(0)),v,10,[]) /[
         x(s(s(0)),n,11,[]) /[ you/[] ],
         x(s(0),v,12,[]) /[
          x(0,v,13,[]) /[],
          x(s(s(0)),v,14,[]) /[
           x(s(s(0)),n,15,[])/[],
           x(s(0),v,16,[]) /[
            x(0,v,17,[]) /[ think/[] ],
            x(s(s(0)),c,18,[]) /[
             x(s(s(0)),a,19,[])/[],
             x(s(0),c,20,[]) /[
              x(0,c,21,[])/[],
              x(s(s(0)),i,22,[]) /[
               x(s(s(0)),n,23,[])/[],
               x(s(0),i,24,[]) /[
                x(0,i,25,[]) /[ (-ed)/[] ],
                x(s(s(0)),v,26,[]) /[
                x(s(s(0)),n,27,[])/[ john/[]],
```

```
x(s(0),v,28,[]) /[
x(0,v,29,[]) /[],
x(s(s(0)),v,30,[]) /[
  x(s(s(0)),v,30,[]) /[
   x(s(s(0)),n,31,[])/[],
   x(s(0),v,32,[]) /[
    x(0,v,33,[]) /[ fix/[] ],
    x(s(s(0)),n,34,[]) /['the car'/[] ]]],
   x(s(s(0)),a,35,[]) /[ how/[] ]]]]]]]]]]]]]]
).
```

Notes

Chapter 1

1. Among computational linguists, Marcus (1980) is probably responsible for inspiring recent widespread interest in functional explanations of universals. The idea is developed further by Berwick and Weinberg (1984), van de Koot (1990) and others, and has been criticized by J.D. Fodor (1983; 1985) among others. Inspired by these functionalist projects, Stabler (1983) presented a rather different alternative to explicit representation theories, arguing that given a good performance model that explicitly represents and uses the grammar to compute certain representations, we could construct another model that computes the very same representations without any explicit representation of the grammar. Of course, the onus is on the defender of such a view to show that the constructed model can do what the original does, and to show that the constructed model does not have any representation of the principles. Unfortunately, the latter idea relies on a concept of representation that that is really not clear. It is notoriously difficult to say when we ought to regard a physical system as representing something. (On this point, cf. Stabler, 1987.) A second problem, though, is that the "original" model of the argument is lacking. That is, we do not yet know how to design a good performance model even given an explicit representation of the grammar!

Chapter 2

1. The basic logical ideas presented here are covered in detail in most of the standard texts on formal logic. My presentation in §2.1 is based on Enderton (1972), and §2.3 on Chang and Keisler (1973), and Ebbinghaus, Flum and Thomas (1984). Only the application of the basic ideas to a simple linguistic domain is original here. The proof sketches presented here all correspond to proofs of results about simple number theories that are presented in detail in these texts.

2. See, for example, Matthews (1979).

3. Our presentation is inspired by the presentation of Tarski's ideas in (Corcoran et al., 1974), where the generalization to various theories of strings was explicitly taken into account. Their formulation also facilitates the comparison with theories of arithmetic, which we will consider below.

4. For further discussion of categoricity in theories of strings, see Tarksi's (1934, 74) remarks. For clear discussions of the need for a second order induction axiom to guarantee categoricity, see Kleene (1952, §75) or Boolos and Jeffrey (1980, §18).

5. Cf. Boolos (1981) on sentences of the form "For every A there is a B." Cf. Stabler and Keenan (1991) for more extensive discussion of inexpressibility and for stronger results about inexpressibility even in finite models.

Chapter 3

1. For better introductions to automatic proof methods see, e.g., Stickel (1986b), Lewis and Papadimitriou (1981, §§8,9), Chang and Lee (1973), Gallier (1986), or Loveland (1978).

2. Some texts reverse the order of term and variable, writing $\{t/X\}$.

3. Surprisingly, most texts do not introduce a notion corresponding to our "answer substitution" for general resolution. The idea is implicit in Green's (1969) work which is discussed in, e.g., Chang and Lee (1973, §11). A more restricted idea is fundamental to SLD resolution and Prolog – see, e.g., Lloyd's (1974) "correct answer" and "computed answer."

4. See for example Chomsky's (1986b) account which is the subject of §10, below, Sportiche's (1990) account discussed in §13, Rizzi (1990, §3.2), and many others.

5. See, for example, Clark (1979) (discussed in §3.5, below), Yahya and Henschen (1985), Chi and Henschen (1988), Rajasekar, Lobo and Minker (1988), Minker and Rajasekar (1988), Lobo, Minker, and Rajasekar (1990), Ross and Topor (1988), and Wakayama and Payne (1988).

6. Since we have mentioned Skolem transforms, it is perhaps worth noting that there are other satisfiability-preserving transforms of theories that "eliminate" equality. See for example Dreben and Goldfarb (1979, §8). Unfortunately, though, these transforms pose the same computational problems as the original theories with equality, since they eliminate logical equality just by introducing an appropriate axiomatization of an equality predicate.

7. See Morris (1969); Digricoli (1983); Digricoli and Harrison (1986).

8. As noted in Stabler (1989), our implementation of SEq resolution is carried out in a "model elimination" theorem prover. This approach is briefly discussed in §3.7 below, and again in §§14,15.

9. Sometimes the ∧ is replaced by a comma, and sometimes the ← is replaced by :-, as in the Prolog listings in §§4.5, 5.5, 5.6.

10. "SLD" is usually thought to stand for Definite clause Linear resolution with a function that Selects the literal to be resolved upon. A nice formal treatment of SLD-resolution is provided by Lloyd (1987).

11. An elegant Horn clause theorem prover Hornlog is proposed by Gallier and Raatz (1987). They use the following example to illustrate the contrast with Prolog. Consider the Horn theory:

$\leftarrow sounds\_great(X) \wedge analog(X)$
$digital(beethoven) \leftarrow$
$analog(bach) \leftarrow$
$analog(mozart) \leftarrow$
$sounds\_great(X) \leftarrow digital(X)$

This theory is inconsistent with $sounds\_great(X) \leftarrow$, but Prolog would not be able to prove this fact. Hornlog finds two refutations with the answer substitutions $\{X/bach\}$ and $\{X/mozart\}$ respectively.

12. Actually, "SLDNF" is usually used to name the previous, unnecessarily strong restriction that all selected negative literals be ground. However, here we use "SLDNF" to refer to this more general, safe strategy described in Lloyd (1987, 94). The extension of standard SLDNF results to this case is straightforward.

13. In the second, revised version of his text, Lloyd (1987, 87) removes the last sentence of the following quoted passage, but it is both correct and important, so I quote the earlier version. There is no *logical* barrier to non-Horn deductions that construct answer substitutions, as indicated by the general results of §3.2 above and Stabler (1990a).

14. Many introductions to first order logic and model theory discuss the possibility of avoiding functions with the use of appropriate relations. For example, in a discussion of these options in axiomatizations of group theory, Bridge (1977, 9-10) describes the situation very clearly: "The structure

$< G, M, e >$ ... is, from a purely formal point of view, simpler than the structure $< G, =, \cdot, e >$ ... The function $\cdot$ is replaced by the relation M. This kind of replacement is always possible when the set of functions $\{f_j\}_{j \in J}$ in the relational structure $\mathcal{U}$ is non-empty. We substitute for the $\mu(j)$-ary function f_j the $\mu(j) + 1$-ary relation R_{f_j} given by $< a_0, \ldots, a_{\mu(j)} > \in R_{f_j}$ iff $f_j(a_0, \ldots, a_{\mu(j)-1}) = a_{\mu(j)}$. We can go one stage further and replace each distinguished constant c by the unary relation $R_c = \{c\}$ so that the resulting structure $\mathcal{U}^{\mathcal{R}} = < A, \{R_i\}_{i \in I} \cup \{R_{f_j}\}_{j \in J} \cup \{R_{c_k}\}_{k \in K} >$ is purely relational. Although purely relational structures are technically simpler ... we prefer, in most cases, to consider structures with the added complexity due to functions and constants. In the transition from a function f to the associated relation R_f the functional character is obscured." (Cf. also Ebbinghaus, Flum and Thomas, 1984 §VIII.1; Enderton, 1972, §2.7.) We prefer to use constants and functions as well - for reasons of readability (to humans), but for proof-theoretic simplicity we can only use functions that are 1-1 in the intended interpretation if we are to restrict ourselves to functions whose denotations are all pairwise distinct in the clausal form. All functions that are not 1-1 must be treated as relations and represented with predicates.

15. The term "selective SLDNF" is taken from Chan (1986), though it is there applied to the more restrictive safe strategy in which negative literals are selected only if they are ground. As before, the extension of results to our more general inference rule is straightforward.

16. We have used an implementation of model elimination modified with special equality rules. Stickel (1986b, §2.12) provides a nice informal introduction to model elimination. A thorough account of the method and its relation to resolution is presented in Loveland (1978). Implementations are described in Fleisig et al. (1974) and Stickel (1986). Our implementation is more similar to that of Fleisig et al., since we have been experimenting with the use of automatically introduced lemmas, etc., as described by Fleisig et al. and Loveland. The special equality rules we added to model elimination are those mentioned in §3.4, above, and described in more detail in Stabler (1989).

Chapter 4

1. It is a good exercise for readers familiar with other methods, such as Jeffrey's (1981) tableaux method or Mates' (1972) natural deduction method, to check this out if it is not immediately obvious, as various transformations are considered. A nice survey of such standard methods and fundamental relations among them is provided by Sundholm (1983).

2. Clark and Tärnlund (1977), Tärnlund (1978), Hansson and Tärnlund (1982).

3. This transformation is essentially the one proposed for "Definite Clause Grammars" (DCGs) by Pereira and Warren (1980). It is often provided as a built in feature of Prolog systems.

4. In this standard notation, the grammar is defined by specifying its nonterminal categories N, its terminal categories Σ, the special nonterminal sentence symbol S, and the set of rewrite rules, or productions, P. For simplicity we assume $N \cap \Sigma = \emptyset$. Since we are considering context-free grammars, each rewrite rule has the form $Cat \rightarrow Cat_1 \ldots Cat_k$, allowing the nonterminal Cat to be rewritten as the (possibly empty) sequence of terminal and nonterminal categories $Cat_1 \ldots Cat_k$.

5. I am one of those people. For a discussion of the error, see, for example, Tomita (1986).

6. This sort of tree notation, using nested function expressions, is quite common. Alternative representations will be discussed in §15.

7. A bijection is a 1-1 onto function.

8. As discussed in Stabler (1990), this feature distinguishes the present approach from Gödel's (1931). The necessarily less intuitive Gödelization approach has been used in a logic programming context by Bowen and Kowalski (1982).

9. This example is slightly modified from Stabler (1990), where a slightly different tree notation and slightly different semantics are used.

10. This point is familiar to logic programmers. For example, Sterling and Shapiro (1986, 38) make the relevant point about "type conditions," but the point is properly semantic. That is, the missing conditions should not really be regarded as a (metalogical) condition on "types," where a "type" is defined as an infinite set of terms, but rather as a (logical) condition needed for the statement to be true when it is universally quantified.

11. Proofs of these propositions appear in Stabler (1990).

12. Cf., e.g., Aho and Ullman (1972).

13. For more rigorous introductions to hyperresolution, see, Robinson (1965a), Chang and Lee (1973, §6.5), McCharen et al. (1976) or Stickel (1986b, §2.6).

14. Other bottom-up approaches to logic programming, similar in spirit to this idea from context-free parsing, have been explored. See, for example, Ramakrishnan (1988). Frisch (1986) considers a bottom-up resolution method for context-free parsing with restricted quantification.

Chapter 5

1. We will follow the standard convention of marking ungrammatical examples with an asterisk.

2. Kripke (1982) has argued that these abstractions yield theories with no empirical content. This challenge to scientific legitimacy has been defused, I think, by Stabler (1987), Chomsky (1986b) and others.

3. See, for example, Marcus (1980), Ford, Bresnan and Kaplan (1982), Briscoe (1983), Crain and Steedman (1985), Pritchett (1988), van de Koot (1990).

4. Cf., e.g., Hopcroft and Ullmann (1979).

5. Manaster-Ramer (1988, 101) notes a technical error in Shieber's formulation of the argument, but indicates a way to avoid the problem.

6. Pullum and Gazdar (1982; 1985) rightly object to arguments that try to draw a conclusion about the capabilities of arbitrary context-free grammars on the basis of a single context-free grammar – a different form of argument from the one just suggested. However, they also seem to object to informal arguments of any kind. In discussing one argument, Pullum and Gazdar (1982, 473) say: "There are several non sequiturs here, the central one being that 'there seems to be no way of using [phrase structure] rules' for some task does not license the inference that no successful phrase structure ... account could be devised." It is of course true that informal arguments may turn out to be incorrect or difficult to formalize, but that is the risk of informal argumentation in general. Fortunately, very many things that seem to be so, even before they are derived in complete formal detail, actually do turn out to be so. For more formal analyses of the conciseness and efficiency of context-free grammars and related systems, see Barton et al. (1987). It is also instructive to look at GPSG attempts to handle the "movement" phenomena discussed below. See, for example, Fodor (1983), Hukari and Levine (1987).

7. In Pereira's treatment, the item added is not * but *close*.

8. These strategies are explored in Stabler (1987a).

9. Stabler (1987) attempts to deal with some of the following problems in the "restricted logic grammar" (RLG) framework. The results are not inspiring, and this led to the much more direct approach of Parts II and III, below.

10. Some of these examples were first pointed out to me by Mike Maxwell.

Chapter 6

1. See §12 below for a proposal about fitting determiners into the X-bar system.

2. Cf., e.g., Radford (1988) for extensive introductory discussion of adjuncts and complements across categories. For a different view about categorial structure, and in particular, about the position of adjunct modifiers, see, e.g., Abney (1986), Larson (1988; 1990; 1991).

3. One popular view is that the precedence ordering is determined, at least in part, by a parameter of case theory which specifies a "direction of case assignment," and by a parameter of θ-theory that specifies "direction of θ-role assignment." See, e.g. Stowell (1981), Koopman (1984), Travis (1984).

4. The attentive reader will notice below one other place where ordering is relevant: our formulation of the adjunction transformation allows for both left and right adjunction. But the distinction is really irrelevant for the syntax.

5. However, the simple idea that the VP is restructured to form a complex verb V+P is rejected by Kayne and Rizzi on the grounds that material can intervene between the V and P, as is almost possible in English: *?? Mary was spoken rudely to.* For this and other reasons, Koster (1986, §§5.5-5.8) rejects the reanalysis stories altogether and proposes a simpler alternative. Burzio (1986, §5) has provided a movement account of the constructions that motivated Rizzi's reanalysis proposal. Baker (1988, 202, 259ff) speculates that a movement analysis can unify the reanalysis constructions with similar incorporation phenomena, allowing P to move to a governing verb – i.e. from a complement PP but not an adjunct PP – arguing that benefactive and instrumental PPs are complements, while temporal, manner and reason PPs are adjuncts. This goes some way towards accounting for the examples displayed above, but apparently faces some trouble with the last 3. Sportiche (1990, §3.4.2) has a similar view and proposes an additional idea to explain why such extractions do not occur in most languages.

6. See Williams (1986) for a critique and alternative to reconstruction stories. See, e.g. Hornstein and Weinberg (1990) for a recent defense of them.

7. This is essentially the idea proposed by Chomsky (1986a, 92n10).

8. See, e.g., Johnson (1990, 1988), Pereira (1987), Moshier and Rounds (1987).

9. The definition of *lexical* will be modified in §10.2 in order to get the account of the ECP to work on some English examples. Chomsky (1986a) does not mention the idea that the set of lexical categories may also vary from one language to another. For example, Huang (1982) and Lasnik and Saito (1984) assume that I is a lexical category in Chinese.

10. Mark Johnson (p.c.) and others have pointed out to me that since each of these two parameters has only two settings, we could use 0-place predicates. We could, for example, allow the setting *head_spec* or ¬*head_spec*. (Cf. Johnson, 1989.) It slightly simplifies our axiomatization, though, to use predicates with arguments as shown here. Notice how the axioms for $x1$ and xp, below, use the argument to these predicates as an indication of the position of the head, where 0 means last in the sequence, and $s(0)$ means first.

11. Here we do not allow for adjunctions to X0, but this may need to be modified for some theories. *Barriers* considers base-generated adjuncts at some length, e.g. in discussing the CED and the "adjunct condition" (see §9.4), but does not provide the X-bar restrictions for such structures. In §12.2, we consider a proposal that assumes that I might have an adjoined V, which would require this account to be changed to allow an X0 adjunct of Y0.

Chapter 7

1. The empty category in *(a)* is a trace, but it turns out that the empty NP position in *(b)* is something with rather different properties, called "PRO." Both types of NPs will be discussed below.

2. Unfortunately, human language is not quite so simple. There also seem to be arguments for the view that binding principles apply before movement, on the basis of examples like *Which pictures of himself does John like?* or *Which friends of each other did they talk about?* or **Whose mother does he love?* To handle these cases, reconstruction analyses have been proposed, according to which binding principles apply after movements, but also after a reconstruction step which can put a phrase back into the position of one of its traces. See, e.g., Chomsky (1976), Lasnik and Uriagereka (1988, §5.2.5), van Riemsdijk and Williams (1986, §13.3). Alternative stories that avoid reconstruction in favor of some other theoretical device are proposed in, e.g., Higginbotham (1980) and van Riemsdijk and Williams (1981).

3. Chomsky's (1981, §3.2.2) discussion of this is worth reading, and Bouchard's (1982) more extended discussion. For a critique see, for example, Postal and Pullum (1982).

4. This approach to move-α is unique to this work, as far as I know. The "SD-SC" (structural description-structural change) transformations of earlier syntactic theories are formalized by Ginsberg and Partee (1969), Peters and Ritchie (1973) and Lasnik and Kupin (1980). The rule move-α is a rather different from the SD-SC rules of earlier theories, and the formalization presented in this chapter of course reflects this. Our approach is also distinctive in that we do not merely express the grammar rules

as operations on formal objects (trees, bracketings, phrase markers or whatever). Here, not only the trees but also the rule move-α is encoded in a declarative formalism. Also, as noted in §6, the worries about restricting the power of transformations – the primary motivation of these earlier formal studies – has been distilled into the problem of appropriately specifying the parameters of language variation, and so is not a concern here. The goal is just to be true to the intentions of the linguists and as elegant as possible. I am indebted to Mark Johnson and David Weir for discussions about formalizing relations as tree transductions.

5. It is important to remember that these productions are not sentences of first order logic. They are more like the rewrite rules of a regular or context-free grammar, except that they use the notion of the states of the transducing device. For rigorous definitions and a survey of results see Gécseg and Steinby (1984). For an informal survey, see Thatcher (1973). Our terribly brief account is nonstandard in that (i) we do not use the standard function notation for trees – our notation has the advantage of allowing complex terms as node labels; and (ii) we do not rank our alphabet as is now usually done in algebraic treatments of tree automata – but it is a trivial matter to associate a ranked alphabet with an arbitrary alphabet, as shown in Gécseg and Steinby (1984) and elsewhere.

6. Notice that the same kind of incompleteness is present in "Definite Clause Grammar" (DCG) representations of context-free grammars discussed in §4 and in Pereira and Warren (1980), and indeed in many other Prolog programs.

7. This kind of predicate is very commonly used in logic programming, where it is often described as being used in the "forward" direction to select a tree from a sequence and then in the "backwards" direction to insert a tree in a sequence. See, e.g., Sterling and Shapiro (1986, 53).

8. Notice that this independence of vocabulary holds only if the logical domain contains only trees that are in both the input and output sets. If the domain contains trees in which a movement of d to $\emptyset$ is possible but which should not be transduced, then our definitions of the states would have to be appropriately conditioned.

9. It should be observed, though, that the axioms could be more concise. Notice in particular the disjunctions on the right-hand-sides of the definitions of $zero\_d$ and d_zero. I have used two existentially quantified variables to form terms $[T0|T0s]$ where I could have used a single existentially quantified variable $Seq0$. This small sacrifice in conciseness does not significantly decrease the readability of the axiom, but it significantly reduces the search for proofs involving the axioms because of the fact that the first disjuncts will only be used when Tree0 dominates a non-empty sequence, and the second disjuncts will only be used when Tree0 dominates an empty sequence. Later axioms will show similar minor departures from elegance when they have this kind of advantage.

10. The first displayed example where renumbering has an effect is Figure 9.4, where node 15 is renumbered because it is no longer a segment of node 13. In order to make the trees easier to read, in many of our figures the node occurrence number of the original D-structure position after the substitution is used as the value of the index for every node in the chain produced by move-α, but this assignment convention cannot be adhered to in all cases. It is sometimes inconsistent with the percolation of indices required by the "amalgamation" of verb and inflection, as described in §9.2, and with the sharing of indices required by "SPEC-head" agreement, as described in §10.5. To allow the conventional assignment whenever it is not in conflict with other principles of the theory, our implementation adds to the definition of $zero\_cat$ a condition which says that either the index is the conventional value or else $x = x$; that is, either assign the conventional value or leave the value unspecified so that it can be fixed as required by other principles.

11. *Barriers* is not actually clear about whether node1 can only be a nonargument maximal projection, or whether it can be maximal only if it is a nonargument. The latter idea, chosen here, fits better with the account of head movement developed later in *Barriers* and discussed in §9.2, below.

12. The renumbering relations do not have special linguistic interest, so their definitions have been left out of the text, but can be found in Appendix B. As mentioned in footnote 10, the relations almost always have the most straightforward instances.

13. The pumping lemma for finite state tree recognizers (Thatcher, 1973) (Gécseg and Steinby, 1984, Lemma 10.1) generalizes immediately to both R-transducers and to frontier-to-root tree transducers ("F-transducers"). David Weir drew my attention to this technique for establishing results about the range of tree transducers. Cf. Vijay-Shanker, Weir, and Joshi (1987).

14. Cf. the discussions of this issue in Huang (1982), Lasnik and Saito (1984), May (1985), and in §10, below.

Chapter 8

1. Cf., e.g., Chomsky (1980a, 1981), Rouveret and Vergnaud (1980), and references cited in these works. A good introduction is provided in van Riemsdijk and Williams (1986).

2. Actually, the case filter has been somewhat discredited. See, for example, Lasnik and Uriagereka (1988, §6.1) for a good review of this recent research.

3. See Chomsky (1986a, 11ff) and references cited there for other arguments that CP is not always a barrier to government. Cf. also the structures of §9.6.

4. Chomsky (1981, §3.2.2) surveys some of the differences between case and θ-role.

5. To achieve the effect of L-marking heads and specifiers, Chomsky (1986a, 24) actually presents the definition of L-marking in terms of agreement, assuming that SPEC-head agreement will make the head and specifier agree, and percolation will ensure that the head agrees with its projections. We formalize SPEC-head agreement in §10.6, but it involves having certain features in common, whereas a stronger relation seems to be required here.

6. For discussion of the requirements on PRO that follow from binding theory, see, e.g. Lasnik and Uriagereka (1988, §2.2).

Chapter 9

1. Once this principle is accepted, one might well wonder why transformations are needed. The answer is that the SPC is actually does not quite say that all structures must be well-formed D-structures, as we will see. Furthermore, transformations link the "moved" constituents to the positions in which they are licensed, and second, the linking of positions that is established in this way is subject to special constraints (e.g. subjacency). We return to consider this still controversial position again in §15.

2. This restriction may turn out to be accounted for by other principles. The projection principle, in particular, seems to overlap. Cf. Emonds' (1985, §3.5) remarks on this point.

3. See §13 for a formalization of Pollock's (1989) account of this, and references cited there for other views.

4. Figures 9.3 and 9.6 do not show the internal structure of the object AP. Stowell (1978; 1981, §4.1) argues persuasively that copular *be* is a raising verb that does not assign θ-roles. On this view, the surface subject originates as subject of an AP small clause, where it gets its θ role, and raises to the specifier of IP. This is one of the proposals that led to regarding a wide range of surface forms as derived by raising the object to subject position: not only with traditional raising verbs, but ergatives (or unaccusatives), middle constructions, etc. are often supposed to be derived in this way. See, e.g. Burzio (1986, §1), Hoekstra (1988), Chomsky (1986a, 78), and §12, below, for similar views.

5. I follow Pollock (1989, §4.1) in assuming that the verb movement in *Barriers* typically involves adjunction, though the movement of I or V-I to an empty C can of course be a substitution. Otherwise, it is hard to make sense of Chomsky's use of Lasnik's principle about affixes, and of Chomsky's (1986a, 94n48) worry about how to block the raising of the head of an NP to the amalgamated V-I. However, Radford (1988, §§8.2-8.3) assumes that all head movements are substitutions, and even suggests that these substitutions are structure preserving in some weakened sense. Radford is apparently inclined toward this view by Koopman's (1984, 42) observation that in Vata, the verb does not raise to I if there is an auxiliary verb, just as in English V-I does not raise to C if there is a complementizer. However, these facts may be explained by other assumptions. Cf., e.g. Koopman (1984, 152n4), Pollock (1989), Chomsky (1988).

6. See, e.g., Baker (1989), Travis (1984), Marantz (1981), Pollock (1989), Chomsky (1988).

7. This tree and the next are adapted from Bennis and Hoekstra (1989, 103,141). Notice that they show the subjects as originating inside the VPs. We explore the idea that subjects are VP-internal in most or all languages, including English, in §13.

8. On these structures in Dutch, see, e.g. Bennis and Hoekstra (1989, §5), den Besten (1983), den Besten and Edmondson (1983), Zaenen (1979), Rutten (1991). On the computational implications of these structures, see Bresnan et al. (1982), Bach et al. (1986), Joshi (1989), Kroch and Santorini (1987).

9. The "counting" aspect of n-subjacency should be clear. The proposal is that structures that satisfy 1-subjacency are good, but the acceptability of structures satisfying n-subjacency for $n > 1$ degrades. With the axiomatization proposed here, to show that a movement of α to β satisfies n-subjacency, we show that there are not $n + 1$ barriers for β that exclude α. It is interesting to compare these ideas about subjacency with proposals to the effect that a version of 1-subjacency is somehow built in to the architecture of the human language processor (Marcus, 1980; Berwick and Weinberg, 1984, §5; Kroch and Joshi, 1985, §6), that the human language processor is unable to "count" (Berwick and Weinberg, 1984, 158f), and that the grammars of human language should be unable to express counting relations. I hope to explore this interesting topic elsewhere.

10. We have not developed the theory of θ-assignment, but notice that Figure 9.8 indicates that the PP is θ marked by N, and the embedded wh-phrase is θ marked by P. Stowell (1981, §3.2) rejects this sort of analysis, suggesting instead that the head noun assigns a θ role to the object of the preposition, but unless other adjustments in the theory were made, this analysis would not fit with Chomsky's account of the extraction possibilities here. The PP would then be a barrier to extraction.

11. These structures are discussed in more detail in §11, below. This idea about the parametric barrier is not a surprise: compare the "tensed S condition" of Chomsky's (1973) "Conditions on Transformations," and the many discussions of this constraint that have followed.

12. In fact, it is not quite clear how improper movements should be handled in the binding theory. Aoun (1985, §2.10.1) proposes that S-bar (CP) breaks an A-chain, while Chomsky (1986a, 93n20) makes the more general suggestion that the embedded trace in the last example would be an A-bar bound R-expression that is A-bound in the domain of its chain, and this should be ruled out by condition C.

Chapter 10

1. Chomsky discussed these examples in a lecture entitled "Language and other Cognitive Systems," delivered at the University of Western Ontario, October 1987. Similar examples are discussed in Chomsky (1986a, §6).

2. It is not quite clear what will happen to empty categories like C at D-structure. Are these to be marked *+pronominal* too, and if so, what happens to this feature when a category moves into it? As indicated below, rather than assuming that the only nonpronominal empty categories are traces, we will assume that at S-structure, the only nonpronominal empty categories with index features are traces.

3. Notice that in the second example, below, if the wh-phrase *how* had come from the position modifying the matrix IP, the structure would be well-formed. It is only the extraction from the embedded adjunct position that is ill-formed, as indicated here.

4. For various views on the category and position of adjunct phrases, see, for example, Huang (1982, 535ff), Lasnik and Saito (1984), Larson (1988; 1990; 1991).

5. This is the "narrower" of the two versions of minimality that Chomsky considers. The examples from Torrego support this version.

6. Chomsky (1986a, 47-48) suggests an alternative formalization of this matter: rather than modifying the definition of minimal government to be insensitive to projections of bare categories, we could say that an intermediate level node is present only when its head is not a bare category with no features. This suggestion would have an equivalent effect on the structures just shown, but it could not be part of X-bar theory or any other constraint on D-structures, since we want to allow bare heads as landing sites for movements. It is not clear where the principle would apply.

7. Chomsky indicates that he wants to regard ($np(2, [index : 9]), v(6, [index : 9]), np(9, [index : 9])$) as an extended chain. Unfortunately, there is a minor technical snag here: this is a chain of the form $(\alpha_1, \ldots, \alpha_{n-1}, \beta, \alpha_n)$ rather than a chain of the form allowed by the definition, $(\alpha_1, \ldots, \alpha_n, \beta)$ In other words, according to the definition given, ($np(2, [index : 9]), v(6, [index : 9]), np(9, [index : 9])$)) is not an extended chain, since ($np(2, [index : 9]), v(6, [index : 9])$)) is not a chain. The minor fix we introduce here, using a special notion of "link" for extended chains, avoids this problem. I think that this captures the effect Chomsky (1986a, 75) intends when he says "the final element of an extended chain ... is properly governed if it is governed by the terminal element of the chain."

8. We leave aside the question of how the verb gets its participial morphology, and how this morphology manages to "capture" the external θ-role of the verb. See, e.g., Jaeggli (1986); Baker and Johnson (1989).

9. Notice that such an addition might also get back the contrast noted at the very beginning of this chapter, which was lost when the disjunctive formulation was rejected. Conjunctive accounts are considered in, e.g., Stowell (1984; 1986); Koopman and Sportiche (1986; 1988; 1990); Aoun et al. (1987); Rizzi (1990). We consider the Koopman and Sportiche proposal in §13.

10. Lasnik and Saito (1984) and Lasnik and Uriagereka (1988) do not need to delete an intermediate trace adjoined to VP to account for examples like *What$_i$ did you believe that Bill [won t$_i$]*, since adjunction to VP is not required in their analyses. However, they do need deletion to account for extractions across *that*, as in *who do you think that Mary said won the race*, and to account for extraction from adjuncts, as in *why do you believe that john [left t]*. They discuss allowing these either by deleting *that* between S-structure and LF or else by deleting an intermediate trace. Deletion of intermediate traces, unless they are otherwise required, is also used in earlier accounts of ECP effects by Stowell (1981) and others.

11. The latter assumption that *combien* is a specifier, a phrase, is particularly questionable. Sportiche (p.c.) points out that *combien* looks more like the head Q of a phrase QP than like a full phrase QP, in which case it is hard to see how it could be fronted on any of the accounts being considered here.

12. Guéron (1981) has suggested that a "complete constituent constraint" rules out "incomplete" structures in which a N1 is left by itself, as in extraction of the QP from English NPs, whereas the similar extraction in French leaves a PP. The insertion of the French preposition is triggered by a [+N] feature on the quantifier *combien*, a feature that most English quantifiers lack. Safir (1985, §2.6) similarly assumes a specific difference between French and English quantifiers. Obenauer (1983, §1.3; 1984) has explored the problem in greater depth, and makes a number of interesting suggestions. See also Obenauer (1976).

Chapter 11

1. Cf., e.g., Szabolcsi (1981; 1987; 1989); Fukui (1986); Speas (1986); Fukui and Speas (1986); Ritter (1990); Valois (1990); Crook (1990).

2. The situation is complicated in a respect that Stowell does not point out: the subjacency-violating derivation also violates the ECP. In Figure 11.5, for example, traces 21 and 16 will get marked -γ. Trace 16 can be deleted but 21 cannot. However, Stowell's (1984; 1986) proposals about the ECP differ from the *Barriers* account. A full consideration of these issues are beyond the scope of this project.

3. Friedin (1978) discusses this kind of problem.

Chapter 12

1. Many competing analyses based on *Barriers*-like assumptions are appearing. See, for example, Chomsky (1988), Ouhalla (1990), Iatridou (1990), Pesetsky (1989), Johnson (1989, 1990). The phenomena discussed here are of course considered in many other theoretical frameworks as well.

2. This raising from small clause analysis extends the idea of Stowell's (1978, 1981) that was mentioned in footnote 4 of §9.2. Pollock does not commit himself to any view about the category of the small clause, but Figure 12.1 follows Stowell's (1989, 1989a) tentative assumption that NP small clauses are NPs. Pollock suggests that the structure of this small clause, not shown in the figure, is something like [P t$_i$ [any money L]] where t$_i$ is the trace of the subject NP and L is an abstract predicate. With regard the assumption of a null θ-role assigning preposition P, Pollock (1989, 388) refers to Kayne (1983, 134-136) and Guéron (1986). The special ability of *have* and *be* to raise then follows on the assumption that the amalgamated structure formed by V-raising to the Modern English Agr blocks the ability of (any element in the chain of) the verb to assign θ-roles. A verb with arguments needing θ-roles would be unable to assign those roles if it raised to Agr, and a θ-criterion violation would result. 3. Dialects of American English which do not allow sentences like *John hasn't any money* are presumably dialects in which *have* assigns θ-roles like a main verb.

4. Pollock (1989, §5.5.5) also considers an alternative view in which Neg is not a head, in which case these adjustments would not be required, though other aspects of the account would be more complicated.

5. Pollock also says that the auxiliary verb must be generated "beyond the VP boundary." This fits with the proposal quoted here, and so it is clear that auxiliaries are not assumed to come from inside the VP. Iatridou (1990, 555) seems to get this aspect of Pollock's account wrong, but is correct in any case in observing that it is unappealing to have verbs that do not project to the phrasal level like main verbs and other lexical items.

6. Pollock (1989, 400n33) proposes that English *do* gets a copy of the θ-grid of the verb it selects, as shown in this figure, but the details are not worked out.

Chapter 13

1. Cf., e.g., Stowell (1981); Williams (1975). The category of the VP small clause shown in Figure 13.1 is VP, following Sportiche (1990), but it is not clear that this is right. Koopman and Sportiche (1990) call it Vmax, and some other linguists call it just SC or VC to signify its small clause status. The basic ideas considered in this chapter could be made to work on any of these assumptions.

2. We could assume, following Larson (1988; 1990; 1991) and others, that there is at most one complement as well, but this gets into complications that we do not need to consider here.

3. To account for some data not considered here, Sportiche (1990) complicates the following definition of barriers slightly, but as we will see, this simple formulation already covers a wide range of facts.

4. As pointed out in footnote 4 of §9.2, there is good reason to suppose that the adjective occurs in an AP small clause in constructions like this, and that *John* originates as the subject of this clause.

5. As we noted in footnote 4 of §9 about Figure 9.6, *john* presumably originates as the subject of the AP small clause, though we have not shown this here.

6. This is essentially the proposal of Sportiche (1988).

7. We have here assumed that the modal verb is "amalgamated" with I in the sense of sharing an index with it, in the underlying structure. Then our definition of L-marks allows $c(22, \ldots)$ to L-mark the trace $np(23, \ldots)$.

8. The RECP differs in this respect from the theory presented in Aoun et al. (1987), where the structure with *that* is counted as an ECP violation. They try to dismiss the judgement of speakers for whom the structure is perfectly acceptable by suggesting that some "analogical process" may make such structures seem grammatical when they really are not (1987, 563-564). Lasnik and Saito (1984, 1988), on the other hand, allow the structure, but only by giving it a rather complex and unintuitive derivation.

9. Of course we are no longer assuming that SPEC-head agreement shares index values, as was done in *Barriers*. The modification in the axiomatization required to make this change is trivial.

Chapter 14

1. The definition of *ss_gamma* is axiom 10.1.5. The other axioms are presented in Appendix B. Here we are concentrating on the *Barriers* axiomatization, but a predicate used in Part III is actually much worse than any of the *Barriers* axioms, namely, the *projection* predicate of §13.2, which holds of triples where the first two elements are nodes in the same projection of some category in the tree that is the third element of the triple. The definition of *projection*, also presented in Appendix B, yields 2032 clauses by itself. The method described below for naming subformulas reduces this to 48.

2. See Plaisted and Greenbaum (1986) and Boy de la Tour (1990) for further discussion of this point.

3. The completeness of proof methods that use such "selection functions" was established independently for certain linear resolution methods by Reiter (1971), Kowalski & Kuehner (1971), and for model elimination by Loveland (1972). A different application of this idea to natural language processing is discussed in Stabler (1989a).

4. In Prolog, of course, the identity predicate is typically eliminated from the Horn part of the definition.

5. In §15.4.2, Proposal 9 (together with other grammatical principles) blocks infinitely large structures without empirical consequences like those of the DAC.

6. See, e.g., Toman (1981) on multiple extractions in Czech; Comorovski (1986) on Romanian; Rudin (1988) on Bulgarian, Serbo-Croatian, and Polish; Engdahl (1986) on Swedish; Mahajan (1990, §3.5.1) on Hindi. In some of these examples, scrambling plus wh-movement could be involved, but Comorovski, McDaniel, and Mahajan argue for multiple (long-distance) wh-movements that apparently threaten either the DAC or some other part of the *Barriers* framework. For example, Mahajan suggests that the Hindi examples might be derived by wh-adjunction to IP of the sort that is explicitly blocked in the *Barriers* framework as discussed in §9.4.

7. This aspect of inductive arguments is one of the things that makes them so hard to automate. See, e.g., Burstall (1969), Wegbreit and Spitzen (1976), Boyer and Moore (1979), Bundy (1988), Elkan and McAllester (1988), Hutter (1990). Rather than automating the introduction of induction principles, as is done with heuristic principles in Boyer and Moore's (1979) work, we rely here on the user to supply the necessary principles and guide these proofs. A search problem only arises if the *user* does not see how the induction ought to proceed!

8. It would be interesting to consider whether this induction principle, and the others considered in the next chapter, could be derived from the basic well-founded induction principles for trees discussed in §2.3.

9. Cf., e.g. Rabin (1961), Kreisel and Wang (1955) for general results about the independence of certain classes of sentences from theories of arithmetic lacking some of the induction principles.

10. The usual proof technique would involve constructing a non-standard model of FB that falsifies the sentence of interest. See, for example, the proofs of Propositions 6 and 8 in §2.3.

11. Baker (1988, 53f), Roberts (1991, 210), Johnson (1989). Baltin (1991, §2) argues that the HMC follows from the ECP when we add the "Like Attracts Like Constraint" which says: "When they move, phrasal categories adjoin to phrasal categories and non-phrasal categories adjoin to non-phrasal categories." But this is explicitly stipulated in *Barriers* (Chomsky, 1986a, 73) and was formalized and enforced in §9.1. Even with this constraint, the HMC does not follow.

12. Thanks to Eric Ristad for reminding me to emphasize this point. Huang (1982, 505, 471) formulates the CED as the claim "A may be extracted out of a domain B only if B is properly governed", where "A properly governs B if and only if A governs B and (a) A is a lexical category, or (b) A is co-indexed with B." So far the proposal sounds like the one formulated here, but in this context Huang (1982, 507-507) deploys two versions of government, one for a constraint on movements and the other for a constraint on representations; he assumes S-bar structures with Comp positions; and so on.

13. In structures where co-indexing can result from other operations, we might need a more complex antecedent, one which holds only when A and C are to be regarded as elements of the same "extended chain." See §§9.3 and 10.7 for further discussion of our representational definition of chains.

Chapter 15

1. Chomsky persuasively argues that, in advance of a characterization of human languages, the basic facts of human linguistic performance provide no reason to assume that the parsing or recognition problem for natural languages must be computable in general (Chomsky, 1981, 11-13; 198b, 120-128), but Ristad's (1990) claim is that, after studying human languages, we find that parsing is an NP-complete problem.

2. This problem has been studied from a number of perspectives, in work on handling ungrammaticality (e.g. Hindle, 1983; Jensen et al., 1983; Weischedel et al., 1983; Mellish, 1989), work on incremental interpretation (e.g. Mellish, 1985; Stabler, 1989a), and work on programming systems (Parker, 1987; 1989; Jaffar and Lassez, 1987).

3. The idea that one subproblem must be completed before the next, one step finished before the next is begun, is called the "pedestrian's assumption" in Stabler (1989a). This assumption should be avoided!

4. Actually, this consequence would not follow from our theory if lexical items were given by axioms of the sort shown in §6.5. Instead of $lexicon(the, d, [...])$ we would need something like $lexicon(the, C, F) \leftrightarrow C = d \wedge F = [...]$.

5. As pointed out in Stabler (1990), unlike ancestral induction, 15.3.11 is not usually given explicit consideration in standard logic or set theory texts. The former induction principle is often used in proving results like this one, but the following argument is the most intuitive I have found. Suppose $r \circ s \subseteq r$. It follows that $r \circ s^* \subseteq r$. Then if the identity relation $i \subseteq r$, it follows that $i \circ s^* \subseteq r$. But $i \circ s^* = s^*$, so $s^* \subseteq r$.

6. Cf., e.g. Rabin (1961) and Kreisel and Wang (1955) on the independence of certain classes of sentences from theories of arithmetic lacking some of the induction principles.

7. Our presentation of this first Theorem 15 is based on Harrison's (1978, Thm 12.2.1) similar result for lengths of derivations.

8. Berwick and Weinberg (1985, Appendix A) argue for a linear bound on (augmented) S-structures, but their argument relies on assumptions that are no longer held: cycle-free D-structures; no structure in empty categories; the strict transformational cycle of the Extended Standard Theory; a particular "landing site" theory; a particular theory of coordinate structures and VP ellipsis; no intermediate adjunction sites. Going slightly further afield, Correa (1988, §4.5) presents results which imply a size bound for his grammar for a small fragment of English. Kroch and Joshi (1985) and others have been developing tree adjoining grammars (with local constraints, etc.) for natural languages, and parsers have been proposed for these grammars (e.g. Vijay-Shanker and Joshi, 1985; Schabes and Joshi, 1988; Harbusch, 1990), but these parsers are like Earley's in that they do not presuppose an upper bound on tree size, but only a bound on the size of the smallest tree. Similar remarks apply to GPSG-like systems that exploit context-free parsing techniques – e.g. Shieber (1983).

9. There is some reason to worry that in some syntactic theories (theories that go well beyond the principles in $FB \cup SEQ_{FB}$), LF sizes will be more problematic than D- and S-structure sizes. Ristad (1990) points out that theories of VP ellipsis which explicitly reconstruct the structure of elided verb phrases at LF are committed to structures that are exponentially larger than S-structures. I hope to explore this interesting issue elsewhere.

10. If the co-indexing and co-numbering of nodes were done not with explicit representations of integers, but with pointers among these nodes, this log factor could be eliminated. This is mentioned again in §15.5.2, below.

11. This is not universally accepted. For example, Pesetsky (1982, §3.1) considers the idea that coordinators like *or* and *and* should be regarded as heads that can select any number of complements.

12. See also, e.g., Rizzi (1986) on Italian. There are various accounts of the many languages which allow missing objects. E.g., Oshima (1979) and Kameyama (1988) on Japanese; Platero (1982) on Navajo; Hale (1983) and Jelinek (1984) on Warlpiri; Heath (1986) on Nunggubuyu (Australia); Authier (1988) on KiNande (Zaire); and Farrell (1990) on Brazilian Portuguese.

13. Recent theories of implicit arguments that are not expressed in syntactic structure have been presented by, e.g., Williams (1990), Bouchard (1987), Di Sciullo (1989).

14. A number of linguists have theories which bring the functional/lexical dichotomy more in line with the dichotomy between semantically significant θ-assigners on the one hand, and the grammatical formatives on the other. For example, Abney (1986) says, "The primary property of functional elements is this: they select a unique complement, which is not plausibly either an argument or an adjunct of the functional element ... And semantically, at least on an intuitive level, C and I contrast with N, V, A, etc., in that they do not describe a distinct object from that described by their complement." Fukui (1986, 27), developing ideas from Abney and from Higginbotham (1985), has a similar perspective: "Items such as Comp and Infl ... act as syntactic heads but do not ... have θ-grids or 'lexical-conceptual structures' in the sense of Hale and Keyser (1985)." These theories have some appeal, and would allow the following proposals to have a more elegant statement.

15. These are essentially Emonds' (1985, §4.6) "designated elements."

16. See e.g., Koopman, 1983 on Kru languages; Chung, 1990 on Chamorro; Baker, 1988 on Mohawk, Tuscarora, Southern Tiwa and other languages.

17. The wording of Proposals 6 and 7 is designed to emphasize that I am not assuming that the grammatical principles which entail them apply at D-structure.

18. Engdahl (1986, §7.1) suggested that the limitations on the number of extractions should come from the performance theory rather than from the grammar, on the grounds that in some languages multiple extractions are quite intelligible (esp. with aids to memory), gradually degrading in acceptability as the number of extractions increases. But the current approach to grammar tries to account for exactly this kind of acceptability judgement, with the cumulative version of n-subjacency and hypotheses about

how severe various grammar violations are. Graded departures from acceptability are no longer the domain of just the performance theories. We can look for a description of the facts first, and then we can consider whether they have a plausible functional explanation. Proposed functional explanations have not fared well, even for the most famous case of center-embedding. Cf., Anderson (1976, 457-8, 471ff); Joshi (1989); Abney and Johnson (1990); Wu (1991).

19. The original, strong form of the HMC which prohibits lowering is also rejected by Chomsky (1988), Pesetsky (1989), and other works cited in §12.

20. See, e.g., Williams (1977) and Zagona (1988, §4.4) for arguments against deletion analyses.

21. Cf. Williams (1978), Sag et al. (1985).

22. See, e.g., Rizzi (1986; 1990). Some first steps towards implementations of this kind of theory have been taken by, e.g. Guasti and Walther (1991).

23. Ristad (1990, §3.4.1) points out that the value of locality can be overemphasized, since if we are free to design a representation however we like, nonlocal relations in recursively enumerable structures can just be recoded as chains of local relations. However, we are not free to design linguistic structure; linguists are in the business of bringing empirical considerations to bear on hypotheses about linguistic structure. Ristad worries about the empirical support for some crucial parts of the *Barriers* framework, saying "any nonlocal relation can always be described as a chain of local relations ... In short, 'locality' has no empirical consequences and cannot be falsified ... A case in point is the intermediate traces of Barriers-type theories, whose only apparent purpose is to allow the iterated local description of nonlocal movement relations ... they do not interact with other components of the grammar." Unfortunately, the substance of Ristad's challenge is beyond the scope of this study. We have not undertaken a thoroughgoing empirical assessment of any of the theories discussed here. Certainly it is true that the intermediate traces would be much better supported if they interacted with many linguistic principles involving a wide range of empirical considerations. And of course, if an alternative theory with simpler, nonlocal chains does as well or better than *Barriers* in accounting for the facts, it is to be preferred.

24. The formal representation of the intended structure is included in Appendix C as τ in the clause of the form $figure(9\text{-}9, \tau)$.

25. Examples include Loveland's (1972, 372) BB, AB, and AA pruning rules. See also the references cited in footnote 15 of §3.7.

26. Smith and Genesereth (1985); Warren (1981); Stabler and Elcock (1983); Seki and Furukawa (1987); Naish, (1985).

27. E.g., van Hentenryck and Dincbas (1987); Rossi (1988).

28. See, e.g., Sterling and Shapiro (1986), Seki and Furukawa (1987), Fujita and Furukawa (1988), Fuller and Abramsky (1988). As pointed out in the logic programming literature (Seki and Furukawa, 1987; Naish, 1985; Smith and Genesereth, 1985).

29. See, e.g., Knuth (1973, §2.3); Aho et al. (1974).

30. Ullman (1973), Aho et al. (1976), Maier (1979).

31. In the logic programming tradition see, e.g., Hirschman and Puder (1985), Hirschman (1986), Stabler (1988), Johnson (1991).

32. Thanks to Verónica Dahl for drawing my attention to this point.

33. Features and agreement relations have been a focus of recent research. Cf., e.g., Johnson (1990, 1988), Pereira (1987), Moshier and Rounds (1987), Saint-Dizier (1991).

34. Cf. Marcus (1981); Berwick and Weinberg (1984); van de Koot (1990).

Bibliography

Abney, S.P. (1986) Functional elements and licensing. Presented at GLOW, 1986.

Abney, S.P. (1987) *The English Noun Phrase in its Sentential Aspect.* MIT Dept. of Linguistics and Philosophy Ph.D. dissertation.

Abney, S.P. (1989) A computational model of human parsing. *J. of Psycholinguistic Research 18*: 129-144.

Abney, S.P. (1991) Parsing by chunks. In R.C. Berwick, S. Abney, C. Tenny, eds., *Principle-based Parsing: Computation and Psycholinguistics.* Boston: Kluwer.

Abney, S.P. and Johnson, M. (1990) Memory requirements and local ambiguities of parsing strategies. Forthcoming in *J. of Psycholinguistic Research.*

Aho, A.V., Hopcroft, J.E. and Ullman, J.D. (1974) *The Design and Analysis of Computer Algorithms.* Menlo Park, California: Addison-Wesley.

Aho, A.V., Hopcroft, J.E. and Ullman, J.D. (1976) On finding lowest common ancestor in trees. *SIAM J. Computing 5*: 115-132.

Aho, A.V. and Ullman, J.D. (1972) *The Theory of Parsing, Translation and Compiling, Volume 1: Parsing.* Englewood Cliffs, New Jersey: Prentice-Hall.

Aho, A.V. and Ullman, J.D. (1977) *Principles of Compiler Design.* Menlo Park, California: Addison-Wesley.

Akmajian, A. and Heny, F. (1975) *Introduction to the Principles of Transformational Syntax.* Cambridge, Massachusetts: MIT Press.

Anderson, J.R. (1976) *Language, Memory and Thought.* Hillsdale, New Jersey: Erlbaum.

Aoun, J. (1985) *A Grammar of Anaphora.* Cambridge, Massachusetts: MIT Press.

Aoun, J., Hornstein, N., Lightfoot, D., and Weinberg, A. (1987) Two types of locality. *Linguistic Inquiry 18*(4): 537-578.

Aoun, J. and Sportiche, D. (1983) On the formal theory of government. *Linguistic Review 2*: 211-236.

Authier, J.-M. P. (1988) Null object constructions in KiNande. *Natural Language and Linguistic Theory 6*: 19-37.

Bach, E., Brown, C. and Marslen-Wilson, W. (1986) Crossed and nested dependencies in German and Dutch. *Language and Cognitive Processes 1*: 249-262.

Baker, M.C. (1988) *Incorporation: A Theory of Grammatical Function Changing.* Chicago: University of Chicago Press.

Baker, M.C. (1989) Object sharing and projection in serial verb constructions. *Linguistic Inquiry 20*: 513-553.

Baker, M.C., Johnson, K. and Roberts, I. (1989) Passive arguments raised. *Linguistic Inquiry 20*: 219-252.

Baltin, M.R. (1982) A landing site theory of movement rules. *Linguistic Inquiry 13*: 1-38.

Baltin, M.R. (1991) Head movements in logical form. *Linguistic Inquiry 22:* 225-250.

Bar-Hillel, Y. and Shamir, E. (1960) Finite state languages: formal representations and adequacy problems. Reprinted in Y. Bar-Hillel, *Language and Information*. Reading, Massachusetts: Addison-Wesley, 1964.

Barton, G.E., Jr., Berwick, R.C., and Ristad, E.S. (1987) *Computational Complexity and Natural Language*. Cambridge, Massachusetts: Bradford/MIT Press.

Belletti, A. and Rizzi, L. (1981) The syntax of 'ne': some theoretical implications. *The Linguistic Review 1*: 117-154.

Belletti, A. and Rizzi, L. (1988) Psych-verbs and θ-theory. *Natural Language and Linguistic Theory 6*: 291-352.

Bennis, H. and Hoekstra, T. (1989) *Generatieve Grammatica*. Dordrecht: Foris.

Berwick, R.C. (1983) A deterministic parser with broad coverage. *Procs. 8th Int. Joint Conf. on Artificial Intelligence, IJCAI 8*: 710-712.

Berwick, R.C., and Weinberg, A.S. (1984) *The Grammatical Basis of Linguistic Performance: Language Use and Acquisition*. Cambridge, Massachusetts: MIT Press.

Bibel, W., Letz, R. and Schumann, J. (1987) Bottom-up enhancements of deductive systems. In I. Plandes (ed.): *AI and Robot Control Systems*. New York: North-Holland.

Bird, C., Hutchison, J. and Kanté, M. (1977) *Beginning Bambara*. Bloomington, Indiana: Indiana University Linguistics Club.

Boolos, G.S. (1981) For every A there is a B. *Linguistic Inquiry 12:* 465-467.

Boolos, G.S. and Jeffrey, R.C. (1980) *Computability and Logic*. (Second edition.) NY: Cambridge University Press.

Bouchard, D. (1982) *On the content of empty categories*. MIT Ph.D. thesis. Also published in Cinnaminson, New Jersey: Foris Publications, 1983.

Bouchard, D. (1987) Gaps as nonprojected arguments. *Procs. NELS 18*.

Bowen, K.A. and Kowalski, R. (1982) Amalgamating language and metalanguage in logic programming. In K.L. Clark and Tärnlund, S.-Å (eds.), *Logic Programming*, NY: Academic Press, 153-172.

Boy de la Tour, T. (1990) Minimizing the number of clauses by renaming. *Procs. 10th Int. Conf. on Automated Deduction, CADE-10:* 558-572.

Boyer, R.S. and Moore, J.S. (1979) *A Computational Logic*. New York: Academic Press.

Bresnan, J. (1975) Transformations and categories in syntax. *Procs. 5th Int. Conf. of Logic, Methodology and Philosophy of Science*.

Bresnan, J. (1976) On the form and functioning of transformations. *Linguistic Inquiry 7*: 3-40.

Bresnan, J., Kaplan, R.M., Peters, S. and Zaenen, A. (1982) Cross-serial dependencies in Dutch. *Linguistic Inquiry 13*: 613-635. Reprinted in W.J. Savitch (ed.), *The Formal Complexity of Natural Language*. Boston: Reidel, 1987.

Bridge, J. (1977) *Beginning Model Theory: The Completeness Theorem and Some of its Consequences*. Oxford: Clarendon Press.

Briscoe, E.J. (1983) Determinism and its implementation in PARSIFAL. In K. Sparck Jones and Y. Wilks (eds.), *Automatic Natural Language Parsing*. New York: Wiley.

Browning, M.A. (1989) ECP ≠ CED. *Linguistic Inquiry 20:* 481-491.

Bundy, A. (1988) The use of explicit plans to guide inductive proofs. *Procs. 9th Int. Conf. on Automated Deduction*, Lecture Notes in Computer Science, Volume 310: 111-120.

Burstall, R. (1969) Proving properties of programs by structural induction. *Computer Journal 12:* 41-48.

Burzio, L. (1986) *Italian Syntax.* Boston: Reidel.

Chan, K.-H. (1986) Representation of negative and incomplete information in Prolog. *Procs. 6th Canadian Conf. on Artificial Intelligence*: 89-93.

Chang, C.C. and Keisler, H.J. (1973) *Model Theory.* Amsterdam: North-Holland.

Chang, C.-L. and Lee, R.C.-T. (1973) *Symbolic Logic and Mechanical Theorem Proving.* New York: Academic Press.

Chi, A. and Henschen, L.J. (1988) Recursive query-answering with non-Horn clauses. *Procs. 9th Int. Conf. on Automatic Deduction*: 294-312.

Chomsky, N. (1955) *The Logical Structure of Linguistic Theory.* New York: Plenum Press, 1975.

Chomsky, N. (1956) Three models for the description of language. *IRE Transactions on Information Theory, IT-2:* 113-124.

Chomsky, N. (1957) *Syntactic Structures.* The Hague: Mouton.

Chomsky, N. (1963) Formal properties of grammars. In R.D. Luce, R. Bush and E. Galanter (eds.), *Handbook of Mathematical Psychology, Volume II.* New York: Wiley.

Chomsky, N. (1965) *Aspects of the Theory of Syntax.* Cambridge, Massachusetts: MIT Press.

Chomsky, N. (1970) Remarks on nominalization. In R. Jacobs and P. Rosenbaum (eds.), *Readings in English Transformational Grammar.* Waltham, Massachusetts: Ginn. Reprinted in N. Chomsky, *Studies on Semantics in Generative Grammar.* The Hague: Mouton, 1972.

Chomsky, N. (1973) Conditions on transformations. In S.R. Anderson and P. Kiparsky (eds.), *A Festschrift for Morris Halle.* New York: Holt, Rinehart and Winston.

Chomsky, N. (1976) Conditions on rules of the grammar. *Linguistic Analysis 2:* 303-351.

Chomsky, N. (1980a) On binding. *Linguistic Inquiry 11:* 1-46.

Chomsky, N. (1980b) *Rules and Representations.* New York: Columbia University Press.

Chomsky, N. (1981) *Lectures on Government and Binding.* Cinnaminson, New Jersey: Foris Publications.

Chomsky, N. (1984) *Some Concepts and Consequences of the Theory of Government and Binding.* Cambridge, Massachusetts: MIT Press.

Chomsky, N. (1986a) *Barriers.* Cambridge, Massachusetts: MIT Press.

Chomsky, N. (1986b) *Knowledge of Language: Its Nature, Origin, and Use.* New York: Praeger.

Chomsky, N. (1988) Some notes on economy of derivation and representation. In I. Laka and A. Mahajan, eds., *Working Papers in Linguistics 10*, Massachusetts Institute of Technology.

Chomsky, N. (1988a) Prospects for the study of language and mind. Forthcoming in E. Kashir, ed., *The Chomskian Turn.*

Chomsky, N. (1990) On formalization and formal linguistics. *Natural Language and Linguistic Theory 8*(1): 143-147.

Chomsky, N. and Lasnik, H. (1977) Filters and control. *Linguistic Inquiry 8*(3): 425-504.

Chung, S. (1990) VPs and verb movement in Chamorro. *Natural Language and Linguistic Theory 8*: 559-619.

Chung, S. and McCloskey, J. (1987) Government, barriers and small clauses in Modern Irish. *Linguistic Inquiry 18*: 173-238.

Church, K. and Patil, R. (1982) Coping with syntactic ambiguity or how to put the block in the box on the table. *Computational Linguistics 8*: 139-149.

Cinque, G. (1990) *Types of $\overline{A}$ Dependencies*. Cambridge, Massachusetts: MIT Press.

Clark, K. (1978) Negation as failure. In H. Gallaire and J. Minker (eds.) *Logic and Data Bases*. New York: Plenum Press.

Clark, K. (1979) Predicate logic as a computational formalism. Research Report 79/59, Department of Computing, Imperial College.

Clark, K., and Tärnlund, S.-Å. (1977) A first order theory of data and programs. *Information Processing, Procs. of IFIP Congress 77*: 939-944.

Comorovski, I. (1986) Multiple WH-movement in Romanian. *Linguistic Inquiry 17*: 171-177.

Contreras, H. (1979) Clause reduction, the saturation constraint, and clitic promotion. *Linguistic Analysis 5*: 161-182.

Corcoran, J., Frank, W. and Maloney, M. (1974) String theory. *Journal of Symbolic Logic, 39*: 625-637.

Correa, N. (1988) *Syntactic Analysis of English with respect to Government-Binding Grammar*. Ph.D. dissertation, Electrical and Computer Engineering, Syracuse University.

Crain, S. and Steedman, M. (1985) On not being led up the garden path: the use of context by the psychological syntax processor. In D.R. Dowty, L. Kartunnen, and A.M. Zwicky (eds.), *Natural Language Parsing: Psychological, Computational, and Theoretical Perspectives*. New York: Cambridge University Press.

Crook, H.D. (1990) *Implications of Universal Grammar for the Constituent Structures of the Bambara Noun Phrase*. UCLA Dept. of Linguistics M.A. thesis.

Curry, H.B. and Feys, R. (1958) *Combinatory Logic*. Amsterdam: North-Holland.

Dahl, V. (1984) More on gapping grammars. *Procs. of the Int. Conf. on Fifth Generation Computing Systems*.

Dahl, V. (1986) Gramáticas discontinuas - una herramienta computacional con applicaciones en la teoría de gobierno y nexo. *Revista Argentina de Lingüística 2*.

Dahl, V. and Abramson, H. (1989) *Logic Grammars*. New York: Springer-Verlag.

Dahl, V. and Saint-Dizier, P. (1986) Constrained discontinuous grammars. Rapports de Recherche No. 309, IRISA, Campus Universitaire de Beaulieu, Rennes, France.

den Bensten, H. (1983) On the interaction of root transformations and lexical deletive rules. In W. Abraham (ed.), *On the Formal Syntax of the Westgermania*. Philadelphia: John Benjamins.

den Bensten, H. and Edmondson, J.A. (1983) The verbal complex in Continental West Germanic. In W. Abraham (ed.), *On the Formal Syntax of the Westgermania*. Philadelphia: John Benjamins.

Digricoli, V.J. (1983) *Resolution by Unification and Equality*. Ph.D. Thesis, Department of Computer Science, New York University.

Digricoli, V.J. and Harrison, M.J. (1986) Equality-based binary resolution. *Journal of the ACM 33*(2): 253-289.

Dijkstra, E.W. (1982) Why naive program transformation systems are unlikely to work. In his *Selected Writings on Computing: A Personal Perspective*. New York: Springer-Verlag.

Di Sciullo, A.-M. (1989) Two types of implicit arguments. *Procs. WCCFL 8*: 94-109.

Dreben, B. and Goldfarb, W.D. (1979) *The Decision Problem: Solvable Classes of Quantificational Formulas*. Don Mills, Ontario: Addison-Wesley.

Earley, J. (1970) An efficient context free parsing algorithm. *Communications of the ACM, 6*(8): 94-102.

Ebbinghaus, H.-D., Flum, J. and Thomas, W. (1984) *Mathematical Logic*. New York: Springer-Verlag.

Elkan, C. and McAllester, D. (1988) Automated inductive reasoning about logic programs. *Procs. of the 5th Int. Conf. and Symp. on Logic Programming*: 876-892.

Emonds, J. (1976) *A Transformational Approach to English Syntax*. New York: Academic Press.

Emonds, J. (1985) *A Unified Treatment of Syntactic Categories.* Cinnaminson, New Jersey: Foris Publications.

Enderton, H.B. (1972) *A Mathematical Introduction to Logic.* New York: Academic Press.

Engdahl, E. (1986) *Constituent Questions: The Syntax and Semantics of Questions with Special Reference to Swedish.* Dordrecht: Reidel.

Epstein, S.S. (1990) Linear encodings of linguistic analyses. *Procs. COLING-90 III:* 108-113.

Farrell, P. (1990) Null objects in Brazilian Portuguese. *Natural Language and Linguistic Theory 8:* 325-346.

Flannagan, T. (1986) The consistency of negation as failure. *Journal of Logic Programming, 3*(2): 93-114.

Fleisig, S., Loveland, D., Smiley, A.K., III and Yarmush, D.L. (1974) An implementation of the model elimination proof procedure. *Journal of the ACM 21:* 124-139.

Fodor, J.A. (1983) *The Modularity of Mind.* Bradford/MIT Press: Cambridge, Massachusetts.

Fodor, J.D. (1983) Phrase structure parsing and the island constraints. *Linguistics and Philosophy 6:* 163-223.

Fodor, J.D. (1983a) Constraints on gaps: is the parser a significant influence? *Linguistics 21:* 9-34.

Fodor, J.D. (1985) Deterministic parsing and subjacency. *Language and Cognitive Processes 1:* 3-42.

Fodor, J.D. (1987) Sentence processing and the mental grammar. Forthcoming.

Fong, S. (1989) A principle-ordering parser. In C. Tenny, ed., MIT Parsing Volume 1988-1989, Center for Cognitive Science, MIT.

Fong, S. (1991) The computational implementation of principle-based parsers. In R.C. Berwick, S. Abney, and C. Tenny, eds., *Principle-based Parsing: Computation and Psycholinguistics.* Boston: Kluwer.

Ford, M., Bresnan, J. and Kaplan, R.M. (1982) A competence-based theory of syntactic closure. In J. Bresnan (ed.), *The Mental Representation of Grammatical Relations.* Cambridge, Massachusetts: MIT Press.

Friedin, R. (1978) Cyclicity and the theory of grammar. *Linguistic Inquiry 9:* 519-549.

Frisch, A.M. (1986) Parsing with restricted quantification: an initial demonstration. *Computational Intelligence 2:* 142-150.

Fujita, H. and Furukawa, K. (1988) A self-applicable partial evaluator and its use in incremental compilation. *New Generation Computing 6:* 91-118.

Fukui, N. (1986) *A Theory of Category Projection and Its Applications.* Ph.D. Dissertation, Department of Linguistics and Philosophy, Massachusetts Institute of Technology.

Fukui, N. and Speas, M. (1986) Specifiers and projection. *MIT Working Papers in Linguistics 8:* 128-172.

Fuller, D.A. and Abramsky, S. (1988) Mixed computation of prolog programs. *New Generation Computing 6:* 119-141.

Gallier, J.H. (1986) *Logic for Computer Science: Foundations of Automatic Theorem Proving.* New York: Harper and Row.

Gallier, J.H. and Raatz, S. (1987) HORNLOG: A graph based interpreter for general Horn clauses. *J. of Logic Programming 4:* 119-155.

Gazdar, G., Klein, E., Pullum, G., and Sag, I. (1985) *Generalized Phrase Structure Grammar.* Cambridge, Massachusetts: Harvard University Press.

Gécseg, F. and Steinby, M. (1984) *Tree Automata.* Budapest: Akadémiai Kiadó.

Ginsberg, S. and Partee, B.H. (1969) A mathematical model of transformational grammar. *Information and Control 15:* 297-334.

Gödel, K. (1931) On formally undecidable propositions of *Principia Mathematica* and related systems I. *Monatshefte für Mathematik und Physik, 38:* 173-198. Reprinted in J. van Heijenoort (ed.), *Frege and Gödel: Two Fundamental Texts in Mathematical Logic.* Cambridge, Massachusetts: Harvard University Press, 1970.

Green, C. (1969) Application of theorem proving to question answering systems. *Procs. 1st Int. Joint Conf. on Artificial Intelligence:* 219-239.

Gries, D. (1981) *The Science of Programming.* New York: Springer-Verlag.

Guasti, M.T. and Walther, C. (1990) Building chains in TPs and DPs. Revised version forthcoming in E. Wehrli, ed., *Procs. of the Geneva Workshop on GB Parsing.*

Guéron, J. (1981) Logical operators, complete constituents, and extraction transformations. In R. May and J. Koster (eds.), *Levels of Syntactic Representation.* Cinnaminson, New Jersey: Foris.

Guéron, J. (1984) Le verbe 'avoir'. In P. Coopmans, I. Bordelois, and B.D. Smith, eds. *Formal Parameters of Generative Grammar II, Going Romance.* Dordrecht: ICG Printing.

Haegeman, L. and van Riemsdijk, H. (1986) Verb projection raising, scope an the typology of rules affecting verbs. *Linguistic Inquiry 17:* 417-466.

Hale, K. (1983) Warlpiri and the grammar of non-configurational languages. *Natural Language and Linguistic Theory 1:* 5-47.

Hale, K. and Keyser, J. (1985) Some transitivity alternations in English. MIT Dept. of Linguistics and Philosophy manuscript.

Hansson, Å., and Tärnlund, S.-Å. (1982) Program transformation by data structure mapping. In K.L. Clark and Tärnlund, S.-Å (eds.), *Logic Programming.* Toronto: Academic Press.

Harbusch, K. (1990) An efficient parsing algorithm for tree adjoining grammars. *Procs. 28th Ann. Mtg. of the Assoc. for Computational Linguistics:* 284-291

Harlow, S. (1981) Government and relativizatio in Celtic. In F. Heny, ed., *Binding and Filtering.* Cambridge, Massachusetts: MIT Press.

Harris, Z. (1951) *Methods in Structural Linguistics.* Chicago, University of Chicago Press.

Harrison, M.A. (1978) *Introduction to Formal Language Theory.* Menlo Park, California: Addison-Wesley.

Heath, J. (1986) Syntactic and lexical aspects of nonconfigurationality in Nunggubuyu (Australia). *Natural Language and Linguistic Theory 4:* 375-408.

Higginbotham, J. (1980) Pronouns and bound variables. *Linguistic Inquiry 11:* 679-708.

Higginbotham, J. (1985) On semantics. *Linguistic Inquiry 16:* 547- 594.

Hindle, D. (1983) Deterministic parsing of syntactic non-fluencies. *Procs. 21st Ann. Mtg. of the Assoc. for Computational Linguistics:* 123-128.

Hirschman, L. and Puder, K. (1985) Restriction grammar: a prolog implementation. In D.H.D. Warren and M. van Caneghem, eds., *Logic Programming and Its Applications.* Norwood, New Jersey: Ablex.

Hirschman, L. and Puder, K. (1986) Conjunction in meta-restriction grammar. *J. of Logic Programming 4:* 299-328.

Hoekstra, T. (1988) Small clause results. *Lingua 74:* 101-139.

Hopcroft, J.E. and Ullman, J.D. (1979) *Introduction to Automata Theory,Languages, and Computation.* Don Mills, Ontario: Addison-Wesley.

Hornstein, N. and Weinberg, A. (1990) The necessity of LF. *The Linguistic Review 7:* 129-167.

Huang, C.-T.J. (1982) *Logical Relations in Chinese and the Theory of Grammar.* Ph.D. dissertation, Massachusetts Institute of Technology.

Hukari, T.E. and Levine, R.D. (1987) Parasitic gaps, slash termination, and the c-command condition. *Natural Language and Linguistic Theory 5:* 197-222.

Hutter, D. (1990) Guiding induction proofs. *Procs. 10th Int. Conf. on Automated Deduction CADE-10:* 147-161.

Iatridou, S. (1990) About Agr(P). *Linguistic Inquiry 21*: 551-577.

Jackendoff, R. (1977) *X̄ Syntax: A Study of Phrase Structure*. Cambridge, Massachusetts: MIT Press.

Jaeggli, O.A. (1986) Passive. *Linguistic Inquiry 17(4)*: 587-622.

Jaeggli, O.A. and Safir, K.J. (1989) *The Null Subject Parameter*. Boston: Kluwer.

Jaffar, J. and Lassez, J.-L. (1987) Constraint logic programming. *Procs. 14th ACM POPL Symp.*.

Jeffrey, R. (1981) *Formal Logic: Its Scope and Limits,* Second Edition. New York: McGraw-Hill.

Jelinek, E. (1984) Empty categories, case and configurationality. *Natural Language and Linguistic Theory 2*: 39-76.

Jensen, K., Heidorn, G.E., Miller, L.A., and Rivin, Y. (1983) Parse fitting and prose fixing: getting a hold on ill-formedness. *Computational Linguistics 9*: 147-160.

Johnson, K. (1989) Clausal architecture and structural case. Forthcoming.

Johnson, K. (1990) On the syntax of inflectional paradigms. Forthcoming.

Johnson, M. (1988) Deductive parsing with multiple levels of representation. *Procs. 26th Ann. Mtg. of the Assoc. for Computational Linguistics*: 241-248.

Johnson, M. (1988a) *Attribute-Value Logic and the Theory of Grammar*. Lecture Notes No. 16, Center for the Study of Language and Information, Stanford University.

Johnson, M. (1989) Parsing as deduction: the use of knowledge of language. *J. Psycholinguistic Research 18(1)*: 105-128.

Johnson, M. (1990) Expressing disjunctive and negative feature constraints with classical first-order logic. *Procs. 28th Ann. Mtg. of the Assoc. for Computational Linguistics*: 173-179.

Johnson, M. (1991) Techniques for deductive parsing. *Procs. 3rd Int. Workshop on Natural Language Understanding and Logic Programming*.

Joshi, A.K. (1989) Processing crossed and nested dependencies: an automaton perspective on the psycholinguistic results. Forthcoming in *Language and Cognitive Processes*.

Joyner, W.H., Jr. (1976) Resolution strategies as decision procedures. *Journal of the ACM, 23(3)*: 398-417.

Kameyama, M. (1988) Japanese pronominal binding: where syntax and discourse meet. In W.J. Poser, ed., *Papers from Second Int. Workshop on Japanese Syntax*. Center for the Study of Language and Information, Stanford Universiity.

Kayne, R.S. (1975) *French Syntax: The Transformational Cycle*. Cambridge, Massachusetts: MIT Press.

Kayne, R.S. (1983) *Connectedness and Binary Branching*. Cinnaminson, New Jersey: Foris Publications, 1983.

Kayne, R.S. (1985) L'accord du participe passé en francais et en italien. *Modeles Linguistiques 7*: 73-80.

Kleene, S.C. (1952) *Introduction to Metamathematics*. New York: North-Holland.

Koopman, H. (1990) The syntactic structure of the verb particle construction. Forthcoming.

Koopman, H. (1984) *The Syntax of Verbs*. Dordrecht: Foris.

Koopman, H. and Sportiche, D. (1986) A note on long extraction in Vata and the ECP. *Natural Language and Linguistic Theory 4*: 367-374.

Koopman, H. and Sportiche, D. (1988) The position of subjects. UCLA manuscript. Forthcoming in *Lingua*.

Koopman, H. and Sportiche, D. (1990) The position of subjects. Forthcoming in *Lingua*.

Koot, J. van de (1990) *An Essay on Grammar-Parser Relations*. Dissertation, University of Utrecht.

Koster, J. (1987) *Domains and Dynasties: The Radical Autonomy of Syntax*. Cinnaminson, New Jersey: Foris Publications.

Kowalski, R. and Hayes, P.J. (1969) Semantic trees in automatic theorem proving. *Machine Intelligence 4*: 87-101. Reprinted in J. Siekmann and G. Wrightson (eds): *Automation of Reasoning 2*, New York: Springer-Verlag.

Kreisel, G. and Wang, H. (1955) Some applications of consistency proofs. *Fundamenta Mathematicae 42*: 101-110.

Kripke, S. (1982) *Wittgenstein: On Rules and Private Language – An Elementary Exposition*. Cambridge, Massachusetts: Harvard University Press.

Kroch, A.S. and Joshi, A.K. (1985) The Linguistic Relevance of Tree Adjoining Grammar. Technical Report, Department of Computer and Information Science, University of Pennsylvania.

Kroch, A.S. and Santorini, B. (1987) The derived constituent structure of the West Germanic verb raising construction. Technical Report MS-CIS-87-25, University of Pennsylvania. Forthcoming in R. Friedin (ed.), *Procs. of the Princeton Workshop on Comparative Grammar*.

Laka, I. (1990) *Negation in Syntax: On the Nature of Functional Categories and Projections*. MIT Ph.D. Dissertation.

Laka, I. (1990a) The structure of inflection: a case study on X0 syntax. Forthcoming manuscript, University of Rochester.

Lakoff, G. (1971) On generative semantics. In D. Steinberg and L. Jakobovits, eds., *Semantics: An Interdisciplinary Reader*. New York: Cambridge University Press.

Langendoen, T. (1976) On the adequacy of type-3 and type-2 grammars for human languages. *CUNY Forum 1*: 1-12. Reprinted in P.J. Hopper (ed.), *Studies in Descriptive and Historical Linguistics*. Amsterdam: John Benjamin.

Larson, R.K. (1988) On the double object construction. *Linguistic Inquiry 19*: 335-391.

Larson, R.K. (1990) Double objects revisited: reply to Jackendoff. *Linguistic Inquiry 21*: 589-632.

Larson, R.K. (1991) *Promise* and the theory of control. *Linguistic Inquiry 22*: 103-139.

Lasnik, H. (1980) Restricting the theory of transformations: a case study. In N. Hornstein and D. Lightfoot, eds., *Explanation in Linguistics*. London: Longmans.

Lasnik, H. (1985) Illicit NP movement: locality conditions on chains? *Linguistic Inquiry 16*: 481-490.

Lasnik, H. and Kupin, J.J. (1980) A restrictive theory of transformational grammar. *Theoretical Linguistics 4*: 173-196.

Lasnik, H. and Saito, M. (1984) On the nature of proper government. *Linguistic Inquiry 15*: 235-289.

Lasnik, H. and Saito, M. (1988) *On the nature of proper government*. Forthcoming.

Lasnik, H. and Uriagereka, J. (1988) *A Course in GB Syntax: Lectures on Binding and Empty Categories*. Cambridge, Massachusetts: MIT Press.

Lewis, H.R. and Papadimitriou, C.H. (1981) *Elements of the Theory of Computation*. Englewood Cliffs, New Jersey: Prentice-Hall.

Lightfoot, D. and Weinberg, A. (1988) Review of *Barriers* by Noam Chomsky. *Language 64*(2): 366-383.

Lloyd, J.W. (1984) *Foundations of Logic Programming*. New York: Springer-Verlag.

Lobo, J., Minker, J., and Rajasekar (1990) Semantics of Horn and disjunctive logic programs. Forthcoming in *Journal of Theoretical Computer Science*.

Longobardi, G. (1985) Connectedness, scope and c-command. *Linguistic Inquiry 16*: 163-192.

Loveland, D.W. (1978) *Automated Theorem Proving: A Logical Basis*. New York: North-Holland.

Macías, B. (1990) *An Incremental Parser for Government-Binding Theory*. Ph.D. Thesis, Cambridge University.

Mackworth, A.K. (1977) Consistency in networks of relations. *Artificial Intelligence 8*: 99-118.

Mackworth, A.K. (1987) Constraint satisfaction. In S.C. Shapiro, ed., *Encyclopedia of Artificial Intelligence*. New York: Wiley.

McCawley, J. (1971) A program for logic. In D. Davidson and G. Harman, eds., *Semantics of Natural Language*. Boston: Reidel.

Maher, M.J. (1986) Equivalences of logic programs. *Procs. 3rd Int. Conf. on Logic Programming:* 410-424.

Maier, D. (1979) An efficient method for storing ancestor information in trees. *SIAM J. Computing 8*: 599-618.

Maloney, M.J. (1969) *Logical and Axiomatic Foundations for the Study of Formal Languages and Symbolic Computation*. Ph.D. thesis, Department of Computer Science, University of Pennsylvania.

Manaster-Ramer, A. (1988) Review of W.J. Savitch, E. Bach, W. Marsh, and G. Safran-Naveh (eds.), *The Formal Complexity of Natural Language. Computational Linguistics 14*(4): 98-103.

Manna, Z. and Waldinger, R. (1985) *The Logical Basis for Computer Programming. Volume 1: Deductive Reasoning*. Menlo Park, California: Addison-Wesley.

Manna, Z. and Waldinger, R. (1990) *The Logical Basis for Computer Programming. Volume 2: Deductive Systems*. Menlo Park, California: Addison-Wesley.

Marantz, A. (1981) *On the Nature of Grammatical Relations*. MIT Ph.D. thesis.

Marantz, A. (1990) Implications of asymmetries in double object constructions. University of North Carolina, Chapel Hill, manuscript. Forthcoming

Marcus, M. (1980) *A Theory of Syntactic Recognition for Natural Language*. Cambridge, Massachusetts: MIT Press.

Mates, B. (1972) *Elementary Logic*, second edition. New York: Oxford University Press.

Matthews, R. (1979) Do the grammatical sentences of a language form a recursive set? *Synthese 40*: 209-224.

May, R. (1985) *Logical Form*. Cambridge, Massachusetts: MIT Press.

McCarthy, J. (1987) Generality in artificial intelligence. *Communications of the ACM 30*(12): 1030-1035.

McCarthy, J. (1962) Towards a mathematical science of computation. *Information Processing, Procs. of IFIP Congress 62*:21-28. Amsterdam: North-Holland.

McCharen, J., Overbeek, R. and Wos, L. (1976) Complexity and related enhancements for automated theorem-proving programs. *Computers and Mathematics with Applications 2*: 1-16.

McDaniel, D. (1989) Partial and multiple wh-movement. *Natural Language and Linguistic Theory 7*: 565-604.

Mellish, C.S. (1985) *Computer Interpretation of Natural Language Descriptions*. New York: Wiley.

Mellish, C.S. (1989) Some chart-based techniques for parsing ill-formed input. *Procs. 27th Ann. Mtg. of the Assoc. for Computational Linguistics:* 102-109.

Miller, G.A. and Chomsky, N. (1963) Finitary models of language users. In R.D. Luce, R. Bush and E. Galanter (eds.), *Handbook of Mathematical Psychology, Volume II*. New York: Wiley.

Minker, J. and Rajasekar, A. (1988) Procedural interpretation of non-Horn logic programs. *Procs. 9th Int. Conf. on Automatic Deduction:* 278-293

Moore, R.C. (1980) Reasoning about knowledge and action. Technical Note 191, SRI International, Menlo Park, California.

Morris, J. (1969) E-resolution: an extension of resolution to include the equality relation. *Procs. 1st Int. Joint Conf. on Artificial Intelligence.*

Moshier, D. and Rounds, W. (1987) A logic for partially specified data structures. *Procs. of the ACM Symp. on the Principles of Programming Languages.*

Mostowski, A., Robinson, R.M. and Tarski, A. (1953) Undecidability and essential undecidability in arithmetic. In A. Tarksi, A. Mostowski and R.M. Robinson, *Undecidable Theories*. Amsterdam: North-Holland.

Naish, L. (1985) Automating control for logic programs. *J. of Logic Programming 3*: 167-183.

Obenauer, H.-G. (1976) *Etudes de syntaxe interogative du français*. Tübingen: Niemeyer Verlag.

Obenauer, H.-G. (1983) Une quantification non canonique: la 'quantification à distance'. *Langue Française 58*: 66-88.

Obenauer, H.-G. (1984) On the identification of empty categories. *Linguistic Review 4*: 153-202.

Oshima, S. (1979) Conditions on rules: anaphora in Japanese. In G. Bedell, E. Kobayashi, and M. Muraki, eds., *Explorations in Linguistics: Papers in Honor of Kazuko Inoue*. Tokyo: Kenkyusha.

Ouhalla, J. (1990) Sentential negation: relativised minimality and the aspectual status of auxiliaries. *The Linguistic Review 7*: 183-231.

Parker, D.S. (1987) Partial order programming. UCLA Dept. of Computer Science Technical Report CSD-870067.

Parker, D.S. (1989) Partial order programming: extended abstract. *Procs. 16th Ann. ACM SIGACT-SIGPLAN Symp. on Principles of Programming Languages*.

Pereira, F.C.N. (1981) Extraposition grammars. *Computational Linguistics 7*: 243-256.

Pereira, F.C.N. (1982) *Logic for Natural Language Analysis*, Ph.D. thesis, University of Edinburgh, Scotland. Also available as Technical Note 275, SRI International, Menlo Park, California.

Pereira, F.C.N. (1987) Grammars and logics of partial information. *Procs. of the Int. Conf. on Logic Programming:* 989-1013.

Pereira, F.C.N. and Shieber, S.M. (1987) *Prolog and Natural Language Analysis*. Chicago: Chicago University Press.

Pereira, F.C.N. and Warren, D.H.D. (1980) Definite clause grammars for natural language analysis. *Artificial Intelligence, 13*: 231-278.

Pereira, F.C.N. and Warren, D.H.D. (1983) Parsing as deduction. *Procs. 21st Ann. Mtg. of the Assoc. for Computational Linguistics:* 137-144.

Pesetsky, D. (1985) *Paths and Categories*. MIT Ph.D. thesis.

Pesetsky, D. (1989) Language-particular processes and the earliness principle. Forthcoming.

Peters, P.S., Jr. and Ritchie, R.W. (1973) On the generative power of transformational grammars. *Information Sciences 6*: 49-83.

Plaisted, D.A. and Greenbaum, S. (1986) A structure-preserving clause form translation. *Journal of Symbolic Computation 2*: 293-304.

Platero, P. (1982) Missing noun phrases and grammatical relations in Navajo. *J. of American Linguistics 48*: 286-305.

Pollock, J.-Y. (1989) Verb movement, universal grammar, and the structure of IP. *Linguistic Inquiry 20*: 365-424.

Postal, P.M. and Pullum, G.K. (1982) The contraction debate. *Linguistic Inquiry 13*: 122-138.

Pritchett, B.L. (1988) Garden path phenomena and the grammatical basis of language processing. *Language 64:* 539-576.

Pullum, G. (1985) Assuming some version of X-bar theory. *Procs. Chicago Linguistic Society Meeting, CLS21.*

Pullum, G. (1989) Formal linguistics meets the boojum. *Natural Language and Linguistic Theory 7*(1): 137-143.

Pullum, G.K. and Gazdar, G. (1982) Natural languages and context-free languages. *Linguistics and Philosophy 4*: 471-504.

Pullum, G.K. and Gazdar, G. (1985) Natural languages and context-free languages. *New Generation Computing 3*: 273-306. Reprinted in W.J. Savitch (ed.), *The Formal Complexity of Natural Language*. Boston: Reidel, 1987.

Pylyshyn, Z.W. (1984) *Cognition and Computation: Toward a Foundation for Cognitive Science*. Cambridge, Massachusetts: Bradford/MIT Press.

Quine, W.V.O. (1946) Concatenation as a basis for arithmetic. *Journal of Symbolic Logic, 11*(4): 105-114. Reprinted in Quine's *The Ways of Paradox and Other Essays*. NY: Random House, 1966.

Quine, W.V.O. (1976) *Mathematical Logic*. Cambridge, Massachusetts: Harvard University Press.

Rabin, M.O. (1961) Non-standard models and the independence of the induction axiom. In *Essays on the Foundations of Mathematics*: 287-299. Jerusalem: Magnum Press.

Radford, A. (1981) *Transformational Syntax: A Student's Guide to Chomsky's Extended Standard Theory*. New York: Cambridge University Press.

Radford, A. (1988) *Transformational Grammar: A First Course*. New York: Cambridge University Press.

Rajasekar, A., Lobo, J. and Minker, J. (1989) Weak generalized closed world assumption. *Journal of Automated Reasoning 5*: 293-307.

Ramakrishnan, R. (1988) Magic templates: a spellbinding approach to logic programs. *Procs. 5th Int. Conf. on Logic Programming*: 140-159.

Raposo, E. and Uriagereka, J. (1990) Long-distance case assignment. *Linguistic Inquiry 21*(4): 505-537.

Reinhart, T. (1976) *The Syntactic Domain of Anaphora*. Ph.D. thesis, Massachusetts Institute of Technology.

Reiter, R. (1965) Equality and domain closure in first-order databases. *Journal of the ACM, 27*: 235-249.

Riemsdijk, H. van and Williams, E. (1981) NP-structure. *The Linguistic Review 1*: 171-217.

Riemsdijk, H. van and Williams, E. (1986) *Introduction to the Theory of Grammar*. Cambridge, Massachusetts: MIT Press.

Ristad, E.S. (1990) *A Computational Complexity Thesis for Human Language*. Technical Report, Princeton University Dept. of Computer Science. (Revised version of his MIT Ph.D. thesis.)

Ritter, E. (1990) Cross-linguistic evidence for number phrase. Forthcoming in C. Lefebvre, J.S. Lumsden, and L. Travis (eds.), *Functional Categories*.

Rizzi, L. (1982) *Issues in Italian Syntax*. Cinnaminson, New Jersey: Foris Publications.

Rizzi, L. (1982a) Comments on Chomsky's "On the representation of form and function." In J. Mehler, E.T.C. Walker, and M. Garrett, eds., *Perspectives on Mental Representation*. London: Erlbaum.

Rizzi, L. (1986) On chain formation. *Syntax and Semantics, Volume 19: The Syntax of Pronominal Clitics*. New York: Academic Press.

Rizzi, L. (1986a) Null objects in Italian and the theory of *pro*. *Linguistic Inquiry 17*: 501-558.

Rizzi, L. (1987) Relativized minimality. Ms distributed at the 1987 Linguistic Institute, Stanford University.

Rizzi, L. (1990) *Relativized Minimality*. Cambridge, Massachusetts: MIT Press.

Roberts, I. (1991) Excorporation and minimality. *Linguistic Inquiry 22*(1): 209-218.

Robinson, J.A. (1965) A machine-oriented logic based on the resolution principle. *JACM 12*: 23-41.

Robinson, J.A. (1965b) Automatic deduction with hyper-resolution. *Int. Journal of Computer Mathematics 1*: 227-234.

Ross, K.A. and Topor, R.W. (1988) Inferring negative information from disjunctive databases. Journal of Automated Reasoning 4: 397-424.

Ross, J.R. (1967) *Constraints on Variables in Syntax*. Ph.D. Dissertation, Massachusetts Institute of Technology.

Rossi, F. (1988) Constraint satisfaction problems in logic programming. *SIGART Newsletter 106*: 24-28.

Rounds, W.C. (1970) Mappings and grammars on trees. *Math. Systems Theory 4*: 257-287.

Rouveret, A. and Vergnaud, J.-R. (1980) Specifying reference to the subject. *Linguistic Inquiry 11*(1): 97-102.

Rudin, C. (1988) On multiple questions and wh-fronting. *Natural Language and Linguistic Theory 6*: 445-501.

Rutten, J. (1991) Infinitival Complements and Auxiliaries. *Amsterdam Studies in Generative Grammar 4*. University of Amsterdam.

Safir, K.J. (1985) *Syntactic Chains*. New York: Cambridge University Press.

Sag, I., Gazdar, G., Wasow, T. and Weisler, S. (1985) Coordination and how to distinguish categories. *Natural Language and Linguistic Theory 3*: 117-171.

Saint-Dizier, P. (1991) Modeling government and move-α by means of a logic-based, typed representation. Revised version forthcoming in E. Wehrli, ed., *Procs. of the Geneva Workshop on GB Parsing*.

Sato, T. and Tamaki, H. (1984) Transformational logic program synthesis. *Procs. of the Int. Conf. on Fifth Generation Computer Systems 1984*, ICOT: 195-201.

Schabes, Y. and Joshi, A.K. (1988) An Earley-type algorithm for tree-adjoining grammars. *Procs. 26th Ann. Mtg. of Assoc. Computational Linguistics*: 258-269.

Seki, H. and Furukawa, K. (1987) Notes on transformation techniques for generate and test logic programs. *Procs. 1987 Symp. on Logic Programming*: 215-223.

Sells, P. (1985) *Lectures on Contemporary Syntactic Theories: An Introduction to Government-Binding Theory, Generalized Phrase Structure Grammar, and Lexical-Functional Grammar*. Stanford, California: Center For the Study of Language and Information, Stanford University.

Shapiro, E.Y. (1984) Alternation and the computational complexity of logic programs. *Journal of Logic Programming, 1*(1): 19-34.

Sheperdson, J.C. (1984) Negation as failure: a comparison of Clark's completed data base and Reiter's closed world assumption. *Journal of Logic Programming, 1*(1): 51-79.

Sheperdson, J.C. (1985) Negation as failure II. *Journal of Logic Programming, 2*(3): 185-202.

Shieber, S.M. (1983) Direct parsing of ID/LP grammars. *Linguistics and Philosophy 7*: 135-154.

Shieber, S. (1985) Evidence against the context-freeness of natural language. *Linguistics and Philosophy 8*: 333-343. Reprinted in W.J. Savitch (ed.), *The Formal Complexity of Natural Language*. Boston: Reidel, 1987.

Shieber, S. (1985) Criteria for designing computer facilities for natural language analysis. *Linguistics 23*: 189-211.

Smith, D.E. and Genesereth, M.R. (1985) Ordering conjunctive queries. *Artificial Intelligence 26*: 171-215.

Speas, M. (1986) *Adjunctions and Projections in Syntax*. Ph.D. Dissertation, Department of Linguistics and Philosophy, Massachusetts Institute of Technology

Sportiche, D. (1988) Conditions on silent categories. UCLA manuscript.

Sportiche, D. (1990) *Movement, Agreement and Case*. UCLA manuscript, forthcoming.

Stabler, E.P., Jr. (1984) Berwick and Weinberg on linguistics and computational psychology. *Cognition 17*: 155-179.

Stabler, E.P., Jr. (1987) Kripke on functionalism and automata. *Synthese, 70*(1): 1-22.

Stabler, E.P., Jr. (1987a) Restricting logic grammars with government-binding theory. *Computational Linguistics 13*(1-2): 1-10.

Stabler, E.P., Jr. (1988) Parsing with explicit representations of syntactic constraints. In V. Dahl and P. Saint-Dizier, eds., *Natural Language Understanding and Logic Programming, II*. New York: North-Holland.

Stabler, E.P., Jr. (1988a) Implementing Government Binding theory. Forthcoming in *Formal Linguistics: Theory and Implementation*, edited by R. Levine and S. Davis.

Stabler, E.P., Jr. (1988b) Notes on model elimination. Technical Report, Department of Computer Science, University of Western Ontario.

Stabler, E.P., Jr. (1989) Syntactic equality in knowledge representation and reasoning. *Proceedings of the First Int. Conf. on Principles of Knowledge Representation and Reasoning, KR '89*: 459-466.

Stabler, E.P., Jr. (1989a) Avoid the pedestrian's paradox. In *MIT Parsing Volume 1988-1989*, edited by C. Tenny, MIT Center for Cognitive Science. Revised version in R.C. Berwick, S. Abney, C. Tenny (1991), eds., *Principle-based Parsing: Computation and Psycholinguistics*. Boston: Kluwer.

Stabler, E.P., Jr. (1990) Representing knowledge with theories about theories. *Journal of Logic Programming*. Also Technical Report #188, Department of Computer Science, University of Western Ontario, 1987.

Stabler, E.P., Jr. (1990a) Parsing as non-Horn deduction. Forthcoming.

Stabler, E.P., Jr. (1990b) Relaxation techniques for Relaxation principles for principle-based parsing. UCLA Center for Cognitive Science Technical Report 90-1. Revised version forthcoming in E. Wehrli, ed., *Procs. of the Geneva Workshop on GB Parsing*.

Stabler, E.P., Jr. and Elcock, E.W. (1983) Knowledge representation in an efficient deductive inference system. *Procs. of the Logic Programming Workshop '83*: 217-228.

Stabler, E.P., Jr. and Keenan, E.L. (1991) Notes on natural language and first order expressibility. Forthcoming.

Sterling, L. and Shapiro, E.Y. (1986) *The Art of Prolog: Advanced Programming Techniques*. Cambridge, Massachusetts: MIT Press.

Stickel, M. (1986) A Prolog Technology Theorem Prover: Implementation by an extended Prolog compiler. *Procs. 8th Int. Conf. on Automated Deduction*, edited by J. Siekmann. Lecture Notes in Computer Science Volume 230. New York: Springer-Verlag.

Stickel, M. (1986a) Automated deduction by theory resolution. *Journal of Automated Reasoning 1*: 333-355.

Stickel, M. (1986b) An introduction to automated deduction. In W. Bibel and Ph. Jorrand, eds., *Fundamentals of Artificial Intelligence: An Advanced Course*. New York: Springer-Verlag.

Stowell, T. (1981) *Origins of Phrase Structure*. Ph.D. Dissertation, Department of Linguistics and Philosophy, Massachusetts Institute of Technology.

Stowell, T. (1984) Null operators and the theory of proper government. Unpublished ms, UCLA.

Stowell, T. (1986) Null antecedents and proper government. *Procs. NELS 16:* 476-492.

Stowell, T. (1989) Subjects, specifiers and X-bar theory. In M.R. Baltin and A.S. Kroch, eds. *Alternative Conceptions of Phrase Structure*. Chicago: University of Chicago Press.

Stowell, T. (1989a) Determiners in NP and DP. Forthcoming in K. Leffel, ed., *Views on Phrase Structure*. Boston: Reidel.

Sundholm, G. (1983) Systems of deduction. In D. Gabbay and F. Guenthner, eds., *Handbook of Philosophical Logic, Volume I*. Boston: Reidel.

Szabolcsi, A. (1981) A possessive construction in Hungarian: a configurational category in a non-configurational language. *Acta Linguistica Academiae Scientiarum Hungaricae 31*: 261-289.

Szabolcsi, A. (1987) Functional categories in the noun phrase. In I. Kenesei (ed.) *Approaches to Hungarian, Volume Two: Theories and Analyses*. Szeged.

Szabolcsi, A. (1989) Noun phrases and clauses: is DP analogous to IP or CP? Forthcoming in J. Payne (ed.), *Procs. of the Colloquium on Noun Phrase Structure*.

Szymanski, T.G. and Williams, J.H. (1976) Noncanonical extensions of bottom-up parsing techniques. *SIAM Journal of Computing 5*: 231-250.

Tärnlund, S.-Å. (1978) An axiomatic database theory. In H. Gallaire and J. Minker (eds.) *Logic and Data Bases*. New York: Plenum Press.

Tarski, A. (1934) The concept of truth in formalized languages. In his *Logic, Semantics and Metamathematics: Papers from 1923 to 1938 by A. Tarski.* Oxford: Clarendon Press.

Thatcher, J.W. (1973) Tree automata: an informal survey. In A.V. Aho, ed., *Currents in the Theory of Computing.* Englewood Cliffs, New Jersey: Prentice-Hall.

Toman, J. (1981) Aspects of multiple wh-movement in Polish and Czech. In R. May and J. Koster, eds., *Levels of Syntactic Representation.* Dordrecht: Foris.

Tomita, M. (1986) *Efficient Parsing for Natural Language: A Fast Algorithm for Practical Systems.* Boston: Kluwer.

Travis, L. (1984) *Parameters and Effects of Word Order Variation.* Ph.D. Dissertation, Department of Linguistics and Philosophy, Massachusetts Institute of Technology.

Ullman, J.D. (1973) Fast algorithms for the elimination of common subexpressions. *Acta Informatica 2*: 191-213.

Valois, D. (1990) The internal syntax of DP and adjective placement in French and English. *Procs. NELS, 1990.*

Van Hentenryck, P. and Dincbas, M. (1987) Forward Checking in Logic Programming. *Logic Programming: Procs. of 4th Int. Conf.* Cambridge, Massachusetts: MIT Press.

Vijay-Shanker, K. and Joshi, A.K. (1985) Some computational properties of tree adjoining grammars. *Procs. 23rd Ann. Mtg. of Assoc. Computational Linguistics*: 82-93.

Vijay-Shanker, K., Weir, D.J., and Joshi, A.K. (1987) Characterizing structural descriptions produced by various grammatical formalisms. *Procs. 25th Ann. Mtg. of Assoc. Computational Linguistics*: 104-111.

Wakayama, T. and Payne, T.H. (1988) Case inference in resolution-based languages. *Procs. 9th Int. Conf. on Automatic Deduction*: 313-322.

Warren, D.H.D. (1981) Efficient processing of interactive relational database queries expressed in logic. *Procs. 7th IEEE Int. Conf. on Very Large Databases.*

Wegbreit, B. and Spitzen, J.M. (1976) Proving properties of complex data structures. *JACM 23:* 389-396.

Weischedel, R.M. and Sondheimer, N.K. (1983) Meta-rules as a basis for processing ill-formed input. *Computational Linguistics 9*: 161-177.

Williams, E. (1975) Small clauses in English. In J. Kimball, ed., *Syntax and Semantics, Volume 4.* New York: Academic Press.

Williams, E. (1977) Discourse and logical form. *Linguistic Inquiry 8*: 101-139.

Williams, E. (1978) Across-the-board rule application. *Linguistic Inquiry 9*: 31-43.

Williams, E. (1985) PRO and subject of NP. *Natural Language and Linguistic Theory 3(3)*: 297-315.

Williams, E. (1985) The Italian null subject. In A.-M. Di Sciullo and A. Rochette, eds., *Binding in Romance: Essays in Honour of Judith McA'Nulty.* Ottawa: Canadian Linguistic Association.

Woods, W. (1970) Transition network grammars for natural language analysis. *Communications of the ACM 13*: 591-606.

Wos, L.A., Overbeek, R.A, and Henschen, L. (1980) Hyperparamodulation: A refinement of paramodulation. *Procs. 5th Conf. on Automated Deduction*: 208-219. New York: Springer-Verlag.

Wu, A. (1991) Center embedding and parsing constraints – a computational approach. UCLA manuscript, forthcoming.

Yahya, A. and Henschen, L.J. (1985) Deduction in non-Horn databases. *Journal of Automated Reasoning 1*: 141-160.

Zaenen, A. (1979) Infinitival complements in Dutch. *Procs. CLS 15*: 378-389.

Zagona, K. (1988) *Verb Phrase Syntax: A Parametric Study of English and Spanish.* Boston: Kluwer.

Index

A

A-bar position, 179, 195, 404
A-position, 179
Abney, S.P., 214, 288, 304, 400, 408–409
Abramsky, S., 409
adjoin, **139**, **343**
adjoin_cat, **140**, **168**, **228**, **343**, **348**, **356**
adjoin_conds, **140**, **163**, **175**, **241**, **343**, **347**, **349**, **360**
adjunction, 112, 118, 121, 127, 133–135, 138–142, 144, 150–151, 161–162, 168, 172–174, 176, 179, 182, 186, 188, 190, 195, 198, 202, 204, 208, 213, 218–219, 225, 230–231, 241, 245–246, 250, 253, 260, 270–273, 278–279, 296, 298, 300, 305–308, 310, 319, 401, 403, 405, 407–408
adjunction structures
  deletions of segments of, 233
  segments of, **118**, 118–119
Affect-alpha, 3, 183, 191, 204, 260, 268, 270, 273–274, 284–286, 289–291, 308, 320, see also Move-alpha; Deletions
affectA, **183**, **351**
affectAn, **183**, **351**
affix-hopping, 163, 234
agree, **355**
agreement, 88–89, 118, 195, 225, 252–253, 320, 403, 409, see also Attribute-value structures
  SPEC-head, 195–198, 208–209, 234–235, 244, 253, 274, 278, 281, 402–403, 406
Aho, A.V., 75, 400, 409
Akmajian, A., xiv
amalgamate, **169**, **228**, **348**, **356**
anaphor, 125, 133, 157
ancestor

in a deduction, **34**
in a tree, **66**, 150
ancestor, **66**, **338**
ancestral induction, 273
Anderson, J R., 409
answer substitution, **35**
ante_governs, **185**, **198**, **353**, **355**
Aoun, J., 150, 404–406
append, **15**
argument, **139**, **343**
arithmetic, 2, 22–23, 52, 268, 282, 291, 397, 407–408
atomic formula, **28**
attribute-value structures, **118**, **120**, see also Phi-features; Psi-features; Index features; Agreement
in movements, 134
percolation of, 195, 403
Augmented Transition Networks (ATNs), 92–93
  HOLD lists of, 92
Authier, J.-M.P., 408
auxiliary verb, 94, 107, 163, 167, 223, 225–226, 237, 303–304, 403, 406
auxiliary verbs, 224
axiomatization, **11**

B

Bach, E., 403
Baker, M.C., 321, 401, 403–404, 407–408
Baltin, M.R., 407
Bambara, 217, 283
Bar-Hillel, Y., 88
barrier, 145, 150, 153, **155**, 155–158, 169–177, 181, 186, 188, 190–191, 194–195, 204–208, 213, 215, 217–219, **226–227**, 227–229, **239**,

239–240, 242–243, 245–246, 248–249, 268, 270, 272, 278–279, 281, 306, 312–313, 403–404, 406
  by inheritance, **155**
  intrinsic, **155**, 191
  minimal, 191
  parametric bounding node, **177**
barrier, **156**, **227**, **240**, **347**, **356**, **359**
Barss, A., 208
Barton, G.E., Jr., 87, 400
Basque, 302
Beghelli, F., xiv
Belletti, A., 149
Ben-shalom, D., xiv
Bennis, H., 403
Berwick, R.C., xiii, 99, 288, 397, 404, 408–409
Bibel, W., xiv, 317
bijection, **399**
binding theory, 3, 97, 125–126, 148, 152–153, 158, 162, 171, 179, 195, 222, 401, 403–404
  Principle A, 126
binds, **152**, **346**
Bird, C., 217
blocking category, **155**
blocking_cat, **156**, **347**
Boolos, G.S., 397–398
Bouchard, D., 304, 401, 408
bounding_parameter, **177**
bounding theory, 97–98, 150, 169–171, see also subjacency
Bousquet, J., 145
Bowen, K.A., 399
Boy de la Tour, T., 259, 406
Boyer, R.S., 273, 407
Bresnan, J., 40, 400, 403
Bridge, J., 398
Briscoe, E.J., 400
Browning, M.A., 278, 281
Bulgarian, 407
Bundy, A., 407
Burstall, R.M., 361, 407
Burzio, L., 321, 401, 403

C

c-command, 97, **150**
c_commands, **151**, **345**
case assignment, 89, 147
case theory, 2–3, 145, 148, 159
  case filter, 146, 148, 159, 403
cat_zero, **136**, **342**
categoricity, 22
ccl, **241**, **360**
center embedding, 1, 85–86

chain, 146, 150, 154, 169–171, 176–177, 179, 185, 195–197, 199, 202, 208, 221–222, 224, 241, 244, 248, 272–273, 278–279, 290–291, 304, 307, 310, 313, 319, 402, 404–405, 409
  extended, **196–198**, 404, 407
Chamorro, 408
Chang, C.-L., 398, 400
Chang, C.C., 397
Chan, K.-H., xiv, 52, 399
Chinese, 237, 283, 401
Chi, A., 398
Chomsky, xiv, 40, 84, 86, 107, 113, 133, 144, 146, 169, 179, 181–182, 220, 246, 271, 304, 398, 401, 403–405, 409
  Aspects of the Theory of Syntax, 41
  Barriers, xiii, 2, 4–6, 9, 107, 110–113, 115, 120, 127, 133, 137–139, 142, 145, 150–158, 161–165, 168–176, 179, 181–182, 185–186, 189–191, 195–196, 198–199, 202, 204–208, 213–215, 217–218, 223, 226–227, 229, 233–235, 237–241, 243–244, 246, 248–250, 257–258, 271–272, 277–281, 285, 297, 300, 302–303, 306, 312–313, 315, 401–407, 409
  Knowledge of Language, 134, 179, 400
  Lectures on Government and Binding, 117, 126, 133, 152, 171, 179, 401, 403, 407
Chung, S., 237, 408
Church, A., see Church's hypothesis; Church's thesis
Church's theorem, 282
Church's thesis, 12
Church, K., 292
Cinque, G., 100
Clark, K., 48, 50–51, 55, 58, 60, 130, 398–399
clausal form, **28**, **30**, 37
  size of, 258–259
clause, in logic, **30**, see also Negative clause; Horn clause; Definite clause; Empty clause
clitics, 116, 127, 149, 252–253, 321
Co-indexing, see Index features
Comorovski, I., 407
complement, **123**, **340**
complements, 3, **109**
Complete Constituent Constraint, 405
completeness, see also Essential incompleteness
  of a proof method, **13**
  of a theory, **11**
completion, of a logical theory, **48–54**
Complex NP constraint, 95, 103
Condition on Chain Links (CCL), **241**, 246, 248
conjunctive normal form, **28**
Constraint on Extraction Domains (CED), 173, 175, 277–278, 280–281, 401, 407

constraint satisfaction, 6, 284, 286, 315, 320, 322
consistency techniques for, 286
context-free grammars, 10, 13–14, 37, 57, 60–61, 64–67, 75, 80, 83–84, 88–92, 113, 167, 244, 249, 293–298, 301, 309, 314, 318, 399–400, 402, 408
for natural languages, 84, 86, 88–90
cycle-free, **294**
derivations from, **61**, 61–64, 69–73, 113
k-bounded cycling, **296**
size of derivations from, 293–297
contraction, 127
Contreras, H., 116
control theory, 133
coordinate structure reduction, 308
Corcoran, J., 22–23, 397
Correa, N., 408
covering grammars, 74–75
Crain, S., 400
Creider, C., xiii
Crook, H.D., 217, 405
Cut, see Factorization

D

D-structure, 2, 112–114, 121, 126, 142, 153, 157, 161, 169, 181–182, 186, 188, 195, 202, 204, 230, 282–283, 287, 289–291, 298, 300–301, 304–305, 308, 312, 319–321, 402–404, 408
psychological relevance of, 321
size bounds on, 299–302, **304–308**
Dahlgren, K., xiii
Dahl, V., xiv, 409
Darlington, J., 361
decidability, 6, 11, 13, 44, 47, 55, 282, 291, 322
Deduction, see Resolution; Model elimination
deduction, natural, 399
definability
of a relation, **11**
semantic limitations on, 23
Definite clause grammars (DCGs), 399, 402
definite clause
in logic, **30**, 44
deleteA, **182**, **349**
delete_conds, **183**, **351**
deletion, see also Trace deletion
instance of affect alpha, 114, 182–183, 225, 232, 249, 260, 268, 272, 285, 289, 291, 300–301, 305, 307–308, 313, 405, 409
Demopoulos, W., xiii
den Besten, H., 403
descendant, in a deduction, **34**
determiner phrases (DP), 213–219, 221–222, 304–305

Di Sciullo, A.-M., 408
difference lists, 57–59, 92–93, 318
and syntactic equality, 59
Digricoli, V.J., 43, 398
Dijkstra, E., 314
Dincbas, M., 409
directly_th_marks, **154**, **346**
do-support, 95–96, 225
dominates, **150**
dominates, **150**, **345**
Double Adjunction Condition (DAC), 272, 407
Dreben, B., 317, 398
Dutch, 116, 165, 167, 209, 403

E

e-unsatisfiability, **42**
Earley, J., 65, 75, 292–293, 297, 408
Ebbinghaus, H.-D., 397, 399
ecp, **185**
Edmondson, J.A., 403
Elcock, E.W., xiii, 409
elementary equivalence, **23**
Elkan, C., 407
Emonds, J., 138, 161, 163, 301, 307, 403, 408
Empty Category Principle (ECP), 3, 100, 168, 178, 181–183, 188–189, 192, 195–196, 198–199, 201–202, 204, 206, 208, 217–218, 225–226, 228, 230, 232–234, 241, 243, 249–250, 274, 277–281, 285, 306–307, 311–312, 320, 401, 405–407
conjunctive formulation, 202, 405
empty clause
in logic, **30**, 44
Enderton, H.B., 397, 399
Engdahl, E., 407–408
Epstein, S.S., 292
equality
standard axiomatization, 17, 42, 398–399
syntactic, 42–44, 56, 257
ergatives, 403
essential incompleteness, **16**
ex_link, **199**, **355**
excludes, **152**, **173**, **346**, **349**
excorporation, 306, see also Head movement
expletives, 308
expressibility
in first order logic, **24**, 398
extra_barrier, **177**, **349**
extra_BC, **177**, **349**

F

factorization, **113**
Farrell, P., 408
feature, 119, **338**
Features, see Attribute-value structures
Flannangan, T., 53–54
Fleisig, S., 399
Flum, J., 397, 399
Fodor, J.A., xiv, 4, 27
Fodor, J.D., xiii, 397, 400
Ford, M., 400
Forster, P., xiv
French, 116, 148, 163, 204–205, 223, 225, 252,
    405
Friedin, R., 405
Frisch, A.M., 400
Fujita, H., 409
Fukui, N., 405, 408
Fuller, D.A., 409
functional categories, **110**
functional explanations, 4, 397, 409
Furukawa, K., 318, 409

G

Gallier, J.H., 398
gamma-assignment, 261, see also Empty cate-
    gory principle
gamma-marking, 182–183, 185–186, 195, 201,
    203
garden path, 1, 87
Gazdar, G., 92, 400
Gécseg, F., 127, 402
general logic program, **47**, 261
Generalized Phrase Structure Grammar (GPSG),
    92, 400, 408
generate-and-test, 286
Genesereth, M.R., 409
German, 89, 116, 167, 206
Ginsberg, S., 401
Gödel, K., 16, 23, 70, 399
Goldfarb, W.D., 317, 398
Gould, S.J., 83
government, 3, 115, 125, 133, 145–146, 148–150,
    154–155, **157**, 157–159, 164–165, 168, 176,
    186, **188–191**, 191–192, 195–196, 202–203,
    206–207, 213, 215, 217–218, 227–229, 231,
    234–235, 237, **239**, 239, 241, 244, 246, 249–
    250, 261–262, 274, 277–281, 291, 301, 306–
    307, 312, 401, 403–404, 407
  antecedent, **185–186**, 189–190, 195, 197–198,
    202, 204, 206, 312
  head, **250–251**

minimal, **191–192**, 194
  proper, 181–182, **185**, 185–186, 188–189, 191,
    194, 198, 202–203, 205–206, 208, 312
  theta-government, **154**, 188–190, 198
governs, **191**
governs, **157**, **192**, **239**, **347**, **353**, **359**
Greenbaum, S., 258–259, 406
Green, C., 398
Gries, D., 2
ground, in logic, **30**
Guasti, M.T., 409
Guéron, J., 405

H

Haegeman, L., 116
Hale, K., 408
Hansson, A., 399
Harbusch, K., 408
Harlow, S., 237
Harnish, R.M., xiv
Harrison, M.A., 408
Harrison, M.J., 398
Harris, G., xiv
Hayes, P.J., 55
Head Movement Constraint (HMC), 161, 165,
    167–168, 227–233, 246, 274, 277, 285, 307,
    313, 407, 409
head movement, 168, 230, 233, 250, 278, 401,
    see also Verb raising; Head Movement Con-
    straint; Excorporation
head_governs, **250**
head_spec, **338**
head_compl, **338**
head_x1, **123**, **340**
head_xp, **123**, **340**
Heath, J., 408
Henschen, L.J., 398
Herbrand, J., see Herbrand interpretation
Herbrand interpretation, 15, 65, 70
Higginbotham, J., 401, 408
Hill, K.M., xiv
Hindemith, P., 161
Hindi, 407
Hindle, D., 407
Hirschman, L., 409
Hirsh, S., xiv
Hirst, G., xiv
hmc, **167**, **233**, **348**, **357**
Hoekstra, T., 403
homomorphism, **23**
Hopcroft, J.E., 400
Horn, A., see Horn clauses
Horn clauses, 6, **30**, 30, 44–47, 54–55, 57, 67–
    69, 260, 263, 317, 398, 401, 406

Hornlog, 398
Huang, C.-T.J., 173, 175, 182, 204, 277–278, 401–402, 404, 407
Hukari, T.E., 400
Hungarian, 216
Hutter, D., 407
Hyperresolution, see Resolution

I

i-command, **239**
i_command, **239**, **359**
I-to-C movement, see Head movement
Iatridou, S., 405–406
imm_dominates, **152**, **346**
improper movement, 179, 195, 245, 404
incorporation, 164–165, 401, see also Verb raising; Head movement
index features, 118–119, 125, 133–134, 137–138, 146, 152–154, 168–169, 195–196, 199, 209, 221–223, 227, 231, 235, 241, 244, 248, 253, 264, 277–278, 299, 306, 320, 406, 408
Indonesian, 167
inductive reasoning, 16, 22, 36, 63, 273–274, 289, 291–292, 294–295, 297, 397, 407–408
inflectional phrases (IP), 110, 125, 142, 147–148, 153, 155, 157, 171, 173–176, 178, 181–182, 186, 188, 191, 204, 223, 237, 239, 241, 244, 246, 250, 268, 272–273, 277–279, 281, 301, 304, 306, 312–313, 403–404, 407
innateness, 5
Irish, 237
island constraints, 173, see also Complex NP Constraint; Condition on Extraction Domains; Weak islands; Strong islands
isomorphism, **23**
Israel, D., xiv
Italian, 116, 149, 176, 237, 281, 301, 408

J

Jackendoff, R., 214
Jaeggli, O.A., 301, 404
Jaffar, J., 407
James, W., 257
Japanese, 167, 237, 408
Jeffrey, R.C., 397, 399
Jelinek, E., 408
Jensen, K., 407
Johnson, K., 404–405, 407
Johnson, M., xiii, 286, 317, 401–402, 409
Joshi, A.K., 402–404, 408–409
Joyner, W.H., Jr., 55

K

Kahn, L., 9
Kameyama, M., 408
Kaplan, R.M., 400
Kayne, R.S., 116, 148, 205–206, 253, 278, 401, 405
Keenan, E.L., xiv, 398
Keisler, H.J., 397
Keyser, J., 408
KiNande, 408
Kleene, S.C., 397
Koopman, H., 116, 163, 182, 237–238, 400, 403, 405–406, 408
Koot, J. van de, 397, 400, 409
Koster, J., 117, 208, 401
Kowalski, R., 55, 399, 406
Kreisel, G., 407–408
Kripke, S., 400
Kroch, A.S., 403–404, 408
Kru languages, 408
Kupin, J.J., 113–114, 401

L

L_dependent, **240**, **359**
L-marking, **154**, 154–155, 157–158, 164–165, 173–174, 186, 188–189, 191, 195, 206, 208, 213, 215, 217, 227–231, 239–240, 242, 245–246, 250, 274, 278–279, 281, 403, 406
L_marks, **155**, **189**, **229**, **240**, **346**, **353**, **357**, **359**
Laka, I., 302
Lakoff, G., 40
Langendoen, T., 88
Larson, R.K., 400, 404, 406
Lasnik, H., xiv, 41, 113–114, 146, 164, 181–182, 185, 198, 278, 307, 401–406
Lassez, J.-L., 407
last-resort principle, 179
last, **121**, **338**
Lee, R.C.-T., 398, 400
Levesque, H., xiv
Levine, R.D., 400
Lewis, H.R., 398
lexical categories, **108**, **188**, 401
lexical, **120**, **188**, **229**, **231**, **338**, **353**, **356–357**
lexicon, **124**, **407**
lf_gamma, **352**
lf_sub_gamma, **352**
LF-movement, 144

LF-structure, 2, 117, 142, 144, 170, 174, 182–
    183, 185–186, 204, 217, 249, 282–283, 285,
    287, 312, 320, 405, 408
linear precedence, in syntax, 115–117
link, **171**, **349**
list notation, semantics of, **15**
list, **15**
literal, **28**
Lloyd, J.W., 48, 50–51, 398
Lobo, J., 398
Local binding, see Binding theory
locality conditions, 3, 145, 169, 202, 238, 291,
    304, 310, 312–315, 322, 409
locally binds, **152**
locally_binds, **152**, **346**
Longobardi, G., 281
Logical form, see LF-structure
lookahead, 6, 75–76, 78–80
Loveland, D.W., 315–316, 326, 398–399, 406,
    409
Löwenheim, L., see Löwenheim-Skolem theo-
    rem
Löwenheim-Skolem theorem, 24
Lowering rules, see Affix-hopping
LR(k) deduction, **78–80**
LR(k) parsing, 75–76, 78–80, 314, 322

M

m-command, **151**, 158, 310
m_commands, **151**, 310, **345**
Mackworth, A.K., 286–287
Maher, M.J., 317
Maier, D., 409
Maloney, M.J., 22
Manaster-Ramer, A., 400
Marantz, A., 115, 403
Marcus, M., 288, 397, 400, 404, 409
Mates, B., 399
Matthews, R., xiv, 397
maximal projection, **108**
maximal, **120**, **338**
Maxwell, M., 400
May, R., xiv, 118, 142, 150, 182, 402
McAllester, D., 407
McCarthy, J., 70, 213
McCawley, J., 40
McCharen, J., 400
McCloskey, J., 237
McDaniel, D., 272, 407
McDowell, J., xiii
Mellish, C.S., 407
member, **66**, **337**
metatheories, 57, 65–73, 103–104
Miller, G.A., 86, 107

Milosz, O.V. de L., 125
minimal, **120**, **338**
minimal_barrier, **191**, **230**, **353–354**, **357**
minimality, 189, 191–195, 202, 205–208, 213–
    214, 228–229, 250, 274, 277, 404
Minker, J., 398
model elimination, 259, 284, 315–316, 326, 398–
    399, 406
Mohawk, 167, 408
Moore, J.S., 273, 407
Moore, R.C., 70
Morris, J., 43, 398
Moshier, D., 401, 409
most general unifier (mgu), **32**
Mostowski, A., 291
move-alpha, 125, 133, **140**, 142, 169, 181–182,
    402, see also Substitution; Adjunction
moveA, **140**, **167**, **344**, **347**
moveAn, **141**, **344**

N

n_subjacent, **171**, **349**
Naish, L., 409
negative clause
    in logic, **30**, 44
no_vacuous_ops, **230**
no_vacuous_ops, **231**, **357**
nominals, derived and gerundive, 107–108
nonargument, **241**, **360**
Nunggubuyu, 408

O

Obenauer, H.-G., 204–206, 208, 405
occurrence numbers, of a category, **118**, 134,
    299
operator, empty (O), 134
Oshima, S., 408
Ouhalla, J., 405

P

Papadimitriou, C.H., 398
parameter, 2, 24, 40–41, 114, 120, 134, 146, 257,
    401–402
    case assignment, 400
    theta assignment, 400
    word order, 109, 112, 120
    bounding theory, 173, 175
parent, **66**, **337**
Parker, D.S., 407
parsing problem, **64–65**, **73**, 73
Pärt, A., 223
Partee, B.H., 401
partial evaluation, 317–318

partitives, 205
passives, 133, 195–196, 198–201, 243, 404
path, through a tree, **113**
Patil, R., 292
Payne, T.H., 398
pedestrian's assumption, 407
Percolation, see Attribute-value structures
Pereira, F.C.N., xiii, 75, 92, 95, 98, 317, 399–402, 409
Pesetsky, D., 405, 408–409
Peters, S., 401
phi, **137, 342**
phi features, 133–134, see also Agreement
phonetic form (PF), 3, 126, 225, 283–284
phrase marker, **113**, 113
  reduced (RPM), 113–114
Plaisted, D.A., 258–259, 406
Platero, P., 408
Polish, 407
Pollock, J.-Y., 144, 223–227, 229–233, 235, 246, 301, 304, 306–307, 403, 405–406
Portuguese, 408
possessive constructions, 216, 219
Postal, P.M., 401
prenex normal form, **28**
prepositional verb constructions, 116
previously_n_subjacent, **177, 349**
Pritchett, B.L., 400
PRO, 126–127, 133, 148–149, 157–159, 167, 204, 214–215, 301, 401, 403
pro, 133, 301–302
program transformations, 57–58, 285, 314, 316–318
projection, **359**
projection principle, **125**, 403
Prolog, 44, 75, 80, 101–102, 361, 398, 406
proof trees, **62**, 62–64, 67–73, 266
Proper analysis, see Factorization
properly_governs, **185, 198, 352, 355**
pseudo-opacity, 204–205
pseudopassives, 116
psi, **138, 343**
Psi-features, 195, see also Agreement
psi-features, **137**
Puder, K., 409
Pullum, G.K., 400–401
put_features, **137, 342**
Pylyshyn, Z., xiv, 1

Q

QR movement, see LF-movement
quantifiers, movement in French, 205–206, 208
Quine, W.V.O., 15, 23, 273

R

Raatz, S., 398
Rabin, M.O., 407–408
Radford, A., 400, 403
raising constructions, 188, 195–196, 198–199, 223–226, 233–235, 237, 242, 244, 277, 306, 308, 403, 405, see also Verb raising; Head movement
super-raising, 198, 200–201, 244
Rajasekar, R., 398
Ramakrishnan, R., 400
Ramanath, M.V.S., xiv
reanalysis, 113, 115–117
recognition problem, **64, 73**
reconstruction, 113, 117, 308, 401
recp, **250**
recursiveness, of natural languages, 12
reflexive pronoun, 125, see also Anaphor; Binding theory
Reinhart, T., 150
Reiter, R., xiv, 406
relative clause, 94, 96–97, 108, 134, 145, 173, 248, see also Wh-movement
representation
  of a context free parsing problem, 74
  of a relation, **12, 36**
Residue of the Empty Category Principle (RECP), 250–252, 406
resolution, 27, **31–33**, 33–35, 37, 40, 42, 45–47, 51–56, 58, 79–80, 257–258, 262–263, 282, 315, 317–319, 325, 398–400, 406, see also Proof trees
  binary, **46**
  E-resolution, 43
  hyperresolution, **79**, 400
  input, **46**
  linear, **46**
  reductions for, 317
  search space size, 260, 315
  selection functions for, 259, 406
  SEq, 40, 42–44, 54, 257–258, 260, 262–263, 266, 315–316, 398
  SLD, **45–47**, 52, 54–56, 59, 61–62, 67, 78, 80, 398
  SLDNF, 46, 48, 50–52, 257, 260–262, 316, 398–399
  soundness and completeness, 34
Restricted logic grammars (RLGs), 97–100, 400
Riemsdijk, H. van, 401, 403
Ristad, E.S., xiv, 87, 284, 407–409
Ritchie, R.W., 401
Ritter, E., 405

Rizzi, L., xiii, 116, 149, 176, 204–205, 207, 281, 398, 401, 405, 408–409
Roberts, I., 144, 306, 313, 407
Robinson, J.A., 34, 79, 400
Robinson, R.M., 291–292
Romani, 272
Rossi, F., 409
Ross, J.R., 95–96
Ross, K.A., 398
Rounds, W.C., 127, 401, 409
Rouveret, A., 403
Rudin, C., 407
Rutten, J., 403

S

S-structure, 2, 115, 146, 170, 182–183, 198, 225, 232, 241, 249–250, 282–283, 285, 287–291, 297–298, 301–304, 307–309, 312–313, 320–321, 404–405, 408
  size bounds on, 282, 299–302, 304–307
Safir, K., 301, 405
Sag, I., 409
Saint-Dizier, P., xiv, 409
Saito, M., 181–182, 185, 278, 307, 401–402, 404–406
Santorini, B., 403
Sato, T., 262
Schabes, Y., 408
Schoenberg, A., 283
Segment, see Adjunction structures
Seki, H., 318, 409
select, **131**, **341**
separate, **121**, **338**
SEq-unsatisfiability, **42**
Serbo-Croatian, 407
Shamir, E., 88
Shapiro, E.Y., 62, 399, 402, 409
Shieber, S.M., 89, 317, 400, 408
sisters, **153**, **189**, **346**, **353**
Skolem, Th., see Skolem functions; Skolem transform; Löwenheim-Skolem theorem
Skolem functions, 29, 39, 43–44, 54, 257, 261, 325, 398
Skolem transform, **29**, 259
SLD, see Resolution
small clause, 214–215, 224, 237, 403, 405–406
Smith, D.E., 409
Spanish, 116, 189
Speas, M., 405
spec_head, **354**
spec_heads, **354**
specifier, **123**, **340**
specifiers, **109**
Spitzen, J.M., 407

Sportiche, D., xiii, 150, 182, 237–239, 241, 249–250, 252–253, 302, 398, 401, 405–406
ss_gamma, **184**, **351**
ss_sub_gamma, **184**, **352**
Stabler, E.P., xiv
Stabler, E.P., Jr., 36, 42, 44, 67, 70, 97, 99, 286–287, 289, 315, 397–400, 406–409
Steedman, M., 400
Steinby, M., 127, 402
Sterling, L., 399, 402, 409
Stickel, M., 326, 398–400
Stowell, T., xiii, 110, 153, 214–215, 217–219, 221–222, 250, 400, 403–406
Strict Cycle Condition (SCC), **219–220**, 220–222, 248, 268, 285, 291
strong islands, 100, see also Complex NP Constraint; Subjacency; Condition on Extraction Domains
structure preservation theorems, 288
Structure Preserving Constraint (SPC), 161, 403
subcategorization, 24, 90–91, 112, 125, 154
subjacency, 2–4, 97, 144, 161, 169–170, 172–173, 176, 178, 181–182, 186, 188, 213, 218–219, 221–222, 241, 246, 249, 266, 268, 272–273, 277–278, 280–281, 285, 306, 311–313, 319–320, 403–405, 408
  and counting, 404
  cumulative version, **176–177**, 177
subjacency, **171**, **349**
subst_conds, **135**, **162**, **341**, **347**
substitute, **135**, **341**
substitution
  for variables, **31**, 31–36, 42, 50–51, 72, 286, 317–319, 398
  instance of move alpha, 127–128, 133–134, 138–141, 161, 169, 173–174, 176, 204, 221, 226, 230, 240, 246, 250, 253, 257, 260, 266, 268, 289, 312, 402–403
subtree, **66**, **347**
Sundholm, G., 399
Swedish, 407
Syntactic equality, see Equality; Resolution, SEq
Szabolcsi, A., 216, 405
Szwarc, M., xiv
Szymanski, T.G., 80

T

take_features, **137**, **342**
Tamaki, H., 262
Tärnlund, S.-A., 58, 399
Tarski, A., 397
Tensed S Condition, 404
tensed, **178**, **349**
th_governs, **154**, **346**

that-trace effects, 192–193, 195, 202, 249
Thatcher, J.W., 402
theory, of a structure, Th(U), **11**
theta criterion, **150**, 226
theta grid, **154**
theta theory, 2–3, 238, see also Theta-marking;
   Government
theta-government, 165
theta-grid, 226
theta-marking, 139, 153, 169, 228
   direct, **154**
Thomas, W., 397, 399
Tiwa, 408
Toman, J., 407
Tomita, M., 80, 399
Topor, R.W., 398
trace deletion, 182, 217, 225, 232, 405
Trace erasure, see Trace deletion; Strict Cycle
   Condition
trace, **133**
Travis, L., 167, 400, 403
tree notation, semantics of, **65**
tree transducers, 127–134, 141, 402
Tuscarora, 408
type conditions, 399

U

Ullman, J.D., 75, 400, 409
unaccusatives, 403
universal grammar, 4–5, 40, 112, 114, 145, 257,
   298–299, 302, 397
Uriagereka, J., 401, 403, 405

V

V-to-I movement, see Verb raising; Head movement
Valois, D., 405
van Riemsdijk, H., 116
variants, **33**
Vata, 116, 403
verb raising, 163–165, 168–169, 209, 223, 225,
   232, 234–235, 278, 302, 405
Vergnaud, J.-R., 403
Vijay-Shanker, K., 402, 408
visible categories, **134**
visible, **135, 341**
VP-ellipsis, 87, 307
VP-internal subject hypothesis, 237, 240–241,
   243, 246, 248, 250–251, 253

W

Wakayama, T., 398
Walther, C., 409
Wang, H., 407–408
Warlpiri, 283, 408
Warren, D.H.D., 75, 92, 337, 399, 402, 409
weak islands, 100, see also Complex NP Constraint; Subjacency; Condition on Extraction Domains
weak representation
   of a context free parsing problem, 73
   of a relation, **12, 36**
Wegbreit, B., 407
Weinberg, A.S., 288, 397, 401, 404, 408–409
Weir, D.J., xiii, 402
Weischedel, R.M., 407
well-foundedness, 266, 268, 270, 273–274, 407
well_formed, **185**
Welsh, 237
wh-movement, 91–93, 98, 125, 127, 171, 179,
   205, 246, 248, 306
wh_ip_violation, **175, 349**
Williams, E., 401, 403, 406, 408–409
Williams, J.H., 80
Wiseman, D., xiv
Wong, N.-Y., xiv
Woods, W., 92
Wright, F.L., 57
Wu, A., xiv, 409

X

X-bar theory, 40, 107–110, 112–113, 115, 118,
   120–121, 153, 205, 213–214, 217, 223, 226,
   285, 289, 299–301, 400–401, 404
x0, **122, 338**
x1, **338**
xp, **123, 338**
xps, **122, 338**

Y

Yahya, A., 398

Z

Zaenen, A., 403
zero_cat, **136, 341**

The MIT Press, with Peter Denning as general consulting editor, publishes computer science books in the following series:

ACL-MIT Press Series in Natural Language Processing
Aravind K. Joshi, Karen Sparck Jones, and Mark Y. Liberman, editors

ACM Doctoral Dissertation Award and Distinguished Dissertation Series

Artificial Intelligence
Patrick Winston, founding editor
J. Michael Brady, Daniel G. Bobrow, and Randall Davis, editors

Charles Babbage Institute Reprint Series for the History of Computing
Martin Campbell-Kelly, editor

Computer Systems
Herb Schwetman, editor

Explorations with Logo
E. Paul Goldenberg, editor

Foundations of Computing
Michael Garey and Albert Meyer, editors

History of Computing
I. Bernard Cohen and William Aspray, editors

Logic Programming
Ehud Shapiro, editor; Fernando Pereira, Koichi Furukawa, Jean-Louis Lassez, and David H. D. Warren, associate editors

The MIT Press Electrical Engineering and Computer Science Series

Research Monographs in Parallel and Distributed Processing
Christopher Jesshope and David Klappholz, editors

Scientific and Engineering Computation
Janusz Kowalik, editor

Technical Communication and Information Systems
Edward Barrett, editor